A World Bank Group Flagship Report

WORLD DEVELOPMENT REPORT 2022

FINANCE FOR AN **EQUITABLE RECOVERY**

WORLD BANK GROUP

ISSN, ISBN, e-ISBN, and DOI:

Softcover
ISSN: 0163-5085
ISBN: 978-1-4648-1730-4
e-ISBN: 978-1-4648-1731-1
DOI: 10.1596/978-1-4648-1730-4

Hardcover
ISSN: 0163-5085
ISBN: 978-1-4648-1759-5
DOI: 10.1596/978-1-4648-1759-5

Cover and interior design: Gordon Schuit, with input from the Design team in the Global Corporate Solutions unit of the World Bank.

Library of Congress Control Number: 2022930708

The cutoff date for the data used in this report was August 31, 2021, unless otherwise indicated.

Contents

Boxes

Figures

Tables

Foreword

This new *World Development Report* focuses on the interrelated economic risks that households, businesses, financial institutions, and governments worldwide are facing as a consequence of the COVID-19 crisis. The Report offers new insights from research on the interconnectedness of balance sheets and the potential spillover effects across sectors. It also offers policy recommendations based on these insights. Specifically, it addresses the question of how to reduce the financial risks stemming from the extraordinary policies adopted in response to the COVID-19 crisis while supporting an equitable recovery.

The unfolding COVID-19 pandemic has already led to millions of deaths, job losses, business failures, and school closings, triggering the most encompassing economic crisis in almost a century. Poverty rates have soared and inequality has widened both across and within countries. Disadvantaged groups that had limited financial resilience to begin with and workers with lower levels of education—especially younger ones and women—have been disproportionately affected.

The response by governments has included a combination of cash transfers to households, credit guarantees for firms, easier liquidity conditions, repayment grace periods for much of the private sector, and accounting and regulatory forbearance for many financial institutions. Although these actions have helped to partially mitigate the economic and social consequences of the pandemic, they have also resulted in elevated risks, including public over-indebtedness, increased financial fragility, and a general erosion in transparency. Emerging economies have been left with very limited fiscal space, and they will be made even more vulnerable by the impending normalization of monetary policy in advanced economies.

This Report highlights several priority areas for action.

First is the need for early detection of significant financial risks. Because the balance sheets of households, firms, financial sector institutions, and governments are tightly interrelated, risks may be hidden. The share of nonperforming loans has generally remained below what was feared at the beginning of the crisis. But this could be due to forbearance policies that delayed debt repayments and relaxed accounting standards. Firm surveys in emerging economies reveal that many businesses expect to be in payment arrears in the coming months, and so private debt could suddenly become public debt, as in many past crises.

The interdependence of economic policies across countries matters as well. Public debt has reached unprecedented levels. As monetary policy tightens in advanced economies, interest rates will need to increase in emerging economies as well, and their currencies will likely depreciate. Higher interest rates make debt service more expensive, reinforcing the trend of recent years, and weaker currencies make debt service more burdensome relative to the size of the economy. Liquidity problems could suddenly morph into solvency problems.

The corporate–government nexus is another potential source of contingent liabilities and hidden debt. State-owned utilities have been asked to delay increases in tariffs and accept arrears in bill collection. Concessions and public-private partnerships have faced dramatic declines in revenue. Sooner or later, the losses could end up on the budget. Meanwhile, borrowing from foreign state-owned enterprises often escapes the surveillance of debt management agencies. These contingent liabilities and parastatal loans can raise significant financial risks in low-income and some emerging market countries.

Second is the need for proactive management of distressed assets. In the absence of effective resolution mechanisms for private sector debt, balance sheet problems last much longer than they should, with loan evergreening keeping "zombie" firms alive and undermining the strength of the recovery. Formal insolvency mechanisms need to be strengthened and alternative dispute resolution systems facilitated. Revamped legal mechanisms can promote debt forgiveness and help protect the long-term reputation of former debtors.

Early detection of risks and proactive management may also reduce the risks associated with the servicing of sovereign debt. Reprofiling allows moving to longer maturities and smoothing out debt-related payments. And the time for it is now, while international interest rates are still low and accessing global financial markets is still an option. Debt management can also help hedge against exchange rate volatility and currency weakness.

The biggest challenge is sovereign debt restructuring. The absence of a predictable, orderly, and rapid process for sovereign debt restructuring is costly, dampening recovery prospects and creating uncertainty. The historical track record shows that the longer the debt restructuring process takes, the larger the "haircut" creditors experience. For debtor countries, delay presents major setbacks to growth, poverty alleviation, and development. Unfortunately, negotiations on debt restructuring for the poorest countries under the G20 Common Framework are currently stalled.

Finally, it is critical to work toward broad-based access to finance. Low-income households are more likely to smooth out their consumption if they can save and borrow. Small businesses are better able to invest and create jobs if they have access to credit. Digital finance can play a critical role in enabling access to finance and fostering new economic opportunities.

Emerging economies need to rebuild their buffers and avoid sacrificing the accumulation of capital—both physical and human—along the way. The path chosen for fiscal consolidation is critically important in this respect. The composition of government spending affects economic growth, and more buoyant economic activity is critical to achieve development goals and debt sustainability in the longer term.

As for advanced economies, they should carefully unwind the extraordinary stimulus policies and avoid creating global turbulence. While reducing the balance sheets of their central banks, they should also rebalance their composition toward shorter-term assets because short-term interest rates matter more for the small and medium enterprises that constitute the backbone of global supply chains.

This new edition of the *World Development Report* charts a road map to tackle the financial vulnerabilities created by the COVID-19 crisis. The World Bank Group will continue to work tirelessly to assist client countries in these efforts.

David Malpass
President
The World Bank Group

Preface

In the midst of exceptional uncertainty, policy makers around the globe are grappling with the delicate task of scaling back the economic support measures put in place during the early stages of the COVID-19 pandemic while encouraging creation of the conditions needed to restore economic activity and growth.

One significant challenge is the lack of transparency—created or reinforced by the pandemic and (unintentionally) exacerbated by policy actions—about the risks in the balance sheets of the private and public sectors. What we *do* know is that the pandemic-induced recession of 2020 led to the largest single-year surge in global debt in decades. Before the pandemic, private debts were already at record highs in many advanced economies and emerging economies, leaving many households and firms poorly prepared to withstand an adverse income shock. Many governments were also facing record-high levels of debt prior to the pandemic, and many more significantly increased their debt burdens to fund vital response policies. In 2020, the average total debt burden of low- and middle-income countries increased by roughly 9 percentage points of the gross domestic product, compared with an average annual increase of 1.9 percentage points over the previous decade. Fifty-one countries (including 44 emerging economies) experienced a downgrade in their sovereign debt credit rating.

What we do not yet know, however, is the extent to which governments and private debtors are harboring hidden risks with the potential to stymie economic recovery. In particular, increased complexity and opacity in sovereign debt markets (as to who holds the debt and under what terms) often make it difficult to assess the full extent of risks in government balance sheets. On the private side, common elements of pandemic response programs, such as moratoria on bank loans, general forbearance policies, and a marked relaxation in financial reporting requirements, have made it difficult to determine whether debtors are facing short-term liquidity challenges or whether their incomes have been permanently affected. For both, the risk is insolvency on a scale and scope that are difficult to gauge in advance.

Within the context of uncertainty, the world is confronting the daunting challenge of continuing to navigate a global pandemic, while managing and reducing financial risks across household, business, financial, and government sectors. Problems in one area can and do reverberate across entire economies through mutually reinforcing channels that connect the financial health of all sectors. What at first blush appears to be an isolated disruption in one sector can very quickly spill over to the rest of the economy. For example, if households and firms are under financial stress, the financial sector faces a higher risk of loan defaults and is less willing or able to provide credit and support economic recovery.

As the financial position of the public sector deteriorates as a result of higher sovereign debt and lower tax revenue, many governments find that they are less able to support economic activity.

Policies that facilitate the early detection and swift resolution of economic and financial fragilities can make all the difference between an economic recovery that is robust and one that falters—or, worse, one that delays recovery altogether. Starting with an in-depth assessment of the severest and most regressive financial and economic impacts of the pandemic, this *World Development Report* puts forward a focused, actionable policy agenda that countries can adopt to cope with some of the harmful and potentially lasting economic effects of the pandemic. Some of these policies seek to reduce opacity in credit markets, for example, by ensuring that banks report accurate, timely indicators of loan quality or by increasing transparency around the scale and terms of sovereign debt. Other initiatives aim to accelerate the resolution of debt distress through improved insolvency proceedings for companies and individuals, and proactive efforts to reprofile or restructure sovereign debt.

Because there is no one-size-fits-all approach to economic recovery, the appropriate policy mix depends critically on prevailing conditions and policy capacity. Few if any governments have the resources and political leeway to tackle simultaneously all of the challenges they face as the pandemic recedes. Countries will need to prioritize. The potential for policy to contribute to a lasting, inclusive recovery will depend on the ability of governments, working in partnership with international financial institutions and other development professionals, to muster the political will for swift action.

Carmen M. Reinhart
Senior Vice President and Chief Economist
The World Bank Group

Acknowledgments

The 2022 *World Development Report* (WDR) was prepared by a team led by its director, Leora Klapper. Martin Kanz served as deputy director, Davida Connon as manager, and Davide Mare as data manager. Laura Starita provided developmental guidance in drafting the Report. Overall guidance was provided by Carmen Reinhart, Senior Vice President and Chief Economist of the World Bank Group (WBG), and leader of its Development Economics (DEC) Vice Presidency, and Aart Kraay, Director of Development Policy of DEC and Deputy Chief Economist of the WBG. The Report is sponsored by DEC and was prepared in partnership with the World Bank's Equitable Growth, Finance, and Institutions (EFI) Vice Presidency (Finance, Competitiveness, and Innovation Global Practice; Macroeconomics, Trade, and Investment Global Practice; and Poverty Global Practice) and with the Financial Institutions Group and the Development Impact Measurement Department of the International Finance Corporation (IFC).

The core author team comprised Momina Aijazuddin, Alexandru Cojocaru, Miquel Dijkman, Juan Pablo Farah Yacoub, Clemens Graf von Luckner, Kathryn Holston, Martin Holtmann, Nigel Jenkinson, Harry Lawless, Davide Mare, Sephooko Ignatius Motelle, Rita Ramalho, Matthew Saal, Beniamino Savonitto, and Mahesh Uttamchandani, together with research analysts Sri Sravya Raaga Akkineni, Francine Chang Fernandez, Michael Gottschalk, Lingaraj Giriyapura Jayaprakash, Mansi Vipin Panchamia, Jijun Wang, and Nan Zhou. Selome Missael Paulos provided the team with administrative support.

Members of the extended team and contributors to the Report's spotlight features are Matthew Gabriel Brown, Pietro Calice, Nadine Chehade, Erik Feyen, Matthew Gamser, Wissam Harake, Meraj Husain, Kira Erin Krown, Christoph Lakner, Camilo Mondragon-Velez, Stephen Rasmussen, Allison Ryder, Valentina Saltane, Alexander Sotiriou, Stefan Staschen, Robert Johann Utz, and Nishant Yonzan.

Additional contributors are Pranjul Bhandari, Fernando Dancausa, Fiseha Haile Gebregziabher, Ashish Gupta, Alexandre Henry, Fernanda Massarongo Chivulele, Collen Masunda, Antonia Menezes, Rachel Chi Kiu Mok, Sergio Muro, Ugo Panizza, Albert Pijuan Sala, Tarun Ramadorai, and Guillermo Vuletin.

Special thanks are extended to the senior leadership and managers of EFI and IFC for their partnership and guidance in preparing the Report, including Paulo de Bolle (Senior Director, Global Financial Institutions Group, IFC), Marcello Estevão (Global Director, Macroeconomics, Trade, and Investment, EFI), Issa Faye (Director, Development Impact Measurement, IFC), Dan Goldblum (Manager, Development Impact Measurement, Financial Institutions, IFC), Cedric Mousset (Acting Practice Manager, Finance, Competitiveness, and Innovation, EFI), and Jean Pesme (Global Director, Finance, Competitiveness, and Innovation, EFI).

The team is also grateful for the guidance, comments, and inputs provided by Tatiana Alonso Gispert, Karlis Bauze, Buddy Buruku, Jennifer Chien, Krishnamurti Damodaran, Hugo De Andrade Lucatelli, Denise Leite Dias, Matei Dohotaru, Ismael Ahmad Fontán, Xavier Gine, Eva Gutiérrez, Samira Kalla, Pamela Lintner, Martin Melecky, Martha Mueller, Juan Ortiz, Alexander Pankov, José Rutman, Venkat Bhargav Sreedhara, Ekaterina Ushakova, and Carlos Leonardo Vicente. The team would also like to thank the many World Bank colleagues who provided written comments during the formal Bank-wide review process. Those comments provided invaluable guidance at a crucial stage in the Report's production. The WDR team also gratefully received suggestions and guidance from the members of a technical advisory board for the Report: Viral Acharya, Muhamad Chatib Basri, Graciela Kaminsky, Odette Lineau, Atif Mian, Jonathan Murdoch, Tim Ogden, Raghuram Rajan, and Kenneth Rogoff.

The WDR team also engaged with and received specific inputs, including policy guidance and data, from the following representatives of academia, international organizations, civil society organizations, private sector companies, and development partners: John Fischer, Jim Rosenberg, and Michael Schlein (Accion); Daniel Osorio (Banco de la República, Colombia); Marcia Díaz and Veronica Gavilanes (Banco Pichincha); Mariusz Cholewa and Paweł Szarkowski (Biuro Informacji Kredytowej S.A.); Nancy Silva Salas (Comisión para el Mercado Financiero); Andrée Simon (FINCA Impact Finance); Amrik Heyer and David Taylor (FSD Kenya); Rafe Mazer (Innovations for Poverty Action); Carlos Arredondo, Nadia Cecilia Rivero Morey, Jeffrey Sadowsky, and Gregorio Tomassi (Konfío); Zhenhua Li, Shi Piao, Xiaodong Sun, and Joey Zhang (MYbank and Ant Group); and Andreas Fuster (Swiss Finance Institute @ EPFL). The team consulted with and received input from the following IFC colleagues: Olawale Ayeni, Jessica Camilli Bluestein, Erica Bressan, Peter Cashion, José Felix Etchegoyen, Bill Gallery, Anushe Khan, Luz María Salamina, Leila Search, and Beatrix Von Heintschel.

Data from the World Bank Business Pulse Surveys used throughout the Report, as well as related analysis, were collected and analyzed by Besart Avdiu, Xavier Cirera, Marcio Cruz, Elwyn Davies, Subika Farazi, Arti Grover, Leonardo Iacovone, Umut Kılınç, Ernesto López-Córdova, Denis Medvedev, Gaurav Nayyar, Mariana Pereira López, Trang Tran Minh Pham, Santiago Reyes Ortega, and Jesica Torres Coronado. The Report also draws on data collected by the World Bank's High-Frequency Phone Surveys conducted during the pandemic. They were led by Benu Bidani, Ambar Narayan, and Carolina Sánchez-Páramo, with the assistance of Sulpice Paterne Mahunan Amonle, Miyoko Asai, Paola Ballon, Gildas Bopahbe Deudibe, Laura Blanco Cardona, Antonia Johanna Sophie Delius, Reno Dewina, Carolina Díaz-Bonilla, Fatoumata Dieng, Julia Dukhno, Ifeanyi Nzegwu Edochie, Karem Edwards, Kristen Himelein Kastelic, Lali Jularbal, Deeksha Kokas, Nandini Krishnan, Gabriel Lara Ibarra, Maria Ana Lugo, Silvia Malgioglio, José Montes, Laura Moreno Herrera, Rose Mungai, David Newhouse, Minh Cong Nguyen, Sergio Olivieri, Bhavya Paliwal, Utz Pape, Lokendra Phadera, Ana Rivadeneira Alava, Laura Rodríguez Takeuchi, Carlos Sabatino, Jeeyeon Seo, Dhiraj Sharma, Siwei Tian, Ikuko Uochi, Haoyu Wu (Tom), Nobuo Yoshida, and Maryam Zia. Data collected through Enterprise Surveys COVID-19 Follow-Up Surveys, made available by the Enterprise Analysis Unit of the DEC Global Indicators Department of the World Bank Group, were used to inform the Report's analysis and recommendations. The team is led by Jorge Rodríguez Meza and coordinated by Silvia Muzi. Adam Aberra, Gemechu A. Aga, Tanima Ahmed, Andrea Suzette Blake-Fough, David Francis, Filip Jolevski, Nona Karalashvili, Matthew Clay

Summers, Kohei Ueda, Domenico Viganola, and Joshua Seth Wimpey all contributed to the data collection and publication of indicators.

The team consulted as well with World Bank Group colleagues, policy makers, and staff from other international organizations, civil society organizations, development partners, donors, financial institutions, and research institutions. Seminars were held with subject matter experts to discuss the technical details of the legal and policy recommendations in the Report. Panelists and co-hosts were Scott Atkins (Chair and Head of Risk Advisory, Norton Rose Fulbright Australia, and President, INSOL International), Juanita Calitz (Associate Professor, University of Johannesburg), Zarin Daruwala (Cluster Chief Executive Officer [CEO], India and South Asia Markets [Bangladesh, Nepal, and Sri Lanka], Standard Chartered Bank), Matthew Gamser (CEO, SME Finance Forum), Juan Carlos Izaguirre (Senior Financial Sector Specialist, Consultative Group to Assist the Poor [CGAP], World Bank), Klaas Knot (President, De Nederlandsche Bank, and Chair, Financial Stability Board), Alexander Sotiriou (Senior Financial Sector Specialist, CGAP, World Bank), Lucia Spaggiari (Innovation Director, MicroFinanza Rating), Kristin van Zwieten (Professor, University of Oxford), and Romuald Wadagni (Minister of Economy and Finance, Benin). Special thanks are extended to CGAP and the SME Finance Forum for facilitating engagement with their networks. The team would also like to thank the German Federal Ministry for Economic Cooperation and Development (BMZ) and its convening authority, the Deutsche Gesellschaft für Internationale Zusammenarbeit (GIZ), for holding a stakeholder workshop on the Report and providing an additional opportunity for the team to collect feedback from development partners.

The Report was edited by Sabra Ledent and proofread by Catherine Farley and Gwenda Larsen. Robert Zimmermann verified the Report's extensive citations. Gordon Schuit was the principal graphic designer. Anugraha Palan, Shane Romig, and Nina Vucenik developed the communications and engagement strategy. Mikael Reventar and Roula Yazigi provided web and online services and related guidance. Special thanks are extended to Mark McClure, who coordinated and oversaw formal production of the Report by the World Bank's publishing program. The team would also like to thank Patricia Katayama and Stephen Pazdan, who oversaw the overall publication process; Mary Fisk, who facilitated the multiple translations of the overview and chapter summaries; Bouchra Belfqih and the Translation team, who translated the texts; and Deb Barker and Yaneisy Martinez, who managed the printing and electronic conversions of the Report and its many ancillary products. Monique Pelloux Patron provided the team with resource management support. The team also extends its appreciation to Maria Alyanak, Marcelo Buitron, Gabriela Calderon Motta, and Maria del Camino Hurtado for their help with coordination and high-level engagement strategies.

Finally, the team apologizes to any individuals or organizations inadvertently omitted from this list and is grateful for the help received from all who contributed to this Report, including those whose names may not appear here. Like many people around the world, team members were working from home during the year it took to prepare this report. Our families deserve full author credit for the encouragement, entertainment, snacks, and distractions they provided throughout the development of this publication.

Abbreviations

ADR	alternative dispute resolution
AI	artificial intelligence
AMC	asset management company
AQR	asset quality review
ASEAN	Association of Southeast Asian Nations
BCBS	Basel Committee on Banking Supervision
BNPL	buy now, pay later
BP	Banco Pichincha (Ecuador)
BRSS	Bank Regulation and Supervision Survey
CAC	collective action clause
CBI	Climate Bonds Initiative
CDBP	consolidated distance to break point
CESEE	Central, Eastern, and Southeastern Europe
CG	credit guarantee
CGAP	Consultative Group to Assist the Poor
CIRP	Corporate Insolvency Resolution Process
COVID-19	coronavirus disease 2019
CRILC	Central Repository of Information on Large Credits (India)
CRSP	credit reporting service provider
DE JURE	Data and Evidence for Justice Reform (World Bank project)
DSA	debt sustainability analysis
DSSI	Debt Service Suspension Initiative
EAP	East Asia and Pacific
ECA	Europe and Central Asia
ECB	European Central Bank
ECL	expected credit loss
ECLGS	Emergency Credit Line Guarantee Scheme
EU	European Union
EWT	early warning tool
FMCG	fast-moving consumer good
FSAP	Financial Sector Assessment Program (World Bank/IMF)
FSB	Financial Stability Board
FV	future value
G20	Group of Twenty
GBP	Green Bond Principles
GDP	gross domestic product
GTSF	Global Trade Supplier Finance Program (IFC)
HIPC	Heavily Indebted Poor Countries Initiative (IMF)

IADI	International Association of Deposit Insurers
IBBI	Insolvency and Bankruptcy Board of India
IBC	Insolvency and Bankruptcy Code (India)
ICMA	International Capital Market Association
IDA	International Development Association
IFC	International Finance Corporation
IMF	International Monetary Fund
LAC	Latin America and the Caribbean
MAS	Monetary Authority of Singapore
MDRI	Multilateral Debt Relief Initiative (IMF)
MENA	Middle East and North Africa
MFB	microfinance bank
MFI	microfinance institution
ML	machine learning
MSEs	micro- and small enterprises
MSMEs	micro-, small, and medium enterprises
NBFI	nonbank financial institution
NBMFC	nonbank microfinance company
NDCs	Nationally Determined Contributions (Paris Agreement)
NPL	nonperforming loan
NPV	net present value
OECD	Organisation for Economic Co-operation and Development
P&A	purchase and assumption
PAYGo	pay-as-you-go
PCGS	public credit guarantee scheme
RBI	Reserve Bank of India
SAR	South Asia Region; special administrative region
SDGs	Sustainable Development Goals
SMEs	small and medium enterprises
SOE	state-owned enterprise
SSA	Sub-Saharan Africa
suptech	supervision technology
UNCITRAL	United Nations Commission on International Trade Law
UTP	unlikely to pay
VAT	value added tax

All dollar amounts are US dollars unless otherwise indicated.
The cutoff date for the data used in this report was August 31, 2021, unless otherwise indicated.

Overview

Introduction

In 2020, as communities around the world were struggling to contain the spread of COVID-19 (coronavirus) and manage the health and human costs of the pandemic, governments implemented a wide range of crisis response policies to mitigate the worst social and economic impacts of the pandemic.

The mobility restrictions, lockdowns, and other public health measures necessary to address the pandemic rapidly produced the largest global economic crisis in more than a century. This was compounded by a drop in demand as the pandemic affected consumer behavior. Economic activity contracted in 2020 in about 90 percent of countries, exceeding the number of countries seeing such declines during two world wars, the Great Depression of the 1930s, the emerging economy debt crises of the 1980s, and the 2007–09 global financial crisis (figure O.1). In 2020, the first year of the COVID-19 pandemic, the global economy shrank by approximately 3 percent,[1] and global poverty increased for the first time in a generation.[2]

To limit the impact of the crisis on households and businesses, governments enacted a swift and encompassing policy response that used a combination of fiscal, monetary, and financial sector policies. The case of India, which like many other countries enacted a large emergency response to the first wave of the pandemic, offers an example of a decisive policy response that used a wide range of policy instruments to mitigate the worst immediate effects of the crisis. When the pandemic first erupted in India in March 2020, the government declared a two-month national lockdown that closed businesses and sent workers home. The lockdown halted all manner of economic activity, and incomes fell in tandem. Small businesses and low-income workers in urban areas and the informal sector were the most severely affected.

The first measure adopted by the Indian government was a fiscal stimulus package that amounted to nearly 10 percent of the gross domestic product (GDP) and included direct support for poor households.[3] Monetary policy reduced interest rates and eased lending conditions for banks and nonbank financial institutions. Financial sector policies were also part of the support plan; India instituted a debt repayment moratorium for households and firms that ultimately lasted six months. In addition, the Indian government introduced a large credit guarantee scheme aimed at ensuring that small and microenterprises would continue to have access to credit.

India's response to the economic crisis was similar to that of many other countries. The strategy recognized that the sectors of its economy—households and businesses, financial institutions, and governments—are interconnected. A large shock to one sector can generate spillover risks that destabilize the economy at large if not addressed promptly and in an integrated manner. As the pandemic rolled on, producing multiple waves of infection, many countries extended relief measures beyond their original timeline. Although these policies have helped limit the worst economic outcomes of the pandemic in the short run, they also bring challenges—such as increased public and private debt burdens—that need to be addressed soon to ensure an equitable economic recovery.

Figure O.1 Economic impact of COVID-19 in historical perspective

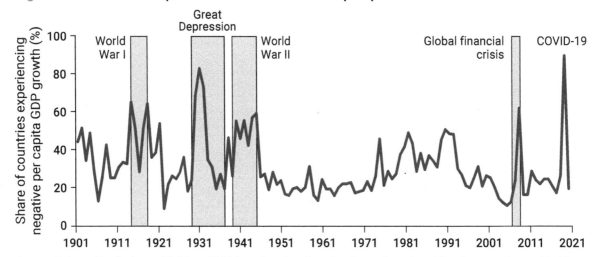

Source: Holston, Kaminsky, and Reinhart 2021, based on data from Groningen Growth and Development Centre, Maddison Project Database 2020, Faculty of Economics and Business, University of Groningen, Groningen, The Netherlands, https://www.rug.nl/ggdc/historicaldevelopment/maddison/releases/maddison-project-database-2020; International Monetary Fund, WEO (World Economic Outlook Databases) (dashboard), https://www.imf.org/en/Publications/SPROLLS/world-economic-outlook-databases.

Note: The figure shows the percentage of countries experiencing negative growth in their per capita gross domestic product (GDP) from 1901 to 2021. Data are as of October 21, 2021.

As the economic effects of the pandemic continue, policy makers aim to strike a balance between providing enough support to mitigate the human costs of the crisis, while limiting the longer-term financial and macroeconomic risks that could emerge from higher debt levels resulting from the crisis. These risks are likely to arise more quickly in emerging economies and especially in low-income countries, where the public and private debt-carrying capacity is much lower than in advanced economies, and where economic conditions were, in many cases, challenging even before the pandemic.[4]

The evidence available so far suggests that the economic effects of the pandemic will be more persistent and severer for emerging economies. For example, after the collapse in per capita incomes across the globe in 2020 (figure O.1), 40 percent of advanced economies recovered and exceeded their 2019 output level in 2021. The comparable share of countries achieving per capita income in 2021 that surpassed their 2019 output is far lower for middle-income countries, at 27 percent, and lower still for low-income countries, at 21 percent, pointing to a slower recovery in poorer countries.[5]

This *World Development Report* examines the central role of finance in the recovery from what has been called a once-in-a-century crisis and charts pathways toward a robust and equitable recovery. Achieving an "equitable recovery" means that all adults, including vulnerable groups such as poor adults, women, and small businesses, are able to recover from losses of jobs, incomes, human capital, and assets.[6] COVID-19 has widened inequality both within and across countries. Addressing financial risks is important to ensure that governments and financial institutions can support the recovery, including through investments in public services, such as health care and education. It is also critical that households and firms do not lose access to financial services that can strengthen resilience to economic shocks, including the loss of income and the unanticipated expenses many are incurring during the pandemic. Success in addressing these risks will help limit the damage to sustainable development outcomes and support an equitable recovery.

This Report incorporates new research, data collected throughout the crisis, as well as country case studies to document the immediate financial and economic impacts of the pandemic, the government responses, and the risks that have materialized or are imminent. These risks include an increase in nonperforming loans and financial sector distress; a lack of options for households and businesses to discharge debts incurred during the pandemic through formal insolvency; tighter access to credit; and elevated levels of sovereign debt. With the goal of directing countries toward options that can support an equitable recovery, this Report then highlights policies that respond to some of the adverse impacts of the crisis and mitigate spillovers of financial risks.

The economic impacts of the pandemic

Interconnected financial risks

Although household and business incomes were most directly affected by the crisis, the consequences of this large shock have repercussions for the entire economy through numerous mutually reinforcing channels that connect the financial health of households and firms, financial institutions, and governments (see figure O.2). Because of this interconnection, elevated financial risks in one sector can easily spill over and destabilize the wider economy if left unchecked. When households and firms are under financial stress, the financial sector faces a higher risk of loan defaults and is less able to provide credit. Similarly, when the financial position of the public sector deteriorates, for example, as a result of higher debt and debt service, its ability to support households and firms may weaken.

However, this relationship is not deterministic. Well-designed fiscal, monetary, and financial sector policies can counteract and reduce these intertwined risks, and help transform the links between sectors of the economy from a vicious "doom loop" into a virtuous cycle (see figure O.3).

Figure O.2 Conceptual framework: Interconnected balance sheet risks

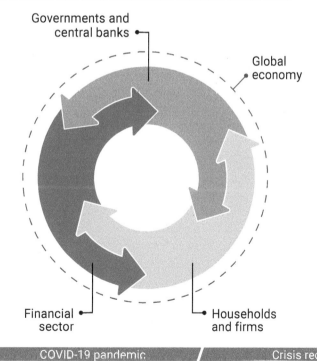

Source: WDR 2022 team.

Note: The figure shows the links between the main sectors of an economy through which risks in one sector can affect the wider economy.

Figure O.3 Conceptual framework: Vicious and virtuous cycles

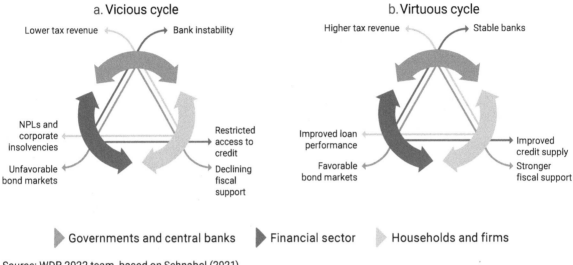

Source: WDR 2022 team, based on Schnabel (2021).
Note: NPLs = nonperforming loans.

One example of policies that can make a critical difference are those targeting the link between the financial health of households, businesses, and the financial sector. In response to lockdowns and mobility restrictions necessary to contain the virus, many governments supported borrowers through direct cash transfers and financial policy tools, including debt moratoria and credit guarantees. As the crisis unfolded, these policies provided much-needed support to households and small businesses and helped avert a wave of insolvencies and loan defaults, which could have threatened the stability of the financial sector. Looking ahead, ensuring that debt burdens for households and businesses are sustainable and that there is continued access to credit is essential for an equitable recovery.

Similarly, governments, central banks, and regulators also used policy tools to assist financial institutions and prevent financial sector risks from spilling over to other parts of the economy. In many countries, central banks lowered interest rates, injected liquidity into the market, broadened access to refinancing facilities, and reduced provisioning requirements. These measures enabled banks and other institutions to continue to offer financing to households and businesses. Like many other central banks, the Central Reserve Bank of Peru, for example, injected liquidity into the banking system through government-backed repurchase (repo) agreements, which reduced the interest rate on new credit. Central banks also made unprecedented use of unconventional monetary policy tools such as asset purchase programs. Twenty-seven emerging economies adopted such programs for the first time in response to the COVID-19 crisis.[7] These measures were aimed at preventing a liquidity crisis and safeguarding financial stability. However, debt moratoria and the provision of additional liquidity for the financial sector do not change the underlying economic conditions of borrowers. The risks now embedded in bank balance sheets will have to be addressed to ensure that the financial sector is well capitalized going into the recovery phase and is able to fulfill its role of providing credit to finance consumption and investment.

The crisis response will also need to include policies that address the risks arising from high levels of sovereign debt to ensure that governments preserve their ability to effectively support the recovery. The support measures adopted to mitigate the immediate impact of the pandemic on households and businesses required new government spending at a time when many governments were already burdened by elevated levels of public debt. High debt levels reduce a government's ability to support the recovery through direct support of households and firms. They also reduce a government's ability to invest in public goods and social safety nets that can reduce the impact of economic crises on poverty and inequality. Managing and reducing high levels of sovereign debt are therefore an important condition for an equitable recovery.

It is also important to recognize that COVID-19 is a crisis within a larger crisis arising from the escalating impacts of climate change on lives and economies. Preserving the ability of governments to invest in the transition to a green economy will be critical to counteract the inequitable impacts of climate change.

Increased inequality within and between countries

The economic impact of the pandemic has been highly unequal within and between countries. As the COVID-19 crisis unfolded in 2020, it became clear that many households and firms were ill-prepared to withstand an income shock of the length and scale of the pandemic. In 2020, more than 50 percent of households globally were not able to sustain basic consumption for more than three months in the event of income losses, while the cash reserves of the average business would cover fewer than 51 days of expenses.[8]

Within countries, the crisis disproportionately affected disadvantaged groups. In 2020, in 70 percent of countries the incidence of temporary unemployment was higher for workers who had completed only primary education.[9] Income losses were similarly larger among youth, women, the self-employed, and casual workers with lower levels of education.[10] Women, in particular, were affected by income and employment losses because they were more likely to be employed in sectors most affected by lockdown and social distancing measures, and they bore the brunt of the rising family care needs associated, for example, with the closures of childcare centers and schools. According to high-frequency phone survey data collected by the World Bank, in the initial phase of the pandemic, up to July 2020, 42 percent of women lost their jobs, compared with 31 percent of men, further underscoring the unequal impacts of the crisis by gender.[11]

The pattern of the crisis having a higher impact on disadvantaged groups applies to both emerging and advanced economies.[12] Early evidence from a number of emerging economies points to significant increases in within-country inequality.[13] It also reveals that initial disparities in job losses did not decline as lockdown and social distancing measures were relaxed. Those who suffered larger initial losses—women, younger workers, urban workers, and those with low levels of formal education—recovered more slowly than their counterparts or were not able to substantially reverse the initial disparities in losses.[14] Not surprisingly, with average incomes contracting and the effects concentrated among the less well-off, the available global data suggest that the pandemic has had a substantial impact on global poverty.[15]

Similar patterns emerge for businesses. Smaller firms, informal businesses, and those with more limited access to the formal credit market were harder-hit by income losses stemming from the pandemic. Larger firms entered the crisis with the ability to cover expenses for up to 65 days, compared with 59 days for medium-size firms and 53 and 50 days for small firms and microenterprises, respectively. Moreover, micro-, small-, and medium-size enterprises were overrepresented in the sectors most affected by the crisis, such as accommodation and food services, retail, and personal services. These businesses were more likely to suffer from supply chain disruptions that limited their access to inventory or supplies. Emerging data from surveys also indicate that affected businesses had to contend with longer payment terms or payment delays from buyers, including the public sector.[16]

These indicators are particularly alarming because in many emerging economies small and informal businesses account for a large share of total economic activity and employment. It is, for example, estimated that the informal economy accounts for about 34 percent of GDP in Latin America and Sub-Saharan Africa and 28 percent of GDP in South Asia.[17] In India, more than 80 percent of the total labor force is employed in the informal sector.[18] The survival of small and informal businesses therefore has a direct impact on the broader economy.

The pandemic also exposed and worsened preexisting fragilities in the financial sector. Similar to that of households and governments, the resilience of banks and financial institutions at the onset of the pandemic varied widely across countries. Some countries that were heavily affected by the 2007–09 global financial crisis had initiated meaningful financial sector reforms in response and ensured that their banking systems were well capitalized.[19] In some countries, such as Ghana, reforms also strengthened regulation and capitalization of the microfinance and nonbank sector. As a result, the financial sector in these countries was better able to weather the strains of the pandemic.

Many emerging economies, however, had failed to address financial sector fragilities in the years prior to the crisis, which compounded the problems of chronically low levels of financial intermediation and credit in the private sector. As a result, the financial sectors of these countries were ill-prepared for a crisis of the magnitude of the COVID-19 recession, which further reduced their ability to finance consumption and productive investment through the recovery.

The economic policy response to the pandemic: Swift but with large variation across countries

There were also marked inequalities in the crisis response across countries, which reflect differences in the resources and policy tools available to governments. As the pandemic intensified in 2020, the size and scope of government support programs varied widely. Many low-income countries struggled to mobilize the resources necessary to fight the immediate effects of the pandemic, or had to take on significant new debt to finance the crisis response. Half of the low-income countries eligible for the Group of Twenty (G20) Debt Service Suspension Initiative (DSSI), for example, were already in debt distress or close to debt distress prior to the pandemic.[20] During the first year of the pandemic, the debt stock of these countries increased from 54 percent to 61 percent of GDP, further limiting their ability to respond to the possibility of a drawn-out recovery.[21] While these debt levels are low by the standards of advanced economies, which have a much higher debt carrying capacity, they have been associated with the onset of debt crises in low-income countries.[22]

Figure O.4 shows the stark variation across countries in the scale of the fiscal response to the pandemic. The magnitude of the fiscal response as a share of GDP was almost uniformly large by any historic metric in high-income countries and uniformly small or nonexistent in low-income countries. In middle-income countries, the fiscal response varied significantly, reflecting marked differences in the ability and willingness of governments to mobilize fiscal resources and spend on support programs.

In many cases, fiscal emergency measures were supported by large monetary policy interventions. Several emerging economy central banks, for example, used unconventional monetary policies such as asset purchase programs for the first time in history. These programs supported the fiscal response and provided liquidity at a time it was most urgently needed. However, the capacity of central banks to support the crisis response in this manner varied dramatically, so that these policy tools were both more widely used and more effective in higher-middle-income countries that had deeper capital markets and a more sophisticated financial sector. By contrast, in most low-income countries governments were constrained in their response to the crisis because monetary policy was not able to play a similarly supportive role.

The initial impact of the pandemic translated into rising inequality across countries in large measure because of the constraints many governments faced in assisting households and businesses.[23] Although

Figure O.4 Fiscal response to the COVID-19 crisis, selected countries, by income group

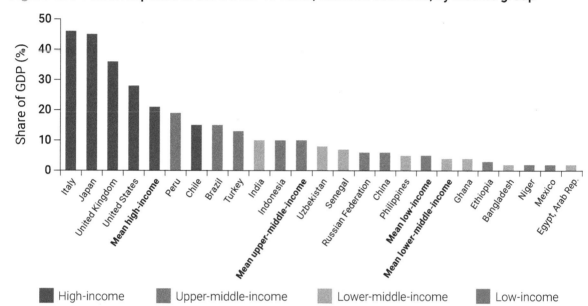

Source: WDR 2022 team, based on IMF (2021a). Data from International Monetary Fund, Fiscal Monitor Database of Country Fiscal Measures in Response to the COVID-19 Pandemic, Fiscal Affairs Department, https://www.imf.org/en/Topics/imf -and-covid19/Fiscal-Policies-Database-in-Response-to-COVID-19.

Note: The figure reports, as a percentage of GDP, the total fiscal support, calculated as the sum of "above-the-line measures" that affect government revenue and expenditures and the subtotal of liquidity support measures. Data are as of September 27, 2021.

poverty increased globally, nearly all of those who have slipped into extreme poverty (measured as the number of people living on less than $1.90 a day) as a result of the crisis live in lower-middle- and low-income countries.[24]

In addition to the scale of the policy response, there has also been wide variation in the combination of policy tools that countries have used to fight the immediate economic effects of the pandemic. This is illustrated by figure O.5, which shows the percentage of countries within country income groups that adopted different types of fiscal, monetary, and financial sector policy measures. The figure highlights some differences in the policy mix that are explained by resource constraints, as well as some differences that are explained by differences in the nature of economic risks faced by different countries. High-income and upper-middle-income economies, for example, made much more extensive use of financial sector policies, such as debt moratoria, given that financial institutions in these countries are much more exposed to household and small business loans, whose credit risk was severely affected by the pandemic.

Figure O.5 also highlights that the immediate response to the pandemic included a number of policy tools that were either untested in emerging economies or altogether unprecedented at this scale. One example are the extensive debt repayment moratoria and freezes on credit reporting that were enacted in many countries around the world. Although these programs have played an important role in mitigating the short-term liquidity issues faced by households and businesses, they did not necessarily address the future ability to repay, and had the unintended consequence of hiding loan losses, thereby creating a new problem: lack of transparency about credit risk and the true health of the financial sector.

Figure O.5 Fiscal, monetary, and financial sector policy responses to the pandemic, by country income group

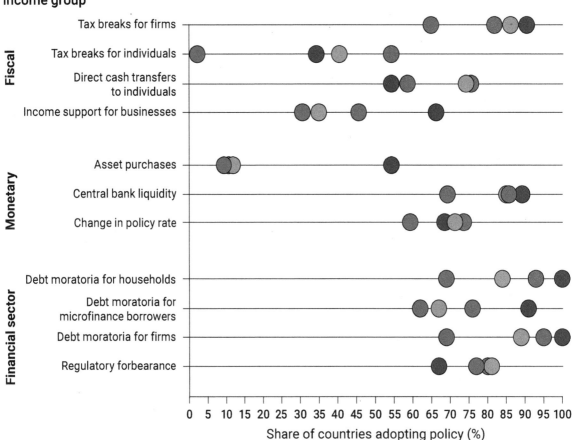

Sources: Fiscal measures: Lacey, Massad, and Utz 2021; monetary measures: World Bank, COVID-19 Finance Sector Related Policy Responses, September 30, 2021, https://datacatalog.worldbank.org/dataset/covid-19-finance-sector-related-policy -responses; financial sector: World Bank, COVID-19 Crisis Response Survey, 2021, http://bit.do/WDR2022-Covid-19_survey.

Note: The figure shows the percentage of countries in which each of the listed policies was implemented in response to the pandemic. Data for the financial sector measures are as of June 30, 2021.

Resolving financial risks: A prerequisite for an equitable recovery

The impact of the COVID-19 economic crisis has created unprecedented financial risks that will force governments, regulators, and financial institutions to pursue short-term stabilization policies and longer-term structural policies to steer their economies toward a sustained and equitable recovery. Traveling this path will require timely action in four policy areas:

1. Managing and reducing loan distress
2. Improving the legal insolvency framework
3. Ensuring continued access to finance
4. Managing increased levels of sovereign debt.

Policy area 1: Managing and reducing loan distress

In many countries, the crisis response has included large-scale debt relief measures, such as debt moratoria and freezes on credit reporting. Many of these policies have no historical precedent; it is therefore difficult to predict their longer-term impacts on the credit market. As governments wind down such support policies for borrowers, lenders should expect to see increases in nonperforming loans (NPLs) of varying magnitudes across countries and sectors.[25] Because many countries have relaxed the rules defining an NPL during the crisis, policy makers now face the challenge of interpreting increasingly opaque balance sheets. Banks' incentives to underplay the true extent of exposure to problem loans will likely increase as moratoria end, other support measures are phased out, and the impact of the pandemic becomes clearer. If not countered by strong bank governance, robust regulatory definitions of NPLs, and careful bank supervision, hidden NPLs can create significant discrepancies between reported asset quality figures and the underlying economic realities. A lack of NPL transparency can stand in the way of a timely identification of potential banking system stress, weaken trust in the financial sector, and lead to reductions in investment and lending, which can hinder an equitable postpandemic recovery.

Banks do have processes to manage NPLs in the normal course of business, but the scale and complexity of the possible increase resulting from the COVID-19 crisis could strain that capacity. This may, in turn, fuel a credit crunch, even in countries with sound financial institutions and, at worst, destabilize the financial sector. Banks confronting a decline in loan quality that severely affects capital tend to limit lending, and those reductions typically hit low-income households and small businesses the hardest. In this way, sharply rising NPLs can give rise to a negative feedback loop between deteriorating financial sector performance and weakening real economic activity, which can also exacerbate economic inequality.

Therefore, managing the risk posed by opacity about rising NPLs should be a priority to enable early and clear diagnosis of emerging financial stress and thus facilitate resolution of the problem, while recognizing that the degrees of stress and capacity to absorb higher NPLs differ across countries (figure O.6).

Microfinance institutions (MFIs) face similar challenges and so warrant the same attention from policy makers. Low-income households and micro-, small, and medium enterprises (MSMEs) in developing economies generally rely on MFIs instead of conventional banks for financial services. Although MFIs have so far weathered the pandemic better than initially expected, the challenges they face in refinancing their own debt and in pressures on their asset quality—which so far have been relatively stable in part because of government support—may increase as moratoria are fully lifted and loans begin to come due.

Figure O.6 Capacity of banking systems to absorb increases in nonperforming loans, by country income group

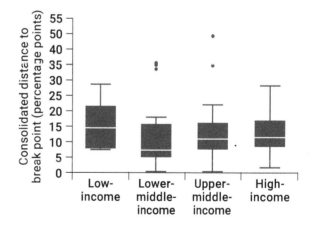

Source: WDR 2022 team, based on Feyen and Mare (2021).

Note: The figure reports the percentage point increase in the nonperforming loan (NPL) ratio at the country level that wipes out capital buffers for banks representing at least 20 percent of banking system assets (see Feyen and Mare 2021). Higher values denote higher capacity to absorb NPL increases. The country distribution of the percentage point increase in the nonperforming loan ratio is shown across country income groups. The underlying bank-level data are from up to July 2021. Dots are values falling outside the whisker range.

Past crises have revealed that without a swift, comprehensive policy response, loan quality issues are likely to persist and worsen over time, as epitomized by the typical increase in loans to "zombie firms"—that is, loans to weak businesses that have little or no prospect of returning to health and fully paying off their debts. Continued extension and rolling over of loans to such firms (also known as evergreening) stifles economic growth by absorbing capital that would be better directed to loans for businesses with high productivity and growth potential.

Some financial institutions may be unable to cope with rising NPLs and will require recapitalization or resolution. If left unaddressed, rising NPLs can set the stage for systemic banking crises, which are associated with severe and prolonged recessions and consequent effects on poverty and inequality. A prompt comprehensive response is therefore critical to preserving the financial sector's ability to support an equitable recovery and avoid mounting losses for the financial system. A strategy that supports timely identification and management of NPLs is necessary. The key elements of such a strategy are transparency, loan resolution, and problem bank resolution.

Improving transparency and supervision and reducing incentives for mismeasurement

An important first step is to establish enforceable rules and incentives that support transparency about the true state of banking assets. Assessing asset quality during the pandemic is complex because of the great uncertainty about economic prospects and the extent and persistence of income losses. The widespread use of debt moratoria and other support measures for borrowers has made it even more difficult for banks to assess the true repayment capacity of both existing and prospective borrowers. Indeed, debt moratoria and other support measures have reduced the comparability of NPL metrics across time both in countries and among countries.

Accurate and timely indicators of loan quality are essential to gauge the overall health of the financial sector and the ability of banks to absorb credit losses that may materialize in the near future.[26] The use of internationally agreed definitions of NPLs is critical for monitoring and assessing banks' asset quality in a consistent manner.[27] The easing of regulatory definitions obscures banks' true asset quality challenges and should be avoided.

Robust regulatory definitions should be underpinned by effective banking supervision. Banking supervisors, responsible for enforcing these regulatory definitions, must ensure that banks comply with prudential rules in an increasingly challenging environment. As pressure on the asset quality of banks increases, they increasingly are susceptible to incentives to step up efforts to disguise the extent of their difficulties in an attempt to avoid a supervisory or market response. Faced with these incentives, some banks may exploit regulatory loopholes or engage in questionable practices such as evergreening loans or transferring loans off balance sheets to present an overly optimistic picture of asset quality, which, in turn, can make a banking supervisor's job significantly more difficult.

Resolving troubled loans through regulatory interventions

Governments and banking supervisors can use various interventions to encourage banks to step up efforts to resolve troubled loans. To manage rising volumes of bad debt, they can require banks to adopt appropriate processes and dedicate sufficient resources to recovering past-due loans. Bank business models, organizational structure, strategy, and internal resources must all reflect a coherent approach to managing rising NPLs, including setting up dedicated internal workout units and devising methodologies to assess borrower viability.

Banks hold primary responsibility for managing distressed loans. Public interventions may be necessary as well, however, if problem loans jeopardize a banking system's capacity to finance the real economy or threaten the stability of the financial system. Individual bank-level strategies may not be sufficient when the increase in NPLs is systemwide, as would be expected after a pandemic. Public policy interventions, such as national NPL resolution strategies for coordinating NPL resolution efforts across stakeholders in the economy, can play a useful role in accelerating the reduction of bad debts. For example, the government of Serbia established a national NPL working group in May 2015 after the banking sector NPL ratio rose to 23.5 percent after the global financial crisis. The working group, which included participants from the public and private sectors, developed and implemented a comprehensive strategy for reducing NPLs,[28] which contributed to a fall in the NPL ratio to a historic low of 3.7 percent in December 2020.

In response to sharp systemic increases in NPL volumes, some countries have established public asset management companies (AMCs) or a systemwide "bad bank" to manage problem loans removed from bank balance sheets. Such a step can help to restore public confidence in the banking sector and prevent unnecessary fire sales. For example, in response to earlier crises, public AMCs were created in Malaysia and Spain in conjunction with publicly funded bank recapitalization schemes to overcome capital space constraints that otherwise would have hindered efforts to recognize the full extent of banks' exposure to problem loans. The case for and effectiveness of public AMCs depend on a country's circumstances and on the soundness of the overall design. This is an area in which emerging economies have in practice often experienced challenges.

Dealing with problem banks

When banks are unable to absorb the additional financial stress from the pandemic and develop a viable recovery plan, authorities must be able to deploy a robust set of early intervention measures to turn around ailing banks and resolve failing ones. Measures for dealing with failing banks should include a legal regime that sets bank failures apart from the general insolvency framework and gives authorities more policy options and greater powers to allocate losses to shareholders and uninsured liability holders, thereby protecting depositors while shielding taxpayers against financial sector losses.

Authorities responsible for handling troubled banks should always prioritize solutions led and funded by the private sector, building to the extent possible on the financial buffers of troubled financial entities. The use of public money to resolve a crisis should be a last resort, deployed after private sector solutions have been fully exhausted and only to remedy an acute and demonstrable threat to financial stability.

Policy area 2: Improving the legal insolvency framework

Many households and businesses are struggling with unsustainable debts as a result of the pandemic. Insolvency proceedings can be an effective mechanism to help reduce excessive levels of private debt. However, a sudden increase in loan defaults and bankruptcies resulting from the crisis (figure O.7) poses a significant challenge for the capacity of insolvency frameworks to resolve bankruptcies in a timely manner, even in advanced economies with strong institutions. This challenge stems, in part, from the complexity of court-led insolvency processes. According to World Bank data, resolution of a corporate bankruptcy case in the average country takes more than two years.[29] Complex liquidations can take even longer, even in well-functioning judicial systems.

For countries with weak insolvency frameworks, retaining the status quo creates the risk that more drastic and costlier action will be needed if NPLs and insolvency filings increase. The absence of effective legal mechanisms to declare bankruptcy or resolve creditor-debtor disputes invites political interference in the credit market in the form of debt relief mandated by the government because such

Figure O.7 Share of enterprises in arrears or expecting to fall into arrears within six months, selected countries, May–September 2020

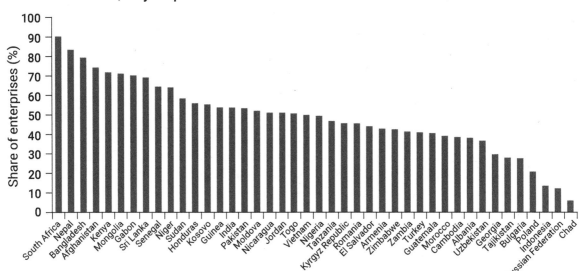

Source: Apedo-Amah et al. 2020, based on World Bank, COVID-19 Business Pulse Survey Dashboard, 2020–21 data, https://www.worldbank.org/en/data/interactive/2021/01/19/covid-19-business-pulse-survey-dashboard.
Note: The figure presents percentages for countries surveyed by the World Bank.

action becomes the only alternative for resolving unsustainable debts. Indeed, emerging economies have made extensive use of politicized debt forgiveness programs. In the past, such programs have often damaged credit discipline and the ability of creditworthy borrowers to obtain loans in the longer term.[30] Even in economies that have effective insolvency laws, debt resolution can be inhibited by a slow, overburdened judicial system with insufficient resources to manage the legal and procedural complexity of the issues.

Improving the institutional capacity to manage insolvency is critical for equitable economic recovery for several reasons. First, when households and businesses are saddled with unsustainable debts, consumption, job creation, and productive investment are suppressed. Second, the longer the time needed to resolve a bankruptcy case, the larger are the losses to creditors. Third, higher creditor losses reduce the availability of credit in the economy and raise its cost.[31] Finally, the longer the bankruptcy process, the more time overindebted "zombie" firms have to absorb resources that could support equitable economic recovery if they were redeployed to more productive firms.

In the aftermath of the COVID-19 crisis, the availability and efficiency of bankruptcy systems will determine how quickly unsustainable debt burdens can be reduced and, consequently, how quickly recovery can be achieved. Studies reveal that improvements in insolvency frameworks are associated with greater access to credit,[32] faster creditor recovery, stronger job preservation,[33] higher productivity,[34] and lower failure rates for small businesses.[35] Cost-reducing reforms can also create the right conditions for nonviable firms to file for liquidation,[36] thereby freeing up resources that could be redirected toward more productive firms with better growth prospects.

The following reforms can help to ease COVID-19 debt distress and facilitate an equitable economic recovery. These reforms can be taken up by economies at varying stages of development, with varying degrees of sophistication in their existing insolvency laws, and at varying levels of institutional capacity, and have been shown to be effective by evidence from numerous countries.

Strengthening formal insolvency mechanisms

A strong formal insolvency law regime defines the rights and behaviors needed for orderly in-court and out-of-court workouts.[37] A well-designed system includes incentives to motivate creditors and debtors to cooperate in the resolution process. Other tenets of a strong system are predictable creditor seniority rules that define the order in which debts are repaid;[38] timely resolution, which creates a positive feedback loop motivating all actors to engage in out-of-court workouts;[39] and adequate expertise in the complexities of bankruptcy law. Finally, early warning tools for the detection of business distress hold great promise to assist in the early identification of debtors in financial difficulty before this difficulty escalates to the point of insolvency.

Facilitating alternative dispute resolution systems

Alternative dispute resolution (ADR) frameworks can provide quicker and cheaper resolution of disputes than the formal court system, while retaining some of the rigor that courts provide. In an ADR process, the debtor and creditor engage directly. The process can be mediated by a third party; resolutions are contractually binding; and participants can maintain confidentiality. Variations of ADR processes include degrees of court involvement. Significant creditor buy-in and cohesion are needed in the ADR process because creditors unwilling to make concessions can bring the process to a halt. Active communications by regulators with the private sector, or legal mechanisms to prevent minority creditors from obstructing progress on a restructuring deal, are two methods that can help address the challenges associated with creditor cohesion.

Establishing accessible in-court and out-of-court procedures for small businesses

Small and medium-size businesses are less well capitalized than large businesses and frequently lack the resources and expertise to effectively understand and use complex, costly insolvency systems. Exacerbating these structural problems, the pandemic has hit small businesses harder than large businesses. Because of these factors, dedicated reforms are needed to design insolvency systems that cater to small and medium-size businesses. Such reforms include increasing the efficiency of debt restructuring for viable firms by simplifying legal processes, allowing debtors to maintain control of their businesses when possible, making fresh financing available, and using out-of-court proceedings to keep costs down. With these reforms, policy makers can help facilitate the survival of viable but illiquid firms and the swift exit of nonviable firms.

Promoting debt forgiveness and long-term reputational protection for former debtors

Job losses, reduced operations, and declining sales stemming from the COVID-19 pandemic have pushed many historically creditworthy individuals and entrepreneurs into delinquency. For small businesses, which are often financed at least in part by debt personally guaranteed by the entrepreneur, business failures can have severe adverse consequences. Because many of these borrowers have been devastated through no fault of their own, courts should try to quickly resolve no-income, no-asset cases, and the law should provide a mechanism for discharge and a fresh start for natural person entrepreneurs. High costs (such as court filing fees) and barriers to access (such as overly burdensome or confusing procedures) should be reduced or eliminated for personal bankruptcy, in particular for no-income, no-asset cases.

Policy area 3: Ensuring continued access to finance

Many households and small businesses are at risk of losing access to formal finance because of multiple factors stemming from the pandemic. Although most lenders have not seen massive pandemic-related liquidity challenges, they anticipate a rise in NPLs, and their ability to extend new loans is constrained by the ongoing economic disruption and the transparency issues discussed earlier. In these circumstances, lenders tend to issue less new credit, and the new credit they do issue goes to better-off borrowers. A review of quarterly central bank surveys on credit conditions in both advanced and emerging economies finds that the majority of economies for which surveys were available experienced several quarters of tightening credit standards after the onset of the crisis (see figure O.8). In periods of tighter credit, the most vulnerable borrowers, including small businesses and low-income households that lack physical collateral or a sufficiently long credit history, tend to be the first cut off from credit.

It is difficult to estimate how long it will take countries to fully recover from the pandemic and its economic repercussions. Because of uncertainty about the economic recovery and the financial health of prospective borrowers, financial institutions find it challenging to assess risk—a prerequisite for credit underwriting. Debt moratoria and freezes on credit reporting, while important for addressing the immediate impacts of the shock, have made it harder for banks to distinguish borrowers experiencing temporary liquidity problems from those that are truly insolvent. As for low-income households and small businesses, their credit risk is difficult to assess even in normal times because they usually lack a credit history and audited financial statements. The widespread disruption of business activity

Figure O.8 **Quarterly trends in credit conditions, by country income group, 2018–21**

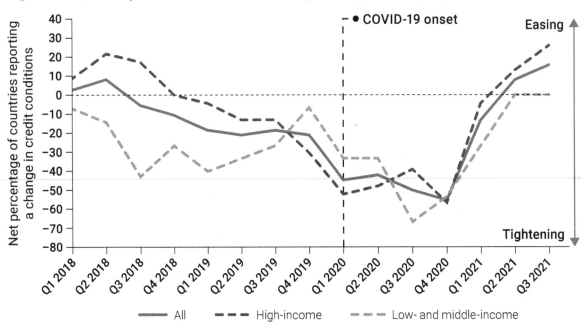

Source: WDR 2022 team calculations, based on data from survey reports by the central banks of 38 countries published or accessed as of December 15, 2021: Albania, Argentina, Austria, Belgium, Canada, Chile, Cyprus, Czech Republic, Estonia, France, Germany, Ghana, Greece, Hungary, India, Indonesia, Ireland, Italy, Japan, Latvia, Lithuania, Mexico, the Netherlands, North Macedonia, the Philippines, Poland, Portugal, Romania, the Russian Federation, Serbia, Spain, Thailand, Turkey, Uganda, Ukraine, the United Kingdom, the United States, and Zambia.

Note: The figure shows the net percentage of countries in which banks reported a change in overall credit conditions in quarterly central bank loan officer or credit condition surveys. The net percentage is the difference between the share of countries that report an overall easing in credit conditions and the share of countries that report an overall tightening of credit conditions relative to the previous quarter. A negative net percentage value indicates an overall tightening of credit conditions in the sample of countries covered. For Chile, Japan, Mexico, Poland, Russia, the United States, and Zambia, the overall credit conditions are estimated from an index of reported credit conditions in business and consumer segments.

and livelihoods has made assessment even more difficult. Banks and nonbank lenders therefore react by tightening credit and reallocating lending—where possible—to observably lower-risk borrowers. Lending innovations that incorporate new approaches for risk measurement and product design can counter this tendency. The accelerated digital adoption that occurred during the pandemic, coupled with the ongoing digital transformation of financial services and financial infrastructure (in a context of consumer and sector protection) could enable those innovations and help lenders better navigate COVID-19–related uncertainty to continue issuing credit.

Mitigating risk by improving visibility and recourse

The pandemic has made it more difficult to assess the credit risk of potential borrowers and limited lenders' recourse when a borrower defaults.

New data and technologies can be used to update existing risk models and increase visibility into a borrower's ability to repay. For example, Konfío—a digital MSME lender that leverages electronic invoices and other alternative data to supplement traditional credit information—adapted its credit algorithm in the early months of the pandemic to integrate granular data on the impacts of COVID-19 on small firms in Mexico. It then doubled its monthly loan disbursements during the pandemic. Other strategies to enhance visibility include temporarily reducing loan tenors and leveraging digital channels to gather high-frequency current transactional data. The use of digital channels can also lower delivery costs to reach small businesses and households more effectively.

Adapting loan product design and product selection can improve recourse in the event the borrower does not repay. Products that allow borrowers to pledge movable assets as collateral or that offer lenders less traditional forms of recourse, such as liens on future cash flows, can help offset the impacts of the pandemic on traditional collateral. Working capital financing that occurs within a supply chain or is embedded in the workflow of a commercial transaction links credit to an existing commercial relationship, as well as to an underlying economic activity and its associated data. Forms of embedded finance are expanding into payments, lending, insurance, and other product areas in various contexts, including e-commerce, logistics, order and inventory management, and other digital platforms. These and other forms of contextual lending provide both better visibility into the financial prospects of the borrower and additional recourse—for example, through automatic repayments from the borrower's revenue through the platform.

Supporting new lending by insuring credit risk

Insuring against loss can help to restore credit growth when sufficient visibility and recourse cannot be achieved using the innovations just described. Credit guarantees give lenders recourse to the guarantor in case of default by the borrower. These instruments may be offered by governments, development banks, or donors to promote lending to priority segments where there are market failures in financing such as small businesses. Guarantees have been a component of pandemic responses in advanced countries and several emerging economies, and partial guarantee schemes may continue to play an important role in the recovery. For example, in Burkina Faso the World Bank helped the government set up a credit guarantee scheme focused on restructured and working capital loans for small and medium enterprises struggling from the COVID-19 crisis, but with potential for long-term profitability. Such programs must be carefully designed to be sustainable. As economic conditions improve, guarantors and their partner lenders can progressively narrow eligibility to the sectors or customer segments that continue to be most in need, and guarantee programs can be leveraged to reduce the risk associated with longer-term investments to support priorities such as job creation and financial flows to low-carbon activities.

Adopting policies to facilitate access and manage risks

Financial innovation has the potential to support responsible delivery of financial services, but unsupervised financial innovation can pose risks for both consumers and financial stability and integrity. Governments and regulators must modernize their policy frameworks to balance the sometimes conflicting imperatives of encouraging responsible innovation while also protecting customers and the financial sector's stability and integrity. Updated regulatory and supervisory approaches should seek to recognize and enable entry into the market of new providers, introduction of new products, and innovations in the use of data and analytics; enhance consumer protection policies and rules around what finance providers can and cannot offer; and facilitate collaboration between regulators and the government authorities overseeing different aspects of digital and embedded finance, as well as competition and market conduct, to prevent regulatory gaps between agencies with overlapping authority. Policies should support modernization of financial infrastructure to facilitate operational resilience and access, including both "hard" infrastructure related to telecommunications networks, payment networks, data centers, credit bureaus, and collateral registries, and "soft" infrastructure around the policies and procedures that dictate standards, access, and rules of engagement. These government policy responses to support digital transformation can help foster a more robust, innovative, and inclusive financial sector.

Policy area 4: Managing higher levels of sovereign debt

The pandemic has led to a dramatic increase in sovereign debt. As shown in figure O.9, the average total debt burdens among low- and middle-income countries increased by roughly 9 percentage points of GDP during the first year of the pandemic, 2019–20, compared with an average increase of 1.9 percentage points over the previous decade. Although interest payments in high-income economies have been trending lower in recent years and account, on average, for a little over 1 percentage point of GDP, they have been climbing steadily in low- and middle-income economies.[40]

Debt distress—that is, when a country is not able to fulfill its financial obligations—poses significant social costs. One study finds that every year that a country remains in default reduces GDP growth by 1.0–1.5 percentage points.[41] During the pandemic, governments accumulated debt to finance current expenditures, but it came at the cost of limiting their ability to spend in the future, including on public goods such as education and public health. Underinvestment in these services can worsen inequality and human development outcomes.[42] High debt and lack of spending flexibility also limit the capacity of governments to cope with future shocks.[43] Moreover, because governments are often the lender of last resort, private sector debts can quickly become public debt if financial and economic stability is threatened in an economic crisis and public assistance is required. Protecting the ability of the government to invest in public goods, to act in a countercyclical manner, and to enable the central bank to deliver on its unique role as the lender of last resort is a central goal of managing sovereign debt.

Managing sovereign debt to free up resources for the recovery

Countries at high risk of debt distress can pursue several policy options to make payment obligations more manageable. The feasibility of these options is shaped by the specifics of the case, including the extent of a country's access to private capital markets, the composition of the debt and creditors, and the debtor country's ability and willingness to negotiate and undertake necessary reforms. The options include modifications of the structure of liabilities and schedule of future payments through negotiations with creditors and the effective use of refinancing tools (debt reprofiling). Proactive debt management can reduce the risk of default and free up the fiscal resources needed to support an equitable economic recovery.

A reprofiling operation could be helpful when a country has multiple loans to be repaid in the same year. The country could issue new debt with a longer or a more even maturity profile. Debt reprofiling

Figure O.9 General government gross debt, by country income group, 2010–20

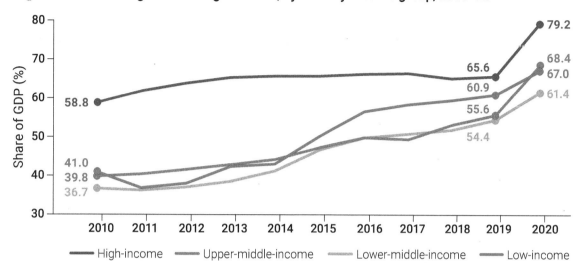

Source: WDR 2022 team, based on data from IMF (2021b); World Bank, World Development Indicators (database), https://datatopics.worldbank.org/world-development-indicators/.
Note: The figure shows the general government debt stock as a share of gross domestic product (GDP) by World Bank income classification.

operations can also help address currency risk, which often adds to debt sustainability concerns. In this case, instead of changing the maturity of the existing debt, the debt reprofiling operation retires the existing debt denominated in one (more expensive or volatile) currency by issuing new debt in another (less expensive or more stable) currency.

Countries facing elevated default risk also have the option of initiating preemptive negotiations with their creditors to reach debt restructuring. This option particularly benefits from transparency around the terms and ownership of the debt. Minimizing the chances of holdouts is important to ensure a speedy resolution. Some evidence shows that a preemptive restructuring is resolved faster than a post-default restructuring, leads to a shorter exclusion of the country from global capital markets, and is associated with a smaller loss in output.[44]

Resolving debt distress

Once a government is in debt distress, the options to treat the problem are more limited and the urgency is greater. A primary tool at this stage is debt restructuring coupled with a medium-term fiscal and economic reform plan. Use of this tool requires prompt recognition of the extent of the problem, coordination with and among creditors, and an understanding by all parties that restructuring is the first step toward debt sustainability. International financial institutions such as the World Bank and the International Monetary Fund (IMF) play an important role in the debt restructuring process for emerging economies by providing the debt sustainability analyses needed to fully understand the problem and often offering the financing to make the deal viable.

A swift, deep restructuring agreement allows a faster and more sustained recovery.[45] The historical track record, however, reveals that resolution of sovereign debt distress is often delayed for years. Even when a country enters negotiations with its creditors, multiple rounds of debt restructuring are often needed for it to emerge from debt distress (see figure O.10). The Democratic Republic of Congo, Jamaica, and Nigeria each had to negotiate seven debt restructuring deals before resolving their debt situations.

Figure O.10 Sovereign debt restructuring and time spent in default, selected countries, 1975–2000

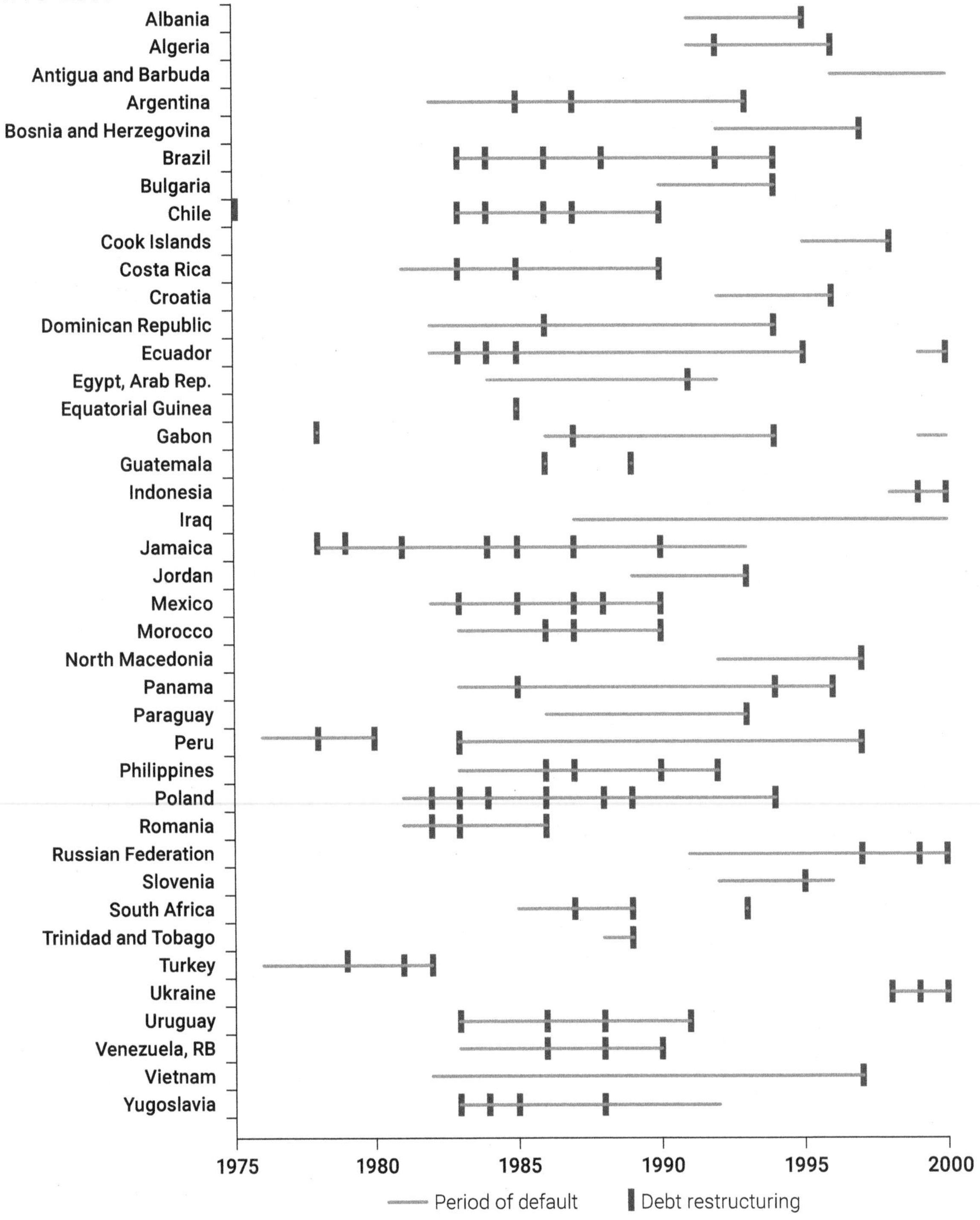

Source: WDR 2022 team, based on Cruces and Trebesch (2013); Farah-Yacoub, Graf von Luckner, and Reinhart (2021); Meyer, Reinhart, and Trebesch (2019); Reinhart and Rogoff (2009).

Note: The figure shows a timeline of sovereign defaults and debt restructuring from 1975 to 2000. The figure excludes countries covered by the International Development Association (IDA) and the Heavily Indebted Poor Countries (HIPC) Initiative.

Restructuring sovereign debt may have become more complex. The creditor community now has a higher share of nontraditional lenders (such as investment companies, bondholders, and official creditors who are not members of the Paris Club[46]). Domestic sources of financing have also increased. Potential off–balance sheet and often unrecorded public sector borrowing from state-owned enterprises and special-purpose vehicles has also trended higher. Collectively, these developments reduce transparency and may complicate the coordination between creditors.

In emerging economies, reducing sovereign debt (particularly external debt) has often required debt restructuring, but governments have also pursued fiscal consolidation (lower expenditures, higher taxes, or both) to improve government revenue, fiscal balances, and debt servicing capacity.

Other ways to reduce domestic currency–denominated debt have included liquidation through inflation or financial repression.[47] Although these approaches have often delivered debt reduction, they frequently come with extremely high social and economic costs that can aggravate poverty and inequality. Inflation is a regressive tax, which would compound the already highly regressive effects of the COVID-19 crisis.

Looking ahead—improving transparency and reducing coordination problems

The surge in sovereign debt during the COVID-19 crisis highlights the need for strategies that can facilitate effective debt management, debt negotiation, and access to capital markets over the longer term. Three broad initiatives stand out: greater debt transparency, contractual innovation, and tax policy and administration reforms.

Effective, forward-looking debt management requires comprehensive disclosure of claims against the government and the full terms of the contracts that govern this debt. Recent debt events have highlighted the problem of "hidden" or undisclosed debt and the possibility of legal disputes about the lack of authority of government and quasi-government entities to enter into debt contracts. Transparency on amounts owed and the contracts themselves does not guarantee a speedy restructuring, but it certainly sets the stage for a more rapid recognition of debt sustainability problems, thereby improving surveillance, and a more favorable entry point for negotiations among the debtors and creditors and the creditors themselves.

Contractual innovations, for their part, can help overcome coordination problems and speed up the resolution of sovereign debt restructuring. These innovations include collective action clauses (CACs),[48] which could lead to faster resolution; state-contingent debt contracts that insure the borrower against disaster risk; and legal reforms that address problematic enforcement practices against states. These innovations offer a positive way forward for new debt contracts. However, they have a more limited role in dealing with debts that require restructuring because state-contingent contracts account for a small share of the outstanding debt contracts of emerging markets. Contracts that include enhanced CACs account for only about half of outstanding contracts.[49]

A well-developed tax policy and administration are essential for debt sustainability. Higher tax revenue arises principally from long-term investments in tax capacity and from structural changes in countries' economies. Taxing wealth through property, income, and capital gains taxes is an underused revenue generation strategy in most emerging economies that would also mitigate the adverse impacts of the COVID-19 crisis on poverty and inequality. Revenue mobilization strategies should also strengthen incentives for businesses to formalize.

As governments pursue changes to manage their debt and promote pro-recovery practices, it is important that they recognize that the COVID-19 pandemic is a crisis within a crisis because of the ongoing impacts of climate change on countries and their economies. Governments' plans to rebuild should place the need for green investments front and center. One promising avenue is issuing sovereign green and social bonds. Pioneering governments are beginning to pave the way for similar debt issuances by the private sector. In 2017, Nigeria became the first African country to issue a sovereign green bond, which was followed by the first green corporate issuance from Access Bank.[50] In 2019, Chile became the first green sovereign bond issuer in Latin America, followed by Banco de Chile, which issued a green bond to raise funds for renewable energy projects.[51] These types of green investments will need to grow as a share of the recovering economy.

Conclusion

The COVID-19 pandemic and the unprecedented worldwide public health crisis it unleashed led to millions of deaths, job losses, business failures, and school closings. The ensuing economic and social disruption both exposed and exacerbated existing economic fragilities, especially in emerging economies, where poverty rates soared and inequality worsened.

Addressing the interrelated economic risks produced by the crisis is a prerequisite for a sustained and equitable recovery. This will require prompt recognition of balance sheet problems, as well as active management of the economic and financial risks. In an ideal situation, governments would implement relevant policies to address each of the risks highlighted by the crisis: financial instability; overindebtedness among households and businesses; reduced access to credit; and rising sovereign debt. However, few if any governments have the resources and political leeway to tackle all of these challenges at once. Countries will have to prioritize the most important policy actions needed. For many low-income countries, tackling unsustainable sovereign debt will be the first priority. Middle-income countries whose financial sectors are more exposed to corporate and household debt may, in contrast, need to focus on policies supporting financial stability.

Although this Report concentrates on the key domestic financial and economic risks produced by the pandemic, a country's recovery prospects will also be shaped by events in the global economy. One example is fluctuations in the price of primary commodities, which are an important source of revenue for many emerging economies. Another example is exchange rate and interest rate risks, which could emerge as economic activity in advanced economies recovers and stimulus programs are withdrawn, resulting in central banks tightening global liquidity and raising interest rates. These global developments expose households, firms, and governments in emerging economies to financial risks. A carefully chosen policy mix must therefore take into account both domestic and global threats to an equitable recovery.

At the same time, the necessity to address the risks created by the pandemic offers an immense opportunity to accelerate the shift toward a more efficient and sustainable world economy. Climate change is a major source of neglected risk in the world economy.[52] Failure to manage these risks will result in the continued mispricing of assets, capital misallocation, and a vicious cycle in which devastating climate disasters are compounded by spikes in financial instability.[53] The financial sector can help activate a virtuous cycle by recognizing and pricing climate risks, so that capital flows toward more sustainable firms and industries.[54] In the aftermath of the COVID-19 pandemic, governments have an opportunity to support the financial sector's ability to perform this role by, for example, mandating risk disclosures and phasing out any preferential tax, auditing, and regulatory policies for environmentally unsustainable industries.

The COVID-19 pandemic is possibly the largest shock to the global economy in over a century. As fiscal, monetary, and financial stimulus programs are withdrawn, new policy challenges will emerge at both the domestic and global levels. Early diagnosis of the economic effects of the crisis and decisive policy action to remedy these fault lines are needed to sustain an equitable recovery. There is no room for policy complacency.

Notes

1. Global real GDP growth in 2020 is estimated at −3.1 percent in the International Monetary Fund's *World Economic Outlook* (IMF 2021c) and −3.5 percent in the World Bank's *Global Economic Prospects* (World Bank 2021a).
2. For more details, see Mahler et al. (2021).
3. Kugler and Sinha (2020).
4. See Reinhart, Rogoff, and Savastano (2003) on "debt intolerance."
5. Holston, Kaminsky, and Reinhart (2021).
6. This definition builds on the broader definition of *equitable development* in World Bank (2005), but it is adapted to the context of the COVID-19 pandemic.
7. Fratto et al. (2021); IMF (2021b).
8. Andersen et al. (2020). Data from World Bank, COVID-19 Business Pulse Survey Dashboard, https://www.world bank.org/en/data/interactive/2021/01/19/covid-19 -business-pulse-survey-dashboard.
9. The difference in the rate of work stoppage between low- and high-educated workers was found to be statistically significant in 23 percent of the countries. For more details, see Kugler et al. (2021).
10. Bundervoet, Dávalos, and Garcia (2021).
11. World Bank, COVID-19 Household Monitoring Dashboard, https://www.worldbank.org/en/data/interactive /2020/11/11/covid-19-high-frequency-monitoring -dashboard.
12. Adams-Prassl et al. 2020; Chetty et al. (2020); Crossley, Fisher, and Low (2021).
13. Mahler, Yonzan, and Lakner (forthcoming).
14. Agrawal et al. (2021).
15. Because of a lack of comprehensive data on many countries, the estimates at the global level assume there are no changes in inequality. Lakner et al. (2020) and Yonzan et al. (2020) estimate the impact of COVID-19 on global poverty using a range of assumptions on inequality within countries.
16. Intrum (2020).
17. Medina and Schneider (2019).
18. See International Labour Organization, "Informal Economy in South Asia," https://www.ilo.org/newdelhi /areasofwork/informal-economy/lang--en/index.htm.
19. World Bank (2020a).
20. WDR 2022 team, based on data from World Bank and International Monetary Fund, Joint World Bank–International Monetary Fund LIC DSF Database (Debt Sustainability Framework for Low-Income Countries), https://www.world bank.org/en/programs/debt-toolkit /dsf.
21. Based on data from IMF (2021b); World Bank, World Development Indicators (database), https://datatopics .worldbank.org/world-development-indicators/.
22. Reinhart, Rogoff, and Savastano (2003).
23. Mahler et al. (2021) based on World Bank, Global Economic Prospects DataBank, https://databank .worldbank.org/source/global-economic-prospects; World Bank, PovcalNet (dashboard), http://iresearch .worldbank.org/PovcalNet/.
24. Ferreira et al. (2021) and Mahler et al. (2021), building on these poverty estimates, estimate a measure of additional poverty years induced by COVID-19. They assume, conservatively, that poverty stemming from the pandemic lasts for one year and show that additional poverty years have a strong downward-sloping relationship with GDP per capita.
25. This observation assumes that the definition of a non-performing loan has remained constant throughout the pandemic. NPLs, as defined by the Basel Committee on Banking Supervision (BCBS 2017), are those loans with lower credit quality in terms of delinquency status (unpaid for a certain period of time) or unlikeliness of repayment.
26. Pancorbo, Rozumek, and Seal (2020).
27. BCBS (2017).
28. NBS and MFIN (2018).
29. World Bank (2020b).
30. Giné and Kanz (2018).
31. Jappelli, Pagano, and Bianco (2005); World Bank (2014).
32. Araujo, Ferreira, and Funchal (2012).
33. Fonseca and Van Doornik (2020).
34. Lim and Hahn (2003); Neira (2017).
35. World Bank (2014).
36. Giné and Love (2006).
37. Based on data from World Bank, COVID-19 Business Pulse Survey Dashboard, https://www.worldbank.org /en/data/interactive/2021/01/19/covid-19-business -pulse-survey-dashboard.
38. Based on data from World Bank, COVID-19 Business Pulse Survey Dashboard, https://www.worldbank.org /en/data/interactive/2021/01/19/covid-19-business -pulse-survey-dashboard.
39. Gadgil, Ronald, and Vyakaranam (2019).
40. Kose et al. (2021).
41. Borensztein and Panizza (2009).
42. Baldacci, de Mello, and Inchauste (2002); Furceri and Zdzienicka (2012); Ravallion and Chen (2009).
43. Mbaye, Badia, and Chae (2018).
44. Asonuma and Trebesch (2016).
45. Reinhart and Trebesch (2016).
46. The Paris Club, a standing committee of official creditor countries formed in 1956, has been instrumental in the majority of sovereign debt restructurings since its creation.
47. See Reinhart, Reinhart, and Rogoff (2015).
48. A collective action clause (CAC) is an article in bond contracts establishing rules in case of restructuring. In particular, if a majority of bondholders agrees to debt restructuring, that agreement becomes legally binding for all bondholders, including those who voted against the restructuring.
49. IMF (2020).
50. Climate Bonds Initiative (2017); Fatin (2019).
51. Climate Bonds Initiative (2019).
52. Gennaioli, Shleifer, and Vishny (2012); Stroebel and Wurgler (2021).
53. Gennaioli, Shleifer, and Vishny (2012).
54. Bolton et al. (2020); Carney (2015); Fender et al. (2020).

References

Adams-Prassl, Abi, Teodora Boneva, Marta Golina, and Christopher Rauh. 2020. "Inequality in the Impact of the Coronavirus Shock: Evidence from Real Time Surveys." *Journal of Public Economics* 189 (September): 104245.

Agrawal, Sarthak, Alexandru Cojocaru, Veronica Montalva, and Ambar Narayan. 2021. "COVID-19 and Inequality: How Unequal Was the Recovery from the Initial Shock?" With inputs by Tom Bundervoet and Andrey Ten. Brief, World Bank, Washington, DC.

Andersen, Steffen, John Y. Campbell, Kasper Meisner Nielsen, and Tarun Ramadorai. 2020. "Sources of Inaction in Household Finance: Evidence from the Danish Mortgage Market." *American Economic Review* 110 (10): 3184–230.

Apedo-Amah, Marie Christine, Besart Avdiu, Xavier Cirera, Marcio Cruz, Elwyn Davies, Arti Grover, Leonardo Iacovone, et al. 2020. "Unmasking the Impact of COVID-19 on Businesses: Firm Level Evidence from across the World." Policy Research Working Paper 9434, World Bank, Washington, DC.

Araujo, Aloisio P., Rafael V. X. Ferreira, and Bruno Funchal. 2012. "The Brazilian Bankruptcy Law Experience." *Journal of Corporate Finance* 18 (4): 994–1004.

Asonuma, Tamon, and Christoph Trebesch. 2016. "Sovereign Debt Restructurings: Preemptive or Post-Default." *Journal of the European Economic Association* 14 (1): 175–214.

Baldacci, Emanuele, Luiz de Mello, and Gabriela Inchauste. 2002. "Financial Crises, Poverty, and Income Distribution." IMF Working Paper 02/4, International Monetary Fund, Washington, DC.

BCBS (Basel Committee on Banking Supervision). 2017. "Prudential Treatment of Problem Assets—Definitions of Non-performing Exposures and Forbearance." Bank for International Settlements, Basel, Switzerland. https://www.bis.org/bcbs/publ/d403.htm.

Bolton, Patrick, Morgan Despres, Luiz Awazu Pereira da Silva, Frédéric Samama, and Romain Svartzman. 2020. *The Green Swan: Central Banking and Financial Stability in the Age of Climate Change.* Basel, Switzerland: Bank for International Settlements.

Borensztein, Eduardo, and Ugo Panizza. 2009. "The Costs of Sovereign Default." *IMF Staff Papers* 56 (4): 683–741.

Bundervoet, Tom, María Eugenia Dávalos, and Natalia Garcia. 2021. "The Short-Term Impacts of COVID-19 on Households in Developing Countries: An Overview Based on a Harmonized Data Set of High-Frequency Surveys." Policy Research Working Paper 9582, World Bank, Washington, DC.

Carney, Mark. 2015. "Breaking the Tragedy of the Horizon: Climate Change and Financial Stability." Address at Lloyd's of London, London, September 29, 2015. https://www.bis.org/review/r151009a.pdf.

Chetty, Raj, John N. Friedman, Nathaniel Hendren, Michael Stepner, and Opportunity Insights Team. 2020. "How Did COVID-19 and Stabilization Policies Affect Spending and Employment? A New Real-Time Economic Tracker Based on Private Sector Data." NBER Working Paper 27431, National Bureau of Economic Research, Cambridge, MA.

Climate Bonds Initiative. 2017. "Nigeria First Nation to Issue a Climate Bonds Certified Sovereign Green Bond." Media release, December 19, 2017. https://www.climatebonds.net/resources/press-releases/2017/12/nigeria-first-nation-issue-climate-bonds-certified-sovereign-green.

Climate Bonds Initiative. 2019. "Banco de Chile." Green Bond Fact Sheet, September 17, Climate Bonds Initiative, London. https://www.climatebonds.net/files/files/2019-08%20CL%20Banco%20de%20Chile.pdf.

Crossley, Thomas F., Paul Fisher, and Hamish Low. 2021. "The Heterogeneous and Regressive Consequences of COVID-19: Evidence from High Quality Panel Data." *Journal of Public Economics* 193 (January): 104334.

Cruces, Juan J., and Christoph Trebesch. 2013. "Sovereign Defaults: The Price of Haircuts." *American Economic Journal: Macroeconomics* 5 (3): 85–117.

Farah-Yacoub, Juan, Clemens Graf von Luckner, and Carmen M. Reinhart. 2021. "The Eternal External Debt Crisis: A Long View." Unpublished manuscript, World Bank, Washington, DC.

Fatin, Leena. 2019. "Nigeria: Access Bank 1st Certified Corporate Green Bond in Africa; Leadership in Green Finance." *Climate Bonds Initiative* (blog), April 2, 2019. https://www.climatebonds.net/2019/04/nigeria-access-bank-1st-certified-corporate-green-bond-africa-leadership-green-finance.

Fender, Ingo, Mike McMorrow, Vahe Sahakyan, and Omar Zulaica. 2020. "Reserve Management and Sustainability: The Case for Green Bonds?" BIS Working Paper 849, Monetary and Economic Department, Bank for International Settlements, Basel, Switzerland.

Ferreira, Francisco H. G., Olivier Sterck, Daniel G. Mahler, and Benoît Decerf. 2021. "Death and Destitution: The Global Distribution of Welfare Losses from the COVID-19 Pandemic." *LSE Public Policy Review* 1 (4): 1–11.

Feyen, Erik, and Davide Salvatore Mare. 2021. "Measuring Systemic Banking Resilience: A Simple Reverse Stress Testing Approach." Policy Research Working Paper 9864, World Bank, Washington, DC.

Fonseca, Julia, and Bernadus Van Doornik. 2020. "Financial Development and Labor Market Outcomes: Evidence from Brazil." Working Paper 532, Research Department, Central Bank of Brazil, Brasília.

Fratto, Chiara, Brendan Harnoys Vannier, Borislava Mircheva, David de Padua, and Hélène Poirson. 2021. "Unconventional Monetary Policies in Emerging Markets and Frontier Countries." IMF Working Paper WP/21/14, International Monetary Fund, Washington, DC.

Furceri, Davide, and Aleksandra Zdzienicka. 2012. "How Costly Are Debt Crises?" *Journal of International Money and Finance* 31 (4): 726–42.

Gadgil, Shon, Bindu Ronald, and Lasya Vyakaranam. 2019. "Timely Resolution of Cases under the Insolvency and Bankruptcy Code." *Journal of Critical Reviews* 6 (6): 156–67.

Gennaioli, Nicola, Andrei Shleifer, and Robert W. Vishny. 2012. "Neglected Risks, Financial Innovation and Financial Fragility." *Journal of Financial Economics* 104 (3): 452–68.

Giné, Xavier, and Martin Kanz. 2018. "The Economic Effects of a Borrower Bailout: Evidence from an Emerging Market." *Review of Financial Studies* 31 (5): 1752–83.

Giné, Xavier, and Inessa Love. 2006. "Do Reorganization Costs Matter for Efficiency? Evidence from a Bankruptcy Reform in Colombia." Policy Research Working Paper 3970, World Bank, Washington, DC.

Holston, Kathryn, Graciela L. Kaminsky, and Carmen M. Reinhart. 2021. "Bust without a Boom? Banking Fragility during COVID-19." Unpublished manuscript, World Bank, Washington, DC.

IMF (International Monetary Fund). 2020. "The International Architecture for Resolving Sovereign Debt Involving Private-Sector Creditors: Recent Developments, Challenges, and Reform Options." Policy Paper 2020/043, IMF, Washington, DC. https://www.imf.org/en/Publications/Policy-Papers/Issues/2020/09/30/The-International-Architecture-for-Resolving-Sovereign-Debt-Involving-Private-Sector-49796.

IMF (International Monetary Fund). 2021a. "Fiscal Monitor Update." January, IMF, Washington, DC.

IMF (International Monetary Fund). 2021b. *World Economic Outlook: Managing Divergent Recoveries.* Washington, DC: IMF.

IMF (International Monetary Fund). 2021c. *World Economic Outlook: Recovery during a Pandemic; Health Concerns, Supply Disruptions, and Price Pressures.* Washington, DC: IMF.

Intrum. 2020. "European Payment Report 2020: Special Edition White Paper." Intrum, Stockholm. https://www.intrum.com/media/8279/epr-2020-special-edition-white-paper_final.pdf.

Jappelli, Tullio, Marco Pagano, and Magda Bianco. 2005. "Courts and Banks: Effects of Judicial Enforcement on Credit Markets." *Journal of Money, Credit, and Banking* 37 (2): 223–44.

Kose, M. Ayhan, Franziska Ohnsorge, Carmen M. Reinhart, and Kenneth S. Rogoff. 2021. "The Aftermath of Debt Surges." Policy Research Working Paper 9771, World Bank, Washington, DC.

Kugler, Maurice, and Shakti Sinha. 2020. "The Impact of COVID-19 and the Policy Response in India." *Future Development* (blog), July 13, 2020. https://www.brookings.edu/blog/future-development/2020/07/13/the-impact-of-covid-19-and-the-policy-response-in-india/.

Kugler, Maurice, Mariana Viollaz, Daniel Duque, Isis Gaddis, David Locke Newhouse, Amparo Palacios-López, and Michael Weber. 2021. "How Did the COVID-19 Crisis Affect Different Types of Workers in the Developing World?" Policy Research Working Paper 9703, World Bank, Washington, DC.

Lacey, Eric, Joseph Massad, and Robert Utz. 2021. "A Review of Fiscal Policy Responses to COVID-19." Equitable Growth, Finance and Institutions Insight, World Bank, Washington, DC. https://openknowledge.worldbank.org/handle/10986/35904.

Lakner, Christoph, Daniel Gerszon Mahler, Mario Negre, and Espen Beer Prydz. 2020. "How Much Does Reducing Inequality Matter for Global Poverty?" Global Poverty Monitoring Technical Note 13, World Bank, Washington, DC.

Lim, Youngjae, and Chin Hee Hahn. 2003. "Bankruptcy Policy Reform and Total Factor Productivity Dynamics in Korea: Evidence from Macro Data." NBER Working Paper 9810, National Bureau of Economic Research, Cambridge, MA.

Mahler, Daniel Gerszon, Nishant Yonzan, and Christoph Lakner [randomized order]. Forthcoming. "The Impacts of COVID-19 on Global Inequality and Poverty." Unpublished manuscript, World Bank, Washington, DC.

Mahler, Daniel Gerszon, Nishant Yonzan, Christoph Lakner, Raul Andrés Castañeda Aguilar, and Haoyu Wu. 2021. "Updated Estimates of the Impact of COVID-19 on Global Poverty: Turning the Corner on the Pandemic in 2021?" *World Bank Blogs: Data Blogs*, June 24, 2021. https://blogs.worldbank.org/opendata/updated-estimates-impact-covid-19-global-poverty-turning-corner-pandemic-2021.

Mbaye, Samba, Marialuz Moreno Badia, and Kyungla Chae. 2018. "Bailing Out the People? When Private Debt Becomes Public." IMF Working Paper 18/141, International Monetary Fund, Washington, DC.

Medina, Leandro, and Friedrich Georg Schneider. 2019. "Shedding Light on the Shadow Economy: A Global Database and the Interaction with the Official One." CESifo Working Paper 7981, Munich Society for the Promotion of Economic Research, Center for Economic Studies, Ludwig-Maximilians-University Munich, and Ifo Institute for Economic Research, Munich.

Meyer, Josefin, Carmen M. Reinhart, and Christoph Trebesch. 2019. "Sovereign Bonds since Waterloo." NBER Working Paper 25543, National Bureau of Economic Research, Cambridge, MA.

NBS (National Bank of Serbia) and MFIN (Ministry of Finance, Serbia). 2018. "NPL Resolution Strategy: Lessons Learned from the NPL Working Group in Serbia." Presentation at FinSAC NPL Resolution Conference, Vienna, May 15–16, 2018. https://thedocs.worldbank.org/en/doc/3c28bd048d78efd27744987253e2c44a-0430012021/original/NPLConferenceDay211MilanKovacMarijaRandelovic.pdf.

Neira, Julian. 2017. "Bankruptcy and Cross-Country Differences in Productivity." *Journal of Economic Behavior and Organization* 157 (January): 359–81.

Pancorbo, Antonio, David Lukas Rozumek, and Katharine Seal. 2020. "Supervisory Actions and Priorities in Response to the COVID-19 Pandemic Crisis." Special Series on Financial Policies to Respond to COVID-19, Monetary and Capital Markets Department, International Monetary Fund, Washington, DC.

Ravallion, Martin, and Shaohua Chen. 2009. "The Impact of the Global Financial Crisis on the World's Poorest." *VoxEU* (blog), April 30, 2009. https://voxeu.org/article/impact-global-financial-crisis-world-s-poorest.

Reinhart, Carmen M., Vincent Reinhart, and Kenneth S. Rogoff. 2015. "Dealing with Debt." *Journal of International Economics* 96 (Supplement 1): S43–S55.

Reinhart, Carmen M., and Kenneth S. Rogoff. 2009. *This Time Is Different: Eight Centuries of Financial Folly.* Princeton, NJ: Princeton University Press.

Reinhart, Carmen M., Kenneth S. Rogoff, and Miguel A. Savastano. 2003. "Debt Intolerance." NBER Working Paper 9908, National Bureau of Economic Research, Cambridge, MA.

Reinhart, Carmen M., and Christoph Trebesch. 2016. "Sovereign Debt Relief and Its Aftermath." *Journal of the European Economic Association* 14 (1): 215–51.

Schnabel, Isabel. 2021. "The Sovereign-Bank-Corporate Nexus: Virtuous or Vicious?" Address at London School of Economics and Political Science public online conference on "Financial Cycles, Risk, Macroeconomic Causes, and Consequences," Systemic Risk Center, Frankfurt, January 28, 2021. https://www.ecb.europa.eu/press/key/date/2021/html/ecb.sp210128~8f5dc86601.en.html.

Stroebel, Johannes, and Jeffrey Wurgler. 2021. "What Do You Think about Climate Finance?" *Journal of Financial Economics* 142: 487–98.

World Bank. 2005. *World Development Report 2006: Equity and Development.* Washington, DC: World Bank; New York: Oxford University Press.

World Bank. 2014. "Debt Resolution and Business Exit: Insolvency Reform for Credit, Entrepreneurship, and Growth." Trade and Competitiveness Global Practice Note 343, World Bank, Washington, DC. https://documents1.worldbank.org/curated/en/912041468178733220/pdf/907590VIEWPOIN003430Debt0Resolution.pdf.

World Bank. 2020a. "COVID-19 and Non-Performing Loan Resolution in the Europe and Central Asia Region: Lessons Learned from the Global Financial Crisis for the Pandemic." FinSAC Policy Note, Financial Sector Advisory Center, World Bank, Vienna. https://pubdocs.worldbank.org/en/460131608647127680/FinSAC-COVID-19-and-NPL-Policy-NoteDec2020.pdf.

World Bank. 2020b. *Doing Business 2020: Comparing Business Regulation in 190 Economies.* Washington, DC: World Bank.

World Bank. 2021a. *Global Economic Prospects, June 2021.* Washington, DC: World Bank.

World Bank. 2021b. *World Development Report 2021: Data for Better Lives.* Washington, DC: World Bank.

Yonzan, Nishant, Christoph Lakner, Daniel Gerszon Mahler, Raul Andrés Castañeda Aguilar, and Haoyu Wu. 2020. "The Impact of COVID-19 on Global Poverty under Worsening Growth and Inequality." *World Bank Blogs: Data Blogs*, November 9, 2020. https://blogs.worldbank.org/opendata/impact-covid-19-global-poverty-under-worsening-growth-and-inequality.

Introduction

The COVID-19 pandemic sent shock waves through the world economy and triggered the largest global economic crisis seen in more than a century. The economic impacts of the pandemic were especially severe in emerging economies. Global poverty increased for the first time in a generation, and disproportionate income losses among disadvantaged populations led to a dramatic rise in inequality within and across countries. Governments responded at the onset of the pandemic with large economic programs that were successful at mitigating the worst human costs in the short run. However, this emergency response has also exacerbated a number of preexisting economic fragilities that may pose an obstacle to an equitable recovery.

Policy Priorities

The economic response to the pandemic will need to address the following areas in which economic fragilities have been highlighted and worsened by the pandemic:

- **Addressing increased inequality within and between countries** resulting from the highly regressive impacts of the crisis.

- **Managing and reducing the interconnected financial risks created by the pandemic** to prevent spillover effects that can threaten the return to economic growth.

- **Ensuring continued access to finance** to help households and businesses weather economic uncertainty and invest in opportunities.

- **Preserving and restoring market transparency** to enable a prompt recognition of economic risks.

Introduction

The COVID-19 (coronavirus) pandemic triggered a global public health crisis that overwhelmed the health systems of many countries with over 200 million cases and close to 5 million deaths worldwide. The outbreak of the pandemic quickly turned into the largest economic crisis seen in more than a century, as countries enacted unprecedented emergency measures, such as travel bans, mobility restrictions, closure of nonessential businesses, limitations on public gatherings, and mandatory home-based work, that severely affected economic activity. In response, household incomes, business revenue, and employment declined dramatically. Small businesses, low-income households, and vulnerable populations were disproportionately affected, and global poverty increased for the first time in a generation.

The economic crisis stemming from the COVID-19 pandemic stands out in its global scale, scope, and severity. In 2020, economic output contracted in 90 percent of countries, while the world economy contracted by approximately 3 percent.[1] The share of countries experiencing negative output growth as a result of the pandemic surpassed that of both world wars and the Great Depression.

The crisis is also distinct in its highly unusual indiscriminate impacts across the globe. Economic crises in the postwar period have typically hit advanced economies and emerging markets unevenly. For example, despite its designation as the global financial crisis, the 2007–09 financial crisis primarily affected advanced economies, whereas emerging markets, whose economies were supported by robust commodity prices and rapid growth in China, were far less affected. As a result, at the height of the global financial crisis in 2009, output contracted in only 63 percent of countries, and the world economy contracted by 2.2 percent, much less than in the first year of the pandemic.[2]

The COVID-19 economic crisis is also unique in its nature and origins. Unlike most crisis episodes in recent decades, the COVID-19 economic crisis did not originate as a financial crisis or as a debt crisis in the public or private sector. Instead, it was the result of a truly exogenous event that generated both an aggregate demand and an aggregate supply shock. By contrast, the economic crises of the 1980s were sparked by government debt and financial crises in emerging markets, and the 2007–09 crisis originated from asset bubbles and financial distress in advanced economies. In most countries, the current crisis therefore does not fit the prototypical pattern in which a long economic expansion is followed by a recession during which borrowers who took out loans in boom times can no longer afford their debt payments. Instead, when the COVID-19 pandemic emerged, most countries had not been experiencing a robust economic expansion. It is not uncommon, however, for one form of crisis to morph into another. Although this economic crisis did not begin as a debt or financial crisis, the large increases in private and public debt incurred from the pandemic could very well turn it into one.[3]

This introduction explores the short- and medium-term implications of the COVID-19 crisis for emerging economies. It begins by documenting the dramatic immediate impacts of the crisis on households and businesses, which were most immediately affected by income losses arising from the pandemic. It then highlights the unequal economic impacts of the crisis within and between countries and the large government responses to the crisis, which made use of many unprecedented policy tools and was relatively successful at mitigating the worst effects of the crisis in the short run but may create longer-term economic risks that pose obstacles to an equitable recovery.

Impacts on households

Household incomes and employment were severely affected by the COVID-19 crisis and the public health measures adopted to contain the effects of the pandemic. Survey data covering 51 countries reveal that 57 percent of firms reduced employment during the first two quarters of the pandemic, directly affecting

Figure I.1 Impacts of the COVID-19 crisis on households, by country income group

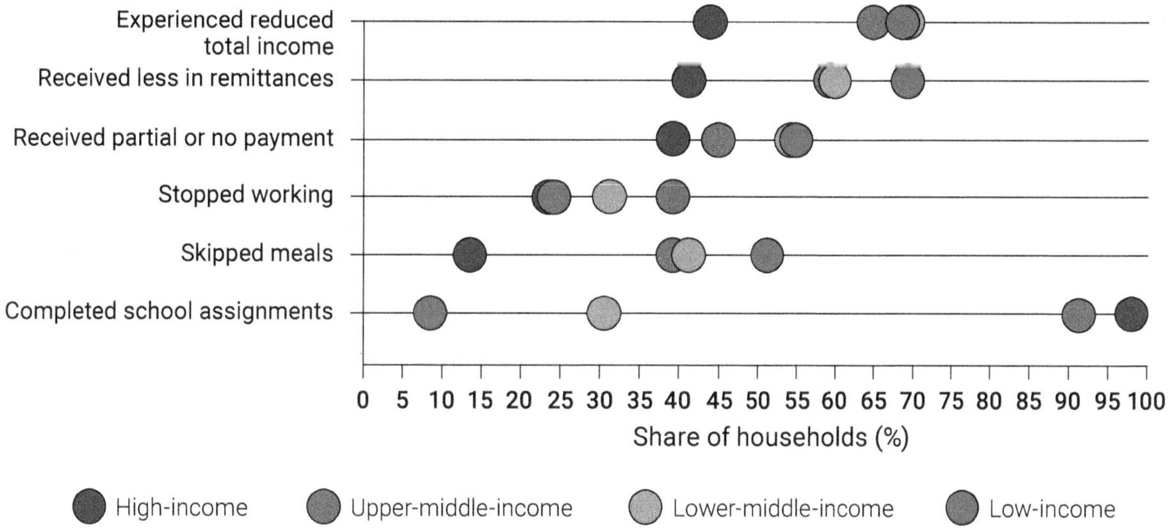

Source: World Bank, COVID-19 Household Monitoring Dashboard, https://www.worldbank.org/en/data/interactive/2020/11/11/covid-19-high-frequency-monitoring-dashboard.

Note: The figure shows survey data summarizing the economic impact of the crisis on households. Data are taken from the first wave of surveys, administered between April and July 2020, to ensure comparability across countries.

household income.[4] Similarly, World Bank high-frequency phone surveys[5] from a sample representative of 1.4 billion adults in 34 low- and middle-income countries found that, on average, more than a third of respondents stopped working because of the pandemic, and 64 percent of households experienced reductions in income.[6] This employment-income effect was compounded by a steep decline in remittances in those countries. Over 60 percent of households reported receiving less in remittances since the onset of the pandemic (figure I.1).[7] The aggregate nature of the economic shock also made it more difficult for low-income households to rely on other risk-sharing mechanisms, such as informal credit and support from social networks.[8]

Rising global poverty

Meanwhile, global poverty increased for the first time in a generation. Figure I.2 shows the annual year-on-year change in the number of poor for the last three decades. In this period, poverty increased only twice: during the Asian financial crisis and the COVID-19 pandemic. The 2007–09 global financial crisis did not lead to an increase in global poverty because its effects were felt primarily in advanced economies, whereas most emerging economies—where the majority of the world's poor live—remained relatively unaffected. Although the full consequences of the COVID-19 crisis on poverty are still highly uncertain, preliminary estimates suggest that COVID-19 will have a significantly greater negative impact than the Asian financial crisis.[9]

This increase in poverty is likely to persist as unequal access to vaccines and the possibility of future waves of the pandemic pose obstacles to the recovery. Figure I.3 shows the global trend in extreme poverty from 2015 to 2021. For the projected years 2020 and 2021, the bars show the change in the poverty rate if prior trends had continued, compared with the estimated poverty rates adjusted for the impact of the COVID-19 crisis. Whereas before the pandemic 635 million people were projected to live in extreme

Figure I.2 Global annual change in extreme poor, 1992–2020

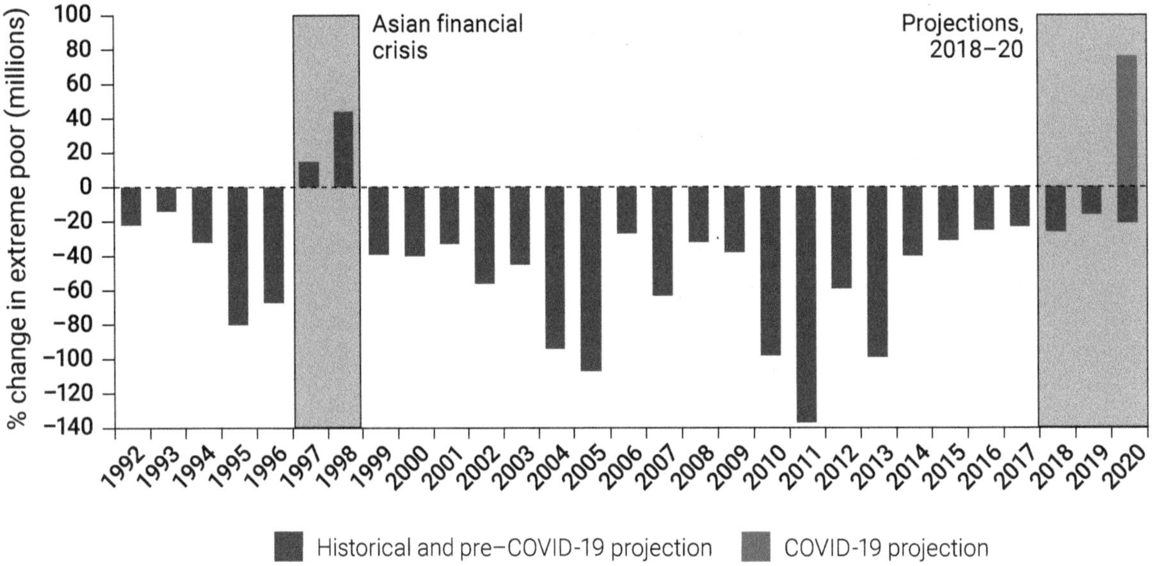

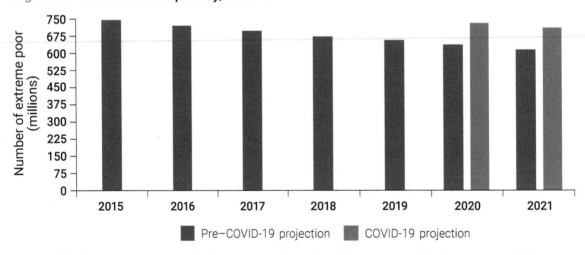

Sources: Lakner et al. 2020; Mahler et al. 2021; World Bank, Global Economic Prospects DataBank, https://databank .world bank.org/source/global-economic-prospects; World Bank, PovcalNet (dashboard), http://iresearch.worldbank.org /PovcalNet/.

Note: The figure shows the global annual year-on-year change in the number of poor in millions, calculated using the international poverty line of $1.90 per person per day. Two growth scenarios are considered: "pre–COVID-19" uses the January 2020 Global Economic Prospects growth rate forecasts (World Bank 2020a), predating the COVID-19 crisis; "COVID-19" uses the June 2021 Global Economic Prospects forecasts (World Bank 2021a).

Figure I.3 Global extreme poverty, 2015–21

Sources: World Bank, Global Economic Prospects DataBank, https://databank.world bank.org/source/global-economic -prospects; World Bank, PovcalNet (dashboard), http://iresearch.worldbank.org/PovcalNet/.

Note: Figures are obtained following the approach developed in Lakner et al. (2020) and Mahler et al. (2021). Poverty is defined using the international poverty line of $1.90 per person per day. The year 2017 is the latest with sufficient population coverage for a global poverty estimate. Subsequent years are projected. Two growth scenarios are considered: "pre–COVID-19" uses the January 2020 Global Economic Prospects growth rate forecasts (World Bank 2020a), predating the COVID-19 crisis; "COVID-19" uses the June 2021 Global Economic Prospects forecasts (World Bank 2021a).

poverty in 2020, after the onset of the pandemic the projected number of poor increased to 732 million. The COVID-19–induced poor, calculated as the difference in poverty trends with and without COVID-19, are thus estimated to be 97 million in 2020 and 2021. These numbers suggest that COVID-19 set back progress on poverty reduction at the global level by nearly half a decade, making the goal of eliminating extreme poverty by 2030 unattainable. If countries return to their historical average growth rates after 2021, about 7 percent of the global population will live below the international poverty line by 2030, or more than double the target level of 3 percent.[10] Put differently, achieving the target would require all economies to grow at 8 percent per capita per year, which is equivalent to about five times the historical growth rates for Sub-Saharan Africa.

Greater inequality across and within countries

The impact of the crisis on households has been highly regressive across and within countries. Early evidence suggests that 2020 per capita gross domestic product (GDP) declined more in higher-income countries.[11] However, these data may not tell the full story.[12] Because many households in low- and middle-income countries work in the informal sector, the impact of the pandemic on them is harder to assess. It is then possible that the impact of the pandemic on those countries is being underestimated. Survey data indicate that the highest share of respondents who stopped working on account of the pandemic was recorded in middle-income countries.[13] One in five of the pandemic-induced poor in 2021 are estimated to reside in low-income countries (which account for 9 percent of the world population), and over 90 percent of those considered newly poor as a result of the crisis reside in low- or lower-middle-income countries.[14] Between 2019 and 2021, the average income of the bottom 40 percent is estimated to have fallen by 2.2 percent, compared with a 0.5 percent decline in the top 40 percent.[15]

Meanwhile, low-income countries experienced a high incidence of income losses and food insecurity, despite having less pronounced disruptions in employment than higher-income countries. Twenty-four percent of households in low-income countries reported work stoppages, compared with 32.3 percent in lower-middle-income countries and 38.7 percent in upper-middle-income countries (figure I.1). This finding stems, in part, from the higher share of the population engaged in agriculture in low-income countries, minimizing the employment effects of lockdown measures. Nonetheless, even among agricultural workers who continued working, many experienced declines in income due to lockdown measures and reduced demand for agricultural products in urban areas. In low- and middle-income countries alike, more than two in three households reported reductions in total income related to the pandemic. More than a third of households in low-income countries and almost half of households in upper-middle-income countries had to reduce their overall consumption. Low- and lower-middle-income countries reported a higher prevalence of food insecurity and of having to resort to coping mechanisms such as selling assets or depleting emergency savings (figure I.4). Such effects of the pandemic increase these countries' vulnerability to shocks that may arise during a protracted recovery and dampen the prospects for an equitable recovery.

The recovery so far has been similarly uneven across countries, with advanced economies faring overall much better than emerging economies.[16] In low-income countries, which face risks to their growth outlook because of unequal access to vaccines and preexisting economic fragilities, GDP growth was forecast to be 2.9 percent in 2021—the second-lowest growth rate (after 2020) in the last 20 years—compared with 5.3 percent in high-income economies.[17] Even if it is assumed that the impact of the pandemic is distributionally neutral, the top 20 percent of the global income distribution was expected to recover around half of its 2020 income losses in 2021, while the bottom 20 percent was expected to lose an additional 5 percent of its income.[18]

Figure I.4 Ways in which households coped with income losses from the COVID-19 crisis, by country income group

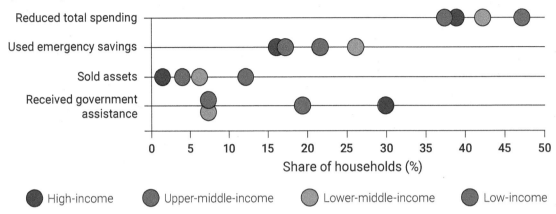

Source: World Bank, COVID-19 Household Monitoring Dashboard, https://www.worldbank.org/en/data/interactive/2020/11/11/covid-19-high-frequency-monitoring-dashboard.

Note: Data from the first wave of surveys, collected between April and July 2020, are used to ensure comparability across countries.

Beyond the immediate impact of the pandemic on incomes and employment, there are also channels through which the crisis is likely to aggravate inequality across countries in the longer term. One such channel is pandemic-related disruptions in access to education. Estimates based on data from 157 countries suggest that the COVID-19 pandemic could lead to a loss of between 0.3 and 0.9 years of schooling, adjusted for quality. Pandemic-related income shocks could force close to 7 million students to drop out of primary and secondary education. And students from the current cohort could face a loss in lifetime earnings equivalent to a 5 percent annual reduction in income.[19] The pandemic has also disproportionately affected female labor force participation, which is another channel through which the crisis aggravates preexisting inequalities.[20]

Within countries, the crisis has disproportionately affected disadvantaged groups. In 70 percent of countries, the incidence of temporary unemployment was higher[21] for workers who completed only primary education.[22] Income losses were similarly larger among youth, women, the self-employed, and casual workers with lower levels of education.[23] These patterns are consistent with those observed in advanced economies.[24] Although the impact of the pandemic on within-country inequality at the global level is not yet known, it seems likely it will increase. The regressive nature of impacts suggests that the impact of the crisis on global poverty is a lower-bound estimate. With a widespread increase in within-country inequality, the crisis would have an even bigger impact on global poverty.[25]

The COVID-19 economic crisis has also been unique in exacerbating gender inequalities. Analysis of firm-level data from the World Bank's Enterprise Surveys reveals that women were more likely than men to be laid off after the onset of the pandemic.[26] According to phone survey data collected during the first months of the pandemic, 42 percent of women stopped working, either temporarily or permanently, compared with 31 percent of men.[27] Women were disproportionately affected by income and employment losses because they were more likely to be employees or owners of firms in the sectors most affected by lockdown and social distancing measures—such as services, hospitality, and retail, where the demand shock was hitting hardest.[28] Indeed, women-owned businesses were, on average, more likely to be closed after the onset of the pandemic, especially microbusinesses and businesses in the hospitality industry. Female-led businesses were also less likely to have received public support.[29]

In addition, women bore the brunt of the higher care needs associated with closures of day-care centers and schools.

Evidence from recent rounds of high-frequency surveys also reveals that the initial disparities in job losses were not reduced with the relaxation of mobility restrictions and other policy measures. Those who suffered larger initial losses—women, younger workers, urban workers, and persons with low levels of formal education—recovered more slowly than their counterparts and were not able to substantially reverse initial disparities in losses.[30] By September 2020, men had recovered 49 percent of their initial employment losses, compared with 30 percent of women. Workers in urban areas had recovered only a third of their initial losses, compared with 58 percent of rural workers. Although the employment recovery was slightly faster for younger workers and those without a college education, this was insufficient to significantly reduce the gaps in job losses relative to older and college-educated workers.[31] Similarly, school closures have been associated with substantial learning losses, particularly for children from low socioeconomic status households. Even with schools reopening, it is not clear whether these children will be able to catch up, thereby exacerbating within-country disparities in the future.

Heightened fragilities on household balance sheets

The impacts of income losses sustained during the pandemic were intensified by the fact that many households were already financially stretched at the beginning of the crisis. Although there was significant within-country and cross-country variation in how well households were positioned to cope with income losses, one pattern that is strikingly similar across advanced and emerging economies is that very few households have the resources to weather substantial income losses for more than a few months.[32] This pattern underscores the immense value of emergency cash transfers for households facing large, prolonged income losses.

Intuitively, households can accommodate income shocks either by financing consumption with liquid financial assets, such as easily accessible savings, or by reducing expenditures to the bare minimum required for food, essential utilities, housing expenses, and debt repayment. Both coping mechanisms do not rely on external sources of funds such as the state or on credit markets, and they have little bearing on households' future ability to borrow. The definition used in this Report therefore considers a household to be fully "resilient" when, in the face of an income shock, it can sustain consumption in the short to medium term using its own liquid financial assets.

Newly available data on household consumption and asset holdings that are comparable across countries make it possible to quantify the resilience of households to income losses as the ratio of a household's total liquid wealth to its monthly consumption expenditure.[33] This measure has a simple interpretation: conditional on an economic shock resulting in a complete loss of income, it is the number of months that a household can maintain its level of consumption by relying solely on its liquid financial wealth. Figure I.5 shows the share of households whose resilience to a total income loss falls below three months, six months, and one year for a sample of 24 emerging and advanced economies for which comparable data are available.[34] The figure reveals that the percentage of households not able to sustain basic consumption beyond three months is higher in emerging economies (50 percent) than in advanced economies (40 percent). However, the percentage of households that cannot self-sustain beyond one year is practically identical, reaching around 70 percent in both emerging and advanced economies.

The same stress test approach can be used to examine how effectively different crisis response policies counteract income losses and enhance household resilience. Figure I.6, which shows the results of this exercise, first considers the effect of debt relief programs on household resilience. It reveals that if all household debt repayments[35] were paused by law, household resilience would improve only marginally

Figure I.5 Household resilience to income losses, selected emerging and advanced economies

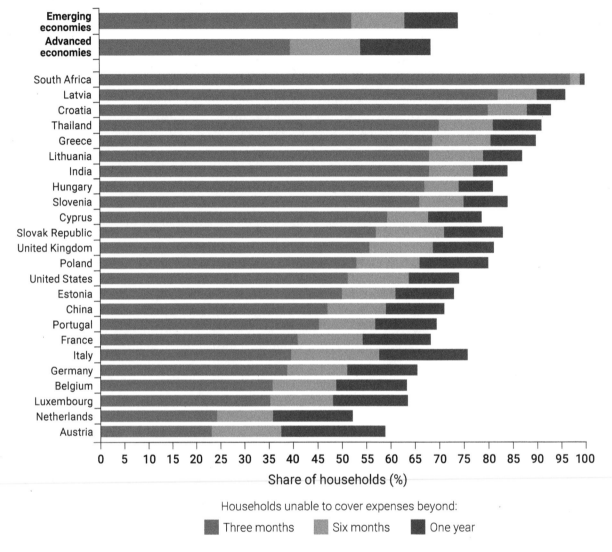

Source: Badarinza et al. 2021.

Note: The figure shows for each economy and economy income group the share of households not able to sustain their baseline consumption with liquid assets for more than three months, six months, and one year in the event of an income loss.

for advanced economies and would be unchanged in emerging economies. Debt relief as a policy tool is largely ineffective because in emerging economies it is mostly the wealthy—and therefore inherently more resilient—households that can access formal credit. This finding also suggests that debt relief may have adverse distributional effects because it benefits primarily wealthier households, while the cost of the policy, through taxation, is borne across the population. Similarly, figure I.6 shows that if households were able to liquidate their *illiquid* financial assets, such as retirement accounts, it would have almost no effect in emerging economies and only short-lived benefits in advanced ones. Roughly 40 percent of advanced economy households would continue to be vulnerable six months after the initial shock. Not surprisingly, a policy instrument that dramatically reduces vulnerability in both emerging and advanced economies is direct income support. Income support replacing 50 percent of regular income brings the

Figure I.6 Impacts of alternative COVID-19 policies and coping strategies at different time horizons, emerging and advanced economies

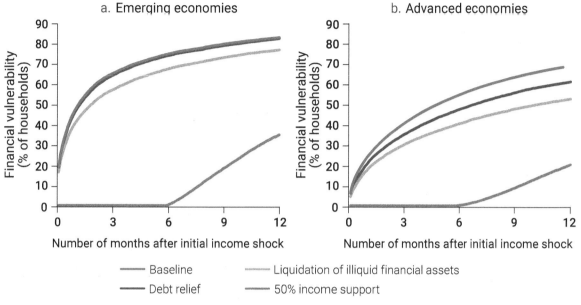

a. Emerging economies

b. Advanced economies

Baseline
Debt relief
Liquidation of illiquid financial assets
50% income support

Source: Badarinza et al. 2021.

Note: The figure shows the impact of alternative support policies and coping strategies—income support, debt relief, and asset liquidation—on household resilience for different time horizons.

total fraction of vulnerable households to near zero for the first six months in both sets of economies. This finding underscores the immense value of the large cash transfers used worldwide to enable households to weather the immediate impacts of the crisis.

Impacts on firms

Business revenue declined dramatically as a result of lockdowns and other public health measures needed to contain the pandemic. Survey data collected from more than 100,000 businesses worldwide show that, overall, 70 percent of businesses closed at the peak of the first wave of the pandemic,[36] and 84 percent of firms reported a drop in revenue. This decline in sales was large in magnitude—on average, firms experienced a 51 percent year-on-year reduction in revenue as a result of the first wave of pandemic-induced mobility restrictions (figure I.7, panel a). Declines in sales and revenues were also persistent—four months after the peak of the pandemic, average revenue was still more than 40 percent lower than in the same period one year earlier. The shock was sufficiently severe and long-lasting to threaten the survival of many firms. In the early stages of the pandemic, 46 percent of firms expected to fall into arrears on their outstanding supplier, wage, or loan payments over the next six months (figure I.7, panel b). The average business reported having cash reserves to cover expenses for less than 51 days. The impacts of business closures and the sharp, persistent decline in business revenue translated into a corresponding reduction in employment, mostly by reducing workers' hours and requiring furloughs (both paid and unpaid). Permanent layoffs were less common. In total, 57 percent of surveyed firms reduced employment.

The impact of the COVID-19 crisis on businesses varied significantly across countries and sectors. Tourism, retail, and parts of the service sector were more severely affected by public health policies

Figure I.7 Impact of COVID-19 on businesses, selected countries

a. Decline in sales

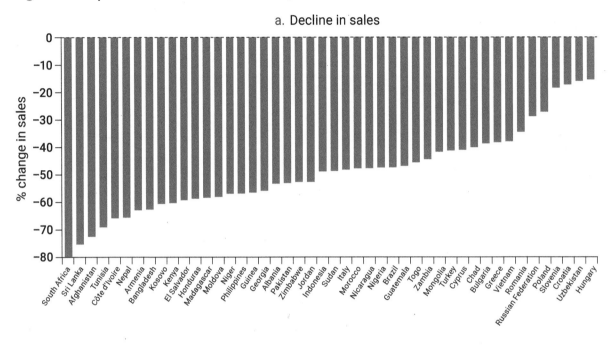

b. Businesses expecting to fall into arrears

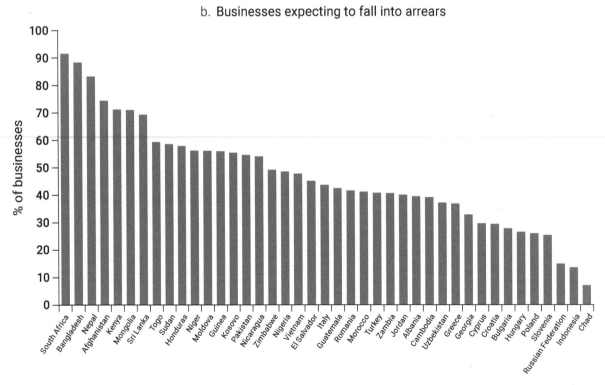

Source: World Bank, COVID-19 Business Pulse Surveys Dashboard, https://www.worldbank.org/en/data/interactive/2021/01/19/covid-19-business-pulse-survey-dashboard.

Note: The figure shows the average predicted percentage decline in sales (panel a) and share of businesses expecting to fall into arrears (panel b) by country. Estimates are obtained from a linear regression that controls for country, firm size, sector, and distance to the first peak of the pandemic. Data are as of July 31, 2021.

limiting mobility or mandating temporary business closures or capacity restrictions. In addition, international supply chains were disrupted, causing input shortages and price fluctuations that rippled through the global economy and eventually also reached sectors not initially affected by the crisis.

Small and informal businesses most severely affected

The impact of the crisis on businesses, like that on households, was highly regressive. Smaller businesses, informal businesses, and businesses with more limited access to the formal credit market were more severely affected. Smaller firms tend to face greater financial constraints, even in advanced economies. In the United States, for example, the median small business has fewer than 15 days in cash reserves.[37] Thus even profitable small businesses can easily fall into arrears and insolvency due to a temporary shock to revenue. The same is true of the impact of the COVID-19 shock on businesses around the world. Larger firms were able to cover expenses for up to 65 days, compared with 59 days for medium-size firms and 53 and 50 days for small firms and microenterprises, respectively. More than 50 percent of all small firms expected to fall into arrears within six months of the onset of the crisis, compared with 45 percent of medium-size firms and 36 percent of large firms. Compounding the challenge, small businesses have far more limited access to external finance than larger firms, and thus were much more likely to be pushed into insolvency by the crisis.[38]

Women-led businesses have been disproportionately affected by the crisis, according to data from the World Bank's COVID-19 Business Pulse Surveys conducted during the first year of the pandemic. Women-owned businesses are, overall, more concentrated in sectors that were harder-hit by lockdowns and mobility restrictions, and even within these sectors women-owned businesses fared worse. Women-owned businesses in the hospitality industry, for example, recorded larger declines in sales revenue than male-led businesses during the same period the previous year (–67.8 percent versus –60.4 percent), were able to cover costs for a shorter period of time (54 days versus 64 days), were more likely to fall into arrears (58 percent versus 51.6 percent), were more likely to reduce work hours (59.6 percent versus 53.7 percent), and had less access to public support (33 percent versus 37 percent).[39] Surveys of some 26,000 business owners in over 50 countries with an active Facebook business page also reveal that the strictness of lockdown measures tended to exacerbate gender gaps in temporary business closures.[40]

Businesses relatively more affected by the initial impact of the COVID-19 pandemic were also experiencing greater difficulties recovering in 2021. Comparisons of first-round (May–November 2020) and second-round (November 2020–May 2021) data from the World Bank's COVID-19 Follow-up Surveys in Europe and Central Asia, for example, show that small, young (founded within the last 10 years), and female-owned firms did not see improvements in sales in 2021, in contrast to larger, older, and male-owned firms. Larger firms were also more likely than smaller firms to receive payment deferrals and fiscal relief.

Persistent economic uncertainty hampering business activity

In addition to revenue losses, business activity has been affected by an uncharacteristically large and persistent increase in uncertainty about future business prospects, despite the presence of large support programs. Studies using data from advanced economies show that, because of its unique nature, the COVID-19 pandemic has generated more uncertainty in business sales and profitability expectations than a conventional economic downturn.[41] The World Bank's COVID-19 Business Pulse Surveys collected comparable data on business expectations worldwide and found strikingly similar results. They confirm that greater uncertainty about business prospects is associated with larger firm-level declines

Figure I.8 Economic uncertainty and employment during the COVID-19 crisis

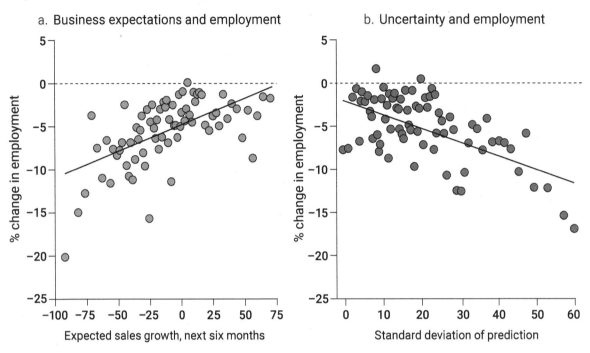

a. Business expectations and employment

b. Uncertainty and employment

Source: Apedo-Amah et al. 2020, based on World Bank, COVID-19 Business Pulse Surveys Dashboard, https://www.world bank.org/en/data/interactive/2021/01/19/covid-19-business-pulse-survey-dashboard.

Note: The figure shows the relationship between expected sales growth and changes in employment (panel a) and uncertainty about sales growth and changes in employment (panel b), based on data from the World Bank's COVID-19 Business Pulse Surveys collected during the first two quarters of the pandemic. The analysis first conditions on the variable on the x-axis and then calculates employment changes for businesses in each bin.

in employment (see figure I.8). Even as pandemic-related risks are gradually resolved, prolonged uncertainty about the recovery of business revenue is therefore likely to suppress job creation and investment by businesses, as well as the availability of credit from their lenders in the longer term.

Heightened fragilities on corporate balance sheets

The precrisis period saw a significant buildup of financial risks in the corporate sector, which became increasingly apparent with the onset of the pandemic. This increase in risks was particularly severe in emerging markets, where an extended period of low interest rates globally had contributed to lending booms and dramatically increased leverage ratios in the corporate sector. Prior to the crisis, many firms in emerging markets were already struggling with unsustainable debt burdens and difficulties covering short-term liabilities.[42] Stress test simulations using precrisis corporate balance sheet data indicate that an economic shock of the size experienced by most emerging from the COVID-19 recession would push a large share of firms in these economies into insolvency (figure I.9).[43] Some of the financial risks that have accumulated among emerging market firms have become apparent as a result of the crisis. Troubled assets in the real estate sector of important emerging markets that have come to light recently are one example of how credit-fueled asset bubbles that accumulate during times of high growth can trigger wider economic instability in the event of an unforeseen adverse shock.[44] This phenomenon is not unique to the current crisis and, in fact, bears many similarities to the asset bubbles and subsequent

Figure I.9 Percentage of corporate debt at risk after a simulated 30 percent shock to earnings, precrisis, selected countries, by income group

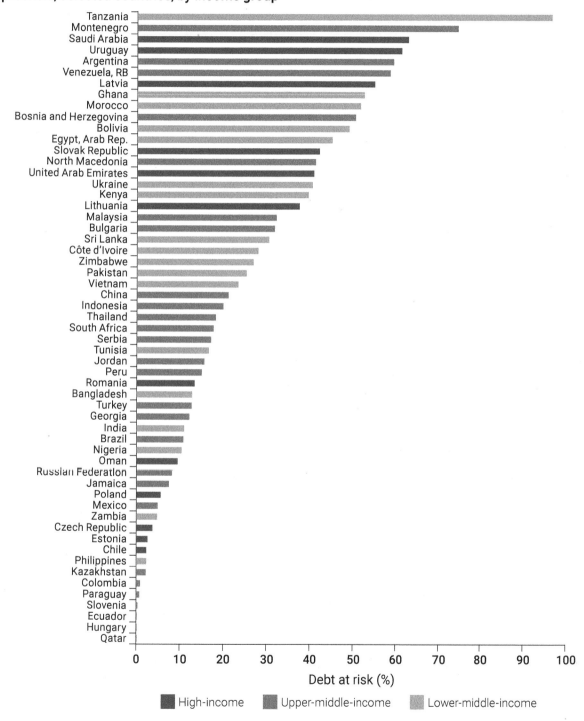

Source: WDR 2022 team, based on Feyen, Dancausa, et al. (2020).

Note: The figure reports the distribution across income groups of the fraction of debt of firms in a country considered "at risk" in terms of interest coverage ratio after a simulated 30 percent shock to earnings. The interest coverage ratio captures the ability of a firm to cover interest expenses with current earnings. A higher value indicates higher debt at risk for corporations in a country.

market corrections in previous crises, such as real estate bubbles in advanced economies prior to the global financial crisis.

In emerging economies, corporate solvency risks have been further exacerbated by a sharp increase in dollar-denominated debt over the past decade. Low interest rates in advanced economies over this period tempted firms to take on foreign rather than local currency debt.[45] Since the beginning of the pandemic, the currencies of many emerging markets have come under pressure. This creates problems for firms that hold significant amounts of foreign currency–denominated debt, which is now more difficult to service because the value of the borrower's local currency revenue has fallen. The exposure to currency risk is likely to become more acute if the recovery proceeds more quickly in advanced economies than in the rest of the world, which will lead to a further weakening of emerging market currencies.

Impacts on the financial sector

In contrast to the immediate large impacts of the COVID-19 crisis on households and firms, the short-term impacts of the crisis on the financial sector were relatively muted because of the large-scale emergency support and forbearance programs for borrowers aimed at preventing a spike in loan defaults.

Moderate initial impacts masking longer-term risks

Although extensive income support and debt forbearance policies have helped to insulate the financial sector from a wave of loan defaults in the short run, few if any countries have the resources to keep these policies in place in the longer term. Therefore, financial institutions around the world are likely to come under significant stress as debt moratoria and other support policies for borrowers are scaled back. In some economies, these risks are already becoming apparent. Loan defaults have been on the rise in India, Kenya, the Philippines, and a growing number of other middle-income countries. These emerging credit risks are also reflected in the worsening outlooks of the main international rating agencies for financial institutions as forbearance policies are lifted.

How well financial sectors around the world are prepared to confront this challenge varies considerably. Some economies that were hard-hit by the global financial crisis of 2007–09 initiated meaningful reforms and ensured that their banking systems were well capitalized. However, given that the global financial crisis affected primarily advanced economies, many emerging economies did not enact such reforms. As a result, their financial sectors are poorly prepared to withstand a crisis of the magnitude of the COVID-19 recession. For example, in emerging economies the average levels of regulatory capital holdings (the risk capital banks are required to hold to protect their balance sheets in the event of loan losses) have remained flat, albeit at a relatively high level, since the global financial crisis.[46] Moreover, bank debt-to-asset ratios, indicating greater balance sheet risk, have increased for smaller banks generally, as well as for banks located in emerging economies.[47]

In many emerging economies, fragilities in the financial sector are compounded by extensive government ownership of banks, misallocation stemming from government-mandated lending programs, and financial repression policies such as the requirement that domestic financial institutions hold government debt, which links the asset quality of the financial sector to that of the government. In the years leading up to the COVID-19 crisis, the Financial Sector Assessment Program, a joint exercise carried out by the World Bank and the International Monetary Fund, highlighted problems in the resolution of nonperforming loans (especially in Sub-Saharan Africa and Eastern Europe), loan classification and provisioning, and bank exposure to the nonbanking sector.

There has also been significant concern about the rapid expansion of lending by nonbank financial institutions (NBFIs) and their links to the formal banking sector in many emerging markets. According to data from the Financial Stability Board, and using a narrow definition of the sector, in 2020 NBFIs accounted for 14.1 percent of the total financial assets of 29 jurisdictions.[48] Nonbank lenders often face greater credit risks than banks, but are typically less regulated and can therefore accumulate significant hidden risks that can threaten financial stability. Regulators have become increasingly aware of these risks and have sought to adapt oversight of nonbank lenders.[49]

The short-term government response and its impact on public finances

The COVID-19 crisis triggered an extraordinarily large government response aimed at stabilizing output and protecting incomes in the short run. Governments enacted comprehensive fiscal, monetary, and financial sector policies, many of which included policy tools that were unprecedented at this scale or had not previously been used in emerging economies. Examples include direct income support measures, debt moratoria, and asset purchase programs by central banks. Most economists welcomed the speed and enormous scale of this response, pointing to the unparalleled scale of the economic shock and the lessons learned from past crises in which gradual approaches had proven less effective at stabilizing output and market expectations.[50]

Wide variation in the scale of the policy response

The fiscal policy response to the COVID-19 crisis was swift and substantial. It consisted primarily of direct emergency payments to the households and firms most acutely affected by a sharp drop in incomes and revenue. Many countries conducted countercyclical fiscal policies during the crisis, a first for most emerging economies. The scale of the response, however, varied significantly across countries, depending on the capacity of governments to mobilize resources, as well as institutional capabilities and the availability of social safety nets, as illustrated by figure I.10. While the extent of the fiscal response was almost uniformly large by any historical measure in high-income countries and uniformly small or nonexistent in low-income countries, there was significant variation in the size of the fiscal responses among middle-income countries. This variation reflects, among other factors, large differences in government debt burdens and the ability to finance the crisis response, as well as differences in the ability of central banks to support government spending through accommodative monetary policy measures. The scale and nature of the fiscal response were also shaped by political economy factors. For example, some recent evidence indicates that less politically polarized governments and societies were able to mobilize more fiscal resources to fight the immediate effects of the pandemic.[51]

In addition to rate cuts, central banks used unconventional monetary policy tools such as asset purchase programs to support the crisis response. Although asset purchase programs had previously been used almost exclusively in advanced economies, 27 emerging economies adopted such programs for the first time in response to the COVID-19 crisis.[52]

In addition to the fiscal and monetary policy response to the crisis, financial regulators around the world also implemented an unprecedented set of measures to prevent financial distress among borrowers and financial institutions. These policies were aimed at maintaining overall financial stability, preserving critical financial market functions, averting preventable insolvencies, and ensuring the continued flow of credit to households and firms. Central banks helped financial institutions maintain liquidity

Figure I.10 Fiscal response to the COVID-19 crisis, selected countries, by income group

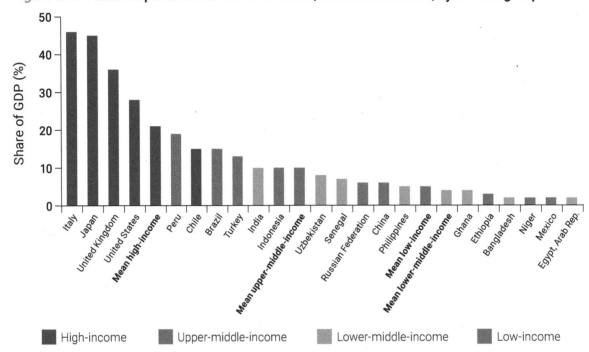

Source: WDR 2022 team, based on IMF (2021a). Data from International Monetary Fund, Fiscal Monitor Database of Country Fiscal Measures in Response to the COVID-19 Pandemic, Fiscal Affairs Department, https://www.imf.org/en/Topics/imf-and-covid19/Fiscal-Policies-Database-in-Response-to-COVID-19.

Note: The figure reports, as a percentage of GDP, the total fiscal support, calculated as the sum of "above-the-line measures" that affect government revenue and expenditures and the subtotal of liquidity support measures. Data are as of September 27, 2021.

through reductions in the policy rate, asset purchase programs, and other interventions intended to quell market turbulence in the early stages of the crisis.

To support borrowers and avert a wave of preventable insolvencies, financial regulators rolled out a variety of temporary debt relief measures for households and businesses, such as debt moratoria and debt restructuring programs. In many countries, these policies ultimately covered a large share of outstanding credit and played an important role in preventing loan defaults among borrowers facing temporary liquidity problems. However, debt moratoria on the scale of those enacted during the pandemic are a largely untested policy, and so far there is very little evidence of their longer-term impacts on borrower behavior and financial stability. One important concern is that, if left in place for too long, debt moratoria can have the unintended effect of masking the true extent of credit risk in the economy and delay rather than prevent the emergence of financial fragilities.

In contrast to previous crises, many countries also implemented so-called regulatory forbearance policies for banks. Regulatory forbearance refers to the relaxation of regulatory requirements and accounting standards in the hope that this will make it easier for lenders to issue new credit. Although some of these policies used the flexibility embedded in existing regulatory frameworks (such as the Basel III regulations), some countries relaxed prudential regulation and accounting standards beyond the emergency measures allowed by these frameworks. This may have created some respite for banks, but could create significant longer-term risks to financial stability. Regulatory forbearance policies reduce bank balance sheet transparency by enabling banks to hide the true extent of their credit risk, delay the resolution of nonperforming loans, and ultimately weaken the ability of the financial sector to provide financing to creditworthy borrowers during the recovery. Because regulatory forbearance policies can lead to the accumulation of significant hidden credit risks, they can also place further burdens on government finances should government intervention be required to support ailing financial institutions once these risks materialize.

In addition to the scale of the short-term crisis response there was also wide variation in the specific combination of policy tools used by different countries (figure I.11). This variation reflects differences in the ability to mobilize resources as well as different priorities for the crisis response. Low-income countries made relatively greater use of simple cash transfer programs, whereas middle- and high-income economies, whose financial sectors are much more exposed to household and small business debt, made more extensive use of financial sector policies aimed at averting financial sector distress.

Figure I.11 **Fiscal, monetary, and financial sector policy responses to the pandemic, by country income group**

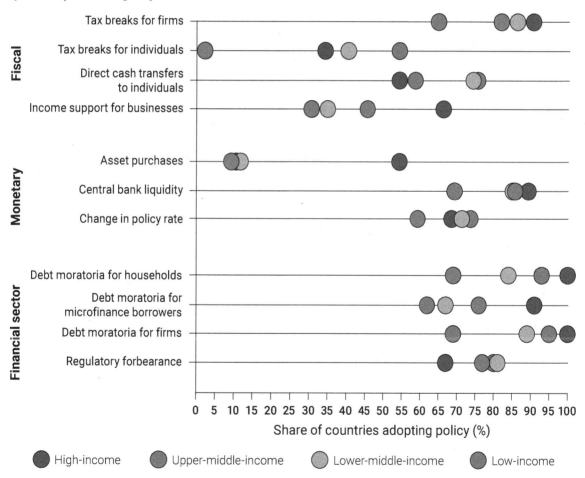

Source: WDR 2022 team, based on Feyen, Alonso Gispert, et al. (2020); Lacey, Massad, and Utz (2021); World Bank, COVID-19 Finance Sector Related Policy Responses, Version 3, https://datacatalog.worldbank.org/search/dataset/0037999.

Note: The figure shows the percentage of countries in which each of the listed policies was implemented in response to the pandemic. Data for the financial sector measures are as of June 30, 2021.

A global increase in government debt triggered by the pandemic

The large crisis response, while necessary and effective at mitigating the worst impacts of the crisis in the short run, led to a global increase in government debt that has given rise to renewed concerns about debt sustainability. Government debt levels have been rising steadily over the last decade in many emerging economies, and several suffered downgrades of their sovereign risk rating prior to the crisis (see figure I.12). In 2020, 51 countries—among them, 44 emerging economies—saw their credit ratings deteriorate. Although advanced economies have not been spared, sovereign downgrades are much more consequential for emerging economies, where credit ratings are at or near junk grade, and where the rating of the sovereign has a direct impact on the ratings of state-owned banks and state-owned enterprises. In more extreme cases, where sovereign restructuring becomes necessary—and these have been on the rise as well—banks and domestic investors will take outright losses on their holdings of government securities. Increases in government debt stemming from fiscal responses to the pandemic are therefore especially consequential for low-income countries.

In emerging and advanced economies, the fiscal response to the pandemic was supported by significant monetary policy measures that made unprecedented use of new policy tools (box I.1). Building on lessons from the global financial crisis, central banks lowered interest rates rapidly rather than through a series of gradual rate cuts. Because advanced economy policy rates were low prior to the crisis, emerging economies had more space to lower interest rates, with several central banks cutting rates by 100–200 basis points. Emerging economies were able to undertake especially ambitious monetary policy responses in part because many were at a low point in the business cycle. With output below potential, there was less concern about overheating the economy and spurring capital outflows. Structural reforms enacted since the global financial crisis helped to create additional flexibility.[53]

Figure I.12 **Global sovereign downgrades, 1980–2020**

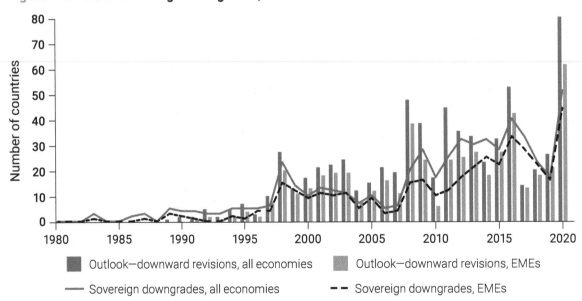

Source: WDR 2022 team, based on Reinhart (2021). Data from Trading Economics, Credit Rating (database), https://trading economics.com/country-list/rating.

Note: The figure shows the total number of sovereigns downgraded in a given year for all economies (gray line) and for emerging market economies (dashed black line) for which ratings data could be obtained. Emerging market economies (EMEs) are defined as in the International Monetary Fund's *World Economic Outlook: A Long and Difficult Ascent* (IMF 2020).

Box I.1 The interplay of fiscal and monetary policy

In response to the pandemic, countries made extensive use of monetary policy to support the large fiscal programs that became necessary to support households and firms. In emerging economies, interest rate cuts were a much more effective tool for stimulating the economy than in advanced economies, where rates had been hovering around the zero lower bound prior to the pandemic. Nonetheless, many emerging economies found themselves constrained in their crisis response because of limited fiscal and monetary policy options arising from high levels of government debt, low policy credibility, or weaker-than-expected effects of rate cuts.

Many economies adopted unconventional monetary policy tools to support the crisis response. The term *unconventional monetary policy* refers to policy instruments that go beyond the traditional regulatory and interest rate-setting powers of a central bank. Examples include asset purchase programs in which the central bank buys government or corporate bonds to inject liquidity into the economy and keep interest rates low; extraordinary liquidity operations, such as the central bank providing the financial sector with liquidity on the condition that it is used to issue new loans; or forward guidance, in which the central bank seeks to influence market expectations to stimulate economic activity.

To mobilize the full set of policy instruments at their disposal, central banks in emerging economies made extensive use of these new monetary policy tools, many for the first time. The most widely used instrument was asset purchase programs (figure BI.1.1), which before the COVID-19 crisis had been used almost exclusively in advanced economies—most notably by the US Federal Reserve Bank and the European Central Bank in the aftermath of the global financial crisis. Where asset purchase programs are aimed at buying government bonds, they increase the demand for longer-term government debt and reduce its cost, which directly supports the government's ability to finance future spending.

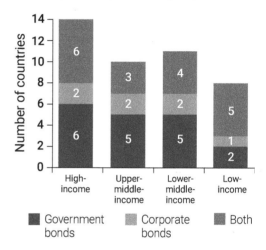

Figure BI.1.1 Asset purchase programs of central banks during the COVID-19 crisis, by country income group

Source: WDR 2022 team, based on Fratto et al. (2021).
Note: The figure shows the number of countries that introduced asset purchase programs in response to the pandemic, by income group, disaggregated by whether the central bank was authorized to purchase government bonds, corporate bonds, or both. Data for the Central Bank of West African States are considered for each individual member state.

In response to the COVID-19 crisis, between March and August 2020, 8 low-income countries, 11 lower-middle-income countries, and 10 upper-middle-income countries initiated asset purchase programs.[a] Examples of countries that initiated asset purchase programs include Angola, the Arab Republic of Egypt, Costa Rica, and Uganda. In several countries, adoption of such programs required changes in the laws governing the operations of the central bank. Brazil, for example, changed its constitution to allow the central bank to carry out monetary financing operations, including the direct purchase of government bonds. Thailand's parliament approved a law to set up a B 400 billion ($12.3 billion) fund to buy corporate bonds.

(Box continues next page)

Box I.1 **The interplay of fiscal and monetary policy** (*continued*)

Although the use of an expanded set of monetary policy tools has been beneficial to the COVID-19 crisis response, it has also increasingly blurred the lines between fiscal and monetary policy and raised the specter of governments trying to influence central banks to accommodate their fiscal needs. In this situation, referred to as "fiscal dominance," the central bank sacrifices price stability to support the government's fiscal policy goals. In the past, this practice has led to episodes of high or hyperinflation, which place a disproportionate burden on the poor and pose a significant obstacle to sustained economic growth in many emerging economies and efforts to tackle climate change and inequality.

The greater interdependence between fiscal and monetary policy foreshadowed by the increased use of new monetary policy tools will require improved coordination between fiscal and monetary authorities, as well as safeguards for central bank independence. In response to these emerging challenges, some emerging economies have introduced rules aimed at isolating central banks from political pressure to finance government outside of emergency situations. In Indonesia, for example, the central bank was prohibited from buying government bonds in the primary market. This prohibition was suspended through emergency legislation but only for a limited time (the prohibition on government financing must be reinstated by law in 2023). However, such rules are not always time-consistent, and it remains to be seen whether they can help countries strike the right balance between enabling an effective policy mix and safeguarding central bank independence.

a. Fratto et al. (2021).

Overall, the swift and decisive policy response to the COVID-19 crisis has mitigated its worst economic impacts in the short run. However, some crisis response measures have also given rise to new risks that may pose an obstacle to an equitable recovery in the longer term. Among these, the most pressing concerns are dramatically increased levels of public and private debt, as well as the significant risk of hidden debts and financial fragilities that will materialize once support and forbearance programs are scaled back. As the immediate effects of the pandemic subside, policy makers face the difficult task of striking the right balance between providing enough support to contain the worst human costs of the crisis, while limiting the longer-term risks that may arise from the crisis response. Given this context, chapter 1 of this Report highlights the mutually reinforcing links between the various sectors of the economy—households, firms, financial institutions, and governments—through which risks in one sector can affect the economy as a whole, and charts policies that can effectively reduce these risks and support an equitable recovery.

Notes

1. Global real GDP growth in 2020 is estimated at −3.1 percent in the International Monetary Fund's World Economic Outlook (IMF 2021b) and −3.5 percent in the World Bank's Global Economic Prospects (World Bank 2021a).
2. See World Bank (2011). Also see Reinhart (2020). Although the COVID-19 pandemic evokes a comparison to the 1918 Spanish influenza pandemic, global economic conditions in the two periods are not comparable because of the wartime production under way during World War I as well as the stark differences in health and economic policy responses (Arthi and Parman 2021).
3. Bordo and Meissner (2016); Reinhart and Rogoff (2009).
4. Apedo-Amah et al. (2020).

5. World Bank, COVID-19 High-Frequency Monitoring Dashboard, https://www.worldbank.org/en/data/interactive/2020/11/11/covid-19-high-frequency-monitoring-dashboard.
6. Bundervoet, Dávalos, and Garcia (2021).
7. The decline in remittances reported by households is at odds with the aggregate data on remittances flows, which show global flows declining only by 1.6 percent in 2020 with respect to the previous year. This difference stems, in part, from migrants switching from informal (carry) to formal (digital) channels of sending remittances in response to mobility restrictions. Even with these changes in the composition of remittances, formal remittances declined by 10 percent or more in the Europe and Central Asia (ECA) and Sub-Saharan Africa (SSA) Regions and by 8 percent in the East Asia and Pacific (EAP) Region. For more details, see World Bank (2021b).
8. Janssens et al. (2021).
9. Measurements of poverty rely on household surveys, which become available with a lag. Data collection for these surveys has also been affected by COVID-19. To estimate poverty for 2020 and 2021, the most recent household surveys have been extrapolated using growth rates from national accounts. This requires additional assumptions: how much of GDP per capita growth feeds through to household consumption or income recorded in the survey and whether there have been any distributional changes. The nowcasts assume that 85 percent of growth in GDP per capita is passed through to household incomes, following Lakner et al. (2020). This pass-through rate is determined by comparing past growth in national accounts and household surveys in a global sample of comparable surveys. In the baseline estimates, it is assumed that all households grow at the same rate, so there are no distributional changes. See the more detailed discussion that follows on the likely distributional changes arising from COVID-19 in selected countries.
10. Lakner et al. (2020); World Bank (2020c).
11. Deaton (2021).
12. Deaton (2021) finds that inequality between countries, measured as the dispersion in per capita GDP without accounting for population size, decreased in 2020. This is consistent with a larger decline in GDP per capita in higher-income countries. However, Deaton finds that this dispersion increases when countries are weighted by their population. Yonzan, Lakner, and Mahler (2021) also find that population-weighted between-country inequality increased in 2020. Their study draws on distributions from household surveys, which are extrapolated using growth in GDP per capita and weighted by population. Both studies agree that the dispersion between countries in 2020 is highly sensitive to the growth forecasts of China and India. The vintages of the growth data also make a difference. Deaton (2021) compares growth forecasts from the October 2019 and October 2020 editions of World Economic Outlook (IMF 2019, 2020), while Yonzan, Lakner, and Mahler (2021) use growth forecasts from the January 2020 and June 2021 Global Economic Prospects (World Bank 2020a, 2021a).
13. Khamis et al. (2021).
14. Mahler et al. (2021) based on World Bank, Global Economic Prospects DataBank, https://databank.worldbank.org/source/global-economic-prospects; World Bank, PovcalNet (dashboard), http://iresearch.worldbank.org/PovcalNet/.
15. Yonzan, Lakner, and Mahler (2021).
16. See note 12.
17. World Bank (2021a).
18. Yonzan, Lakner, and Mahler (2021).
19. Azevedo et al. (2020).
20. See de Paz, Gaddis, and Müller (2021).
21. The difference in the rate of work stoppage between low- and high-educated workers was found to be statistically significant in 23 percent of the countries. For more details, see Kugler et al. (2021).
22. Kugler et al. (2021).
23. Bundervoet, Dávalos, and Garcia (2021).
24. Adams-Prassl et al. (2020); Chetty et al. (2020); Crossley, Fisher, and Low (2021).
25. Because of a lack of comprehensive data for many countries, the estimates at the global level assume there are no changes in inequality. Lakner et al. (2020) and Yonzan et al. (2020) estimate the impact of COVID-19 on global poverty with a range of assumptions on within-country inequality.
26. See de Paz, Gaddis, and Müller (2021).
27. Bundervoet, Dávalos, and Garcia (2021).
28. Goldstein et al. (2020).
29. Torres et al. (2021).
30. Agrawal et al. (2021); de Paz, Gaddis, and Müller (2021); Kugler et al. (2021).
31. Agrawal et al. (2021).
32. Gomes, Haliassos, and Ramadorai (2021); RBI (2017).
33. Badarinza, Balasubramaniam, and Ramadorai (2019). Measuring consumption and asset holdings at the household level is challenging for two reasons: (1) representative surveys often lack sufficiently detailed data on assets and consumption, and (2) where such data are available, they are often difficult to compare across countries. Some recent research has managed to bridge this gap by collating a broad set of household surveys for emerging and advanced economies.
34. Badarinza et al. (2021).
35. Measured in the surveys as part of consumption expenditure, including self-reported exposure to informal loans.
36. World Bank, COVID-19 Business Pulse Surveys Dashboard, https://www.worldbank.org/en/data/interactive/2021/01/19/covid-19-business-pulse-survey-dashboard. Data for the first wave of the survey were collected between April and November 2020.
37. Federal Reserve Bank of New York (2021).
38. Emerging evidence also suggests there is a gender component to the impact on businesses. In response to the pandemic, women-owned businesses closed at a higher rate than those owned by men. See, for example, Goldstein et al. (2020) and Torres et al. (2021).
39. Torres et al. (2021).

40. Goldstein et al. (2020).
41. Altig et al. (2020); Baker et al. (2020).
42. Acharya et al. (2015); Alfaro et al. (2019).
43. Feyen, Dancausa, et al. (2020).
44. Bottelier (2010); Rogoff and Yang (2021).
45. Especially low rates in the United States, as described by Bruno and Shin (2017).
46. World Bank (2020b).
47. Anginer et al. (2021).
48. FSB (2020).
49. India, for example, has introduced a new regulatory framework for nonbank lenders that will come into effect in October 2022. See RBI (2021).
50. For example, see Gopinath (2020) and other essays in Baldwin and Weder di Mauro (2020).
51. Aizenman et al. (2021).
52. IMF (2021b), based on Fratto et al. (2021).
53. Aguilar and Cantú (2020); Arslan, Drehmann, and Hofmann (2020); Cantú et al. (2021).

References

Acharya, Viral, Stephen G. Cecchetti, José De Gregorio, Şebnem Kalemli-Özcan, Philip R. Lane, and Ugo Panizza. 2015. "Corporate Debt in Emerging Economies: A Threat to Financial Stability?" September, Centre for International Governance Innovation, Waterloo, Ontario; Brookings Institution, Washington, DC. https://www.brookings.edu/wp-content/uploads/2016/07/CIEPR2015toWeb.pdf.

Adams-Prassl, Abi, Teodora Boneva, Marta Golina, and Christopher Rauh. 2020. "Inequality in the Impact of the Coronavirus Shock: Evidence from Real Time Surveys." *Journal of Public Economics* 189 (September): 104245.

Agrawal, Sarthak, Alexandru Cojocaru, Veronica Montalva, and Ambar Narayan. 2021. "COVID-19 and Inequality: How Unequal Was the Recovery from the Initial Shock?" With inputs by Tom Bundervoet and Andrey Ten. Brief (June), World Bank, Washington, DC.

Aguilar, Ana, and Carlos Cantú. 2020. "Monetary Policy Response in Emerging Market Economies: Why Was It Different This Time?" *BIS Bulletin* 32 (November), Bank for International Settlements, Basel, Switzerland.

Aizenman, Joshua, Yothin Jinjarak, Hien Nguyen, and Ilan Noy. 2021. "The Political Economy of the COVID-19 Fiscal Stimulus Packages of 2020." NBER Working Paper 29360, National Bureau of Economic Research, Cambridge, MA.

Alfaro, Laura, Gonzalo Asis, Anusha Chari, and Ugo Panizza. 2019. "Corporate Debt, Firm Size, and Financial Fragility in Emerging Markets." *Journal of International Economics* 118 (May): 1–19.

Altig, et al. 2020. "Economic Uncertainty before and during the COVID-19 Pandemic." *Journal of Public Economics* 191 (November). https://www.sciencedirect.com/science/article/pii/S0047272720301389.

Anginer, Deniz, Ata Can Bertay, Robert Cull, Asli Demirgüç-Kunt, and Davide S. Mare. 2021. "Bank Capital Regulation and Risk after the Global Financial Crisis." *Journal of Financial Stability*. Published ahead of print, May 17, 2021. https://doi.org/10.1016/j.jfs.2021.100891.

Apedo-Amah, Marie Christine, Besart Avdiu, Xavier Cirera, Marcio Cruz, Elwyn Davies, Arti Grover, Leonardo Iacovone, et al. 2020. "Unmasking the Impact of COVID-19 on Businesses: Firm Level Evidence from across the World." Policy Research Working Paper 9434, World Bank, Washington, DC.

Arslan, Yavuz, Mathias Drehmann, and Boris Hofmann. 2020. "Central Bank Bond Purchases in Emerging Market Economies." *BIS Bulletin* 20 (June 2). https://www.bis.org/publ/bisbull20.htm.

Arthi, Vellore, and John Parman. 2021. "Disease, Downturns, and Wellbeing: Economic History and the Long-Run Impacts of COVID-19." *Explorations in Economic History* 79 (January): 101381.

Azevedo, João Pedro, Amer Hasan, Diana Goldemberg, Syedah Aroob Iqbal, and Koen Geven. 2020. "Simulating the Potential Impacts of COVID-19 School Closures on Schooling and Learning Outcomes: A Set of Global Estimates." Policy Research Working Paper 9284, World Bank, Washington, DC.

Badarinza, Cristian, Vimal Balasubramaniam, Louiza Bartzoka, and Tarun Ramadorai. 2021. "How Has the Pandemic Affected Household Finances in Developing Economies?" *Economics Observatory: Families and Households* (blog), June 29, 2021. https://www.economicsobservatory.com/how-has-the-pandemic-affected-household-finances-in-developing-economies.

Badarinza, Cristian, Vimal Balasubramaniam, and Tarun Ramadorai. 2019. "The Household Finance Landscape in Emerging Economies." *Annual Review of Financial Economics* 11 (December): 109–29.

Baker, Scott R., Nicholas Bloom, Steven J. Davis, and Stephen J. Terry. 2020. "COVID-Induced Economic Uncertainty." NBER Working Paper 26983, National Bureau of Economic Research, Cambridge, MA. https://www.nber.org/papers/w26983.

Baldwin, Richard, and Beatrice Weder di Mauro, eds. 2020. *Mitigating the COVID Economic Crisis: Act Fast and Do Whatever It Takes*. London: CEPR Press.

Bordo, Michael D., and Christopher M. Meissner. 2016. "Fiscal and Financial Crises." NBER Working Paper 22059, National Bureau of Economic Research, Cambridge, MA.

Bottelier, Pieter. 2010. "Beijing's New Challenge: China's Post-Crisis Housing Bubble." Policy Outlook, July 1, Carnegie Endowment for International Peace, Washington, DC.

Bruno, Valentina, and Hyun Song Shin. 2017. "Global Dollar Credit and Carry Trades: A Firm-Level Analysis." *Review of Financial Studies* 30 (3): 703–49.

Bundervoet, Tom, María Eugenia Dávalos, and Natalia Garcia. 2021. "The Short-Term Impacts of COVID-19 on Households in Developing Countries: An Overview Based on a Harmonized Data Set of High-Frequency Surveys." Policy Research Working Paper 9582, World Bank, Washington, DC.

Cantú, Carlos, Paolo Cavallino, Fiorella De Fiore, and James Yetman. 2021. "A Global Database on Central Banks' Monetary Responses to COVID-19." BIS Working Paper 934, Monetary and Economic Department, Bank for International Settlements, Basel, Switzerland.

Chetty, Raj, John N. Friedman, Nathaniel Hendren, Michael Stepner, and the Opportunity Insights Team. 2020. "How Did COVID-19 and Stabilization Policies Affect Spending and Employment? A New Real-Time Economic Tracker Based on Private Sector Data." NBER Working Paper 27431, National Bureau of Economic Research, Cambridge, MA.

Crossley, Thomas F., Paul Fisher, and Hamish Low. 2021. "The Heterogeneous and Regressive Consequences of COVID-19: Evidence from High Quality Panel Data." *Journal of Public Economics* 193 (January): 104334.

Deaton, Angus S. 2021. "COVID-19 and Global Income Inequality." NBER Working Paper 28392, National Bureau of Economic Research, Cambridge, MA.

de Paz, Carmen, Isis Gaddis, and Miriam Müller. 2021. "Gender and COVID-19: What Have We Learnt, One Year Later?" Policy Research Working Paper 9709, World Bank, Washington, DC.

Federal Reserve Bank of New York. 2021. "Open Market Operations during 2020." May, Federal Reserve Bank of New York, New York. https://www.newyorkfed.org/markets/annual_reports.

Feyen, Erik H. B., Tatiana Alonso Gispert, Tatsiana Kliatskova, and Davide S. Mare. 2020. "Taking Stock of the Financial Sector Policy Response to COVID-19 around the World." Policy Research Working Paper 9497, World Bank, Washington, DC.

Feyen, Erik H. B., Fernando Dancausa, Bryan Gurhy, and Owen Nie. 2020. "COVID-19 and EMDE Corporate Balance Sheet Vulnerabilities: A Simple Stress-Test Approach." Policy Research Working Paper 9324, World Bank, Washington, DC.

Fratto, Chiara, Brendan Harnoys Vannier, Borislava Mircheva, David de Padua, and Hélène Poirson. 2021. "Unconventional Monetary Policies in Emerging Markets and Frontier Countries." IMF Working Paper WP/21/14, International Monetary Fund, Washington, DC.

FSB (Financial Stability Board). 2020. "Global Monitoring Report on Non-Bank Financial Intermediation 2020." December 16, FSB, Basel, Switzerland. https://www.fsb.org/2020/12/global-monitoring-report-on-non-bank-financial-intermediation-2020/.

Goldstein, Markus P., Paula Lorena Gonzalez Martinez, Sreelakshmi Papineni, and Joshua Wimpey. 2020. "The Global State of Small Business during COVID-19: Gender Inequalities." *Let's Talk Development* (blog), September 8, 2020. https://blogs.worldbank.org/developmenttalk/global-state-small-business-during-covid-19-gender-inequalities.

Gomes, Francisco, Michael Haliassos, and Tarun Ramadorai. 2021. "Household Finance." *Journal of Economic Literature* 59 (3): 919–1000.

Gopinath, Gita. 2020. "Limiting the Economic Fallout of the Coronavirus with Large Targeted Policies." In *Mitigating the COVID Economic Crisis: Act Fast and Do Whatever It Takes*, edited by Richard Baldwin and Beatrice Weder di Mauro, 41–47. London: CEPR Press.

IMF (International Monetary Fund). 2019. *World Economic Outlook: Global Manufacturing Downturn, Rising Trade Barriers*. Washington, DC: IMF.

IMF (International Monetary Fund). 2020. *World Economic Outlook: A Long and Difficult Ascent*. Washington, DC: IMF.

IMF (International Monetary Fund). 2021a. "Fiscal Monitor Update." January, IMF Washington, DC.

IMF (International Monetary Fund). 2021b. *World Economic Outlook: Recovery during a Pandemic; Health Concerns, Supply Disruptions, and Price Pressures*. Washington, DC: IMF.

Janssens, Wendy, Menno Pradhan, Richard de Groot, Estelle Sidze, Hermann Pythagore Pierre Donfouet, and Amanuel Abajobir. 2021. "The Short-Term Economic Effects of COVID-19 on Low-Income Households in Rural Kenya: An Analysis Using Weekly Financial Household Data." *World Development* 138 (February): 105280.

Khamis, Melanie, Daniel Prinz, David Locke Newhouse, Amparo Palacios-López, Utz Pape, and Michael Weber. 2021. "The Early Labor Market Impacts of COVID-19 in Developing Countries: Evidence from High-Frequency Phone Surveys." Policy Research Working Paper 9510, World Bank, Washington, DC.

Kugler, Maurice, Mariana Viollaz, Daniel Vasconcellos Archer Duque, Isis Gaddis, David Locke Newhouse, Amparo Palacios-López, and Michael Weber. 2021. "How Did the COVID-19 Crisis Affect Different Types of Workers in the Developing World?" Policy Research Working Paper 9703, World Bank, Washington, DC.

Lacey, Eric, Joseph Massad, and Robert Utz. 2021. "A Review of Fiscal Policy Responses to COVID-19." Macroeconomics, Trade, and Investment Insight 7, Equitable Growth, Finance, and Institutions Insight Series, World Bank, Washington, DC.

Lakner, Christoph, Daniel Gerszon Mahler, Mario Negre, and Espen Beer Prydz. 2020. "How Much Does Reducing Inequality Matter for Global Poverty?" Global Poverty Monitoring Technical Note 13 (June), World Bank, Washington, DC.

Mahler, Daniel Gerszon, Nishant Yonzan, Christoph Lakner, Raul Andrés Castañeda Aguilar, and Haoyu Wu. 2021. "Updated Estimates of the Impact of COVID-19 on Global Poverty: Turning the Corner on the Pandemic in 2021?" *World Bank Blogs: Data Blogs*, June 24, 2021. https://blogs.worldbank.org/opendata/updated-estimates-impact-covid-19-global-poverty-turning-corner-pandemic-2021.

RBI (Reserve Bank of India). 2017. *Indian Household Finance*. Report of the Household Finance Committee. Mumbai: RBI. https://rbidocs.rbi.org.in/rdocs/PublicationReport/Pdfs/HFCRA28D0415E2144A009112DD314ECF5C07.PDF.

RBI (Reserve Bank of India). 2021. "Revised Regulatory Framework for NBFCs A Scale Based Approach." Discussion paper, RBI, Mumbai.

Reinhart, Carmen M. 2020. "Debt and Financial Crises: Implications for the Post-COVID Landscape." Mundell-

Fleming Lecture, International Monetary Fund virtual 21st Jacques Polak Annual Research Conference, "Living in the Extreme: Economics of Pandemics, Climate Change, and Tail Risks," November 5–6, 2020. https://www.imf.org/en/News/Seminars/Conferences/2020/11/05/2020AnnualResearchConference.

Reinhart, Carmen M. 2021. "From Health Crisis to Financial Distress." Policy Research Working Paper 9616, World Bank, Washington, DC.

Reinhart, Carmen M., and Kenneth S. Rogoff. 2009. "The Aftermath of Financial Crises." *American Economic Review* 99 (2): 466–72.

Rogoff, Kenneth S., and Yuanchen Yang. 2021. "Has China's Housing Production Peaked?" *China and World Economy* 29 (1): 1–31.

Torres, Jesica, Franklin Maduko, Isis Gaddis, Leonardo Iacovone, and Kathleen Beegle. 2021. "The Impact of the COVID-19 Pandemic on Women-Led Businesses." Policy Research Working Paper 9817, World Bank, Washington, DC.

World Bank. 2011. *Global Economic Prospects: Navigating Strong Currents*. Vol. 2. Washington, DC: World Bank.

World Bank. 2020a. *Global Economic Prospects, January 2020: Slow Growth, Policy Challenges*. Washington, DC: World Bank.

World Bank. 2020b. *Global Financial Development Report 2019/2020: Bank Regulation and Supervision a Decade after the Global Financial Crisis*. Washington, DC: World Bank. https://www.worldbank.org/en/publication/gfdr/report.

World Bank. 2020c. *Poverty and Shared Prosperity 2020: Reversals of Fortune*. Washington, DC: World Bank.

World Bank. 2021a. *Global Economic Prospects, June 2021*. Washington, DC: World Bank.

World Bank. 2021b. "Resilience: COVID-19 Crisis through a Migration Lens." Migration and Development Brief 34, Global Knowledge Partnership on Migration and Development, World Bank, Washington, DC.

Yonzan, Nishant, Christoph Lakner, and Daniel Gerszon Mahler. 2021. "Is COVID-19 Increasing Global Inequality?" *World Bank Blogs: Data Blogs*, October 7, 2021. https://blogs.worldbank.org/opendata/covid-19-increasing-global-inequality.

Yonzan, Nishant, Christoph Lakner, Daniel Gerszon Mahler, Raul Andrés Castañeda Aguilar, and Haoyu Wu. 2020. "The Impact of COVID-19 on Global Poverty under Worsening Growth and Inequality." *World Bank Blogs: Data Blogs*, November 9, 2020. https://blogs.worldbank.org/opendata/impact-covid-19-global-poverty-under-worsening-growth-and-inequality.

Emerging risks to the recovery

The immediate economic effects of the COVID-19 pandemic were felt most acutely by households and firms, which experienced dramatic income losses. Financial risks resulting from these income losses can ultimately affect the entire economy through multiple, mutually reinforcing links that connect the financial health of households, firms, the financial sector, and government. Because of this interconnection, elevated financial risks in one sector can spill over and destabilize the economy as a whole. For example, income losses among businesses and households can create spillover risks for the financial and public sectors through rising loan defaults and reduced tax revenue. Similarly, the governments of many emerging economies were already heavily indebted before the pandemic and further increased borrowing to finance their crisis response. These relationships between sectors of an economy are not, however, deterministic. Well-designed fiscal, monetary, and financial sector policies can counteract and reduce these risks over time to support an equitable recovery.

Policy Priorities

The pandemic has increased economic risks for households, firms, financial institutions, and governments. Counteracting these risks to ensure an equitable recovery will require policy action in the following areas:

- **Recognizing and resolving asset distress in the financial sector** as support measures for households and firms are scaled back before economic activity has fully recovered.

- **Supporting insolvent households and businesses** that are unable to resolve their debts in countries with limited or no formal insolvency mechanisms.

- **Ensuring continued access to finance** in the face of tightening lending standards resulting from increased economic uncertainty and greater opacity about the true financial health of borrowers.

- **Managing and reducing high levels of government debt,** especially in countries that entered the pandemic with a high risk of debt distress.

Introduction

The COVID-19 (coronavirus) pandemic sent shock waves through the world economy and heightened concerns about high levels of private and public sector debt. Although the immediate government response to the crisis was largely effective at stabilizing output and protecting incomes, it also aggravated some preexisting financial risks to household, firm, financial sector, and public sector balance sheets that may pose a threat to an equitable recovery in the longer term. These financial risks do not exist in isolation; rather, they are connected through a series of direct and indirect links, as illustrated in figure 1.1.

This chapter outlines a conceptual framework that offers an encompassing view of the interrelated financial risks that will shape the economic recovery. The framework recognizes the important role of preexisting fragilities and global economic factors in the recovery prospects of emerging economies and highlights the important complementarities that exist between policies aimed at addressing the financial risks that have accumulated across the economy.

Addressing the economic risks that have arisen from the pandemic is important not only to ensure a return to economic growth, but also to counteract the dramatic impacts of the COVID-19 crisis on poverty and inequality. Reducing overindebtedness among households and firms is, for example, important in its own right, but it also reduces the risk of a credit crunch that disproportionately affects small businesses and low-income households. Similarly, managing and reducing elevated levels of government debt preserve the ability of governments to assist vulnerable populations and support social safety nets that can mitigate the effects of the crisis on poverty and inequality in the longer term. The following

Figure 1.1 Conceptual framework: Interconnected balance sheet risks

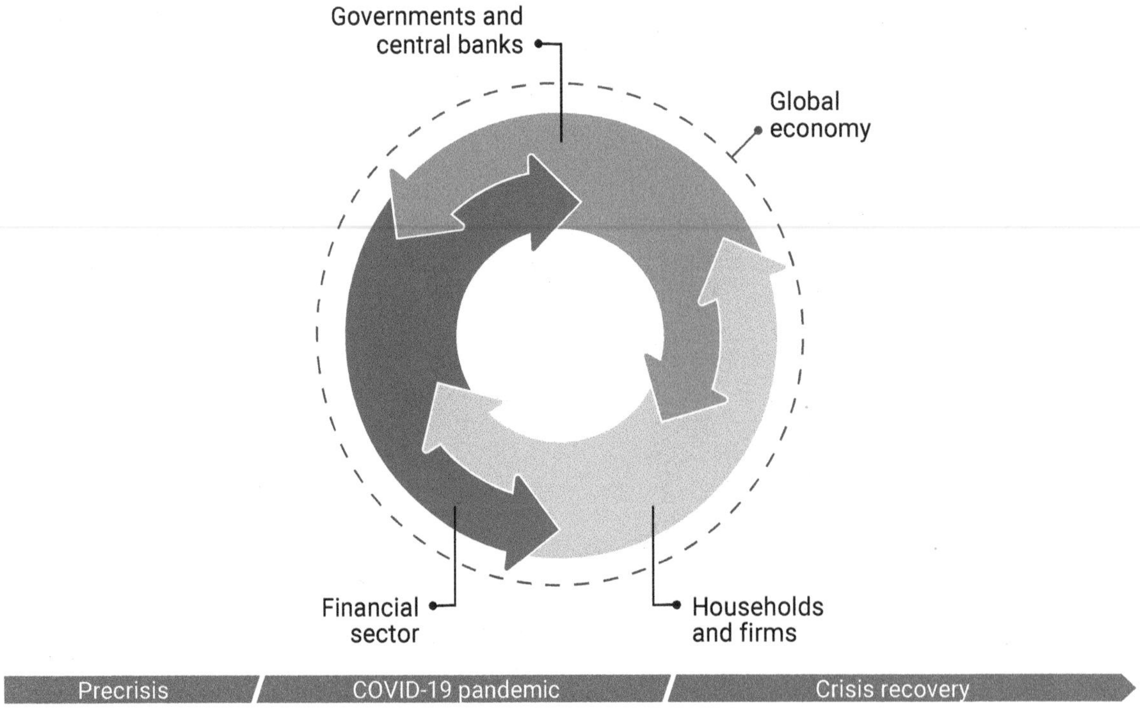

Source: WDR 2022 team.

Note: The figure shows the links between the main sectors of an economy through which risks in one sector can affect the wider economy.

chapters apply this conceptual framework to the various areas where balance sheet risks have accumulated as a result of the pandemic and highlight priority areas where decisive policy action can support an equitable recovery.

Interconnected financial risks across the economy

The initial impacts of the COVID-19 crisis were felt most directly by households and firms, which saw a sharp decline in income and business revenue. These income losses are likely to have repercussions for the wider economy through several mutually reinforcing channels that connect the financial health of households, firms, financial institutions, and governments.

Economic links between sectors create spillover risks

The financial health of households is connected to the larger economy through the so-called household–financial sector nexus and household–government nexus. When the financial health of households deteriorates, it can directly affect the financial sector through a rise in loan defaults and an increase in loan provisioning requirements, which reduce the ability of banks to issue new loans to creditworthy borrowers. Similarly, when balance sheet conditions in the financial sector worsen, banks supply households with less credit and charge higher interest rates, which depresses economic activity.

The financial health of households is similarly connected with that of governments because governments can provide households with direct support in the form of transfer payments, social safety nets, insurance, and employment. These support measures can help households weather the effects of an economic downturn, or an aggregate shock such as the COVID-19 crisis, that overwhelms conventional insurance mechanisms. Governments, in turn, rely on households as a source of tax revenue, which declines when incomes are low, unemployment is high, and household balance sheets are under stress.

Similarly, the corporate sector is connected to the wider economy through links with the financial sector—the so-called corporate–financial sector nexus—and through links with the public sector—the corporate–government nexus. The financial condition of the corporate sector affects banks and non-bank financial institutions directly through insolvency and loan defaults. The health of the financial sector, in turn, affects firms through the availability of credit: when there is stress on financial sector balance sheets, banks extend less credit and charge more for it.

There are multiple feedback loops that can reinforce these links. First, banks are often tempted to delay recognition of nonperforming loans (NPLs) and keep channeling credit to firms that are de facto insolvent. Such "zombie lending" misallocates credit to unproductive firms, reduces the access of profitable firms to financing, and has historically been an important factor in prolonged periods of low economic growth. Second, in times of economic crisis lenders may not be able to distinguish between firms that face temporary liquidity problems and those that are truly insolvent. They may, then, ration credit to both, thereby further depressing economic activity.[1] In emerging economies, government ownership of banks and the greater opacity of market information make these feedback loops more pronounced.

The financial health of the corporate sector is also connected to that of the government. Government spending supports economic activity in the corporate sector directly through public procurement and indirectly through transfers, guarantees, infrastructure investments, and other support schemes, often aimed at priority sectors such as agriculture or small enterprises. Similarly, tax policy can stimulate economic activity and set incentives for the efficient allocation of resources. Through this channel, tax policy has a direct impact on productivity in the corporate sector. The financial health of the corporate sector, in turn, affects governments directly through the taxation of firms and indirectly through the taxation of labor income and economic growth, which expands the tax base of the economy as a whole.

The connection between the government and financial sectors has received the most attention in recent economic crises[2] and is especially important in emerging economies where government debt and banking crises have often coincided.[3] The domestic financial sector is connected to the financial health of the government through two direct and two indirect channels, collectively known as the government–financial sector nexus. As for the direct channels, first, banks are directly exposed to the government's default risk if they hold government securities.[4] Through this channel, a deterioration in the government's financial position directly affects financial institutions' balance sheets, increasing borrowing costs and reducing banks' ability to supply credit. Conversely, banks are an important source of funding for the government through the purchase of government bonds. When financial sector balance sheets are weak, funding costs go up, making it difficult for governments to refinance existing short-term debt (known as rollover risk) and to finance new expenditures.[5] The absence of well-functioning bank resolution and crisis management frameworks can amplify negative feedback loops, particularly if the government's ability to support the financial system becomes compromised.

Second, governments and central banks have in place explicit arrangements, such as emergency liquidity assistance, to support ailing albeit solvent banks in well-circumscribed conditions. These commitments are more extensive in countries with substantial state ownership of banks. There, the government is directly exposed to losses in the financial sector through reduced dividends and losses in its equity holdings and is expected to provide liquidity and other types of support in times of crisis. However, even in countries with little or no state involvement in the financial sector, governments typically are not able to abstain from bailing out systemically important financial institutions in a crisis. Such bailouts for "too big to fail" institutions can have a significant direct impact on the government's financial position. The mere expectation of such bailouts can worsen fragilities in the financial sector by encouraging excessive risk-taking among banks.[6]

Risks to financial sector and government balance sheets are also connected through two indirect channels and feedback loops. First, the two sectors are connected through interactions between the fiscal and real (nonfinancial) sectors of the economy. A deterioration in the government's financial position will ultimately require fiscal consolidation (mobilizing tax revenue and reducing expenditures), which dampens economic activity. This, in turn, may increase insolvencies and put pressure on the financial sector. Second, the financial sector and government are connected through interactions between the banking and real sectors of the economy. The production of goods and services depends on access to credit, which is reduced when the financial sector is distressed. This reduction slows economic activity, triggers automatic stabilizers such as countercyclical welfare expenditures, and lessens the government's ability to raise tax revenue. In addition, many governments support specific sectors of the economy, such as agriculture and small businesses, through financial sector programs such as partial credit guarantees, directed lending, or public-private partnerships. When business conditions worsen, governments can be exposed to credit losses in these loans.

In emerging economies, the interconnected risks of households, firms, the financial sector, and government are exacerbated by external factors stemming from developments in the global economy. For example, in many small, open economies, households, firms, and government borrow in foreign currency. When the value of the local currency depreciates, foreign currency debt becomes more expensive and often unsustainable relative to the local currency income of the borrower. Low- and middle-income countries, and low-income countries in particular, are also more dependent on commodity exports (32 percent of high-income countries are commodity-dependent, compared with 91 percent of low-income countries).[7] Global economic crises, such as the COVID-19 shock, often coincide with a decline in commodity prices. This disproportionately affects government revenue in low-income countries, further reducing their ability to counteract the crisis through expansionary fiscal policy (higher government spending or tax reductions).

Effective policies can counteract risks to the recovery

Although the economic risks faced by households, firms, the financial sector, and government are interconnected, the relationship between these risks is not predetermined (figure 1.2). Well-designed fiscal, monetary, and financial sector policies can turn the links between sectors of the economy from a vicious cycle into a virtuous cycle. In response to the COVID-19 crisis, for example, many governments immediately used fiscal resources to support the balance sheets of households and businesses in order to prevent a wave of loan defaults and a spillover of the economic shock to the financial sector. Similarly, countries made extensive use of monetary and financial sector policies to strengthen the resilience of the financial sector and ensure that well-capitalized banks were in a position to continue supplying the economy with credit.

However, the extent to which governments can mitigate the longer-term risks arising from the COVID-19 crisis differs dramatically across countries because of wide variation in preexisting economic fragilities and access to resources. This disparity makes an unequal recovery within and across countries a very likely outcome. For example, preventing a spillover of household and corporate balance sheet risks to the financial sector requires direct fiscal support to households and firms whose incomes have been affected by the pandemic. But given high preexisting levels of government debt and declining tax revenue during the crisis, few emerging economies had the capacity to finance such anticyclical policies. The result was one of two pitfalls: countries either were not able to enact support policies comprehensive enough to prevent a surge in insolvencies, loan defaults, and spillovers from households and firms to the financial sector, or the scale of support programs required significant new government borrowing, which will constrain the ability of governments to provide ongoing support in the event of a drawn-out recovery.

Figure 1.2 **Conceptual framework: Vicious and virtuous cycles**

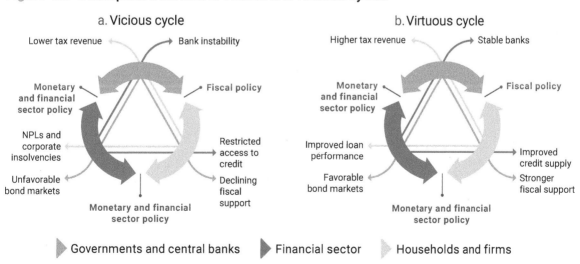

Source: WDR 2022 team, based on Schnabel (2021).
Note: NPLs = nonperforming loans.

In addition to different degrees of policy space, there is also wide variation in structural factors, such as the extent of informality in the economy, the quality of the legal system, the independence of the central bank, and the access to financial and nonfinancial technologies that can help or hinder the reduction of economic risks that may threaten the recovery.

The COVID-19 pandemic is also the first crisis in which access to digital technology and infrastructure plays an important role in determining both the severity of the crisis impacts and the speed of the crisis recovery. In economies with a strong digital infrastructure, a larger share of the workforce was able to work remotely, thereby reducing economic disruptions and job losses arising from the pandemic. Moreover, digital payment channels were used where they were available to disburse support payments to households and firms, allowing beneficiaries to receive relief payments more quickly. A strong digital infrastructure will also be an important factor in the crisis recovery because digital payments, e-commerce, and digital communications reduce the need for in-person interactions and enable normal economic activity to resume faster. New financial technologies can also reduce information asymmetries, support sound risk management, and allow lenders to support the recovery through the uninterrupted provision of credit to households and businesses.

Where governments are able to enact effective crisis response policies, these policies can act as a circuit breaker that lessens balance sheet risks and gives rise to a virtuous cycle with positive spillovers between the sectors. Where governments are unable to enact effective policies, or where such policies are hampered by structural factors beyond their control, a vicious cycle can emerge in which risks in each sector accumulate and reinforce each other over time.

From health crisis to financial distress: Emerging risks to the recovery

The COVID-19 crisis and many of the policies enacted to counter it have reinforced the economic links between households and firms, the financial sector, and government. Although the immediate government response to the crisis was swift and largely effective at mitigating the worst human costs of the pandemic, it also exacerbated preexisting financial fragilities by, for example, triggering a dramatic increase in private and public sector debt. These fragilities, if not addressed decisively, could pose a threat to a strong and equitable recovery in the longer term. One challenge policy makers face is that many of the policies undertaken during the COVID-19 crisis are altogether novel (such as central bank asset purchase programs in emerging economies), have not previously been used at this scale (such as debt moratoria and regulatory forbearance), or have the potential to create various longer-term risks to the recovery, such as hidden debts and contingent liabilities, which may become apparent only much later. As the immediate effects of the pandemic subside, policy makers face the difficult task of scaling back these policies without dampening the recovery or worsening the already highly regressive impacts of the crisis.

Households and firms

Despite the extensive fiscal support measures taken by governments worldwide, the pandemic has led to a significant tightening of household balance sheets. Although many countries enacted cash transfer and income support measures to support households and prevent spillovers to the financial sector, many of these programs were not sufficient to compensate for the full extent of income losses. As highlighted in the introduction to this Report (figure 1.5), the majority of households in both emerging and advanced economies do not have enough liquid assets to sustain basic consumption for more than three months in the face of a large income shock, and most governments lack the fiscal resources to maintain income support programs for a substantial amount of time. As a result, many income support programs had to be phased out before household earnings fully recovered. This was especially true in countries that were hit by multiple waves of the pandemic, lacked strong automatic stabilizers such as unemployment insurance and other social safety nets, and were unable to mobilize external fiscal resources for prolonged support measures. These factors increase the vulnerability of households, as well as the risk of spillovers to financial institutions through increases in nonperforming loans.

Household incomes were especially hard-hit in countries with limited social safety nets (see figure 1.3) and a large share of employment in the informal sector. Because of the aggregate nature of the shock,

Figure 1.3 Social safety nets and income losses during the COVID-19 crisis, by country income group

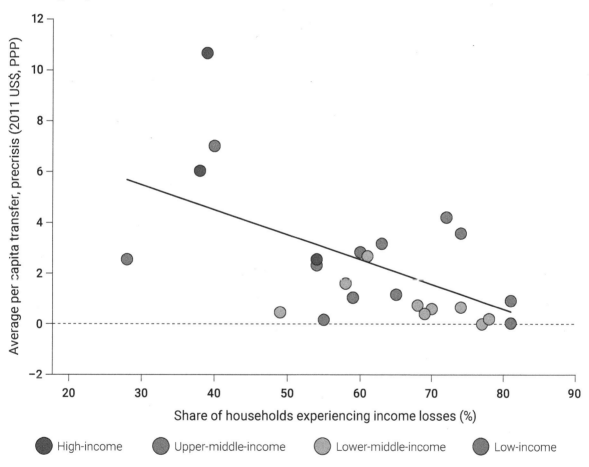

Source: WDR 2022 team, based on data from World Bank, ASPIRE (Atlas of Social Protection Indicators of Resilience and Equity) (dashboard), http://datatopics.worldbank.org/aspire/; World Bank, COVID-19 Household Monitoring Dashboard, https://www.worldbank.org/en/data/interactive/2020/11/11/covid-19-high-frequency-monitoring-dashboard.

Note: The figure shows the average per capita transfer of social protection payments, including transfer payments from social assistance, social insurance, and labor market programs. For each household, the per capita average transfer is the total amount of transfers received (constant 2011 US dollars adjusted for purchasing power parity, PPP) divided by household size, for the latest precrisis year available for each country. Data on income losses were collected between April and December 2020.

informal insurance mechanisms that could have mitigated the impact of the economic shock, such as borrowing from family and friends, were largely ineffective. In the majority of emerging economies, government transfer payments could not compensate for the sharp decline in incomes and were an insufficient substitute for these informal insurance mechanisms. Moreover, access to available support schemes often varied dramatically across population groups and did not reach households employed in the informal sector or households without access to a formal financial account, who were among those most severely affected by the crisis. This uneven access to support programs is likely to increase poverty and inequality and weaken the resilience of households in the longer run (see spotlight 1.1).

To ward off an immediate spike in defaults on consumer debt and spillovers to the financial sector, many governments supplemented income support measures with far-reaching debt forbearance policies. Many of these debt relief measures also included a freeze on credit reporting—that is, borrowers who were late on their loan payments were not reported to credit bureaus and did not suffer a deterioration of their credit score. Such policies create a difficult trade-off. On the one hand, they can be useful in the face of a transitory shock because they reduce the likelihood that borrowers are forced to default on their loans or lose access to credit as a result of temporary liquidity problems. However, such forbearance policies may not be sufficient to prevent spillovers to the financial sector if they are lifted prematurely, forcing defaults among otherwise creditworthy borrowers whose income has not yet recovered. On the other hand, if debt relief policies are left in place too long, they can hide the true extent of nonperforming loans and mask credit risks that materialize once debt moratoria are lifted. Box 1.1 describes how debt moratoria were used as part of the short-term response to the pandemic in India and were successful in warding off a large spike in loan defaults in the early stages of the crisis.

Similarly, a broad range of policies have been enacted to provide liquidity to the corporate sector in the hope that, because the public health crisis will be temporary, so, too, will be the financial distress of firms. These policies have included direct grants and transfer payments, tax breaks, as well as credit subsidies and guarantees. Although the extension of direct support to businesses is sensible in the short run to prevent insolvencies of viable firms and associated job losses, it is important that support policies be designed in a way that does not distort the allocation of resources in the longer term. The pandemic has triggered structural changes in the world economy, which will ultimately necessitate a reallocation of resources between sectors. Some areas such as tourism and corporate real estate are expected to take a long time to recover to their precrisis levels, while areas such as e-commerce, services, and information technology are expected to expand their relative shares of the economy. Temporary support programs that are left in place for too long, or that target specific industries through preferential tax treatment, transfers, or credit subsidies, run the risk of channeling scarce resources to sectors and firms that the crisis has rendered unviable. Evidence from past crises shows that this type of misallocation tends to benefit large firms in stagnating sectors to the detriment of smaller and more efficient firms, as well as sectors with higher growth potential. Emerging evidence on the impacts of COVID-19 support programs suggests that this pattern also holds in the current crisis, with support programs disproportionately benefiting less productive firms in politically favored sectors.[8] This discrepancy could slow the economic recovery and delay the reallocation of resources to more sustainable sectors.

The financial position of households and firms will also be affected by feedback effects from the government and the financial sector. Governments that entered the crisis with elevated debt and limited fiscal resources were either unable to mobilize sufficient resources for the crisis response or will have to phase out support programs prematurely. Data from the World Bank's COVID-19 Crisis Response Survey reveal that the fiscal response to the pandemic was significantly constrained by limited access to domestic borrowing in 72 percent of low-income countries and 57 percent of lower-middle-income countries, by limited access to foreign borrowing in 83 percent of low-income countries and 61 percent

The world over, governments and regulators responded to the COVID-19 crisis with financial sector policies aimed at supporting borrowers and reducing risks to financial stability. Many of these policies, such as debt moratoria, had never been used on this scale. It is possible to draw some first lessons about the effectiveness of these policies from the experience of countries that were confronted with multiple waves of the pandemic and introduced several rounds of support programs in response.

The case of India offers an especially instructive example. India's government and financial regulators put forth a large, decisive policy response to the first wave of the pandemic that used a variety of monetary and financial sector policies aimed at stabilizing the financial sector and supporting households and firms.

Monetary policy tools: Effective but cannot be targeted

In March 2020, the Reserve Bank of India (RBI) approved a first monetary stimulus totaling some $75 billion. This stimulus was expanded in later rounds, and by the end of 2021 the RBI had introduced monetary policy measures totaling $231 billion.[a] The first round of liquidity measures reduced interest rates by 100–200 basis points across the yield curve and successfully averted financial distress among banks and nonbank lenders. Figure B1.1.1 shows how the RBI implemented the monetary stimulus through the repurchase agreement (repo) market and how this action lowered interest rates and shifted the yield curve.

Debt moratoria: Covered 50 percent of all loans in India, most stabilized

India's first COVID-19 package also included a generous debt repayment moratorium for households and firms. Participation in this moratorium, which granted borrowers a freeze on loan repayments for 90 days, was voluntary, but nearly 50 percent of bank loans were eventually covered by the program. As lockdowns continued, another 90-day

Figure B1.1.1 **Use of monetary policy to reduce interest rates in India**

a. Effects of monetary stimulus through repo market, 2018–21

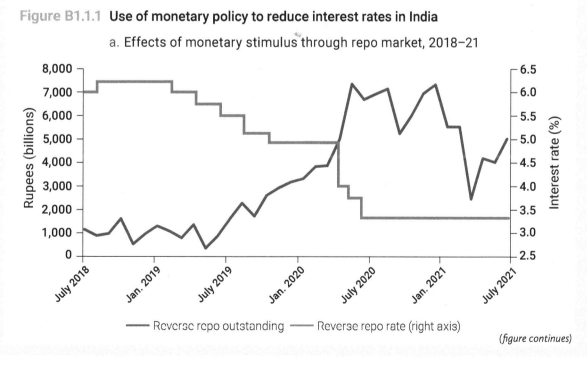

— Reverse repo outstanding — Reverse repo rate (right axis)

(figure continues)

(Box continues next page)

Figure B1.1.1 **Use of monetary policy to reduce interest rates in India** *(continued)*

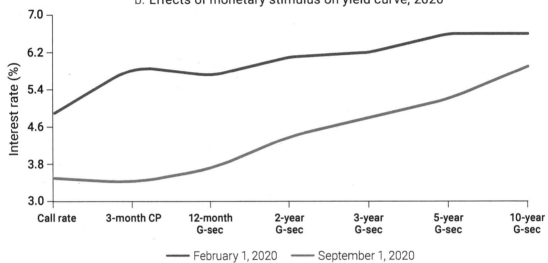

b. Effects of monetary stimulus on yield curve, 2020

Source: Reserve Bank of India.

Note: The figure shows the effects of the Reserve Bank of India's intervention in the repurchase agreement (repo) market. Panel a indicates its importance as a source of financing for financial institutions. Panel b indicates the shift in India's yield curve (that is, the reduction of interest rates at different maturities) that resulted from liquidity infusion through this channel and other actions of the central bank. CP = commercial paper; G-sec = government security.

extension of the program was introduced, which ultimately covered 40 percent of all outstanding loans in India.[b] As the moratorium was eventually being phased out, the central bank opened up a special restructuring window for loans to consumers, micro-, small, and medium enterprises (MSMEs), and larger firms to facilitate the reduction of debt burdens.

Although banks were concerned about the high share of loans covered by the moratorium, the outcomes were relatively benign. In the six months after the moratorium, banks managed to contain additional nonperforming loans to 2–4 percent.[c] However, this relative stability masked considerable differences across segments, with consumer loan delinquency rising while nonperforming loans among MSMEs and larger firms remained stable.

Loan performance in segments such as microfinance was the most severely affected, with nonperforming loans increasing from 1 percentage point to more than 5 percentage points.

Although India's experience with a debt moratorium was overall favorable, applying such a measure repeatedly is challenging because it may affect borrowers' behavior. India later enacted another debt moratorium as part of its response to the severe second wave of the pandemic from March to June 2021. However, the possible effects on hidden debts and credit discipline were a much-debated issue.

Guarantee schemes: Well targeted, but a potential source of contingent liabilities
The Indian government also introduced a partial credit guarantee scheme, the Emergency Credit

(Box continues next page)

Box 1.1 **Case study: Supporting borrowers and the financial sector in India** *(continued)*

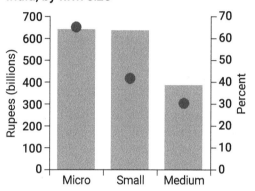

Figure B1.1.2 **Support for new lending through partial credit guarantees in India, by firm size**

Value of loans disbursed under ECLGS

Share of outstanding loans benefiting from ECLGS (right axis)

Source: Reserve Bank of India.
Note: The figure shows the amount of new lending to micro-, small, and medium enterprises under India's credit guarantee scheme initiated in response to the pandemic. ECLGS = Emergency Credit Line Guarantee Scheme.

Line Guarantee Scheme (ECLGS). This scheme enabled the government to provide the economy with additional liquidity with a minimal immediate effect on its fiscal position (figure B1.1.2). Initially, guarantees of Rs 3 trillion ($40 billion) were

announced, and most of the Rs 2.5 trillion ($34 billion) allocated under this scheme went to small and microenterprises.

However, the true cost of these guarantees to the government will only become clear in the longer term. Although India's economic recovery from the first waves of the pandemic has been remarkably robust and the immediate fiscal impact of credit guarantee schemes is low, credit guarantees always carry the risk of turning into a liability for the government if an economic downturn causes loan defaults to rise. This risk is of particular concern in the context of the COVID-19 crisis, in which business prospects across countries and sectors of the economy remain uncertain in the face of possible future waves of the pandemic.

Rising inequality despite a strong crisis response
Although a large spike in insolvencies and loan defaults has been averted thanks to India's ambitious policy response,[d] inequality has increased. While agricultural incomes have been remarkably resilient, the 40 percent of India's informal workforce outside the agriculture sector has suffered the brunt of the economic distress caused by the pandemic.[e] This is not unique to India and mirrors developments in many other countries where the pandemic has worsened inequality despite extensive policy measures aimed at protecting the incomes of the poor.[f]

a. RBI (2021).
b. RBI (2020a, 2020b).
c. Even when the 2 percent of loans under the special restructuring window are included, the total addition in problem loans was only 5 percent of banks' total loan portfolios.
d. RBI (2021).
e. See Azim Premji University (2021), CMIE (2021), and Dhingra and Ghatak (2021). While the data show stark increases in poverty and inequality during India's first lockdown, some recent evidence suggests that these trends may have been more muted and partly reversed later in the pandemic (Gupta, Malani, and Woda 2021).
f. World Bank (2021b, 2022).

of lower-middle-income countries, and by concerns about the overall sustainability of government debt in 83 percent of low-income countries and 70 percent of lower-middle-income countries (figure 1.4). Governments facing such tight fiscal limitations will be unable to protect households and firms from adverse events during the recovery. These include external economic shocks, which are a very real prospect for low- and middle-income countries, where the recovery is highly dependent on a favorable international

Figure 1.4 Fiscal constraints to the COVID-19 response, by country income group

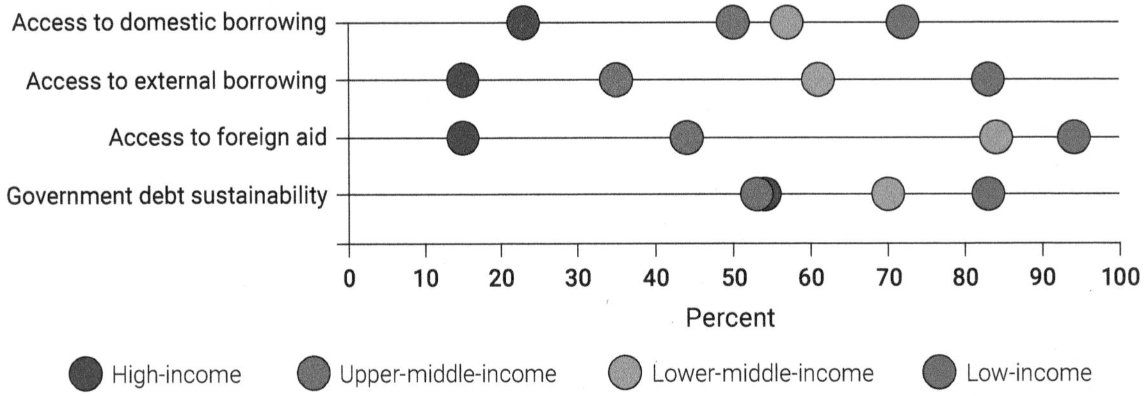

Source: World Bank, COVID-19 Crisis Response Survey, 2021, http://bit.do/WDR2022-Covid-19_survey.
Note: The figure shows the percentage of countries in which each of the listed factors was identified as a significant or moderate constraint to the response to the pandemic. Data are as of June 30, 2021.

environment. Similarly, the survival of many viable firms depends on an ongoing supply of credit, which may be threatened if the financial sector comes under stress from external shocks, exposure to the government risk, or an increase in loan defaults as government support programs are phased out.

Households and businesses are also exposed to tightening public sector balance sheets through government arrears. As a result of the crisis, many governments, particularly in low-income countries, have resorted to suspending or delaying the payments for goods, services, and works procured from the private sector. Some governments have also suspended or delayed paying the salaries of public sector employees. In Sub-Saharan Africa, for example, the government is one of the biggest purchasers of goods and services, and public procurement averages 12 percent of gross domestic product (GDP). Government arrears stood at a staggering 4.26 percent of GDP prior to the COVID-19 pandemic (figure 1.5).[9] The economic contraction stemming from the pandemic has only aggravated the problem. Conservative estimates for the region suggest government arrears increased by nearly 2 percent of GDP during the first year of the pandemic.[10] Financing relief and recovery programs by accumulating arrears is economically costly because it directly counteracts stimulus efforts by depriving households of income and reducing firm revenue at a time when liquidity is crucial for their survival. The accumulation of government arrears is a prime example of an economic link between the public and private sectors that has been exacerbated by the crisis, has an asymmetrically larger adverse effect on small and informal firms, and poses a very real threat to the recovery.

Financial sector

In contrast to earlier crises, the COVID-19 recession did not originate in the financial sector and was not set off by a specific event, such as the failure of a systemically important institution. Nonetheless, a gradual deterioration of asset quality in the aftermath of the pandemic could lead to a longer-term outcome that looks very similar to that after a traditional financial sector crisis.

Mandated by governments and regulators, financial institutions worldwide have granted grace periods and moratoria for loan repayments on an unprecedented scale (figure 1.6). These forbearance policies play an important role in preventing avoidable defaults among creditworthy borrowers suffering temporary liquidity problems. However, if left in place too long these policies can lead to credit market distortions and make it difficult for banks to distinguish between creditworthy and noncreditworthy borrowers, ultimately reducing new lending.

Figure 1.5 Government arrears in Sub-Saharan Africa

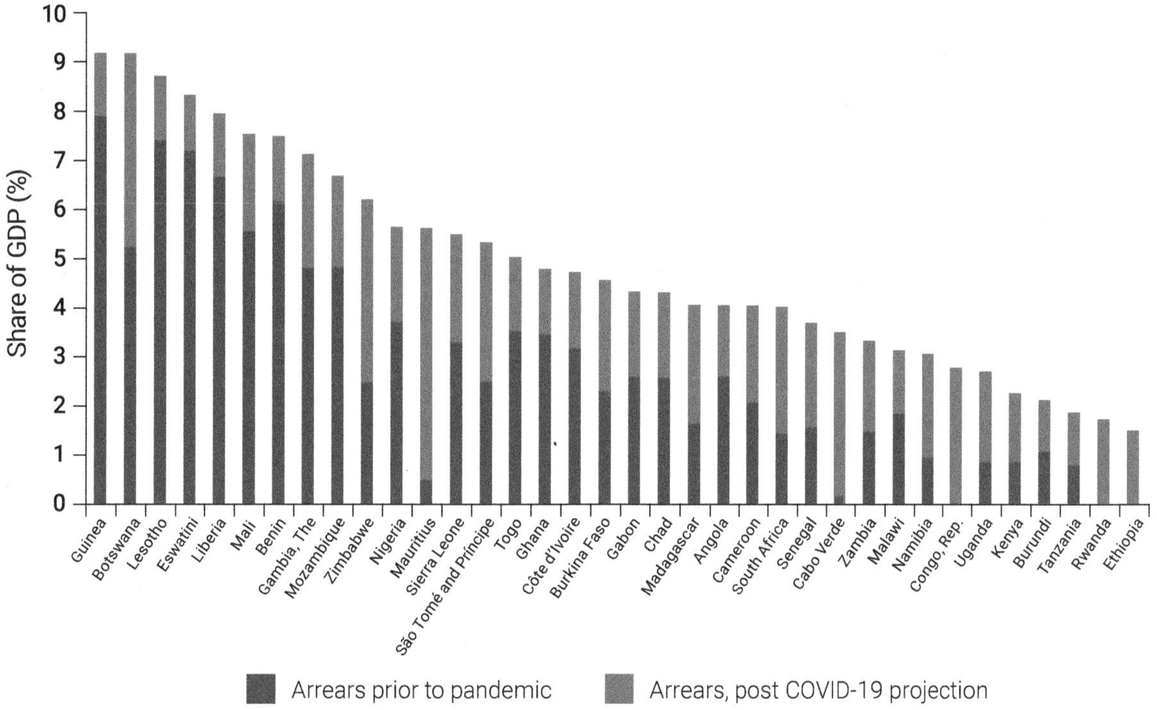

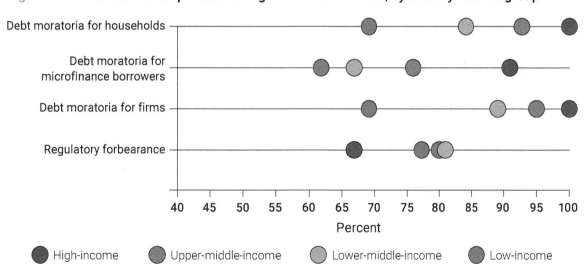

Legend: ■ Arrears prior to pandemic   ■ Arrears, post COVID-19 projection

Source: WDR 2022 team, based on Bosio, Ramalho, and Reinhart (2021).

Note: The arrears are computed using the ratio of the number of days required to process payment beyond 45 days to the number of days in a year, multiplied by total public procurement as a percentage of GDP. Projections are based on data from the October 2020 IMF World Economic Outlook. See International Monetary Fund, WEO (World Economic Outlook Databases) (dashboard), https://www.imf.org/en/Publications/SPROLLS/world-economic-outlook-databases.

Figure 1.6 Financial sector policies during the COVID-19 crisis, by country income group

Legend: ● High-income   ● Upper-middle-income   ● Lower-middle-income   ● Low-income

Source: World Bank, COVID-19 Crisis Response Survey, 2021, http://bit.do/WDR2022-Covid-19_survey.

Note: The figure shows the percentage of countries in which each of the listed policies was implemented in response to the pandemic. Data are as of June 30, 2021.

Some debt moratoria enacted in response to the COVID-19 crisis were accompanied by a freeze on credit reporting—that is, regulators instructed banks to not report delinquent borrowers to credit bureaus for the duration of the moratorium. Although such a measure protects borrowers from being excluded from the credit market because of a temporary liquidity shock, it complicates the task of assessing the true credit risk on bank balance sheets. So long as forbearance programs are in place, banks are largely unable to distinguish illiquid from insolvent borrowers, which may make them more reluctant to issue new credit. This pattern may already be evident in some economies. Since the fourth quarter of 2019, the percentage of loans to total assets has fallen, and lending standards have tightened in countries that were more severely affected by emergency measures (see chapter 2 for a discussion).

Finally, debt forbearance programs always carry the risk of creating incentives for evergreening and zombie lending—that is, they tempt lenders to extend credit to insolvent borrowers to avoid having to classify these loans as nonperforming. Through the financial sector–corporate nexus and the financial sector–household nexus, evergreening and zombie lending have negative effects on the real economy because they depress lending to creditworthy households and viable firms. As a result, households and firms are less resilient to the adverse shocks that may arise during the crisis recovery period and are less able to finance new consumption and investment.

In addition to debt moratoria, many countries have relaxed banking regulations, accounting standards, and capital provisioning rules for bad loans in an effort to stimulate lending and prevent a credit crunch (see box 1.2). Although international regulatory standards, such as the Basel III framework, allow for some flexibility to enact such regulatory forbearance measures, some regulators relaxed prudential regulation beyond international standards in response to the crisis. This is an extremely problematic policy choice because the relaxation of prudential oversight encourages financial institutions to originate poorly screened loans. This contributes to the accumulation of loans whose true credit risk is unknown, but likely much higher than accounted for by those institutions. In addition, numerous political economy factors will make it extremely difficult to reverse the relaxation of regulatory standards once the crisis subsides, especially in countries with weaker institutions and limited central bank independence. In the longer run, the use of regulatory forbearance policies that go beyond the flexibility embedded in international frameworks will magnify financial sector risks and increase the vulnerability of countries to financial crises. This is illustrated by previous crisis episodes in which such policies were used on a much more limited scale than in the COVID-19 crisis and had far-reaching negative consequences, including zombie lending and excessive risk-taking invited by lax regulatory oversight.

In many emerging markets, nonbank financial institutions account for a high share of private credit. They are typically less regulated than banks and may therefore accumulate credit risks that are less apparent than the risks to bank balance sheets. Nonbank lenders—including microfinance institutions and fintech lenders—also account for a large share of lending to consumers and small businesses, which have been especially hard-hit by the pandemic. When the balance sheets of nonbank lenders come under stress, there are far-reaching repercussions for the real economy. In the Indian microfinance crisis of 2010–11, for example, the aggregate loan portfolio of microfinance lenders contracted by 20 percent. This contraction had severe negative effects on household wage earnings and consumption.[11]

Nonbank lenders in emerging economies are also much more exposed to risks originating in the global economy. Unlike deposit-taking commercial banks, nonbank lenders refinance themselves in domestic and international markets, sometimes in foreign currency, which means their ability to supply credit is directly affected by exchange rate fluctuations and the international interest rate environment. Because nonbank lenders in emerging economies deal predominantly with low-income consumers and

Box 1.2 The unintended consequences of regulatory forbearance

During the COVID-19 crisis, many countries experimented with regulatory forbearance policies that relaxed capital requirements or accounting standards for banks in the hope they would provide borrowers with temporary relief.[a] Although it is too early to assess the impact of these regulatory forbearance policies, past experiences can serve as a useful illustration of the longer-term risks such policies can pose to financial stability and economic growth.

One especially instructive example is India, which lowered capital provisioning requirements in response to the 2007–09 global financial crisis. In 2008, the Reserve Bank of India (RBI) announced it would apply "special regulatory treatment" to loans under temporary liquidity stress. The policy relaxed asset risk classification rules that govern capital provisioning requirements for financial institutions with the intent of making it easier for banks to provide forbearance to firms that had suffered temporary cash-flow shocks during the crisis.

With the new regulation, banks were no longer required to automatically downgrade the asset quality of loans to substandard because of a missed principal or interest payment. They could claim that delinquent firms merely faced temporary liquidity problems and place these assets into a new "restructured" category. Under normal circumstances, all loans in the restructured category would be subject to immediate downgrades to substandard, and capital provisioning requirements would increase proportionately and substantially, as table B1.2.1 illustrates. In other words, banks would be required to increase their capital reserves to protect themselves against the higher default risk of these loans.

The RBI regulation did not provide explicit criteria for identifying liquidity-constrained firms, leaving it up to the banks to decide which loans to assign to the new restructured category. Banks took full advantage of this ambiguity and extensively used the restructured category to avoid having to add to their capital reserves. In this way, the policy gave banks an incentive to obscure the true asset quality of the loans on their books and offered them a route to continually postponing or altogether avoiding recognition of troubled assets.

Table B1.2.1 Provisioning requirements by loan category, India, 2008

Asset category	NPL duration (months)	Provisioning rate (%)
Standard	—	0.25–1
Substandard	<12	10
Doubtful	12–24	20
	25–48	30
	>48	100
Loss	—	100

Source: Reserve Bank of India.

Note: The table lists provisioning requirements on various categories of loans as defined by the Reserve Bank of India. The provisioning requirements for standard assets depend on the industry sector of the loan, and thus the table indicates the range of provisioning rates across all industries. NPL = nonperforming loan.

This situation led to a significant buildup of stressed assets in the Indian banking system. State-owned banks, in particular, saw their stressed assets pile up—a problem that became apparent once the regulation was withdrawn (see figure B1.2.1).[b] The marked difference in the accumulation of stressed assets between private and state-owned banks indicates that the negative consequences of the policy are not uniform and may be exacerbated by poor corporate governance.

The rise in nonperforming loans (NPLs) resulting from diminishment of the crisis had a large impact on asset quality in the Indian financial sector. Prior to the global financial crisis, India had the lowest NPL ratio (2 percent) of all G20 nations. Between 2008 and 2018, the share of nonperforming and restructured loans in India's banking system rose dramatically, and by 2018 India had the highest NPL ratio (11 percent) among this group of countries.

Contrary to the intention of the policy, regulatory forbearance also encouraged banks to channel credit to low-liquidity and low-solvency borrowers. As a result, zombie firms emerged on a large scale in the Indian corporate sector. In 2016, approximately 40 percent of nonfinancial firms in India had

(Box continues next page)

Box 1.2 The unintended consequences of regulatory forbearance *(continued)*

Figure B1.2.1 Nonperforming loans in India, 2005–16

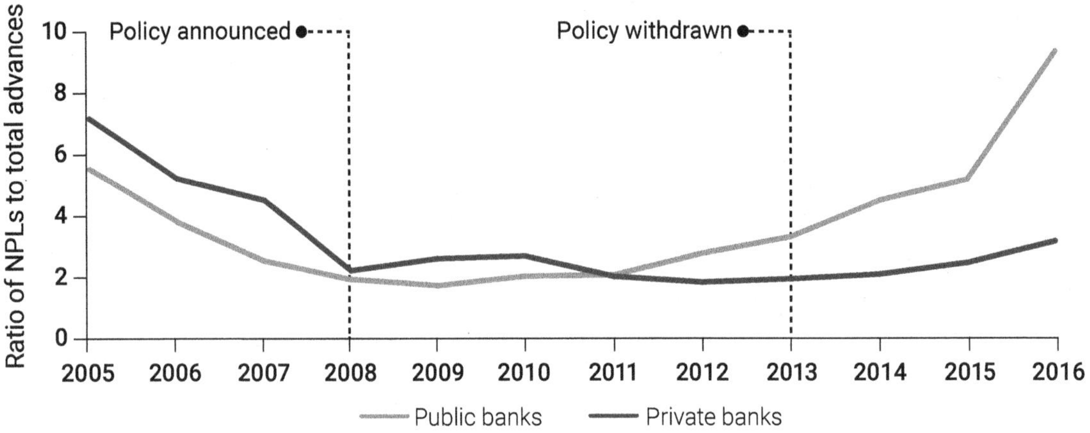

Source: Chari, Jain, and Kulkarni 2021.

Note: The figure shows the ratio of nonperforming loans (NPLs) to total advances for state-owned banks and private banks in India between 2005 and 2016. Dashed lines mark the announcement and withdrawal of the regulatory forbearance policy.

an interest coverage ratio (the ratio of revenue to interest payments) of less than 2, and 21 percent of firms had an interest coverage ratio of less than 1, meaning that they were unable to cover their debt payments with current revenue. The average interest coverage ratio of Indian firms fell by nearly half, from 6.92 in 2007 to 3.38 by 2015. At the same time, overall debt levels remained unchanged, suggesting that the debt service capacity of the Indian corporate sector had sharply declined. This increase in zombie lending also made it more difficult for healthy firms to obtain loans from banks, with obvious negative implications for economic growth.

Meanwhile, regulatory forbearance functioned as an implicit subsidy for the financial sector that allowed the government to delay costly bank recapitalization. Recognizing loan losses in a timely fashion would have undoubtedly weakened bank balance sheets and necessitated large bank recapitalizations. Because state-owned banks account for approximately 70 percent of the Indian banking sector, recognition would have entailed significant costs for the government relative to budget-neutral forbearance schemes.

In light of the many regulatory forbearance policies enacted in the wake of the COVID-19 crisis, India's experiment with regulatory forbearance in a past crisis serves as a cautionary tale. It may be challenging to unwind improperly designed temporary forbearance measures, and many of these policies will have long-lasting negative effects on access to credit, industry structure, and financial stability even after a policy is withdrawn. As economies recover, active and costly intervention may be needed to address some of these longer-term legacies, such as zombie lending and the undercapitalization of banks.

a. Acharya, Engle, and Steffen (2021).
b. Chari, Jain and Kulkarni (2021).

small businesses, the impacts of external shocks on their ability to supply credit will have a disproportionately negative effect on these vulnerable segments of the population.

Financial fragilities in the postcrisis period could also arise from a tightening of the government–financial sector nexus (figure 1.7). Many governments have financed their COVID-19 response by issuing new debt that is held by domestic financial institutions. As the government's fiscal position worsens and

Figure 1.7 Government debt and banking sector fragility during the COVID-19 crisis, by country income group

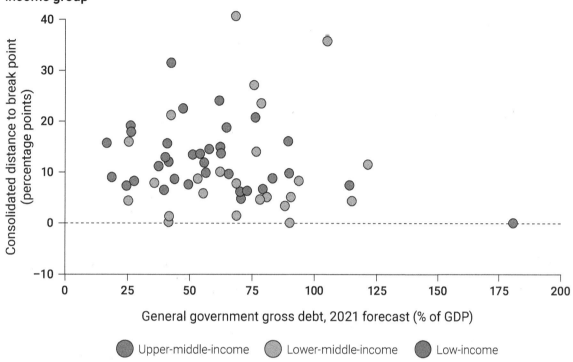

Source: WDR 2022 team, based on Feyen and Mare (2021); World Bank Macro-Fiscal Model Data Base, see Burns and Jooste (2019); Burns et al. (2019).

Note: The consolidated distance to break point is the percentage point increase in the nonperforming loan ratio that wipes out capital buffers for banks representing at least 20 percent of banking system assets (see Feyen and Mare 2021). GDP = gross domestic product.

its credit rating falls, asset quality in the financial sector deteriorates. This deterioration in asset quality has negative feedback effects on the wider economy because it limits the ability of banks to support the recovery through new lending. This situation raises the possibility of mutually reinforcing crises of government finances and the financial sector. In Tunisia and several other countries, for example, international rating agencies, reacting to the crisis, downgraded both the government's issuer ratings, as well as the outlook for some of the country's largest banks. The government–banking sector nexus could also become more precarious because of increases in the relative size of the banking sector, which makes it more difficult for governments to resolve systemwide distress in the event of a crisis.[12]

Governments

In emerging economies, the challenges created by the pandemic go beyond household and firm balance sheets and encompass the financial position of the government. The large fiscal support programs enacted in response to the crisis led to a dramatic increase in government debt, with average debt loads increasing by roughly 7.4 percentage points of GDP since the beginning of the COVID-19 crisis, compared with an average of 1.8 percentage points over the previous decade. This increase in government debt was uneven in several respects (see table 1.1). First, higher-income countries were able to access financing more easily than lower-income countries. Second, upper-middle-income countries relied on international markets to mobilize resources for the crisis response, while, relative to the previous decade, lower-middle-income

Table 1.1 Change in average central government debt stocks, by country income group, 2010–20

Share of GDP (%)

Change in average total debt to GDP ratio	Low-income	Lower-middle-income	Upper-middle-income	High-income	All
Total debt					
Average, 2010–19	2.88	1.82	1.46	1.20	1.84
2020	3.81	6.69	5.55	13.63	7.42
Domestic debt					
Average, 2010–19	0.79	0.59	0.97	−0.30	0.51
2020	0.86	3.04	1.80	9.24	3.73
External debt					
Average, 2010–19	2.09	1.23	0.49	1.41	1.30
2020	3.03	3.66	3.74	4.54	3.74

Source: Barrot 2021.

Note: The table shows the changes in government total, domestic, and external debt stocks for the period 2010–19 and in 2020. GDP = gross domestic product.

countries relied more heavily on domestic debt. Finally, low-income countries with market access turned mostly to external financing to meet increased funding needs for the response to the pandemic.

In addition to increased global debt loads, other indicators point to latent risks that may endanger the financial position of governments. In 2020, five governments defaulted on their obligations to external private creditors, a worrying increase compared with the norm over the post–World War II period. In the previous decade, an average of two governments defaulted every year. Moreover, more than half of the countries eligible for relief under the G20 Debt Service Suspension Initiative (DSSI) are in debt distress or at high risk of debt distress. These heightened risks at the government level have direct implications for poverty and inequality, as well as for the economic resilience of households and firms. Governments that face dramatically increased debt loads may be unable to finance social safety nets and essential public goods, such as health care and education, and may not be able to mobilize the resources to support households and firms that have been directly affected by the crisis.

The deteriorating financial position of governments will not be easily reversed because it is the combined effect of the fiscal response to the crisis, a dramatic decline in tax revenue (averaging almost 1.5 percent of GDP in 2020), the widespread use of tax forbearance schemes, and, in many emerging economies, the worsening balance sheets of state-owned enterprises. Many countries are counting on a rebound in economic activity and tax revenue to mitigate the economic damage resulting from the pandemic. However, unequal access to vaccines, the need to keep public health measures in place longer than anticipated, and a worsening international economic environment have cast doubt on the prospects for a quick recovery. Following a positive trend in the fiscal position of governments, the onset of the pandemic brought about a dramatic reversal as GDP and tax revenue collapsed, widening primary deficits and undoing much of the progress in revenue mobilization efforts implemented in recent years (figures 1.8 and 1.9).

Limited fiscal resources may require many governments to phase out fiscal support for households and firms and resume revenue mobilization efforts, including tax collection, before incomes and employment have fully rebounded. This effort to raise revenue could put further pressure on household and firm balance sheets and threaten hard-won gains in poverty reduction. Historically, episodes of high

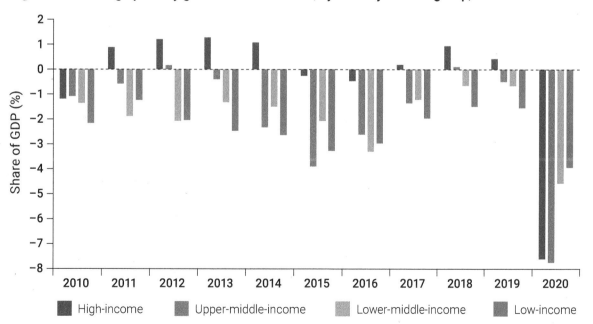

Figure 1.8 Change in average government revenue, by country income group, 2011–20

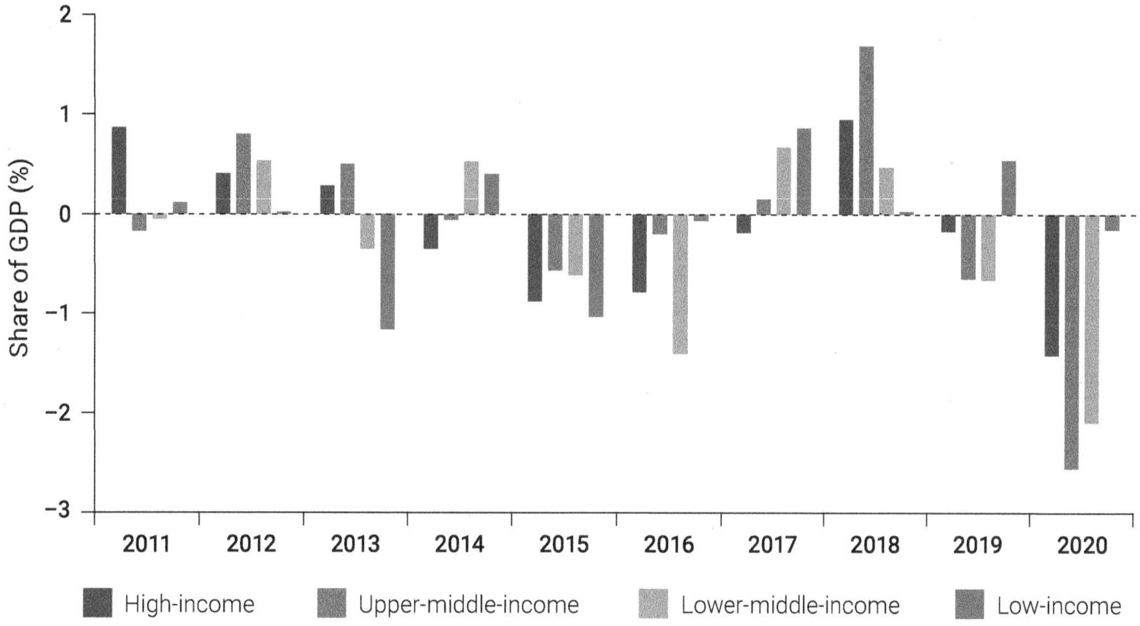

Source: WDR 2022 team, based on data from IMF (2021b).
Note: The figure shows the difference relative to the prior year in average revenue as a share of the gross domestic product (GDP) for each country group.

Figure 1.9 Average primary government balances, by country income group, 2010–20

Source: WDR 2022 team, based on data from IMF (2021b).
Note: The figure shows the difference relative to the prior year in average primary balance (noninterest revenue minus non-interest expenditures) as a share of the gross domestic product (GDP) for each country group.

fiscal deficits and significant increases in the stock of domestic debt have also been associated with higher inflation, which acts as a highly regressive tax on low incomes and exacerbates the impacts of a crisis on poverty and inequality.

Elevated government risks can also spill over to the financial sector, particularly in low- and middle-income economies. Recent studies have evaluated the potential fallout from rising government debt levels. One study finds that about half of identified episodes of rapid debt accumulation across country groups are associated with financial crises, which tend to be severer than those occurring without the presence of a debt buildup in the public sector.[13] Another study finds no association between debt build-ups and a higher likelihood that high-come economies undergo a financial crisis, but it confirms that debt buildups are associated with worse outcomes in the financial crises that do occur.[14] Increases in government debt are thus potentially associated with a heightened risk of financial crises in emerging economies, and, once they occur, large debt loads pose a significant obstacle to crisis resolution.

Against this backdrop, it is important to note that the fiscal response to the COVID-19 crisis has been significantly financed with domestic debt held by local investors such as banks, pension funds, and other financial institutions, thereby tightening the link between government and financial sector balance sheets. Government risk downgrades thus lead to a direct deterioration of asset quality on the balance sheets of financial institutions and reduce the financial sector's ability to support the recovery. During 2020, one-third of the governments assessed by the three main rating agencies suffered a downgrade in their risk rating.[15] This deterioration can, in turn, require governmental intervention to recapitalize financial institutions and potentially trigger shocks to government budgets through contingent liabilities and further increases in the debt stock.

Recent research on the fiscal costs of contingent liabilities can help to quantify these risks. One study finds that when contingent liabilities materialize (such as when a government needs to rescue a state-owned enterprise or subnational entity), the average fiscal cost is 6 percent of GDP. The fiscal costs are even higher for contingent liabilities in the financial sector, where bailouts can cost as much as 40 percent of GDP.[16] State-owned enterprises, which account for a large share of the corporate revenue base and essential services in many countries, are a source of significant contingent liability risks for governments. For example, in 2018 Angola faced downward pressure on its government credit ratings after an unexpected one-off support payment of $8 billion (7 percent of GDP) to Sonangol, the national oil company, became necessary.[17] Similarly, Indonesia's largest utility company required a bailout at a cost of 4 percent of GDP to the taxpayer in 1998. In the same way, financial pressures on state-owned enterprises increased considerably during the pandemic. Many of the largest state-owned enterprises, especially in low-income countries, export natural resources, which are vulnerable to the commodity price shocks and exchange rate fluctuations that will occur during the crisis recovery period.

Meanwhile, some COVID-19 crisis response programs have given rise to new contingent liabilities altogether. Many governments extensively used credit guarantee schemes to continue the flow of credit to households and firms during the crisis. Such programs are attractive in the short run because they have no immediate fiscal cost to the government, but they can create significant longer-term risks to government finances if loans covered by the program default. The magnitude of contingent liabilities stemming from credit guarantee schemes is typically difficult to estimate, but it can be substantial, as evidence from past crises illustrates.[18]

The global economy

External factors will play an important role in shaping the recovery prospects of emerging economies (box 1.3). The COVID-19 crisis has taken place against the backdrop of a relatively benign economic environment characterized by historically low interest rates globally, which remained low because of

Box 1.3 External factors in the recovery: Will this "taper tantrum" be different?

The link between developments in the global economy and the crisis recovery in emerging economies is well illustrated by the withdrawal of stimulus policies in the United States after the 2007–09 global financial crisis, which triggered an event that would later be known as the "taper tantrum."

In response to the global financial crisis, the US Federal Reserve enacted in 2008 a massive monetary policy stimulus. The stimulus relied largely on quantitative easing, a form of unconventional monetary policy in which the central bank purchases securities on the open market to increase the money supply and keep interest rates low. In 2013, the Fed contemplated winding down the program, and Federal Reserve chairman Ben Bernanke hinted at the Fed's intentions in a hearing before Congress.

This statement had an immediate effect on emerging markets, including Brazil, India, Indonesia, South Africa, and Turkey (known as the "fragile five"). Stock prices fell, bond yields rose sharply, and exchange rates depreciated significantly. The fragile five were hit the hardest because their economies shared some important vulnerabilities: large current account deficits financed with a high share of liquid portfolio investments rather than foreign direct investment, large capital inflows, and a sharp appreciation in exchange rates while the US stimulus was in place.[a]

In Indonesia, one of the most severely affected emerging markets, the taper tantrum reversed economic trends (figure B1.3.1). Faced with pressure in financial markets, Indonesia's government and central bank pursued a "stabilization over growth" approach to reducing the current account deficit. Among other measures, the government cut fuel subsidies, a large item in the national budget. As a result, the cost of fuel increased by an average of 40 percent. The central bank raised the base rate by 175 basis points and allowed the Indonesian rupiah to depreciate. These classical expenditure-reducing and expenditure-switching policies successfully stabilized the economy in a relatively short time. Net capital inflows turned positive again in early 2014, less than a year after the onset of the taper tantrum.

In the aftermath of the COVID-19 crisis, emerging economies are likely to face a very similar scenario. As stimulus policies in advanced economies are scaled back, interest rates will increase, leading to an exit of portfolio investment, exchange rate depreciation, and refinancing problems for firms and governments. However, because of the lack of economic growth, it is unlikely that the same recipe applied to the taper tantrum can be applied in the aftermath of the COVID-19 crisis. In 2012, the Indonesian economy grew at 6.2 percent. By contrast, in 2020 the economy shrank by 2.1 percent. Tightening fiscal and monetary policy in this scenario threatens newly recovering economic growth. Economic stabilization when growth is low is not a good option.

At the same time, the risk of recurring taper tantrums seems lower than in 2013: Indonesia experienced large capital outflows at the beginning of the crisis, making it less vulnerable to capital flight than in 2013.[b] In addition, the crisis led to a decline in production and investment. Because more than 90 percent of Indonesia's imports consists of raw materials and capital goods, imports have sharply fallen, resulting in a much smaller current account deficit than in 2012–13. Since the taper tantrum, several other emerging markets, such as India, have also markedly improved their external vulnerability indicators, such as the short-term debt to GDP ratio and the current account to GDP ratio.

Still, several issues must be anticipated. The pandemic has disrupted economic activity, increasing the risk of nonperforming loans (NPLs). To assist businesses and the financial sector, Indonesia has relaxed credit through regulatory forbearance, which may mask the true extent of NPLs. The withdrawal of the stimulus in high-income economies will also increase risks for highly leveraged companies that are exposed to exchange rate risks and "rollover risk" (the risk that a firm cannot refinance short-term debt at higher interest rates). As in other emerging economies, this is especially true for state-owned enterprises, and it increases the risk of contingent liabilities for the government.

In addition, increases in the federal funds rate will create a dilemma for central banks in emerging economies, such as Bank Indonesia. On the one

(Box continues next page)

Figure B1.3.1 **Impacts of the "taper tantrum" on the Indonesian economy, 2005–15**

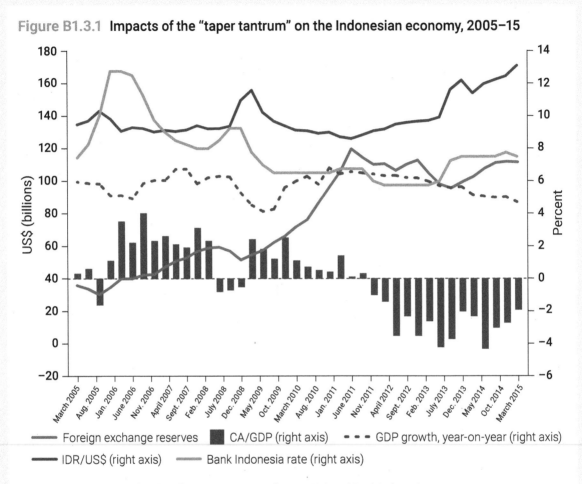

Source: Basri 2017, based on data from Economist Intelligence Unit and Bank Indonesia.

Note: The figure shows the growth of GDP, the Bank Indonesia reference rate, the Indonesian rupiah to US dollar exchange rate, and currency reserves in the Indonesian central bank from 2005 to 2015. CA/GDP = current account/gross domestic product; IDR = Indonesian rupiah.

hand, if banks do not follow the US Federal Reserve in raising interest rates, there is a risk of depreciation of the local currency from capital outflows. On the other hand, if interest rates increase, the risk of insolvencies will increase, disrupting the recovery. The Indonesian government plans to return to the budget deficit limit of 3 percent in 2023. It must do so cautiously, however, because the combination of concurrent fiscal and monetary tightening poses a risk to the recovery. The timing of the stimulus withdrawal is crucial and must be based on economic developments.

a. In several countries such as Brazil, China, India, Indonesia, Mexico, and Turkey, the capital inflow was greater than the absorption capacity of their national economies (Sahay et al. 2014).

b. The share of foreign holders of Indonesian government bonds fell from 32 percent in April 2020 to 23 percent at the end of May 2021.

the massive monetary policy response to the pandemic. As the economic recovery proceeds and stimulus measures are gradually withdrawn in advanced economies, interest rates will rise. This increase could threaten the solvency of firms, financial institutions, and governments in emerging economies that have benefited from short-term financing at low interest rates and will face higher refinancing costs going forward. Rising interest rates in high-income economies will also put pressure on the currencies of emerging economies, which increases the financial burdens faced by firms, financial institutions, and governments that have debt denominated in a foreign currency.

In addition to a less benign interest rate environment, the recovery in emerging economies will also be affected by the lower growth of the world economy. In the aftermath of the global financial crisis, low-income economies were only moderately affected, largely due to robust growth in important emerging markets, particularly China, which accounts for a sizable share of bilateral lending and direct investment in low-income economies. By contrast, the economic effects of the COVID-19 crisis have been felt globally, and lower economic growth in China and other emerging markets could affect low-income countries through several channels, including commodity prices and a reduction in bilateral lending and direct investment.

Conclusion

Although the immediate crisis response, which included extensive efforts to provide households and firms with liquidity, was essential to mitigate the hardships caused by income losses from the pandemic, few governments have the resources to sustain these programs until economic activity has fully recovered. This gives rise to the possibility that risk spillovers among the household, firm, financial, and government sectors of the economy will aggravate preexisting economic fragilities and pose a threat to an equitable recovery. Interconnected risks to the recovery are a concern, especially in emerging economies where such fragilities were already more pronounced at the onset of the pandemic.

Well-designed fiscal, monetary, and financial sector policies can help reduce these risks and prevent them from affecting the wider economy. The following chapters explore the primary risks that affect each of the main sectors of the economy and propose policies that can counteract these risks with the goal of supporting an equitable recovery.

Beginning with the concern that many households and firms will continue to face income losses resulting in loan defaults once debt moratoria are lifted, chapter 2 turns to the risk to the financial sector posed by uncertainty about the true extent of credit risk and the quality of assets on the balance sheets of financial institutions. The chapter examines the steps regulators can take to proactively increase transparency about credit risk and deal with distressed assets and, if necessary, troubled banks. Chapter 3 takes a closer look at how the establishment and reform of insolvency frameworks can help the recovery by allowing private sector borrowers to reduce their debts to sustainable levels. Chapter 4 then explores how financial institutions can continue to provide credit to households and firms through the recovery. It focuses on approaches to managing and mitigating risks in the face of heightened economic uncertainty, which limits the ability of lenders to form an accurate assessment of credit risk and reduces the recourse they have in the event of default. Chapter 5 discusses the risks posed by the dramatic increase in levels of government debt and describes policies that can improve debt management and avoid debt distress. Chapter 6 concludes the Report by outlining policy priorities for the recovery.

Notes

1. Stiglitz and Weiss (1981).
2. Acharya, Drechsler, and Schnabl (2014); Brunnermeier et al. (2016); Gennaioli, Martin, and Rossi (2014).
3. Feyen and Zuccardi Huertas (2019); Laeven and Valencia (2018); Reinhart and Rogoff (2009, 2011).
4. Regulation often forces banks to hold government bonds. In Ethiopia, banks must invest 27 percent of their loan portfolio in government bonds. Emergency measures of this kind were also introduced in response to the COVID-19 crisis. For example, in Ethiopia commercial banks were mandated to invest annually at least 1 percent of their loan portfolio in bonds issued by the National Bank of Ethiopia (NBE 2021), and insurance companies were required to invest at least 40 percent of their assets in treasury bills (Tadesse 2020).
5. Farhi and Tirole (2018).
6. Acharya, Mehran, and Thakor (2016).
7. UNCTAD (2019).
8. See, for example, World Bank (2021a).
9. Bosio et al. (2020); IMF (2019, 2020).
10. Bosio, Ramalho, and Reinhart (2021).
11. Breza and Kinnan (2021).
12. Feyen and Zuccardi Huertas (2019).
13. Koh et al. (2020).
14. Jordà, Schularick, and Taylor (2016).
15. Based on Reinhart (2021) and Standard & Poor's, Moody's, and Fitch ratings, 51 countries—among them 44 middle-income and 4 low-income countries—suffered a downgrade in 2020 of their sovereign risk rating. See Trading Economics, Credit Rating (database), https://tradingeconomics.com/country-list/rating.
16. Bova et al. (2016).
17. Moody's Investors Service (2019).
18. In the United Kingdom, for example, the Office of Budget Responsibility estimates that up to 40 percent of participants in one of its most popular guarantee programs, the Bounce Back Loans Scheme, may default (Browning 2021). Also see IMF (2021a).

References

Acharya, Viral V., Itamar Drechsler, and Philipp Schnabl. 2014. "A Pyrrhic Victory? Bank Bailouts and Sovereign Credit Risk." *Journal of Finance* 69 (6): 2689–739.

Acharya, Viral V., Robert F. Engle, III, and Sascha Steffen. 2021. "Why Did Bank Stocks Crash during COVID-19?" NBER Working Paper 28559, National Bureau of Economic Research, Cambridge, MA.

Acharya, Viral V., Hamid Mehran, and Anjan V. Thakor. 2016. "Caught between Scylla and Charybdis? Regulating Bank Leverage When There Is Rent Seeking and Risk Shifting." *Review of Corporate Finance Studies* 5 (1): 36–75.

Azim Premji University. 2021. *State of Working India, 2021: One Year of COVID-19.* Bengaluru, India: Aziz Premji University.

Barrot, Luis-Diego. 2021. "The Debt of Nations: Government Debt Composition around the World 1900–2020." Presentation at the National Bureau of Economic Research virtual conference, "Summer Institute 2021: International Finance and Macroeconomic Data Sources," July 15. https://conference.nber.org/conf_papers/f150929.slides.pdf.

Basri, Muhamad Chatib. 2017. "India and Indonesia: Lessons Learned from the 2013 Taper Tantrum." *Bulletin of Indonesian Economic Studies* 53 (2): 137–60.

Bosio, Erica, Simeon Djankov, Edward L. Glaeser, and Andrei Shleifer. 2020. "Public Procurement in Law and Practice." NBER Working Paper 27188, National Bureau of Economic Research, Cambridge, MA.

Bosio, Erica, Rita Ramalho, and Carmen M. Reinhart. 2021. "The Invisible Burden: How Arrears Could Unleash a Banking Crisis." *VoxEU* (blog), March 22, 2021. https://voxeu.org/article/how-arrears-could-unleash-banking-crisis.

Bova, Elva, Marta Ruiz-Arranz, Frederik Toscani, and H. Elif Ture. 2016. "The Fiscal Costs of Contingent Liabilities: A New Dataset." IMF Working Paper WP/16/14, International Monetary Fund, Washington, DC.

Breza, Emily, and Cynthia Kinnan. 2021. "Measuring the Equilibrium Impacts of Credit: Evidence from the Indian Microfinance Crisis." *Quarterly Journal of Economics* 136 (3): 1447–97.

Browning, Steve. 2021. "Coronavirus: Business Loans Schemes." Contributing author, Georgina Hutton. Research Briefing 8906 (November 4), House of Commons Library, London. https://researchbriefings.files.parliament.uk/documents/CBP-8906/CBP-8906.pdf.

Brunnermeier, Markus K., Luis Garicano, Philip R. Lane, Marco Pagano, Ricardo Reis, Tano Santos, David Thesmar, Stijn Van Nieuwerburgh, and Dimitri Vayanos. 2016. "The Sovereign-Bank Diabolic Loop and ESBies." *American Economic Review* 106 (5): 508–12.

Burns, Andrew, Benoit Campagne, Charl Jooste, David Stephan, and Thi Thanh Bui. 2019. "The World Bank Macro-Fiscal Model: Technical Description." Policy Research Working Paper 8965, World Bank, Washington, DC.

Burns, Andrew, and Charl Jooste. 2019. "Estimating and Calibrating MFMod: A Panel Data Approach to Identifying the Parameters of Data Poor Countries in the World Bank's Structural Macro Model." Policy Research Working Paper 8939, World Bank, Washington, DC.

Chari, Anusha, Lakshita Jain, and Nirupama Kulkarni. 2021. "The Unholy Trinity: Regulatory Forbearance, Stressed Banks, and Zombie Firms." NBER Working Paper 28435, National Bureau of Economic Research, Cambridge, MA.

CMIE (Centre for Monitoring Indian Economy). 2021. "Consumer Pyramids Household Survey." https://consumerpyramidsdx.cmie.com.

Dhingra, Swati, and Maitreesh Ghatak. 2021. "How Has COVID-19 Affected India's Economy?" Economics

Observatory. https://www.economicsobservatory.com/how-has-covid-19-affected-indias-economy.

Farhi, Emmanuel, and Jean Tirole. 2018. "Deadly Embrace: Sovereign and Financial Balance Sheets Doom Loops." *Review of Economic Studies* 85 (3): 1781–1823.

Feyen, Erik H. B., and Davide Salvatore Mare. 2021. "Measuring Systemic Banking Resilience: A Simple Reverse Stress Testing Approach Using Bank-Level Data." Policy Research Working Paper 9864, World Bank, Washington, DC.

Feyen, Erik H. B., and Igor Esteban Zuccardi Huertas. 2019. "The Sovereign–Bank Nexus in EMDEs: What Is It, Is It Rising, and What Are the Policy Implications?" Policy Research Working Paper 8950, World Bank, Washington, DC.

Gennaioli, Nicola, Alberto Martin, and Stefano Rossi. 2014. "Sovereign Default, Domestic Banks, and Financial Institutions." *Journal of Finance* 69 (2): 819–66.

Gupta, Arpit, Anup Malani, and Bartek Woda. 2021. "Explaining the Income and Consumption Effects of COVID in India." NBER Working Paper 28935, National Bureau of Economic Research, Cambridge, MA.

IMF (International Monetary Fund). 2019. *IMF Annual Report 2019: Our Connected World*. Washington, DC: IMF.

IMF (International Monetary Fund). 2020. *A Year Like No Other: IMF Annual Report 2020*. Washington, DC: IMF.

IMF (International Monetary Fund). 2021a. *Fiscal Monitor: Strengthening the Credibility of Public Finances*. Washington, DC: IMF.

IMF (International Monetary Fund). 2021b. *World Economic Outlook: Managing Divergent Recoveries*. Washington, DC: IMF.

Jordà, Òscar, Moritz Schularick, and Alan M. Taylor. 2016. "Macrofinancial History and the New Business Cycle Facts." Working Paper 2016-23, Federal Reserve Bank of San Francisco.

Koh, Wee Chian, M. Ayhan Kose, Peter S. Nagle, Franziska L. Ohnsorge, and Naotaka Sugawara. 2020. "Debt and Financial Crises." Policy Research Working Paper 9116, World Bank, Washington, DC.

Laeven, Luc, and Fabian Valencia. 2018. "Systemic Banking Crises Revisited." IMF Working Paper WP/18/206, International Monetary Fund, Washington, DC.

Moody's Investors Service. 2019. "Sovereigns, Emerging Markets: Risks from Financial Misreporting Vary, Disclosure Has Major Credit Implications." Sector In-Depth (March 21), Report 1146743, Moody's, New York. https://asianeximbanks.org/images/trainingprogram/EM%20Sovs%20in%20depth%2019.pdf.

NBE (National Bank of Ethiopia). 2021. "Licensing and Supervision of Banking Business." Investment on DBE Bonds Directive SBB/81/2021, NBE, Addis Ababa. https://nbebank.com/wp-content/uploads/pdf/directives/bankingbusiness/sbb-81-2021.pdf.

RBI (Reserve Bank of India). 2020a. *Financial Stability Report*. June. Mumbai: RBI.

RBI (Reserve Bank of India). 2020b. *Report on Trend and Progress in Banking in India*. Mumbai: RBI.

RBI (Reserve Bank of India). 2021. *Annual Report 2020–21*. Mumbai: RBI. https://www.rbi.org.in/Scripts/AnnualReportPublications.aspx?year=2021.

Reinhart, Carmen M. 2021. "From Health Crisis to Financial Distress." Policy Research Working Paper 9616, World Bank, Washington, DC.

Reinhart, Carmen M., and Kenneth S. Rogoff. 2009. "The Aftermath of Financial Crises." *American Economic Review* 99 (2): 466–72.

Reinhart, Carmen M., and Kenneth S. Rogoff. 2011. "From Financial Crash to Debt Crisis." *American Economic Review* 101 (5): 1676–706.

Sahay, Ratna, Vivek Arora, Thanos Arvanitis, Hamid Faruqee, Papa N'Diaye, Tommaso Mancini-Griffoli, and IMF Team. 2014. "Emerging Market Volatility: Lessons from the Taper Tantrum." IMF Staff Discussion Note SDN/14/09, International Monetary Fund, Washington, DC.

Schnabel, Isabel. 2021. "The Sovereign–Bank–Corporate Nexus: Virtuous or Vicious?" Address at London School of Economics and Political Science public online conference, "Financial Cycles, Risk, Macroeconomic Causes, and Consequences," Systemic Risk Center, Frankfurt, January 28, 2021. https://www.ecb.europa.eu/press/key/date/2021/html/ecb.sp210128~8f5dc86601.en.html.

Stiglitz, Joseph E., and Andrew Weiss. 1981. "Credit Rationing in Markets with Imperfect Information." *American Economic Review* 71 (3): 393–410.

Tadesse, Fasika. 2020. "Ethiopia: Central Bank Compels Insurers to Invest in T-Bills." *Addis Fortune*, December 5, 2020. https://allafrica.com/stories/202012080756.html.

UNCTAD (United Nations Conference on Trade and Development). 2019. *World Investment Report 2019: Special Economic Zones*. Geneva: UNCTAD.

World Bank. 2021a. *Competition and Firm Recovery Post-COVID-19*. Europe and Central Asia Economic Update (Fall), Office of the Chief Economist. Washington, DC: World Bank.

World Bank. 2021b. *Global Economic Prospects, June 2021*. Washington, DC: World Bank. doi:10.1596/978-1-4648-1665-9.

World Bank. 2022. *Global Economic Prospects, January 2022*. Washington, DC: World Bank. doi:10.1596/978-1-4648-1758-8.

Spotlight 1.1

Financial inclusion and financial resilience

*F*inancial resilience is an important aspect of financial inclusion—that is, when one has access to the appropriate financial tools (such as bank accounts, savings, credit, and digital payments) that can be used safely in a well-regulated environment to meet one's needs. Financial resilience *refers to the ability of people and firms to recover from adverse economic shocks, such as job loss or unanticipated expenses, without suffering a decline in living standards.*

Before the pandemic, only half of the adult population of emerging economies said they could come up with emergency funds within the next month.[1] The shares were smaller for women (45 percent) and poorer adults (34 percent). Among adults in emerging economies who said they could access emergency funds, a third said they would come up with the money by picking up extra shifts at work or by borrowing from their employer—options that may be impossible or undesirable during a crisis like COVID-19 (coronavirus).

COVID-19 underscored the importance of strengthening financial resilience. The crisis disproportionately hit micro-, small, and medium enterprises (MSMEs) and vulnerable groups, who typically have meager cash buffers. These vulnerable groups are overrepresented in sectors that suffered the most from the crisis.[2] Job and income losses driven by lockdowns and mobility restrictions were deeply felt by individuals and entrepreneurs,

depleting already limited savings and assets.[3] The World Bank predicted that poverty would worsen in low-income countries and that about 100 million people would fall into poverty in 2021.[4]

Access to financial services is essential for resilience and economic recovery. Digital payments, savings, credit, and insurance allow businesses and individuals to manage risk, smooth expenses, and invest. Evidence shows that households and businesses that have access to such financial services are better able to withstand adverse financial shocks than those that do not.[5] Mobile money helps people manage economic shocks by making it easier to borrow money in an emergency from a wider geographic and social network of family and friends.[6] Research from Kenya found that mobile money services allowed families to become less poor in the long term.[7] Savings accounts boost financial resilience by providing a buffer against unexpected expenses.[8] Mobile credit can boost financial resilience as well, to the extent that borrowing can help address the immediate impact of a shock, although these products also raise consumer protection concerns.[9] Lack of access to credit, on the other hand, can reduce resilience; in India, a reduction in microfinance was associated with significant decreases in wages, income, and consumption.[10]

One study found that sustained credit flows in the United States during periods of stringent financial constraints can boost small firms' resilience by shielding their sales and employment.[11] A review of the literature suggests that MSMEs in Organisation for Economic Co-operation and Development countries with access to credit are more likely to survive as employers and creators of economic value.[12] And, as revealed in an analysis of the early impacts of COVID-19, a decline in output is less common among firms in low- and middle-income countries that had better access to finance before the pandemic (although firms with stronger fundamentals might have better access to credit).[13] Financial inclusion also helps governments deliver services cheaper and faster.[14] As the COVID-19 crisis erupted in 2019, countries with higher rates of financial inclusion were able to leverage that infrastructure to rapidly roll out government support, as evidenced by the experiences of China, Colombia, and India.[15]

In recent years, millions of adults have gained access to accounts and other tools that help build financial resilience—but exclusion remains widespread. Worldwide, over 1 billion adults lack access to a transaction account. Lower-income adults in emerging economies access credit and savings largely through informal channels, with very limited access to insurance. For example, access to crop insurance is practically nonexistent among small farmers, despite widespread risk in the agriculture sector.[16] At least 41 percent (130 million) of formal MSMEs in emerging economies lack access to credit, which is viewed as a top obstacle to business survival and growth.[17]

Because MSMEs and the informal sector are the largest source of employment and livelihoods in emerging economies, their resilience is at the core of any economic recovery effort.[18] Access to credit, in particular, is central to the ability of businesses to manage working capital and investment needs. Low-income households and businesses typically do not have enough discretionary savings or insurance coverage to carry them through an adverse income shock. Instead, they often rely on credit instruments to help smooth consumption and safeguard business continuity. Research from Africa and the United States confirms that access to short-term credit can help consumers smooth consumption in the face of idiosyncratic shocks. This research offers evidence that credit—if delivered responsibly—*can* be an important tool in ensuring the resilience of households with limited ways to manage risk.[19] It is less clear that credit can play a significant role in helping MSMEs and lower-income people cope with the impacts of large systemic shocks. Borrowing as a resilience strategy relies on a timely recovery that restores the income needed to repay debts.

The COVID-19 crisis was characterized by a large, rapid deployment of government initiatives aimed at helping residents and businesses weather the economic shock, including through extensive loan repayment moratoria, credit guarantees, and cash transfers.[20] As chapter 1 describes, however, the ability of governments to support these measures was time-bound and limited for lower-income countries, and programs often failed to reach all segments of the population. MSMEs, especially those operating informally, often did not receive commensurate support. As the broader recovery takes hold, however, the judicious use of credit could enable some enterprises and households to bridge cash-flow gaps. The residual uncertainty around the timing of localized recovery suggests that government guarantees could play a useful role. From a fiscal perspective, linking further expenditures to the actual realization of a negative outcome (such as yet another downturn in which credit guarantees are triggered) is less costly than blanket government support.

As the health crisis diminishes and consumer demand increases, credit for MSMEs and low-income households becomes an essential element of the ability of businesses to invest in economic recovery. However, the ability of private sector lenders to lend has been reduced by weakening revenue and lenders' reduced visibility into the economic prospects and creditworthiness of borrowers. Economic shifts stemming from the pandemic have indeed rendered some borrowers less creditworthy, but the uncertainty has caused lenders to lose their appetite for risk, and lending even to creditworthy borrowers may be affected. As discussed in chapter 4, innovations that improve lenders' visibility into borrower viability and improve their ability to realize value from collateral can encourage safer lending. Carefully crafted guarantee programs could also bridge the gap between backward-looking risk aversion and future credit performance.

Notes

1. Demirgüç-Kunt et al. (2018). Respondents were asked if they could come up with the equivalent of 5 percent of the gross national income per capita, equal to approximately $3,000 in the United States.
2. OECD (2020); Vardoulakis (2020).
3. Gomes, Haliassos, and Ramadorai (2020).
4. Mahler et al. (2021).
5. Breza, Kanz, and Klapper (2020); Moore et al. (2019).
6. When hit with an agricultural shock, Kenyan households with no mobile money access suffered a 7 percent drop in the use of goods and services, while those who did have mobile money experienced no such drop on average (Jack and Suri 2014). In Tanzania, rainfall shocks resulted in 6 percent lower consumption on average, but mobile money users were able to maintain consumption due to improved risk-sharing (Riley 2018).
7. El-Zoghbi, Holle, and Soursourian (2019); Suri and Jack (2016).
8. In Chile, women who received free savings accounts reduced their reliance on debt and improved their ability to make ends meet during an economic emergency (Kast, Meier, and Pomeranz 2018). Women in Nepal who received free savings accounts with no withdrawal fees were better able to manage unexpected health expenses than those who did not receive accounts (Prina 2015).
9. Bharadwaj, Jack, and Suri (2019).
10. Breza and Kinnan (2021).
11. Chodorow-Reich (2014).
12. Bakhtiari et al. (2020).
13. Amin and Viganola (2021).
14. In a recent pilot in Albania, the World Bank estimated that digitalizing 75 percent of the current paper-based transactions could potentially achieve savings of about 0.4 percent of GDP. Lund, White, and Lamb (2017) estimate that emerging economies could save as much as 0.8–1.1 percent of GDP annually ($220–$320 billion) by digitalizing government payments alone, with benefits for both governments and recipients.
15. Agur, Peria, and Rochon (2020).
16. A Global Findex survey of economies in Sub-Saharan Africa found that, on average, one in three adults grows crops or raises livestock to produce their main household income, but only about 5 percent had purchased agricultural insurance in the previous five years. Yet roughly two-thirds of these adults faced a crop loss or significant loss of livestock in the last five years, and only a tiny share received any kind of financial payout to help deal with the loss (Klapper et al. 2019).
17. International Finance Corporation, MSME Finance Gap (database), SME Finance Forum, https://www.smefinanceforum.org/data-sites/msme-finance-gap.
18. Ayyagari, Beck, and Demirgüç-Kunt (2003).
19. Bharadwaj and Suri (2020); Collins et al. (2009); Karlan and Zinman (2010); Morse (2011).
20. Gentilini et al. (2020).

References

Agur, Itai, Soledad Martinez Peria, and Celine Rochon. 2020. "Digital Financial Services and the Pandemic: Opportunities and Risks for Emerging and Developing Economies." Special Series on COVID-19, Monetary and Capital Markets Department, International Monetary Fund, Washington, DC.

Amin, Mohammad, and Domenico Viganola. 2021. "Does Better Access to Finance Help Firms Deal with the COVID-19 Pandemic? Evidence from Firm-Level Survey Data." Policy Research Working Paper 9697, World Bank, Washington, DC.

Ayyagari, Meghana, Thorsten Beck, and Asli Demirgüç-Kunt. 2003. "Small and Medium Enterprises across the Globe: A New Database." Policy Research Working Paper 3127, World Bank, Washington, DC.

Bakhtiari, Sasan, Robert Breunig, Lisa Magnani, and Jacquelyn Zhang. 2020. "Financial Constraints and Small and Medium Enterprises." IZA Discussion Paper 12936, Institute of Labor Economics, Bonn, Germany.

Bharadwaj, Prashant, William Jack, and Tavneet Suri. 2019. "Fintech and Household Resilience to Shocks: Evidence from Digital Loans in Kenya." NBER Working Paper 25604, National Bureau of Economic Research, Cambridge, MA.

Bharadwaj, Prashant, and Tavneet Suri. 2020. "Improving Financial Inclusion through Digital Savings and Credit." *AEA Papers and Proceedings* 110 (May): 584–88.

Breza, Emily, Martin Kanz, and Leora Klapper. 2020. "Learning to Navigate a New Financial Technology: Evidence from Payroll Accounts." NBER Working Paper 28249, National Bureau of Economic Research, Cambridge, MA.

Breza, Emily, and Cynthia Kinnan. 2021. "Measuring the Equilibrium Impacts of Credit: Evidence from the Indian

Microfinance Crisis." *Quarterly Journal of Economics* 136 (3): 1447–97.

Chodorow-Reich, Gabriel. 2014. "The Employment Effects of Credit Market Disruptions: Firm-Level Evidence from the 2008–9 Financial Crisis." *Quarterly Journal of Economics* 129 (1): 1–59.

Collins, Daryl, Jonathan Morduch, Stuart Rutherford, and Orlanda Ruthven. 2009. *Portfolios of the Poor: How the World's Poor Live on $2 a Day.* Princeton, NJ: Princeton University Press.

Demirgüç-Kunt, Asli, Leora F. Klapper, Dorothe Singer, Saniya Ansar, and Jake Hess. 2018. *The Global Findex Database 2017: Measuring Financial Inclusion and the Fintech Revolution.* Washington, DC: World Bank. https://doi .org/10.1596/978-1-4648-1259-0.

El-Zoghbi, Mayada, Nina Holle, and Matthew Soursourian. 2019. "Emerging Evidence on Financial Inclusion: Moving from Black and White to Color." CGAP Focus Note, Consultative Group to Assist the Poor, Washington, DC. https://www.cgap.org/research/publication/emerging -evidence-financial-inclusion.

Gentilini, Ugo, Mohamed Almenfi, Ian Orton, and Pamela Dale. 2020. *Social Protection and Jobs Responses to COVID-19: A Real-Time Review of Country Measures.* Washington, DC: World Bank. https://socialprotection .org/discover/publications/social-protection-and-jobs -responses-covid-19-real-time-review-country.

Gomes, Francisco J., Michael Haliassos, and Tarun Ramadorai. 2020. "Household Finance." IMFS Working Paper 138, Institute for Monetary and Financial Stability, Goethe University, Frankfurt.

Jack, William, and Tavneet Suri. 2014. "Risk Sharing and Transactions Costs: Evidence from Kenya's Mobile Money Revolution." *American Economic Review* 104 (1): 183–223.

Karlan, Dean S., and Jonathan Zinman. 2010. "Expanding Credit Access: Using Randomized Supply Decisions to Estimate the Impacts." *Review of Financial Studies* 23 (1): 433–64.

Kast, Felipe, Stephan Meier, and Dina Pomeranz. 2018. "Saving More in Groups: Field Experimental Evidence from Chile." *Journal of Development Economics* 133 (July): 275–94.

Klapper, Leora F., Dorothe Singer, Saniya Ansar, and Jake Hess. 2019. "Financial Risk Management in Agriculture: Analyzing Data from a New Module of the Global Findex Database." Policy Research Working Paper 9078, World Bank, Washington, DC.

Lund, Susan, Olivia White, and Jason Lamb. 2017. "The Value of Digitalizing Government Payments in Developing Economies." In *Digital Revolutions in Public Finance*, edited by Sanjeev Gupta, Michael Keen, Alpa Shah, and Geneviève Verdier, 305–23. Washington, DC: International Monetary Fund.

Mahler, Daniel Gerszon, Nishant Yonzan, Christoph Lakner, Raul Andrés Castañeda Aguilar, and Haoyu Wu. 2021. "Updated Estimates of the Impact of COVID-19 on Global Poverty: Turning the Corner on the Pandemic in 2021?" *World Bank Blogs: Data Blogs*, June 24, 2021. https:// blogs.worldbank.org/opendata/updated-estimates -impact-covid-19-global-poverty-turning-corner -pandemic-2021.

Moore, Danielle, Zahra Niazi, Rebecca Rouse, and Berber Kramer. 2019. "Building Resilience through Financial Inclusion: A Review of Existing Evidence and Knowledge Gaps." Financial Inclusion Program, Innovations for Poverty Action, Washington, DC. https://www.poverty -action.org/publication/building-resilience-through -financial-inclusion-review-existing-evidence-and -knowledge.

Morse, Adair. 2011. "Payday Lenders: Heroes or Villains?" *Journal of Financial Economics* 102 (1): 28–44.

OECD (Organisation for Economic Co-operation and Development). 2020. *Financing SMEs and Entrepreneurs 2020: An OECD Scorecard.* Paris: OECD. https://doi.org/10.1787 /061fe03d-en.

Prina, Silvia. 2015. "Banking the Poor via Savings Accounts: Evidence from a Field Experiment." *Journal of Development Economics* 115 (July): 16–31.

Riley, Emma. 2018. "Mobile Money and Risk Sharing against Village Shocks." *Journal of Development Economics* 135 (November): 43–58.

Suri, Tavneet, and William Jack. 2016. "The Long-Run Poverty and Gender Impacts of Mobile Money." *Science* 354 (6317): 1288–92.

Vardoulakis, Alexandros P. 2020. "Designing a Main Street Lending Facility." Finance and Economics Discussion Series 2020-052, Board of Governors of the Federal Reserve System, Washington, DC. https://doi.org/10 .17016/FEDS.2020.052.

Resolving bank asset distress

Debt moratoria, loan forbearance, and the relaxation of classification and provisioning rules during the COVID-19 crisis have created a lack of transparency about the health of bank balance sheets, particularly in the recognition of nonperforming loans (NPLs). Although not yet visible in reported asset quality indicators, rising borrower distress is likely to translate into rising NPL levels. If left unaddressed, high levels could reduce overall lending volumes and affect the financial sector's capacity to support economic activity. Such an outcome can be particularly harmful to small businesses and lower-income households. To reduce these risks, banks should identify and report problem loans accurately and manage revealed exposures while under strong supervisory oversight.

Policy Priorities

The pandemic and the related government policies have reduced the transparency of bank balance sheets. For banking sectors vulnerable to rapid increases in NPLs, the following timely corrective policies to preserve financial stability will help to support the continued provision of credit:

- **Ensuring clear, consistent practices for reporting on asset quality,** enforced by effective supervision and with strong incentives to encourage speed and transparency.

- **Developing the capacity to manage nonperforming loans** to avoid a rapid increase in bad loans impairing the capacity of banks to finance the real economy.

- **Dealing with problem banks swiftly** to prevent broad distress in the financial system, misallocation of financial resources, and failure in the provision of credit.

Introduction

The pandemic and the associated policy responses have significantly affected the financial position of households, firms, and governments. The payment and enforcement moratoria described in chapter 1 have supported borrowers by allowing a temporary halt in their bank repayment obligations. In applying these moratoria, banks have been able to help mitigate the economic fallout from COVID-19 (coronavirus).

It is not yet clear which borrowers will be permanently affected by the pandemic and how debtors will adjust to the structural changes in the economy. It is evident, however, that many borrowers are facing financial difficulties that go beyond liquidity stress. This situation is an unprecedented challenge for banks and bank supervisors because the magnitude of the ongoing shock, the uncertainty of the impact, as well as the ensuing government support have made the screening, monitoring, and management of risk extremely difficult.

Rising borrower distress is widely expected to translate into increases in nonperforming loans (NPLs) in the banking sector, although this is not yet clearly evident in reported NPL ratios. Data suggest that as of August 2021 the ratio of reported NPLs to total loans in most countries was broadly stable (figure 2.1).[1] However, for several reasons the data may not reflect the full reality of NPL levels:

- Moratoria and other borrower support measures were still in place in many countries in the second quarter of 2021,[2] as were fiscal and monetary interventions aimed at cushioning the impact of the pandemic on households and firms (chapter 1).
- Relatively tranquil global financial markets have also influenced countries' domestic financing conditions, especially by easing pressure on government debt refinancing.
- NPL data are often made available with a significant time lag.
- Many countries continue to apply regulatory definitions of NPLs that are predominantly based on payment arrears (and are therefore backward-looking).

Notwithstanding the seemingly positive data, bankers and policy makers anticipate that NPLs will increase significantly when governments lift moratoria and borrowers become obligated to repay their loans according to their original repayment schedules. Some countries are already reporting significant increases in special-mention loans (loans with potential weaknesses in repayment prospects, but not yet considered nonperforming) and an acceleration of preemptive loan restructuring that may delay the recognition of credit losses. These developments suggest that rising pressures on asset quality are forthcoming.

Banks have processes to manage NPLs in the normal course of business, but the scale and complexity of the expected increase in NPLs could overwhelm the capacity of the banking system, creating pressures that affect the broader economy. For example, when dealing with large and rising volumes of NPLs, banks often stop financing both the supply side of the economy by denying lending to viable firms for investment and working capital and the demand side by declining to finance consumption and household credit. For banks highly exposed to slow-growing, low-productivity firms, capital can become tied up in low-performing sectors at the expense of high-growth ones. Looking ahead, then, a rise in NPLs could affect the banking sector's capacity to support the economic recovery with fresh lending, while increasing the risk of bank failures. The concern is greater for emerging economies that are heavily exposed to credit risk and that tend to rely on bank credit to finance the real economy.[3]

If unaddressed, high NPL levels may thus severely dampen recovery from the pandemic. To preserve capital and manage uncertainty in periods of economic and financial distress, credit intermediaries are incentivized to ration credit extended to higher-risk borrowers such as micro-, small, and medium enterprises (MSMEs) and underserved, vulnerable households. Similarly, international credit for low-income frontier markets, which have been especially hard-hit by the pandemic, may also dry up as potential lenders lower their risk exposure to preserve their capital. Taking early, decisive action to address NPLs and to sustain, and where necessary restore, the strength of the banking system is critical to ensure that banks and other lenders have sufficient capital to finance a strong, equitable recovery.

Addressing rising volumes of NPLs is therefore critical to maintaining a healthy financial sector that can support recovery from the pandemic.[4] This chapter describes policy measures aimed at effective, timely resolution of bank asset distress. Experience shows that asset quality issues do not resolve on their own without a swift, comprehensive policy response. If ignored, NPLs tend to grow, creating mounting losses for the financial system. If distress becomes systemic, losses in output are typically highly persistent, especially for the least developed countries.[5]

A comprehensive NPL resolution strategy is thus essential for governments and banking sectors to manage bad loans in a way that

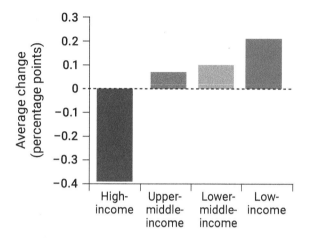

Figure 2.1 Changes in nonperforming loan ratios, by country income group, 2020–21

Source: WDR 2022 team, based on data from International Monetary Fund, FSIs (Financial Soundness Indicators) (dashboard), https://data.imf.org/?sk=51B096FA-2CD2-40C2-8D09-0699CC1764DA.

Note: For the 106 countries represented in the figure, the latest observed data are from December 2020 (27 countries), February 2021 (1 country), March 2021 (27 countries), April 2021 (2 countries), May 2021 (5 countries), June 2021 (41 countries), July 2021 (2 countries), and August 2021 (1 country).

protects viable borrowers, while swiftly dealing with nonviable ones so that they do not absorb productive capital. Three components of an effective strategy are covered in this chapter:

- *Identifying NPLs*—clear-cut, consistent practices for banks to use in reporting on asset health, reinforced by effective supervision and strong incentives to encourage speed and transparency.
- *Developing operational capacity for addressing NPLs*—techniques to segment NPLs according to viability and complexity and to deploy the right management method.
- *Handling problem banks*—decisive policies for dealing with banks at risk of failure.

Banks are primarily responsible for resolving NPLs, and yet supervisory authorities should have a clear diagnostic of the factors driving the deterioration of a bank's asset quality. Specifically, they should have accurate data gauging the NPL exposure of individual banks, as well as a breakdown between households and firms and between credit for investment and consumption, together with details on the sectoral composition of credit.[6] Resolving NPLs also requires a legal system that balances the interests of creditors and borrowers and supports debt restructuring and reorganization of viable firms, as well as an orderly exit of unviable ones (the legal system is addressed in chapter 3).

The themes discussed are commonly accepted building blocks of an effective NPL resolution strategy, but country-level priorities may vary, depending on the sophistication and strength of countries' banking sectors, the severity of the economic impact of the pandemic, the capacity of firms to adjust, and developments in the legal, regulatory, and institutional environments. Administrative capacity is another important factor because countries vary in their ability to undertake complex and comprehensive legal, regulatory, supervisory, and taxation policies in a coordinated manner and in conjunction with public and private sector stakeholders.

Policy makers and bank leaders should act with urgency on the advice laid out in this chapter as best fits their capacity—ideally *before* support measures are lifted and distressed asset levels rise—because developing the systems and capacity needed to deal with NPLs takes time.[7] Those who prefer to wait and see risk missing the opportunity to get ahead of the problem. Such a delay not only prevents recovery of viable capital, but also can lead to long-term low investment across an economy.

Why do NPLs matter?

High NPL levels burden all levels of an economy. For borrowers, failure to repay a debt may lead to the loss of assets and business opportunities and jeopardize future access to credit, which has negative spillover effects on the broader economy. For banks, asset quality problems can lead to capital misallocation, higher funding costs, and lower profitability.[8] These issues can drive up the cost of finance for borrowers and impair a bank's ability to run a viable, sustainable business. Banks may respond by reducing lending volumes, which often leads to the exclusion of underserved, higher-risk groups such as MSMEs, women, and the poor.[9]

At the aggregate level, high NPLs depress economic growth. Because capital is tied up in underperforming sectors, growing sectors may have limited access to new capital, and so market confidence suffers.[10] Banks with high exposure to NPLs and narrow capital buffers may be inclined to reduce the provision of credit[11] and continue to finance weak or insolvent borrowers—so-called zombie lending.[12] When banks' capital is locked up in troubled sectors and companies, some second-round business failures may be prevented, but it also diverts funds from more productive sectors of the economy. Inefficient firms could thus have a dominant impact on the functioning of input and output markets, translating into lower economic output, investment, and employment.[13]

The challenge is particularly acute following financial crises when bank exposure to problem assets often persists at elevated levels because of a lack of incentives and frameworks to resolve them. The ensuing weak growth, in turn, reduces fresh lending and slows the reduction in NPLs.[14] The experiences of countries in Central, Eastern, and Southeastern Europe (CESEE)[15] in the aftermath of the 2007–09 global financial crisis reveal the long-term problems and severer recessions that can result (see online annex 2A[16]). The increase in NPLs in the CESEE region was rooted in excess credit growth and lax underwriting practices by banks, whereas in the COVID-19 crisis the pressures on asset quality arise from an unprecedented economic shock and restrictions in economic activity that affect borrowers' incomes and weaken their debt-weathering capacity. Another difference is that under the current circumstances governments' ability to contain the impacts of the pandemic on firms and households affects which borrowers remain viable. Weaknesses in the macroeconomic, institutional, corporate, and banking sectors that have driven past crises are a factor as well.

The experiences of the CESEE countries following the global financial crisis nonetheless clearly illustrate the dangers of a delayed initial policy response.[17] By allowing the underlying problems to fester, countries compromised the capacity of their banking sector to finance the real economy and ultimately were left trapped in a bad equilibrium of low growth linked to a weak financial system. Avoiding a repeat of this scenario is a priority for policy makers everywhere. Despite important differences in the two crises in the underlying causes and the starting positions of individual countries, the key lesson from the CESEE region, as well as from other regions and at other times, is that rising NPLs require a prompt, comprehensive policy response.

This negative cycle of high NPLs leading to low economic growth is not inevitable. Evidence comparing countries that have proactively pursued strong measures to reduce the stock of NPLs in the wake of an economic crisis with those that have taken a more passive approach reveals that the former approach results in superior economic and credit growth recovery.[18] Sound ex ante policies play an important role in preventing NPL problems from building, while robust corporate governance, effective supervision, and regulation of banks facilitate NPL resolution. Policy makers and bankers can expedite financial recovery by addressing fragilities at both the individual bank level and banking system level, beginning with rules and incentives around transparency about the true state of banking assets.

Identifying NPLs: Asset quality, bank capital, and effective supervision

Accurate, timely indicators of bank asset quality are essential to assessing borrowers' capacity to meet repayment obligations to their lenders and whether such capacity has been significantly and permanently eroded, leading to credit losses for banks. Policy makers need this information to understand the scale of emerging asset quality problems and thus articulate a well-informed policy response and an NPL resolution strategy, including judgments on whether to extend temporary moratoria and other forms of support to affected households, firms, and industries. This information is also critical to separating weak banks from healthy ones, instilling public trust in the integrity of reported bank financial statements, avoiding disorderly runs and panics arising from opacity, and initiating timely supervisory action on weak banks.

The support measures discussed in chapter 1 have eased short-term pressures on borrowers. But by their very nature, they have also made it harder to determine which borrowers are experiencing financial distress likely to result in repayment difficulties once support is withdrawn.[19] Uncertainty about future policy support—such as when moratoria will be lifted or whether new support may be added—may create incentives for banks to hold back on detailed credit risk monitoring and management of emerging loan performance problems as they wait for additional information. This situation may only amplify the incentives for a bank to underestimate the deterioration of its asset quality. It will then report a stronger financial position because as soon as it classifies loans as under- or nonperforming, it must set aside provisions for anticipated credit losses, which lowers earnings and absorbs capital. These incentives are stronger for lower-capitalized banks—losses may signal financial weakness and trigger supervisory intervention and the need for new capital.[20] This context of uncertainty and mixed incentives puts the onus on supervisors to establish a set of requirements for the asset quality indicators that banks must monitor and share.

But setting such requirements is complicated. And national practices vary for many reasons.[21] Nonetheless, banks and supervisory authorities are not entirely on their own. The Basel Committee on Banking Supervision (BCBS) has published helpful guidance on defining nonperformance that highlights the importance of assessing borrower payment capacity (the unlikely-to-pay criterion), as well as payment performance—in particular, the degree of delinquency or number of days payments are past due, with 90 days past due an important threshold (see box 2.1).[22]

Standard setters have provided helpful additional guidance on the application of regulatory frameworks during the pandemic, promoting greater consistency.[23] According to the BCBS, (1) periods of repayment moratoria should not be counted in days past due for assessing loan performance; (2) judgments of the ability to meet payment obligations should focus on the borrower's ability to meet the requirements of rescheduled payments after the moratorium ends; and (3) borrower acceptance of a repayment moratorium or other relief measures such as guarantees should not automatically lead to the loan being categorized as forborne.[24] To support their judgments on the ability of borrowers to meet rescheduled payments, banks must during the moratoria continue to monitor the financial health of borrowers and

Box 2.1 International guidance on loan classification and problem assets

No agreed-on international standard exists for loan classification or the treatment of problem assets. Nonetheless, countries' approaches have common features such as formal loan classification schemes based on loan quality.[a] To support greater convergence, the Basel Committee on Banking Supervision (BCBS) published detailed guidance on defining nonperforming exposures (as well as forbearance), giving supervisors clear reference points (BCBS 2016).

Two principal criteria guide nonperformance: (1) *delinquency*—material exposures that are more than 90 days past due (that is, unpaid), and (2) *unlikely to pay (UTP)*—full repayment under the contractual terms (original or modified) is unlikely without the bank's realization of collateral, regardless of whether the exposure is current and regardless of the number of days the exposure is past due.

The presence of arrears or evidence of UTP defines an exposure as nonperforming. Although the availability of collateral affects the amount

that banks must provision, it does not affect the assessment of whether a loan is nonperforming. In addition, if a bank has a significant exposure to a corporate borrower that is nonperforming, then all exposures (on- and off-balance sheet) to the borrower should also be considered nonperforming regardless of actual repayment status.

Assessments of repayment likelihood should draw on a comprehensive analysis of the financial situation of the borrower based on specific indicators. The BCBS also provided guidance on how to recategorize nonperforming exposures as performing should the counterparty's situation improve and full repayment is likely (as evidenced by successful payments during a probationary period). Related to forbearance, the guidance provides that forbearance applies where there is *financial difficulty*—a borrower is experiencing difficulty meeting its financial commitments—and *a concession*—a bank grants a concession that it would not otherwise consider.

a. The following is an example of a hierarchy of loan quality categories: normal, special mention (or watch), substandard, doubtful, and loss. For details at the country level, see World Bank, BRSS 2019 (Bank Regulation and Supervision Survey, 2019) (dashboard), https://www.worldbank.org/en/research/brief/BRSS.

conduct rigorous assessments of their repayment capacity and likely longer-term viability using a range of financial and economic indicators.[25]

Judgments about borrowers' capacity to meet future debt service obligations can be challenging under the best of circumstances, let alone during a pandemic and a highly uncertain economic outlook. Still, this challenge should not discourage banks from proactively identifying borrowers that are likely to face solvency challenges, recognizing credit losses, and classifying and provisioning for such loans. In short, uncertainty and lack of an international standard need not prevent supervisors from requiring banks to adhere to rigorous criteria for defining and reporting on asset quality, with the BCBS definitions providing a useful basis on which to build.

Seeking accurate asset quality metrics for the banking system

Asset quality is fundamental to analyzing a bank's capital position and financial health. It highlights exposure to credit risk, especially whether borrowers are likely to fail to fulfill their repayment obligations, creating losses for the bank. High-quality indicators that enable banks and their supervisors to assess borrowers' payment performance and capacity, and thus the quality of the bank's loan assets, are essential elements of strong bank management and effective supervision (see table 2.1), particularly in emerging markets that tend to have relatively simple, bank-centric financial systems.[26] Drawing on the 2019 Bank Regulation and Supervision Survey (BRSS), which uses 2016 data, table 2.1 summarizes key features of asset classification systems in emerging economies prior to the guidance supplied by the BCBS.[27] Most respondents deployed a consistent asset classification scheme, applied the principle that the availability of collateral does not affect the classification of loan performance, and required successful performance of restructured loans over a probationary period before classification could be upgraded.

Such indicators underpin financial statements recording performance as well as financial strength. Indicators of deteriorating asset quality also serve as an early warning system for loan performance problems. They enable banks to take preemptive action to resolve problems and avoid the deadweight costs of nonperforming assets. Supervisory authorities also rely on asset quality data and corresponding measures of capital strength to gauge a bank's capacity to absorb credit losses and its ability to supply new credit for a vigorous economic recovery.

Underappreciation of a deterioration in underlying loan quality, and thus inadequate provisioning, leads to overstated capital levels. An overstatement hampers policy analysis, encourages complacency by banks and policy makers, and affects market functioning. At the onset of the pandemic, banks' reported capital levels in many countries were higher than in the past because they had been bolstered by stronger regulatory standards following the global financial crisis. Nonetheless, significant differences across jurisdictions and regions (as well as within them) reflect the differing capacity of banking systems to absorb the pandemic shock.

Table 2.1 **Countries' adoption of selected indicators of asset classification systems, by country income group**

Share of countries answering "yes" (%)

Indicator	Low-income	Lower-middle-income	Upper-middle-income
Asset classification system under which banks have to report the quality of their loans and advances using a common regulatory scale	88	88	95
Availability of collateral allows banks to avoid classifying a loan as nonperforming	6	9	18
Banks allowed to upgrade the classification of a loan or advance immediately after it has been restructured	13	18	21

Source: Data from World Bank, BRSS 2019 (Bank Regulation and Supervision Survey, 2019) (dashboard), https://www.worldbank.org/en/research/brief/BRSS.

Note: The fifth iteration of the BRSS collects information on 160 jurisdictions and the European Central Bank. This table reports information on low- and middle-income countries. It excludes both high-income countries and jurisdictions with a population of less than 500,000. The breakdown of countries by income level is low-income, 16; lower-middle-income, 34; and upper-middle-income, 38.

Figure 2.2 Capacity of banking systems to absorb increases in nonperforming loans, by World Bank region and country income group

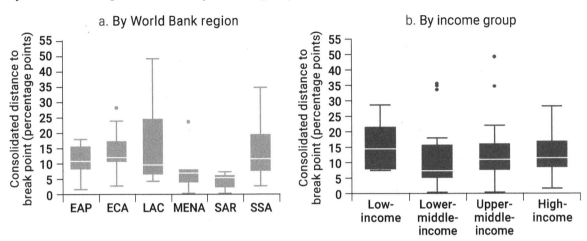

Source: WDR 2022 team, based on Feyen and Mare (2021).

Note: The figure reports the percentage point increase in the nonperforming loan (NPL) ratio at the country level that wipes out capital buffers for banks representing at least 20 percent of banking system assets (see Feyen and Mare 2021). Higher values denote a higher capacity to absorb NPL increases. The horizontal line dividing each box is the median value of each group. The height of the box is the interquartile range. The whiskers span all data within the 1.5 interquartile range of the nearer quartile. Dots represent values outside the whiskers. Panel a shows the distribution of the percentage point increase in the NPL ratio across World Bank regions. Panel b illustrates the distribution of the percentage point increase in the NPL ratio across country income groups. The underlying bank-level data are from up to July 2021. EAP = East Asia and Pacific; ECA = Europe and Central Asia; LAC = Latin America and the Caribbean; MENA = Middle East and North Africa; SAR = South Asia Region; SSA = Sub-Saharan Africa.

Figure 2.2, which is based on data up to July 2021, shows the percentage point increase in NPLs—known as the consolidated distance to break point (CDBP)—at which banks representing at least 20 percent of banking system assets would become undercapitalized.[28] Countries with smaller CDBP values have banking systems with less capital space to absorb increases in NPLs and therefore are more vulnerable to a credit shock. The South Asia Region (SAR) is the most vulnerable, followed by the Middle East and North Africa (MENA) and Latin America and the Caribbean (LAC) Regions (figure 2.2, panel a). The weakest banks in the Sub-Saharan Africa (SSA) and Europe and Central Asia (ECA) Regions could, on average, sustain higher increases in NPLs before capital is depleted.[29] In terms of income groups (figure 2.2, panel b), lower-middle-income countries show the greatest vulnerability because a smaller increase in NPLs (for the median country of approximately 7 percentage points) would deplete capital buffers for a significant portion of banking system assets.

Asset quality indicators not only give banks insight into the existing portfolio, but also serve as the foundation of strong credit risk management standards, including underwriting of new credit. Robust standards increase the likelihood that available funds finance productive new investments. They also guard against competing pressures to prop up unviable borrowers, and thus support the efficient reallocation of capital to support the recovery. The need for strong underwriting standards is particularly relevant in countries with state-owned banks that expanded credit provision during the pandemic. Some countries also rolled out extensive additional public credit guarantee schemes to help support the economy through the pandemic. Care is needed to ensure that public funds help address market failures—for example, to extend credit to MSMEs facing temporary liquidity distress arising from the pandemic or to provide longer-term infrastructure financing that would strengthen the supply capacity of the economy during the recovery. Authorities should avoid the temptation to lower underwriting standards and weaken credit assessments because such a step would increase potential losses, misallocate resources, and distort competition with private commercial banks.

Guarding against incentives for mismeasurement

Banks underreport the magnitude and extent of asset quality problems in several ways. For example, they may delay recognizing the failure of particular borrowers to pay and instead evergreen loans by simply rolling them over at maturity to "extend and pretend" rather than designate the loan as past due and nonperforming. Even when a bank has recognized that a borrower is facing a repayment problem, it may underrecord the severity of the problem in the hope that the borrower's repayment capacity will improve over time. A bank may also place a high value on the collateral posted as security for a loan instead of seeking additional protection when market values decline. Meanwhile, banks can obscure their exposure to problem loans by transferring NPLs to off–balance sheet affiliates not reported in their consolidated financial position. Because this act is often conducted less than transparently to escape supervisory scrutiny, consolidated and cross-border supervision are particularly important in curbing this kind of arbitrage. Supervisors will need to develop a full understanding of financial groups' business(es) and main shareholders, economic interests, and intragroup transactions following the principle of economic substance over legal form.

Incentives to underplay the true extent of exposure to problem loans will likely increase as moratoria end and other support measures are phased out. Weak banks face a particularly strong incentive to disguise problems because full recognition of credit losses may push their capital below the regulatory requirements, triggering reputational risks, an adverse impact on the costs and availability of funding, as well as heightened scrutiny and supervisory intervention to restore the bank's position.[30]

If not countered by strong bank internal governance and intense, intrusive bank supervision, such incentives can create significant discrepancies between reported asset quality figures and the underlying economic realities, as illustrated by the asset quality reviews (AQRs) in countries facing banking stress in the aftermath of the global financial crisis.[31] For example, following the AQR by the European Central Bank (ECB) when it assumed responsibility for banking supervision,[32] a special diagnostic review conducted in Serbia in 2015 identified an additional 4.7 percentage points of NPLs in the total loan book (lowering the capital adequacy ratio by 1.76 percentage points).[33] Similarly, an AQR in India in 2015–16 identified an additional 2.5 percentage points of bank advances as nonperforming.[34] AQRs may become useful once there is more clarity about the longer-term economic impact of the pandemic. At this point, not all businesses are fully operational, relief measures are still in place, and there is major uncertainty about the ultimate credit losses stemming from the COVID-19 crisis.

Recognizing the role of supervision

Bank supervisors play a key role in establishing and upholding consistent, robust standards of credit risk management and loan asset classification. Policy makers and academics agree about the importance of strong, independent banking supervision in maintaining public trust in the banking system. The role of supervisors is especially important under the current circumstances because the growing pressures on asset quality may require them to take firm action.

After the global financial crisis, the supervisory community strengthened frameworks for identifying and managing problem assets. The BCBS reinforced its "Core Principles for Effective Banking Supervision," which set out a minimum baseline for sound practices designed to be of universal applicability for all countries. To facilitate global application, the principle of proportionality underlying the requirements recognizes that practices should be commensurate with the risk profile and systemic importance of the banks being supervised (see spotlight 2.1 for a discussion of the challenges facing microfinance institutions and their supervisors).[35]

The principles lay out clear expectations about the treatment of problem assets, provisions, and reserves, which were strengthened as part of the overall reinforcement.[36] They clarify that supervisors should be granted, and where necessary apply, powers and remedial measures to ensure that loan classification is appropriate and that provisioning, reserves, and capital are sufficient. In practice, this clarification entails conveying powers to a supervisor to require higher provisions when judged necessary and to set additional capital requirements to cover the risks of high levels of NPLs where remediation strategies appear weak.[37] Notwithstanding the recent improvements, further progress in strengthening approaches in this area remains a priority. Detailed assessments of supervisory practices and processes undertaken during the joint World Bank/International Monetary Fund (IMF) Financial Sector Assessment Program (FSAP) reveal that supervisors continue to fall short in meeting the standards of sound practice.[38] Undertaking a speedy self-assessment of conformance to the high-level criteria set out for the identification and management of problem assets may help authorities to make the needed improvements in view of the pervasive weaknesses in supervisory frameworks and the pressing urgency from the pandemic.

Although supervisory reporting has been streamlined during the pandemic, banks must frequently report reliable, detailed, up-to-date information on credit quality. This information should cover the performance of loans that have benefited from borrower relief measures in order to contribute to high-quality prudential supervision and broader policy analysis of the impact of the pandemic. Supervisors can also build on their information base using high-frequency digital data on economic activity and financial prospects, as well as technology that facilitates analysis of data from a wide range of sources (see box 2.2). To support this process, credit bureaus, lenders, and supervisory authorities in some countries are exploring and expanding the use of alternative credit data such as account data and rental data (when permitted by the customer), in combination with advanced digital technology, to enhance the accuracy of credit scoring. The results have been positive, although the need to ensure compliance with consumer protection and privacy regulations remains critical (see chapter 4).[39] Techniques such as stress tests may also supplement financial analysis and help identify emerging risk exposures.

Even where moratoria are still in place, supervisors should encourage banks to undertake thorough assessments of borrowers' likeliness to pay. Moratoria dampen signals of deterioration in repayment performance. Credit assessments can thus inform decisions on the need for, as well as the terms of, restructuring loans to viable borrowers. They can also guide early actions by banks to enforce and recover their claims when borrowers face high risks of insolvency. Banks should be required to perform periodic assessments and report a set of standard indicators on credit risk (such as the availability and quality of collateral and the repayment behavior prior to the pandemic). Using these indicators, supervisors can monitor the performance of these loans. Such information will contribute to policy judgments on whether to temporarily extend loans and on targeting of moratoria, regulatory, and supervisory measures, as well as additional borrower support.[40]

Although the questions of when and how to phase out measures such as moratoria do not have simple answers, the general principle should be to unwind them as soon as economic circumstances and the pandemic allow. Decisions on extensions of moratoria should also be based on a thorough understanding of the financial position and debt-carrying capacity of borrowers. And not least, the financial impact of moratoria on banks needs to be carefully considered. An extension implies that banks must forego regular debt repayments on a possibly significant part of their loan portfolio, which may affect their liquidity.

Box 2.2 The use of financial technology in banking supervision (suptech) during the pandemic

Some advanced economies that had developed suptech tools before the pandemic have been able to use these tools to monitor the impact of the pandemic on the health of their financial sector. The Central Bank of the Netherlands, for example, is developing an interactive reporting dashboard designed to give supervisors insight into banks' exposure to COVID-19–related risks. This tool draws on a variety of data sources and enables the monitoring of relevant indicators for specific banks, as well as peer group analysis. Planned improvements in suptech include incorporating public COVID-19 information and analyzing comment fields using textual analysis.

The Monetary Authority of Singapore (MAS) has deployed automation tools using natural language processing to gather international news and stay abreast of COVID-19–related developments. MAS has also used NLP to analyze consumer feedback on COVID-19 issues and to monitor vulnerabilities in customer and product segments. Meanwhile, as the pandemic unfolded MAS collected weekly data from regulated institutions to track the take-up of credit relief measures. Data aggregation and transformation were automated and visualized for monitoring. In the United States, a Federal Reserve Bank is currently developing an NLP tool to analyze public websites of supervised regulated institutions to identify information on "work with your customer" programs in response to the pandemic.

At the same time, phasing out the measures will likely lead to an increase in total NPL volumes and provisioning charges, which will affect capital, particularly if banks operate with thin capital buffers.[41]

All this will create a more challenging environment for banking supervisors. As pressures on asset quality build, banks may step up efforts to disguise the extent of their difficulties. Supervisory work programs will likely shift toward thematic examinations and in-depth on-site inspections focusing on credit risk. These efforts will be necessary to clarify the true extent of the deterioration of asset quality and the corresponding credit losses. These challenges may be compounded by pressures on the operational independence of prudential supervisors. In the face of mounting stress on bank asset quality, supervisors may be pushed to soften judgments and enforcement or to weaken regulatory standards altogether.

Supervisors should also ensure that legitimate supervisory information needs are met, while avoiding unnecessary burdens. Formally assessing likeliness to pay is more challenging than counting days past due because it requires a more detailed analysis and judgment. In practice, then, some banks and supervisors may have placed more weight on the days past due in identifying NPLs and assessing provisions. However, taking full account of likeliness to pay is important, particularly under the current circumstances. Indeed, the judgments involved in assessing payment capacity on an ongoing basis over the full credit life cycle are an integral part of effective credit risk management, as again highlighted by the "Core Principles."

Illustrating the recommended approach, banks in India and Malaysia, encouraged by their regulators, increased provisions preemptively in 2020 during the moratorium, recognizing that underlying asset quality was deteriorating and that additional performance problems were likely to crystallize at the end of the repayment standstill.[42] The National Bank of Rwanda also highlighted the supervisory expectation that banks proactively assess borrowers' repayment capacity even if not more than 90 days past due in order to accurately determine the level of problem loans, appropriately classify and provide for them, and ultimately assess the adequacy of capital.[43]

While emphasizing the flexibility embedded in the regulatory framework to relieve the pressures of the pandemic, the BCBS and the Financial Stability Board (FSB)[44] have noted the importance of upholding agreed-on minimum standards and applying consistent definitions and classifications. Some countries, however, have not complied fully with these recommendations. They have instead diluted definitions and weakened the application of loan quality standards. For example, Argentina and Turkey relaxed definitions and diverged from international standards by stretching the 90 days past due criterion. Meanwhile, recognizing emerging problem loans, some banks in Colombia reset days past due to zero at the start of the pandemic for borrowers already experiencing repayment arrears. In other cases, supervisors are treating restructured, forborne NPLs as new loans, without undergoing the normal probationary reentry period requiring borrowers to successfully make rescheduled repayments for one year.[45] The various pressures to weaken loan quality standards apply equally to jurisdictions that have not yet had the capacity to implement the international guidelines.

Resisting pressures to lower regulatory standards and soften supervision is critical. Although easing standards may lower measured NPLs, it does not address the underlying problem of banks' exposure to troubled assets. It also weakens the comparability and consistency of reported data, and it creates opacity about the financial position of borrowers and banks that can lower trust in the financial sector. The risk is that neither banks nor supervisors see emerging asset quality problems in time to resolve them before they become embedded and much costlier to address. Where standards have been relaxed during the pandemic, supervisors should clarify that this relaxation is temporary and have plans to restore prudential standards of asset quality.

Fortunately, such relaxation is rare. The majority of supervisors have maintained consistent regulatory approaches and have provided helpful guidance on how to utilize the flexibility in the supervisory and regulatory frameworks, while taking account of moratoria and other temporary support measures.[46] Nonetheless, until the pandemic and the economic crisis are over, political and industry pressures to dilute regulatory norms, soften supervisory enforcement, or challenge the independence of regulatory agencies may continue to increase as banks' asset quality deteriorates.

Supervisors in countries that traditionally have relied heavily on state-owned banks for economic management, and where the state acts not only as regulator but also as owner and promoter of a large part of the banking sector, may be in a particularly difficult position to fend off these pressures (see box 2.3). This is especially true when state-owned banks provide countercyclical lending to mitigate the

Box 2.3 Bank supervision and state ownership of banks

The state continues to play a prominent role in the financial sector of many countries.[a] State-owned banks comprise financial intermediaries that range from strictly commercial to purely developmental. In general, commercial banks operate in competition with the private sector, target profit maximization, take deposits from the public, and extend loans directly to their customers without a specific policy mandate. At the other extreme, development state-owned banks typically operate under a narrow policy mandate, may not collect deposits, and rely on direct lending instruments, as well as the provision of technical assistance. Commercial state-owned banks are usually under the purview of the banking regulatory agency, whereas their development counterparts are often not regulated. The latter may act as providers of public money to private banks, or they may, in some cases, also lend directly.

(Box continues next page)

Box 2.3 **Bank supervision and state ownership of banks** *(continued)*

A high degree of government ownership and strategic control implies a direct and significant influence over the allocation of financial resources. Although state-owned banks can be a helpful vehicle in mitigating the economic impacts of severe shocks, the debate over their pros and cons continues.[b] For example, conflicts about incentives can arise from the multiple (and often opposing) roles of the state as the owner, promoter, and regulator, impairing efforts by authorities to regulate and supervise the financial system.[c] Bank supervisors may face political pressures that prevent them from applying the full range of supervisory tools—such as the replacement of management and board—thereby impairing their ability to enforce rules and standards. The enduring presence of the state may also create issues for privately owned banks, such as reinforcing perceptions of implicit guarantees, discouraging thorough credit risk analysis at loan origination, weakening financial discipline, and distorting resource allocation. These issues are particularly acute when the government routinely backstops weak enterprises, financial institutions, and asset markets.

Many state-owned banks were asked to extend credit and provide guarantees to ease the burden of COVID-19 on companies and households and to help cushion the immediate economic impacts.[d] The long-term effect, however, depends crucially on the quality of underwriting standards and the income-generating capacity of investment projects. Weaknesses in these areas increase the risk that guarantees will be called on and the credit stimulus will resurface in the form of pressures on asset quality. This risk also highlights the importance of corporate governance and risk management arrangements in state-owned banks, as well as supervisory independence and effective enforcement of sound regulatory standards.

a. Panizza (2021).
b. For an overview of the literature, see Cull, Martínez Pería, and Verrier (2018); Panizza (2021); and World Bank (2012).
c. Barth et al. (2003).
d. Medas and Ture (2020).

economic impact of the pandemic (figure 2.3)[47] because in these circumstances asset quality deterioration could be underestimated for some time. State ownership of banks underscores the importance of the legal and operational independence of the supervisory agency and a mandate to focus solely on the safety and soundness of the financial sector, robust legal protection for supervisors, and sufficient powers to address emerging banking vulnerabilities, among other things. Recent FSAP assessments indicate a relatively widespread need to further strengthen these supervisory foundations.[48]

Ensuring a robust regulatory and supervisory framework

Although it is widely recognized that strong regulatory and supervisory frameworks are critical for timely identification of NPLs, many emerging economies continue to face serious challenges in this area. These challenges often stem from a combination of factors, including deep-rooted institutional constraints such as lack of enforcement powers, skill shortages, and weaknesses in the financial sector that predate the pandemic.[49] Under these circumstances, implementing the full range of regulatory and supervisory policies outlined in this chapter can be a tall order. Putting the essential building blocks in place offers a practical way forward.[50]

The logical starting point is to establish a sound institutional base for banking supervision. This base is a legal framework that protects banking supervisors from political and industry pressures and

Figure 2.3 Comparison of accumulation of nonperforming loans at public banks and private banks after adverse shock

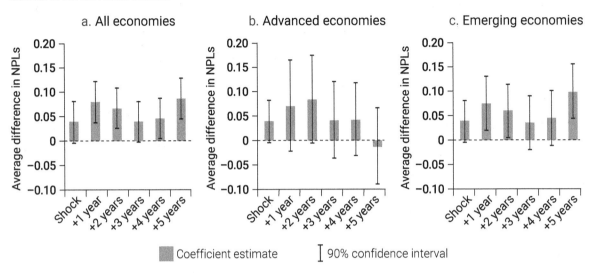

a. All economies b. Advanced economies c. Emerging economies

Coefficient estimate   90% confidence interval

Source: WDR 2022 team, based on Panizza (2021).

Note: The graphs plot for three groups of economies the differential response of state-owned and private banks to a given GDP growth shock over the five years following the shock. A positive coefficient indicates that state-owned banks accumulate higher nonperforming loans after such a shock. GDP = gross domestic product; NPLs = nonperforming loans.

when they undertake acts in good faith, endows the agency responsible for banking supervision with a clear mandate, provides supervisors with an appropriate set of powers, and grants the agency the resources needed to attract and maintain a critical mass of qualified staff. Although these attributes are foundational to the effectiveness of banking supervision, they are often lacking, and efforts to put them in place are forcefully resisted by vested interests. Countries where political elites own or control important parts of the banking sector, or where the state's role as owner and promoter of the banking sector outweighs its role as prudential regulator, may be particularly challenged in laying a sound institutional base.

The second step is to introduce NPL regulatory definitions aligned with international standards. Many emerging economies entered the pandemic with weakly defined NPLs and generous allowances that enabled banks to avoid rigorous loan classifications through questionable restructuring practices.[51] In some countries, these allowances were further weakened in response to the pandemic. It is important to revert to prepandemic standards as soon as possible, while mapping out a transition to definitions aligned with international standards. In addition to the hard backstop of 90 days past due, standards should include the qualitative unlikely-to-pay (UTP) criterion and forbearance definitions aimed at preventing low-quality loan restructuring that aims to delay recognition of inevitable credit losses. Although application of the UTP criterion will require an element of judgment by banks, supervisors should ensure that banks proactively apply consistent approaches to making that assessment and classify loans and provision accordingly on this basis.

Sound regulatory definitions will have to be enforced by banking supervisors. Enforcement will often require developing the capacity of supervisors to support an upgrade from compliance-driven supervisory approaches to approaches that tailor attention and responses to assessed risks. Supervisors must also have the skills needed to challenge common practices that banks often use to underrepresent NPLs, such as overvalued collateral, "extend and pretend" loan restructuring, and transfers of losses to unconsolidated but de facto affiliated entities. Moreover, supervisors will need to understand the broader business interests of the bank's owners. Rigorous application of high-quality corporate governance standards and constraints on lending to related parties are essential steps.

In the most challenged countries, reforms along these lines will take time and must be sustained over several years. Although the task can seem daunting, the rewards will be plentiful. Indeed, in recent years some countries have made remarkable progress in a comparatively short period of time. For example, with extensive World Bank support Uzbekistan introduced a new banking law in 2019 to prepare authorities for the transition to a banking sector with a more prominent role for private capital. The law established a "gatekeeper function" aimed at giving the central bank expanded powers to ensure that private investors seeking to enter the banking sector met common fit and proper standards, de facto ownership structures are well understood and monitored continually, and related party lending would be contained. Another priority was to allow the central bank to legally exercise supervisory judgment in fulfilling its mandate in the face of dynamically evolving banking risks. This change was a drastic and sometimes controversial one because the former legal framework prioritized compliance checks with administrative requirements over the mitigation of risks. The new banking law has had a galvanizing effect on financial sector reform in Uzbekistan. Building on the momentum for financial sector reform, the World Bank has continued to support the central bank in overhauling the corpus of prudential regulations and undertaking extensive capacity building to upgrade supervisory practices.[52]

Building capacity to manage rising volumes of bad debts

In normal times, banks routinely manage NPLs. They know their clients and their capacity to repay and thus are in the best position to restructure, collect, and sell NPLs. Bank capacity to manage NPLs may be insufficient when the volume of NPLs increases significantly across the board, which is very likely in response to the pandemic. Strengthening the capacity of banks to deal with NPLs is critical because of the urgency of addressing bad debts. The recovery prospects for bad loans diminish quickly, and delays in the initial policy response will allow the underlying problems to build, with the risk of overwhelming banks once pressures on asset quality begin to increase.

Methods to manage, recover, and resolve NPLs

Banks can reduce NPLs through a combination of loan restructuring, legal action, write-off, and sale to third parties (see table 2.2).[53] Bank decisions about how they manage NPLs and when to escalate from one method to another should be guided by the expected asset recovery for each method using net present value (NPV) calculations.[54] These calculations should be based on conservative estimates for recovery, discount rates, and carrying costs. Poorly functioning insolvency regimes, for example, translate into lower recovery rates that banks must reflect in their calculations.

Challenges in addressing NPLs in practice

The ease with which banks can work out, collect, write off, or sell bad loans depends on the strength of the enabling environment, particularly the strength of creditor rights, enforcement mechanisms, and

Table 2.2 Nonperforming loan (NPL) reduction measures

Instrument	Subcategory	Typology	Prerequisite	Description
Loan restructuring	Short-term restructuring	Rescheduling	Borrower is experiencing short-term liquidity difficulties. Borrower is cooperative.	Deferment of borrower's debt service obligations to a future date, usually in a net present value (NPV)–neutral manner.
	Concessional restructuring	Workout	Borrower is distressed, but viability can be restored with restructuring that entails debt relief. Borrower is cooperative.	Loan restructuring that entails a NPV reduction.
Legal action	Collateral enforcement	Collection	Debtor receives notice of default from bank, which complies with the prescribed notice periods.	Enforcement of the collateral or guarantee pledged against the loan by taking in-court or out-of-court action to repossess and then sell collateral.
	Insolvency process		Debtor is unable to pay debt as it matures or has liabilities in excess of assets.	Initiation of an insolvency petition to the borrower to reorganize or move toward liquidation. Or the debtor may voluntarily file for insolvency, forcing the bank to prove its claim.
Write-off		Disposal	No realistic prospect of recovery. Loan is fully provisioned. Bank must demonstrate that all other measures have been exhausted.	Transfer of fully provisioned NPL to off–balance sheet records. A write-off does not imply that a bank is forfeiting its claim on the borrower, nor does it involve debt forgiveness. A write-off is instead a formal acknowledgment of uncollectability.
Sale	To a commercial distressed asset investor	Disposal	Bank and distressed debt investor agree on pricing and terms of sale for the bank's NPLs. Ownership rights are transferred to the investor.	Sale of NPL on commercial terms to an investor. Investor continues collection effort, which may require establishment of a servicing platform. A sale can be structured in various ways, the most common of which is a "true" sale, but profit sharing and securitization are practiced as well.
	To a public asset management company		Used in systemic crises to complement the efforts of individual banks.	Transfer of NPL to a centralized agency that manages recovery efforts.

Source: Adapted from Baudino and Yun (2017).

insolvency and debt restructuring frameworks (figure 2.4). This is an area in which many emerging economies stumble, resulting in low and unpredictable recovery prospects for lenders and restricting the range of methods for reducing NPLs. Borrowers may also be less inclined to repay according to their full financial capacity if they are able to delay enforcement proceedings. The result can be elevated, persistent NPLs.[55] The financial crises in Asia—and globally a decade later—brought home the need for comprehensive reforms to address weaknesses in debt resolution, insolvency, and creditor rights, with separate tracks for corporate and retail bankruptcies. Because of their complexity and breadth, these reforms tend to be time-consuming and are therefore best initiated early on, before banks' balance sheets become severely burdened with increasing NPLs.[56]

Poorly functioning enforcement and insolvency frameworks can also discourage banks from dealing forcefully with nonviable or uncooperative borrowers. Absent reliable mechanisms, banks may not be able to steer such borrowers toward an orderly exit through legal action. Political pressure, too, may stand in the way of decisive handling of nonviable state-owned enterprises or national champions. Banks may be pressured to keep such borrowers afloat through frequent rounds of loan restructuring, or they may be restricted in their ability to encourage distressed firms to undertake the operational measures needed to restore financial sustainability and commercial viability. The result can be questionable loan restructuring practices (such as long grace periods, bullet payments,[57] or frequent rescheduling) that exacerbate allocative inefficiencies by locking up the credit stock in highly indebted, underperforming economic sectors at the expense of more promising ones.[58] Although unviable and uncooperative borrowers need to be dealt with resolutely, the depth of the recession puts a high premium on efforts

Figure 2.4 Nonperforming loan reduction flowchart

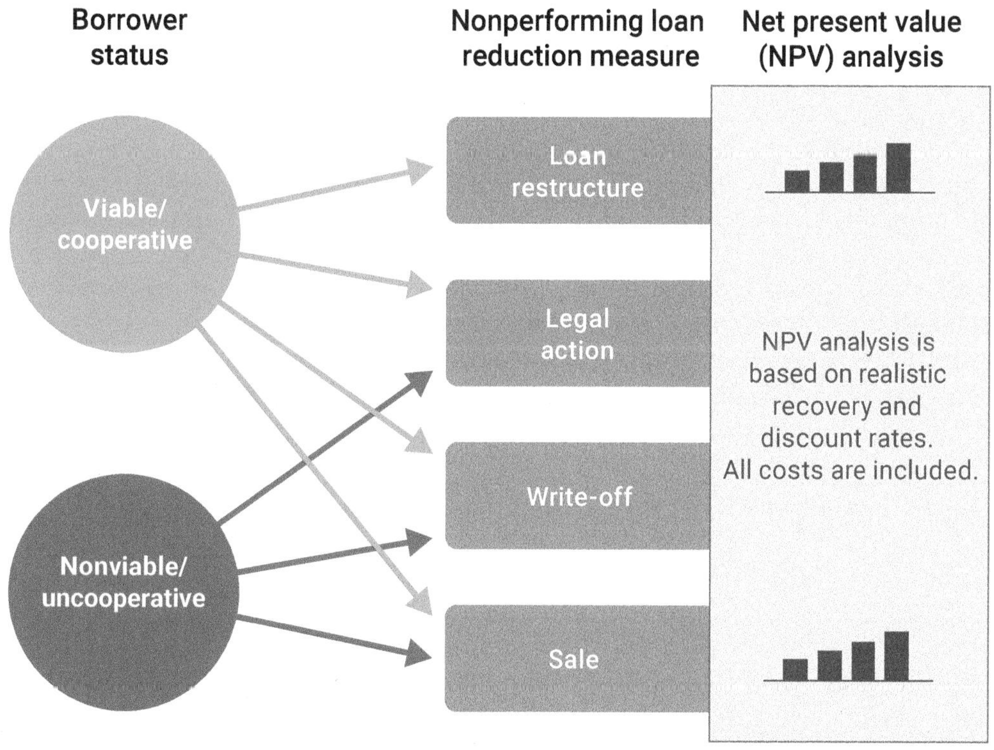

Source: WDR 2022 team.

to ensure that distressed but viable borrowers are given an opportunity to rehabilitate. Support from banks, underpinned by infrastructure that facilitates the efficient restructuring and workout of claims (as highlighted in chapter 3), is important.

The quality of legal and institutional systems for recovering debt is also an important factor in determining the feasibility of developing for distressed assets secondary markets that can play an important role in reducing NPL ratios.[59] Efforts to develop secondary markets have been most effective for unsecured problem loans such as retail loans and credit card debt. Because no collateral is needed, they are easier to price. Successful loan sales require a legal framework that enables a "true sale" of distressed assets so that (1) investors in those assets can acquire the same legal enforcement rights as the originating bank; (2) these legal rights can be transferred to the investor without the debtor's consent; and (3) investors can enforce and collect on these loans. Bank secrecy and data protection laws must not hinder due diligence by prospective investors.

Although market development for distressed assets has largely been limited in most emerging economies, some in the ECA Region made important strides following the global financial crisis. Between 2015 and 2019, total NPL sales in countries that are part of the Vienna Initiative[60] amounted to €14.5 billion. Although in the region the more developed member countries of the European Union (EU) such as Bulgaria, Croatia, Hungary, Romania, and Slovenia account for the bulk of the transactions, smaller deals have also taken place in less developed frontier markets in the Western Balkans. The latter is noteworthy because prospective investors in distressed assets must make sizable up-front investments in servicing platforms and market due diligence, and the opportunities to recoup these up-front costs are limited by the small size of domestic markets in the Western Balkans. The World Bank has supported efforts by client countries to develop secondary markets for distressed assets, including by bolstering in selected countries in Latin America and the Philippines a strong loan servicing ecosystem (specialized companies that for a fee make the collection effort on behalf of the investor in distressed assets).

Faced with a challenging environment for legal enforcement and fledgling markets for NPLs, banks in emerging economies have typically relied heavily on write-offs to dispose of fully provisioned older vintages of NPLs (so-called legacy NPLs) for which there is no realistic prospect of recovery. Banks are often able to write off loans only after demonstrating that all other measures have been exhausted. Full tax deductibility may be granted only after obtaining a court ruling, which can be difficult and time-consuming. It is not unusual for banks to keep significant stocks of full-loss legacy NPLs on their balance sheets. Write-offs tend to be particularly problematic for state-owned banks, as bank managers risk accusations of mishandling state property.

Accelerating write-offs can help bank management turn its attention to fresh lending. Onerous requirements can be streamlined, which many countries in the EU and ECA Region did in the aftermath of the global financial crisis.[61] Going a step further, Ireland, Portugal, Slovenia, and Spain introduced regulatory requirements mandating the write-off of legacy NPLs. Some emerging economies have taken similar steps. For example, in 2017 Malawi required banks to write off NPLs from their balance sheets, which helped to lower NPLs from 15.7 percent at the end of 2017 to 3.6 percent in September 2019.[62]

Organizational needs to manage rising volumes of NPLs

To manage rising volumes of bad debt, banks will have to step up efforts to reclaim past loans—efforts that will have important repercussions for business models, organizational structure, strategy, and internal resources. By starting preemptively to strengthen the internal capacity to work out rising volumes of

Box 2.4 Addressing problematic loans to micro-, small, and medium enterprises in Slovenia

In 2017, the World Bank helped the Bank of Slovenia develop a handbook for the management and workout of problematic loans to micro-, small, and medium enterprises (MSMEs).[a] After resolving the nonperforming loans (NPLs) of large firms through establishment of a national asset management company (AMC), the Bank of Slovenia gradually moved to working out the problem loans of the MSMEs that are the backbone of Slovenia's economy.

According to the Bank of Slovenia, in mid-2016 MSME loans accounted for more than 70 percent of banks' remaining NPL stock, totaling €1.5 billion, or around 4 percent of the gross domestic product (GDP). MSME NPLs were often small (36.5 percent were for less than €10,000) and frequently heavily in arrears. The handbook, developed as part of a European Union–funded technical assistance project completed in 2016, aimed to give banks guidance in working out MSME NPLs.

The exercise highlighted how ill-equipped banks were to work out such NPLs. In view of the small size of the country and its banking system, the scope for substantially expanding its workout units was deemed limited. The problem was exacerbated by skill shortages. At the same time, access to NPL servicing and collection companies had improved and NPL markets had begun to develop, attracting interest from professional NPL investors.

The handbook recommended that banks place MSME NPLs below €10,000 (so-called microexposures) in a separate portfolio during the initial NPL segmentation process. The threshold at €10,000 was based on careful analysis of the MSME NPL portfolio in Slovenia. Because of the vintage of the NPL stock and low number of recoveries expected, a streamlined approach was adopted to enable banks to focus scarce internal workout capacity on larger, more complex cases. This approach entailed a prompt write-off after full provisioning or sale of a portfolio to a third party. Taken together, these measures accelerated the reduction of MSME NPLs.

a. The handbook is available online. See World Bank and BoS (2017).

NPLs, banks can avoid becoming overwhelmed once moratoria are phased out and asset quality issues emerge on their balance sheets. The urgency to do so stems from the fact that building up internal workout capacity takes time, and the pandemic has disproportionately affected households and MSMEs, creating large volumes of small retail loans that are labor-intensive to resolve (see box 2.4).

Banks may not have the skills or incentives to build their internal NPL workout capacity. Some advanced countries have adopted a hands-on approach and require banks with asset quality difficulties to articulate NPL reduction strategies—that is, comprehensive action plans to achieve quantitative NPL reduction targets, which their supervisor must approve. The ECB has required banks to embed their NPL reduction strategies in their risk and capital strategies, review them annually, and ensure that a bank's management body endorses them.[63] The ECB guidelines are based on a sophisticated risk-based supervisory framework and may be difficult to replicate in full in less developed jurisdictions.

Nonetheless, emerging economies may benefit from a more proactive supervisory engagement in banks' NPL reduction efforts and could consider introducing parts of the ECB framework. A good starting point is to require banks with problematic NPL exposures to move problem loans away from the original relationship managers (who, with their focus on new loans, generally lack the knowledge and incentives to work out problematic exposures) to a dedicated workout unit. Creating an independent unit to deal with NPLs will help to eliminate potential conflicts of interest between the originating officer and the troubled borrower and build up expertise. [64] In workout units, separate teams are typically responsible for different loan vintages and groups and for selecting the appropriate management method. Banks have often established a 90-day past due trigger for mandatory transfer to the workout unit (in practice the transfer may take place before reaching this point). In fact, some emerging economies relied on this approach before the pandemic. The Bank of Tanzania, for example, required the country's commercial banks to set up separate workout units as part of a broader strategy introduced in 2018 to lower NPLs.[65]

Banks will need to take the following steps to make their workout units fully functional:

- Allocate the human and financial resources that workout units need for full functionality.[66] The skills needed to deal with NPLs are often in short supply, particularly when demand for those skills surges in the face of systemwide stress on asset quality. Skill gaps can be filled by retraining loan origination staff, using external experts on a contractual basis, or, for subsidiaries from foreign-owned banking groups, using staff from elsewhere within the group.
- Supply workout units with suitable information systems, which can be a challenge in banks with low levels of loan file digitalization.
- Develop internal policies for the management and resolution of NPLs, including assessment of borrower viability, which determines whether a borrower should be considered for loan restructuring.

Assessing borrower viability is particularly challenging under the current circumstances because the viability prospects for many borrowers depend to a large extent on the duration of the pandemic. But it is critical that, despite the uncertainty, banks pursue such assessments, starting with the identification of borrowers that are manifestly nonviable and so should be steered toward an orderly exit.[67] Although banks usually develop their own approaches, regulators could guide the design of these internal methodologies to disseminate best practices and weed out perfunctory analyses by banks.

If a bank decides to put a distressed borrower forward for concessional loan restructuring, it will have to conduct an affordability assessment to determine the debt level consistent with the borrower's ability to pay based on the borrower's liabilities, including debts owed to other creditors. To gather this information, banks can consult private credit bureaus, public registries, or other external sources, where available. Increasing the coverage of borrowers and of credit exposures can help to manage credit risk and problem exposures, as experienced recently in India.[68] Banks also must compile a conservative assessment of the expected income of corporate borrowers, based on an analysis of financial statements and cash flows and adjusted for expenses and taxes. The bank can then determine a debt level consistent with the borrower's debt-shouldering capacity and reduce the debt accordingly. Banks should seek to match rearranged repayment schedules with the borrower's expected future income flows to avoid recurring repayment difficulties. Where struggling borrowers have exposures to multiple banks, efficient procedures for ensuring creditor coordination are important, as described in chapter 3.

Systemwide NPL resolution

Under normal circumstances, banks have primary responsibility for managing distressed loans. In the wake of a crisis, however, countries may resort to public policy interventions to complement banks' NPL reduction efforts, especially if banks' exposure to problem loans jeopardizes their capacity to finance the real economy or threatens the stability of the financial system.

One intervention is to set up national NPL resolution strategies that establish policy priorities and coordination mechanisms based on a comprehensive diagnosis of obstacles to NPL resolution. Experience

Figure 2.5 Ratio of nonperforming loans to total loans, Serbia, 2010–20

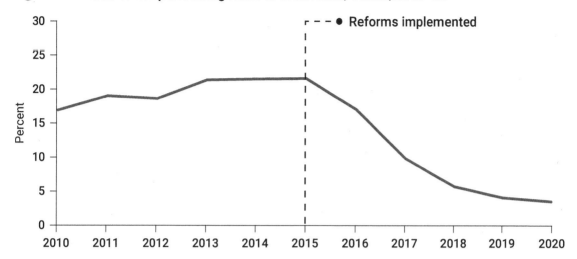

Source: WDR 2022 team, based on data from National Bank of Serbia, https://www.nbs.rs/export/sites/NBS_site /documents-eng/finansijska-stabilnost/pregled_grafikona_e.pdf.

has shown that banks, left to their own devices, are slow to reduce elevated NPLs.[69] Reducing high NPLs requires the participation of a broad range of stakeholders to align policies: representatives of private sector entities (banks, institutional investors, and third-party service providers), national authorities (central banks and banking supervisory agencies, finance and justice ministries), civil society groups (consumer organizations), and occasionally international financial institutions.

Experiences in several ECA countries after the global financial crisis confirmed the importance of policy coordination. For example, Serbia established a national NPL working group in May 2015 that included as core members representatives of the Ministries of Economy, Finance, and Justice and the National Bank of Serbia, and as members representatives of the Chamber of Commerce and the Deposit Insurance Agency. In addition, the World Bank, IMF, International Finance Corporation (IFC), and European Bank for Reconstruction and Development were invited to play an active role in the working group and in the design of the strategy. The working group identified four strategic priorities: (1) improving bank capacity to deal with NPLs; (2) enabling conditions for development of the NPL market; (3) improving and promoting out-of-court restructuring; and (4) improving an in-court debt and mortgage resolution framework. Progress was reviewed and discussed on a quarterly basis. The strategy contributed to a rapid decrease in the NPL ratio, which reached a historic low of 3.7 percent in December 2020 (figure 2.5).[70]

Public asset management companies

In addition to establishing systemwide policies, some regions and countries, including the European Union and Ukraine, have considered establishing public asset management companies (AMCs) to complement bank NPL reduction efforts.[71] Public AMCs allow removal of NPLs from the financial system, while still maximizing the recovery value of these assets.[72] Indonesia, the Republic of Korea, Malaysia, and Thailand, among other countries, used public AMCs in the Asian financial crisis in the late 1990s to clean bank balance sheets and to restructure distressed banks.[73] Advanced economies such as Ireland, Slovenia, and Spain also used public AMCs in the aftermath of the global financial crisis. And more recently, some countries, such as Vietnam (in 2013), Angola (in 2016), and India (in 2021),[74] set up public AMCs to help address NPL problems.[75]

Public AMCs offer important benefits to banks and regulators seeking to resolve high NPL levels.[76] Besides removing problem loans from bank balance sheets, public AMCs give regulators additional leverage to force banks to recognize credit losses—an important step toward restoring public confidence in the banking sector and a critical one in countries where the integrity of reported indicators of asset quality is little trusted. Meanwhile, because of their size and specialization in certain kinds of loans and in recognizing the value of and selling these types of distressed assets, public AMCs can provide economies of scale in the management of distressed assets and greater cost efficiency. This is particularly true if public AMCs can focus on a set of large, complex loans, such as those for real estate development. In addition, by gathering a large volume of homogeneous, distressed assets, public AMCs can help to overcome complex, multicreditor collective action problems and package the assets for sale to outside specialist investors. Public AMCs benefit from enhanced bargaining power with both buyers and sellers, and from having time to realize the value of these assets, thereby avoiding the unnecessary losses associated with fire sales. Setting up a public AMC requires the availability of fiscal resources because finance ministries typically provide (part of) the initial capital and often a partial guarantee on the bonds that banks receive in exchange for the transferred assets.

Achieving these benefits requires a well-designed public AMC, and this is an area in which emerging economies have experienced serious challenges. Without an appropriate design, public AMCs can be vulnerable to political interference in the form of pressure to support well-connected borrowers, strategic sectors, or state-owned enterprises; pressure to include political appointees rather than seasoned workout experts; and rules that allow the public AMC to buy distressed assets at a premium over market prices, which gives banks a subsidy and discourages them from adhering to strong underwriting practices when they originate loans. The outcome could be a buildup of significant contingent liabilities for taxpayers. Emerging economies have also struggled to make public AMCs time-bound. Sunset clauses help to encourage banks to quickly transfer bad loans to a public AMC and incentivize public AMCs to work out these assets within a reasonable time frame, mitigating the risk that they become warehouses for bad assets.

In summary, although a public AMC is an option for NPL resolution, it is not a silver bullet. Public AMCs are most effective when they focus on a relatively homogeneous pool of large corporate loans; include a sunset clause; embrace robust governance, transparency, and disclosure arrangements; and are embedded in a comprehensive NPL resolution strategy, as advocated throughout this chapter.

Dealing with problem banks

Despite the best efforts of banks and governments to prepare for rising NPLs, some banks—especially if they were weak or failing before the pandemic—may be unable to absorb the additional pressure. Dealing expeditiously with these banks is essential to support a strong, sustainable recovery. A powerful lesson from previous episodes of severe banking stress is that delay is costly for two interrelated reasons. First, delay typically increases the scale of the problem.[77] Weak banks generally become weaker absent remedial action: they face both higher funding costs and the risk of losing higher-quality clients and depositors due to a loss in confidence. In the worst case, the result will be bank runs and failure, contagion across the system, and financial crisis. Second, weak banks tend to both misallocate and restrict the supply of credit, which hold back the recovery and dampen future growth.[78] Preserving financial system health by quickly addressing any bank distress that arises is critical to ensure the efficient and prompt provision of the credit needed to spur investment and to foster employment and growth as economies recover from the pandemic.

Building capital strength to absorb losses and finance recovery

Banks were encouraged during the pandemic to utilize buffers above the minimum regulatory standards—notably, countercyclical capital buffers designed to be released in a downturn. Use of such buffers enables banks to continue to extend credit to viable firms facing temporary stress and to finance new, productive investment, while also absorbing the pressures from weakening asset quality.[79] Yet the amount of capital available varies across banks and countries, creating differences in the ability of banks to play this supportive role.[80]

In the years following the global financial crisis, many banks strengthened their balance sheets and built up capital and liquidity buffers, buttressed by the toughening of global regulatory standards.[81] As highlighted earlier, however, reported capital adequacy figures must be interpreted with some caution because of the possibility of underreported credit risk, which inflates measured capital. In addition, in some countries the improvement in reported capital adequacy ratios may have been driven by a shift in bank lending toward assets that carry a low risk weight.[82] Nonetheless, the consensus is that regulatory reforms have, on the whole, contributed to stronger buffers that have helped banks weather the crisis and continue to provide credit.

In countries with banking systems suffering from preexisting vulnerabilities, however, pressures from a sharp increase in problem loans may be increasingly difficult to absorb. Although reported NPLs and capital measures currently seem reassuring, credit losses may increase rather quickly once moratoria are discontinued, affecting capital. The phasing out of public credit guarantee schemes could exacerbate these pressures because banks would face increasing risk.[83] Over time, some banks may struggle to meet capital adequacy requirements, creating the need for viable capital restoration and recovery plans to retain market confidence. And indeed, some banks will be at risk of failing, potentially jeopardizing financial stability if authorities do not quickly and carefully resolve them.

Taking early action to bolster the capital strength of the banking system helps to guard against undercapitalization and potential distress. In this vein, some countries have used favorable global financing conditions as a window of opportunity to raise capital. Furthermore, utilizing this window to raise longer-term finance would also strengthen the funding position of banks that draw on external wholesale markets as a source of finance. In countries such as India, market conditions were sufficiently favorable to support raising bank capital during the pandemic. Moreover, at the outset of the pandemic many authorities took action to encourage the preservation of capital by temporarily limiting and restricting bank dividend payments.[84] Although the restriction temporarily reduces shareholder cash flow and may increase the cost of raising new equity, it sustains reserves within the bank to absorb potential losses.[85] Some authorities subsequently lifted these restrictions for demonstrably strong banks, but retaining the restrictions during the continuing high uncertainty would provide helpful additional capital buffers.

Recent evidence suggests that a failure to respond speedily and effectively to an undercapitalization of the banking system can be very costly to an economy.[86] In addition to causing broader financial instability, weak banks with little chance of recovery tend to take excessive risks. With little to lose, they "gamble for resurrection" in the hope that an unlikely bet will pay off and thus allow the bank's survival.[87] But the costs and downsides of such risk-taking are borne by depositors and other creditors, not by bank management and shareholders. Moreover, such behavior affects the sustainable pricing of risk and thus could spill over and distort decisions by healthy banks. Finally, as noted earlier, weak banks are more likely than strong banks to misallocate credit by continuing to support insolvent borrowers (zombie lending) in the faint hope they will eventually recover and by restricting credit to new, productive uses to preserve dwindling capital.[88]

To guard against the risk of a lackluster recovery due to weak and distorted credit availability, bank supervisors should intensify their monitoring and analysis of individual banks, in addition to the overall banking system's financial position and outlook. Beyond the usual wide range of tools for monitoring and evaluation, including financial analysis, scenario analysis, and stress tests, supervisors can draw on the tools needed to measure longer-term financial risks (such as climate-related and environmental) to align with emerging international good practices.[89] Upon detecting an impending breach of the regulatory capital standard, supervisors should urgently conduct an in-depth assessment rather than rely mechanically on the automatic supervisory triggers embedded in some regulatory systems. An in-depth assessment will reveal whether the breach is temporary and resolvable with a viable plan to restore capital strength over the medium term under strict supervisory oversight.

The credibility and feasibility of medium-term recapitalization and restoration plans to facilitate recovery from the pandemic will vary according to characteristics such as ownership structure, financial position and business model of the bank, financial market conditions, and economic outlook. For domestic, privately owned banks, recapitalization prospects are likely to depend heavily on market conditions and the risk appetite of investors, which, in turn, will depend on the bank's business plan and the outlook for the banking system. Although the same variables will influence the recapitalization prospects for subsidiaries of foreign-owned banks, the financial position and business strategy of the parent bank may be a stronger driver.[90] In financial sectors dominated by a state bank, the ability to transfer losses to private creditors, shareholders, or uninsured depositors is limited. Governments are thus directly exposed to financial sector losses, underscoring the critical role played by effective supervisory and financial stability frameworks, as well as a proper separation of ownership and supervisory functions to minimize conflicting objectives. Decisions on recapitalizing state-owned banks may figure in the overall government policy response, depending on the perceived role of such banks in the financial system, as well as on available fiscal resources and government debt sustainability.

Strengthening frameworks to address bank failures

The 2007–09 global financial crisis vividly demonstrated the inadequacies of the banking regulatory and supervisory frameworks at the time for dealing with bank failures. The standard corporate insolvency framework had limited options for addressing the specific issues raised by banking sector problems and proved ill-suited to address significant failures because of the tight financial and reputational connections within the financial sector and associated risks of contagion. How to maintain confidence in the banking sector and how to sustain access to funds and ensure continuity of key financial services are two questions that must be answered to manage failing banks.

Moreover, deposit-taking banks fundamentally differ from nonfinancial companies and thus require different approaches to insolvency.[91] Unlike failures of nonfinancial companies, bank failures can generate significant wealth losses across the economy (such as by uninsured depositors) and can be associated with a disruption in the provision of critical financial services. In addition, a failed bank may cause knock-on effects that may destabilize the rest of the financial system by, for example, producing loss of depositor confidence and runs on multiple banks, lack of access to key banking services, and impacts on financial counterparties and markets. It is therefore problematic in the context of financial institutions that corporate insolvency measures can generally only be initiated at the point of insolvency. This timing would inhibit an early and decisive preemptive intervention designed to forestall banking sector problems that may quickly become systemic. Another limitation of the corporate insolvency framework when applied to financial institutions is that it does not recognize the particular position of bank depositors, who, unlike creditors of nonfinancial companies, are numerous and not professional market participants, and who have claims on banks that play a major role in the wider functioning of the economy. Application of the corporate insolvency law could thus aggravate systemwide losses and jeopardize financial stability.[92]

The expectation that public authorities will step in to prevent bank failure and preserve financial stability creates moral hazard, whereby banks increase leverage and take excessive risks, assuming they will benefit from the potential upside, while taxpayers underwrite potential major losses on the downside.[93] Thus for regulators, the introduction of effective crisis management frameworks has been an important priority in recent years, complementing the multiple initiatives to strengthen the resilience of financial institutions and the system as a whole. The overarching objective has been to resolve financial institutions without severe systemic disruption and with minimal exposure of taxpayers to losses, while sustaining vital economic functions and preserving financial stability.

International guidelines are useful in developing and implementing national frameworks. In 2014, the Financial Stability Board issued "Key Attributes of Effective Resolution Regimes for Financial Institutions," together with guidance on information sharing and sector-specific implementation.[94] The FSB framework defines the powers and associated legal safeguards, funding arrangements, and requirements for planning and cross-border cooperation needed to facilitate effective bank resolution. In parallel with international efforts to strengthen bank resolution schemes, the International Association of Deposit Insurers (IADI) developed core principles for deposit insurance schemes.[95]

Institutional and legal arrangements that vest in a national agency the responsibility, intervention powers, and tools required to undertake an orderly resolution of failing banks are pivotal. The designated resolution authority (either an existing agency or a new one) should be given the legal authority to pursue financial stability by initiating resolution when it judges that a bank is, or is likely to be, no longer viable and has no reasonable prospect of becoming so.[96] The resolution authority should have policy options and tools at its disposal, including stabilization options that support the continuity of key financial functions and liquidation options that enable the orderly winding down of parts or all of a firm's business. As also described in table 2.3, the main tools would be the following:

- *Partial asset and liability transfer (also known as purchase and assumption).* The resolution authority transfers the insured deposit book to a healthy bank, typically alongside a corresponding volume of performing assets. The remaining "bad" book of the failing bank can then be wound down over time.
- *Bridge bank.* The resolution authority transfers performing assets and a proportion of liabilities to a government-owned bridge bank, while the remaining book is liquidated. The bridge bank can subsequently be sold or privatized.
- *Bail-in.* The resolution authority has the power to write down and convert loss-absorbing liabilities of the bank in resolution into equity.
- *Liquidation.* The resolution authority has the power to liquidate part or all of a bank's book, enabling the separation and management of good assets and the continuity of key financial services, as well as supporting market discipline.

Strong safeguards are integral to resolution frameworks because the use of intervention tools overrides shareholders' and managers' normal decision-making powers and affects creditors' interests. Key safeguards are that the hierarchy of claims in liquidation must be respected, and no creditor will be worse off from undertaking the resolution than under the fallback option of liquidation. Otherwise,

Table 2.3 Principal bank resolution tools

Tool	Description	Objective	Prerequisites
Partial asset and liability transfer (also known as purchase and assumption, P&A)[a]	Transfer the insured deposit book to a healthy bank, with a corresponding volume of performing assets.[b] The remaining "bad" book is wound down.[c]	Avoid the costs of and risks to financial stability of liquidation and depositor payout, as well as lower the risk of a fire sale of assets.	Enabling legal powers for the resolution authority. Willing healthy bank prepared to take over the insured deposit book and performing assets.
Bridge bank[d]	Transfer performing assets and a proportion of liabilities (at a minimum, insured deposits) to a government-owned bridge bank, while the remaining book is liquidated. The bridge bank can thereafter be sold or privatized.	Avoid the costs and risks to financial stability of liquidation and depositor payout, as well as lower the risk of a fire sale of assets.	Enabling legal powers. Used to buy time when there is insufficient notice or time to find a healthy bank to undertake an immediate P&A.
Bail-in[e]	Write down and convert the loss-absorbing liabilities of the bank in resolution into equity.	Restore the balance sheet and maintain bank continuity. For large and complex banks, avoid the costs and execution risk of P&A and bridge banks.	Enabling legal powers. Bank has sufficient loss-absorbing capacity for confidence to be sustained.[f]
Liquidation[g]	Liquidate part or all of a bank's book. Pay out insured depositors if not previously transferred to another bank under P&A.	Support market discipline. May be used alongside other tools.	Enabling legal powers. Sufficient protections to avoid runs and instability.[h]

Source: WDR 2022 team.

a. Examples: Bradford and Bingley (UK, 2008); Washington Mutual, WaMu (US, 2008).

b. With, if necessary and feasible, the deposit insurance fund to cover any gap in value (judged on the basis of least cost to the fund).

c. The "bad" book is wound down over time either through transfer to a public or private asset management company, for example, or through the standard liquidation process.

d. Examples: Independent National Mortgage Corporation, IndyMac (US, 2008); Consolidated Bank (Ghana, 2018).

e. Examples: Bank of Cyprus (Cyprus, 2013); Banco Espirito Santo (Portugal, 2014); Banco Popular (Spain, 2017).

f. The experience in Cyprus in 2013 highlights how this approach can damage confidence when loss-absorbing capacity is inadequate. Regulatory initiatives to increase loss-absorbing capacity for globally systemic banks and for major domestic banks in some jurisdictions help to address this problem by implementing the international standard for total loss-absorbing capacity set out by the Financial Stability Board in 2015 (FSB 2015).

g. Liquidation is used to wind down residual books that have not been transferred after P&A or use of a bridge bank, or for very small banks.

h. Penn Square Bank (US, 1982) is an example of where this failed to apply.

compensation would be due. Taxpayer interests should also be protected if, in the event of a systemic banking crisis, public funds are needed to preserve financial stability and to support orderly resolution.[97]

The FSB's "Key Attributes" set out the international standard for bank resolution[98] and form part of the IMF and World Bank's Standards and Codes Initiative and Financial Sector Assessment Program. Although many of the "Key Attributes" are broadly applicable to any bank resolution regime in any jurisdiction, some of the elements focus on the challenges in resolving complex, globally systemic banks with extensive cross-border operations. A recent World Bank paper provides advice and guidance on how the "Key Attributes" may be applied proportionately in light of the structure and complexity of banking systems and the capacity of authorities to achieve the desired objective—financial stability without loss of public funds—without imposing undue or unjustified operational burdens on authorities and financial institutions or creating market distortions.[99] Thus some tailoring is needed.[100] The following attributes appear to be appropriate to all jurisdictions and all types of banks: the power to remove management, appoint an administrator, operate and resolve a firm, override shareholder rights, transfer assets and liabilities, suspend creditor payment, impose a temporary stay on early termination rights, and liquidate an institution. However, the following attributes address issues found more commonly in large, complex banks: the power to ensure continuity of essential services that support critical functions, to establish a bridge bank, and to bail in shareholders and creditors.

Planning for dealing with failing banks

Planning is essential to ensure that the resolution authority has the information and tools to support orderly implementation. The "Key Attributes" require jurisdictions to establish an ongoing process for recovery and resolution planning, covering, at a minimum, domestically incorporated firms that could have systemic impacts if they fail. Requiring major firms to produce robust recovery and resolution plans under authorities' oversight is a must for effective contingency planning.

Over the last decade, authorities worldwide have made significant progress in developing and implementing resolution frameworks. They have also taken steps to strengthen other key aspects of the financial safety net, such as deposit insurance schemes, which help to support depositor confidence in the banking system.[101] Stronger frameworks have supported authorities in addressing failing banks and in restructuring and strengthening the banking system, which has helped improve resilience to meet the financial pressures from the pandemic (see box 2.5).

Further progress, nonetheless, remains critical. Surveys by IADI suggest that, notwithstanding expansion of the available tools over time, significant gaps remain in the ability of some authorities to deal with problem banks (see figure 2.6). For example, only about half of the reporting sample of low-income countries had instruments other than liquidation available in their toolkit.[102]

Moreover, there may also be some practical challenges in applying the policy instruments, particularly in a context of widespread asset quality weakness and systemwide distress. Open bank bail-in strategies, for example, may prove difficult to execute because of the general lack of loss-absorbing financial instruments that can be bailed in, coupled with the difficulty of issuing eligible liabilities at times of high market volatility. Uninsured deposits are then the only feasible liability class that can be bailed in, which is politically unpopular and can jeopardize depositor and market confidence. Purchase and assumption (P&A) strategies that seek to transfer assets to stronger banks may be difficult to arrange if the entire sector is financially stressed and the appetite for takeovers is limited. And, if set up, bridge banks may be hard to unwind if no ready buyers emerge. Care should be taken that they do not become the "bridge to nowhere." As experienced in the aftermath of the Penn Square Bank case in 1982,[103] liquidation of a bank may prompt depositor runs and financial instability.

Box 2.5 Restructuring the financial system in Ghana

In recent years, Ghanaian authorities have overseen a major restructuring of Ghana's financial system to address weaknesses.[a] This restructuring delivered a smaller but stronger and better capitalized banking system, as well as a stronger microfinance and nonbank sector.

A detailed asset quality review (AQR) in 2015–16 revealed Ghanaian banks' significant underprovisioning and capital shortfalls. In response, authorities implemented a series of reforms to strengthen the regulatory framework, as well as resolution powers and tools, supported by assistance from the International Monetary Fund (IMF) and World Bank.[b] Authorities also introduced Basel II/III,[c] strengthened corporate governance, and took steps to reinforce the regulatory framework for write-offs, large exposures, and related party lending; improve the effectiveness of reporting to credit bureau(s); and facilitate loan and collateral recovery by bolstering the legal infrastructure for insolvency and debt enforcement. In addition, authorities raised the minimum capital adequacy level from 10 percent to 13 percent, with the new level serving as a benchmark for bank viability. Some banks raised capital to meet the new benchmark, while others merged and some closed. Capital was also injected into some state-owned banks. Meanwhile, authorities used a range of tools to support the system restructuring, including purchase and assumption, a bridge bank, and liquidation. Fiscal assistance was provided to sustain depositor confidence (a formal deposit insurance scheme was only introduced in 2019), including by funding shortfalls on asset transfers, funding the bridge bank, and providing some capital injections.

The reforms strengthened overall banking system capital in Ghana, which rose from 18 percent in 2014 to almost 22 percent in 2018 before dipping slightly to close to 21 percent in 2019. At the same time, the number of banks fell from 36 at the start of 2017 to 24 in 2019 (nine closed while others merged). The reforms also helped to reduce nonperforming loans (NPLs)—and actions are ongoing to address legacy problems, as well as to strengthen the underlying framework for NPL resolution. The reforms also addressed weaknesses elsewhere in the financial system. A comprehensive restructuring of special deposit institutions led to the revocation of licenses of almost 400 microfinance and microcredit institutions, as well as intervention in 23 savings and loan firms and finance houses.

The reforms and cleanup have helped the Ghanaian financial sector to weather the impact of the pandemic.[d] Although NPLs had edged up to 17 percent of gross loans by the end of June 2021 and remain at a high level, the regulatory capital ratio stood at 20.8 percent, well above the regulatory minimum and comparing favorably with ratios of other emerging economies.

a. IMF (2019).
b. Cleaning up the banking system was one of the three elements of the IMF Extended Credit Facility Program for Ghana agreed on in 2015. IMF and the World Bank have also provided technical assistance on bank resolution and ongoing advice on bank supervision and the regulation and supervision of special-deposit institutions.
c. Sets of international banking regulations issued by the Basel Committee on Banking Supervision.
d. IMF (2021).

Authorities responsible for handling troubled banks should prioritize private sector–funded solutions, building as much as possible on the financial buffers of troubled financial entities and the scope for extending them. Such an approach preserves market incentives and discipline and avoids the risks and costs to taxpayers associated with fiscal support. Completing the development of resolution frameworks to provide additional policy options is thus an important priority. To facilitate this work, the World Bank and IMF can help develop the capacity to identify and address weak banks and to strengthen resolution and crisis management frameworks proportionately.

Figure 2.6 Financial safety net and bank resolution powers, by country income group, 2016–20

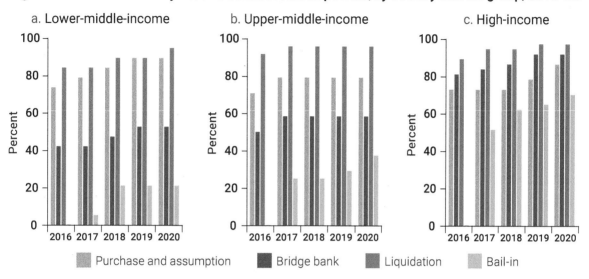

a. Lower-middle-income

b. Upper-middle-income

c. High-income

Purchase and assumption   Bridge bank   Liquidation   Bail-in

Source: WDR 2022 team, based on data from International Association of Deposit Insurers (IADI), Deposit Insurance Surveys (dashboard), Bank for International Settlements, Basel, Switzerland, https://www.iadi.org/en/research/data-warehouse/deposit-insurance-surveys/.

Note: Percentages are computed for the total number of countries in each IADI survey year. Because of the scarcity of data for low-income countries, low- and lower-middle-income countries are reported together.

The use of public money should be a last resort—deployed after private sector solutions have been fully exhausted, and only to remedy an acute, demonstrable threat to financial stability and critical financial services that cannot be taken over easily by other providers. In these circumstances, authorities need to consider the case for additional fiscal support, notwithstanding the additional pressures on fiscal resources, as well as the risks of moral hazard and of a further tightening of the government–financial sector nexus (see chapter 1). In cases of severe systemic stress, where private sector resources are insufficient on their own or the policy tools and options currently available to authorities within the resolution framework are limited, government funds, such as temporary capital injections and resolution funding, may be needed to preserve confidence and financial stability and to drive an orderly and speedy restructuring process, thereby facilitating the rebuilding of financial system health.[104]

A clear assessment of the extent of the asset quality problems and the potential capital shortfall in individual troubled banks and across the system as a whole is an important input into decisions on whether temporary public sector support is warranted. Banks should be adequately recapitalized to support productive new lending and avoid the risk that they engage in evergreening to stay afloat.[105] If time permits, an independent asset quality review, as well as stress tests, may be helpful in supporting policy decisions on bank capital recovery plans and in sizing any temporary public support. Strong safeguards are essential to protect taxpayers' interests.

An important first step is to ensure that all losses are recognized (and equity capital written down) before any government capital injection to avoid bailing out shareholders. Governance and management of the troubled bank should be enhanced and reinforced under strict supervisory oversight, and agreement should be reached on a comprehensive restructuring plan and timetable to restore the viability of the bank. The public sector ownership stake, which at times could extend to temporary nationalization, may be best managed by the finance ministry or a separate body rather than by the supervisor or central bank, both of which may have conflicts of interest. The public sector's stake should be remunerated to limit moral hazard and to maintain a level playing field, and it should be managed at arm's length to avoid the risk of politicization of day-to-day management decisions. To ensure strong accountability, there should be transparency on the extent and cost of the public support (and of recovery), as well as a clear plan for exit.[106] The arrangements should also be buttressed by ensuring that resolution regimes, funding arrangements, and contingency planning build in sufficient flexibility to enable scope for later recovery of resources from the banking industry in the event of a deficit. Improving frameworks to address troubled banks will pay dividends because greater flexibility in the crisis management policy toolkit, combined with strong contingency planning and the development of robust recovery and resolution plans for major firms, will reduce the need for additional support and minimize the costs.

Conclusion

Dealing promptly and comprehensively with distressed assets and problem banks is essential for a well-functioning banking system and healthy, sustainable growth. History has shown that a strong initial response prevents problems from festering, maintains the capacity of the banking sector to finance the real economy, fosters market and public confidence, and reduces the risk that countries become trapped in an equilibrium of low growth and lackluster financial sector performance.

Avoiding such a scenario should be a top priority. Replicating the full range of policies discussed in this chapter may be particularly demanding for countries that face a combination of institutional constraints and serious preexisting financial sector vulnerabilities. Under these circumstances, some sequencing of measures is likely to be necessary, while some of the more complex reforms may need to be simplified.

Whatever the situation, effective resolution of the banking sector must begin with an accurate understanding of the scale of the problem. The starting point is full transparency about bank exposures to troubled assets, supported by a robust regulatory and supervisory framework so that banks properly identify NPLs and provision for credit losses. Supervisors must ensure that banks have sufficient capital buffers to support lending growth and economic recovery, while absorbing credit losses to minimize the risk that insolvency problems materialize and become a threat to financial stability. Encouraging banks to use favorable global financing conditions to strengthen capital and balance sheet resilience can support this process.

Some countries, however, entered the pandemic with lax regulatory definitions and ineffectual supervision. In these countries, it is critical that regulators and supervisors do not succumb to pressures to further dilute regulatory standards and soften supervisory enforcement. Instead, they should consider reversing any recent dilution of asset classification definitions and developing and implementing a plan for gradually introducing internationally agreed-on definitions for NPLs and forborne exposures to ensure rigorous monitoring of banks' asset quality. That effort should be buttressed by ongoing efforts to strengthen the effectiveness of supervision.

Supervisors should require banks with excessive NPL exposures to adopt NPL resolution strategies and reinforce their operational readiness to resolve rising volumes of bad loans. The creation of dedicated workout units tasked with handling problematic exposures is a good starting point. Banks will also need to implement internal policies to manage and resolve NPLs and to assess the viability of distressed borrowers. The latter is vital to avoid questionable loan restructuring that delays the recognition of inevitable credit losses.

At the national level, the government should coordinate the participation of public and private sector stakeholders and civil society representatives in resolving banking sector problems. Such institutional coordination would be particularly useful in jurisdictions where efforts to accelerate NPL resolution face major legal impediments and taxation obstacles. In countries with a long history of unresolved asset quality problems, the establishment of a coordination body could signal authorities' newfound determination to clean up bank balance sheets and gain public and financial industry support for critical legal and regulatory reforms. Such a body could also help to prioritize policy actions, sustain momentum over a likely multiyear process, and ensure that reforms remain on track.

Where helpful, IMF and the World Bank could provide assistance and advice on strengthening financial supervision, including on NPL identification and strategies to resolve them. Strong crisis management frameworks that include a resolution toolkit for handling bank failures, as well as contingency planning for dealing with potential problems, will help to protect taxpayers while ensuring continuity in financial services. Reforms to develop such frameworks and strengthen crisis management planning have been a policy priority in recent years. Building on this progress to ensure that authorities have a broad range of policy tools remains important to ensure that banking systems are able to support a strong, sustainable, equitable recovery.

Notes

1. However, early signs of distress are already visible in some countries. For example, in India bad loans as a share of gross loans surpassed 10 percent in the first half of 2021 (Sanglap 2021). In the Philippines, the nonperforming loan ratio is expected to double to 8.2 percent in 2022 (Villaneuva 2021).
2. The World Bank COVID-19 Crisis Response Survey (http://bit.do/WDR2022-Covid-19_survey) indicates that as of June 2021, 25 upper-middle-income, 14 lower-middle-income, and 6 low-income countries had in place credit forbearance policies for individuals. Also in response to the pandemic, 25 upper-middle-income, 20 lower-middle-income, and 6 low-income countries had in place credit forbearance policies for small businesses and firms.
3. The impact of the COVID-19 crisis on asset quality in the banking sector varies across countries and depends on a complex interplay of factors, including the severity of the pandemic, the duration and rigor of containment measures, the importance of hard-hit economic sectors, as well as the financial capacity of banks to absorb rising credit losses and their operational readiness to work out rising volumes of bad debt. Some countries will be hit harder than others.
4. Aiyar et al. (2015) document that NPLs in several European countries exceeded 10 percent between 2008 and the end of 2014. By reporting NPLs at their historical average, the authors estimate that banks could have provided new lending of up to 5.3 percent of the gross domestic product (GDP) of the countries in their sample at the end of 2014. The same authors also argue that persistent, excessive NPLs are associated with a private debt overhang, which entails weaker investment and slower economic recovery after a recession. In addition, the negative economic effects associated with high NPLs may be amplified by a previous large buildup of excessive credit, eventually leading to a severer economic recession and slower recovery (Jordà, Schularick, and Taylor 2013).

5. Cerra and Saxena (2008).
6. Analysis of the sectoral heterogeneity can reveal how COVID-19 is having a differential impact across and within loan portfolios. For example, Müller and Verner (2021) find that credit booms driven by household credit and credit to the nontradable sector are associated with lower growth in the medium term.
7. Countries enacting measures to support borrowers have stressed their extraordinary and temporary nature. Deciding when and how to unwind them is nonetheless challenging. Withdrawing measures before the pandemic and the macroeconomic outlook have stabilized can permanently reduce economic growth potential through unnecessary insolvencies and unemployment, increasing NPLs and credit losses and triggering disorderly adjustments of asset prices (Kongsamut, Monaghan, and Riedweg 2021). On the other hand, extending support measures risks distorting resource allocation and asset prices, weakening repayment discipline, postponing structural adjustment in the economy, and draining fiscal resources. Policy dilemmas about whether to extend, amend, or end support measures will likely become acuter as the pandemic persists. Further discussion of the timing and strategy for unwinding fiscal and monetary supports appears in chapter 6. See also FSB (2021).
8. A useful distinction is between high levels (*stock*) of NPLs and increases in NPL ratios (*flows*). High levels of NPLs may influence permanently the provision of credit through regulatory restrictions, funding costs stemming from market pressures, and risk-taking behavior such as the tendency to invest in riskier assets to "gamble for resurrection" (Rochet 1992). Increases in NPL ratios temporarily affect income statements and may modify lending policies while banks adjust provisioning (see Balgova, Nies, and Plekhanov 2016).
9. To keep bad loans in check and limit capital absorption due to higher regulatory requirements, banks may

try to limit lending to riskier borrowers such as MSMEs (as described by DeYoung et al. 2015). The most vulnerable borrowers may be also affected by, for example, not providing collateral (which lowers both risk weights and the proportion of a loan that needs to be provisioned) against requested financing. See Cucinelli (2015).

10. Diwan and Rodrik (1992).

11. As discussed in chapter 4, lower lending entails negative real effects. For example, Granja and Moreira (2021) document a decrease in product innovation in the consumer goods sectors following disruptions in the supply of credit.

12. Evidence from Japan indicates that following the bursting of the asset price bubble in the early 1990s, banks with lower capital buffers were more reluctant to write off loans and more likely to provide frequent rounds of loan restructuring—also known as evergreening (Giannetti and Simonov 2013; Peek and Rosengren 2005). European banks, in the aftermath of the global financial crisis, exhibited similar behavior (Acharya et al. 2018, 2019; Andrews and Petroulakis 2019; Blattner, Farinha, and Rebelo 2019; Bonfim et al. 2020; Schivardi, Sette, and Tabellini 2021). European banks with thin capital buffers have reduced their exposures to weak borrowers significantly less than to stronger ones (Dursun-de Neef and Schandlbauer 2021). Recent evidence points to similar patterns in some emerging economies, particularly for government-owned banks. See, for example, Chopra, Subramanian, and Tantri (2021) and Kulkarni et al. (2021) for the case of India and Tan, Huang, and Woo (2016) for the case of China.

13. Acharya et al. (2019); Adalet McGowan, Andrews, and Millot (2018); Banerjee and Hofmann (2018); Blattner, Farinha, and Rebelo (2019); Caballero, Hoshi, and Kashyap (2008).

14. According to Ari, Chen, and Ratnovski (2021), out of 92 banking crises in 82 countries since 1990, 30 percent of the crises saw NPLs exceed 7 percent of total loans. In these countries, output growth six years after a crisis was 5 percent lower than in countries with a relatively low NPL level (that is, below 7 percent of total loans). In earlier research, Reinhart and Rogoff (2009a, 2009b) found that the peak-to-trough output decline after a banking crisis is approximately 9 percent.

15. CESEE countries are Albania, Belarus, Bosnia and Herzegovina, Bulgaria, Croatia, the Czech Republic, Estonia, Hungary, Kosovo, Latvia, Lithuania, Moldova, Montenegro, North Macedonia, Poland, Romania, the Russian Federation, Serbia, the Slovak Republic, Slovenia, Turkey, and Ukraine.

16. Annex 2A can be found at http://bit.do/WDR2022 -Annex2A.

17. World Bank (2020a).

18. That approach may include measures that promote identifying unrecognized NPLs, building banks' capacity to handle rising volumes of bad debt, adopting systemwide NPL resolution mechanisms such as "bad banks" and public asset management companies, and strengthening the enabling legal framework. See Ari, Chen, and Ratnovski (2021).

19. Dijkman and Salomao Garcia (2020).

20. Recapitalization may be unpalatable to shareholders because the new capital would be used primarily to stabilize bank liabilities. In addition, external discipline on bank risk-taking behavior could be also hindered by the presence of a formal financial safety net (such as a deposit guarantee system) and implicit guarantees of uninsured creditors (World Bank 2020b). Appropriate supervision is therefore key to prevent banks from delaying recognition of losses and engaging in zombie lending and evergreening—see Acharya (2020) and Chopra, Subramanian, and Tantri (2021) for the case of India.

21. These reasons include whether jurisdictions apply accounting or regulatory rules in determining provisioning requirements; the different methods for valuing collateral; and the differences in the regulatory treatment of the accrual of interest income on nonperforming loans and asset write-offs (Baudino, Orlandi, and Zamil 2018).

22. BCBS (2016). In its guidance, the Basel Committee on Banking Supervision has also advocated use of the term *nonperforming exposures* (NPEs), which covers a broader range of problem assets than the term *nonperforming loans*. NPEs comprise NPLs, as well as nonperforming debt securities, other amounts due (including interest and fees), and certain off–balance sheet items such as loan commitments and financial guarantees. In practice, however, most countries continue to use NPLs as the metric.

23. BCBS (2020); FSB (2020a).

24. BCBS (2020).

25. BCBS (2020).

26. In the majority of emerging economies, financial intermediation occurs primarily through banks, as opposed to through nonbank institutions such as credit unions, peer-to-peer lending solutions, asset-backed lenders, and microfinance institutions. Credit risk in the form of losses resulting from a borrower's failure to repay a loan is the main risk that banks in these economies encounter. Data as of year-end 2019 reveal that the country median value of the claims of deposit money banks on the domestic real sector is 63 percent of GDP, compared with 18 percent of GDP of the claims of nonbank financial institutions. See World Bank, GFDD (Global Financial Development Database), https://www.worldbank.org/en/publication/gfdr/ data/global-financial-development-database.

27. BCBS (2016).

28. The 20 percent threshold of banking system assets is associated with systemic banking crises. See Feyen and Mare (2021) for details.

29. The analysis uses a so-called reverse stress test approach, assessing for the most fragile banks in the system how much NPLs would have to rise before capital ratios are depleted. See Feyen and Mare (2021) for details.

30. These may include measures to raise capital levels and restrictions on the payout of dividends and executive bonuses and on the launch of new products.

31. An asset quality review is a detailed forensic assessment of underlying loan quality (Gutierrez, Monaghan, and Piris 2019). This point-in-time assessment of the accuracy of the book value of a bank's assets can be a useful tool to bring much-needed transparency on the financial position of banks and to underpin strategies for the restructuring of weak or failing banking systems.

32. The AQR led to a significant increase in the stock of nonperforming loans. See ECB (2014).

33. NBS (2015).

34. RBI (2016).

35. BCBS (2012).

36. In particular, principle 18 specifies that "the supervisor determines that banks have adequate policies and processes for the early identification and management of problem assets, and the maintenance of adequate provisions and reserves" (BCBS 2012, 12). To guide this determination, the principle specifies 12 essential criteria for supervisors to fulfill, covering, among other things, the quality, timeliness, accuracy, and prudence of bank loan classification schemes and provisioning policies.

37. Caruso et al. (2021); D'Hulster, Salomao Garcia, and Letelier (2014); Gaston and Song (2014).

38. For example, significant weaknesses in asset classification and provisioning frameworks were noted in about 65 percent of the 29 detailed FSAP assessments of emerging economies conducted since 2012, and practices for valuing collateral, upgrading restructured loans, supervisory definitions, and supervisory oversight also fall short of best practices in some 25–40 percent of the same assessments (Dordevic et al. 2021).

39. The Hong Kong Monetary Authority and the Hong Kong Applied Science and Technology Research Institute have outlined a strategy and road map for the use of alternative credit data to support credit risk assessment for MSMEs (HKMA and ASTRI 2020). In a recent survey in the United States, 96 percent of the participating financial institutions agree that in times of economic stress alternative credit data allow them to more closely evaluate consumers' creditworthiness and therefore reduce their credit risk exposure (Experian 2020).

40. Kongsamut, Monaghan, and Riedweg (2021).

41. World Bank (2020a).

42. Bank Negara Malaysia (BNM 2021) notes that around 40 percent of additional provisions in 2020 were from application of management overlays by banks over and above the expected credit loss (ECL) model provisions. This development reflects the ongoing challenges faced by banks in incorporating forward-looking information into the measurement of ECL given the prevailing uncertainties about the economic recovery path and reduced visibility into the debt servicing capacity of borrowers under loan moratoria.

43. BNR (2021).

44. The Financial Stability Board (FSB) brings together and coordinates national financial authorities and international standard-setting bodies as they work toward developing strong regulatory, supervisory, and other financial sector policies.

45. Shortening or eliminating this period allowed banks to release provisions and thus present a superficially stronger financial position.

46. This is in line with recommendations and guidance in IMF and World Bank (2020).

47. Bertay, Demirgüç-Kunt, and Huizinga (2015); Levy Yeyati, Micco, and Panizza (2007).

48. Dordevic et al. (2021).

49. Dordevic et al. (2021).

50. The Basel Committee on Banking Supervision's "Core Principles for Effective Banking Supervision" set out a universally applicable framework for regulation and supervision (BCBS 2012).

51. Dordevic et al. (2021).

52. Dijkman and Gutierrez (2019).

53. World Bank (2020a). Following a sale of NPL portfolios, the buyers—often investors that specialize in collecting on bad debts—step up collection efforts by initiating legal action, and a write-off typically takes place only after a creditor has attempted to recover the debt through legal action.

54. To determine the net present value of an asset, the annual net cash flow (cash payments of principal, interest, and fees minus the bank's out-of-pocket costs for legal fees, consultants, and so forth) is calculated. Each of these amounts, or future values (FVs), is then discounted to the present by using an appropriate market-based discount rate. The sum of the FVs equals the NPV.

55. World Bank (2021).

56. On the demand side, it is often a challenge to encourage borrowers to reach out to banks once they anticipate repayment difficulties. A late start of negotiations between debtors and banks generally increases losses and reduces the chances of a successful rehabilitation.

57. A lump sum payment with repayment at maturity of the contract.

58. World Bank (2020a).

59. There are information asymmetries between buyers and sellers of distressed assets. Buyers would fear that the assets they are bidding for are of low quality and bid at a correspondingly low price. The sellers, being able to distinguish between low- and high-quality assets, trade only in the former—the lemons—whereas the market for the remaining assets fails (ECB 2016). One approach to lessen this problem is the development of standardized "data tapes," which provide full details of the terms and conditions governing the assets as well as the payment performance.

60. The Vienna Initiative monitors NPL transactions for Albania, Bosnia and Herzegovina, Bulgaria, Croatia, the Czech Republic, Estonia, Hungary, Latvia, Lithuania, Montenegro, North Macedonia, Poland, Romania, Serbia, the Slovak Republic, and Slovenia.

61. In absence of a full provision, the act of writing off a loan would lay bare an additional credit loss for the bank—the uncollateralized portion of the loan (Bauze 2019).

62. Eyraud et al. (2021). Although write-offs remove NPLs from bank balance sheets, they do not imply debt relief for the borrower. The social and economic benefits of allowing good faith debtors to make a fresh start must be balanced against the need to ensure that they are incentivized to repay to their full financial capacity. Ideally, these borrowers should undergo a formal liquidation process, with a court-ordered discharge at the end of the process for a natural person debtor. Automatic discharge could be considered for first-time debtors, followed by extinction of the debt. In some cases, a limitation period could be considered before the extinction to avoid the sudden discovery of assets after discharge of the borrower's debt.

63. See ECB (2017) and EBA (2018).

64. Banks can go a step further by transferring NPLs, together with all related support staff, into a legally separate entity, a so-called bad bank. NPLs are, however, likely to be transferred at prices below their book value, crystallizing losses that could necessitate raising new capital. The bad bank also needs its own funding and must expend resources to comply with regulatory requirements. Therefore, bad banks are typically only considered after exhausting measures to deal with NPLs in-house.

65. BoT (2018).

66. Officers of the workout units are often assigned an excessive number of cases, which risks undermining the effectiveness of collection efforts and can backfire in the form of lower recoveries and longer recovery terms (World Bank 2016; World Bank and BoS 2017).

67. Although the appropriate benchmarks depend on country-specific circumstances and industry features (such as the capital intensity of the sector), as a rule of thumb a debt to EBITDA (earnings before interest, taxes, depreciation, and amortization) ratio of more than 5, an interest rate coverage of less than 1 for a sustained period of time (such as greater than two years), and persistent negative operating income are common red flags.

68. The Reserve Bank of India set up a Central Repository of Information on Large Credits (CRILC) in 2014 to collect, store, and disseminate credit data to lenders. The CRILC addresses the problem of cross-bank information asymmetry and inconsistencies in asset classification.

69. EBCI (2012).

70. NBS (2021).

71. A public asset management company is a statutory body or corporation, fully or partially owned by the government, usually established in times of financial sector stress to assume the management of distressed assets.

72. Although this section is devoted to public AMCs, private AMCs can be found in some countries, such as Turkey, where local private AMCs are effectively the only category of buyers of distressed assets. The business model of private AMCs often focuses on rapid disposal and generation of returns through margins on resale rather than buy-and-hold strategies with workouts of troubled assets. Reliance on short-term funding can exacerbate pressure to generate quick returns and may preclude time-consuming workouts. See Cerruti and Neyens (2016).

73. Lindgren et al. (1999).

74. India's National Asset Reconstruction Company Ltd (NARCL), incorporated as a bank-sponsored asset reconstruction company (ARC), is one of several ARCs authorized by the Reserve Bank and in operation since 2002.

75. Some public AMCs, such as Danaharta (Malaysia) and SAREB (Spain), were created in conjunction with publicly funded bank recapitalization schemes to overcome capital space constraints that otherwise would have hindered efforts to recognize transparently the full extent of banks' exposure to problem loans. Banks weakened from the burden of NPLs were given a one-off opportunity to recapitalize with public support, so that prudential banking regulations would not be breached. In exchange, banks that benefited from the scheme underwent significant restructuring to secure their long-term viability.

76. Dobler, Moretti, and Piris (2020).

77. See, for example, Claessens et al. (2011) and Homar and van Wijnbergen (2017).

78. See, for example, the discussion in Schwert (2018) and references therein.

79. BCBS (2020); FSB (2020b); IMF and World Bank (2020).

80. Some banks have been unwilling to use their capital buffers as a response to real or perceived financial market pressure. Bondholders may require banks to maintain higher capital ratios to reduce default risk, while shareholders may lean on banks to continue dividend payments rather than use excess capital to lend or to absorb losses.

81. IMF (2020) notes that banks in Europe and in emerging markets significantly strengthened their capital position in the decade following the global financial crisis. Moreover, according to Hohl et al. (2018), the vast majority of countries have adopted or are considering adoption of stricter definitions of capital.

82. See Anginer et al. (2021) and World Bank (2020b) and references therein.

83. Ehrentraud and Zamil (2020).

84. Feyen et al. (2021).

85. Awad et al. (2020).

86. Acharya, Borchert, et al. 2020; Acharya, Crosignani, et al. 2020; Andrews and Petroulakis (2019); Blattner, Farinha, and Rebelo (2019); Giannetti and Simonov (2013).

87. Rochet (1992).

88. Acharya, Lenzu, and Wang (2021); Ben-David, Palvia, and Stulz (2019); Bonaccorsi di Patti and Kashyap (2017).

89. For example, see the Basel Committee on Banking Supervision for a discussion of the causal chains from climate risk drivers to financial risk (BCBS 2021) and the Network for Greening the Financial System on how to design scenarios to model the impact of climate

change and climate policy (Scenarios Portal, Paris, https://www.ngfs.net/ngfs-scenarios-portal/).

90. In addition to parent banks based in advanced countries, new players from World Bank client countries have accounted for much of the growth in cross-border banking in recent years. This has led in a few cases to establishment of holding companies (such as Ecobank in Togo and Colombian banks in Panama) in jurisdictions where the group has a limited footprint and the home authority limited incentives to financially support cross-border subsidiaries (World Bank 2018).

91. See box 1 of Brierley (2009) for a more detailed discussion of the reasons why corporate insolvency law is inappropriate for banks.

92. Limited use of the framework in the early phase of the 2007–09 global financial crisis (such as for Lehman Brothers) exacerbated systemwide stress and amplified the crisis. Authorities were forced to provide massive public sector support and assistance to backstop the financial system and prevent collapse. For example, UK authorities had to nationalize the bank Northern Rock in the absence of an effective resolution mechanism to preserve its financial stability. Similar approaches were taken by other countries in response to bank failures during the global financial crisis.

93. *Financial leverage* is the fraction of assets funded through debt. The higher the reliance on debt to finance bank activities, the higher is the risk of default (because a larger share of profits would be devoted to paying debt obligations) and the lower is the share of capital to absorb losses.

94. FSB (2014).

95. IADI (2014).

96. Various arrangements have been successfully applied—for example, assigning the resolution authority function to the central bank, supervision authority, or the deposit insurer. An important element in all arrangements is addressing potential conflicts of interest and balancing operational independence for the resolution function with approaches that facilitate the synergies with the supervision function (Baudino, Sánchez, and Walters 2021; Dobler, Moretti, and Piris 2020).

97. Dell'Ariccia, Detragiache, and Rajan (2008).

98. FSB (2014).

99. Nolte and Hoelscher (2020).

100. Tailoring may also be applied in other areas—for example, resolution funding and cross-border arrangements (Nolte and Hoelscher 2020).

101. As of April 1, 2021, 146 jurisdictions had deposit insurance in place. See International Association of Deposit Insurers, Deposit Insurance Systems Worldwide (dashboard), Bank for International Settlements, Basel, Switzerland, https://www.iadi.org/en/about-iadi/deposit-insurance-systems/dis-worldwide/.

102. Even among the larger emerging economies that are members of the FSB, progress has been mixed. According to the latest Resolution Report, no jurisdiction in emerging economies has yet applied all the elements (FSB 2020b).

103. Penn Square Bank was liquidated in 1982 following poor underwriting practices on energy loans. The failure prompted queues of uninsured depositors and contagion of other banks exposed to Penn Square, including Continental Illinois Bank, which failed in 1984 and was at that time the largest bank failure in US history. The failures prompted a tightening of US financial regulations.

104. Dobler, Moretti, and Piris (2020).

105. Brei, Gambacorta, and von Peter (2013); Giannetti and Simonov (2013); Homar (2016).

106. Dobler, Moretti, and Piris (2020).

References

Acharya, Viral V. 2020. *Quest for Restoring Financial Stability in India*. New Delhi: Sage Publications.

Acharya, Viral V., Lea Borchert, Maximilian Jager, and Sascha Steffen. 2020. "Kicking the Can Down the Road: Government Interventions in the European Banking Sector." *Review of Financial Studies* 34 (9): 4090–131.

Acharya, Viral V., Matteo Crosignani, Tim Eisert, and Christian Eufinger. 2020. "Zombie Credit and (Dis-)Inflation: Evidence from Europe." NBER Working Paper 27158, National Bureau of Economic Research, Cambridge, MA.

Acharya, Viral V., Tim Eisert, Christian Eufinger, and Christian W. Hirsch. 2018. "Real Effects of the Sovereign Debt Crisis in Europe: Evidence from Syndicated Loans." *Review of Financial Studies* 31 (8): 2855–96.

Acharya, Viral V., Tim Eisert, Christian Eufinger, and Christian W. Hirsch. 2019. "Whatever It Takes: The Real Effects of Unconventional Monetary Policy." *Review of Financial Studies* 32 (9): 3366–3411.

Acharya, Viral V., Simone Lenzu, and Olivier Wang. 2021. "Zombie Lending and Policy Traps." *VoxEU* (blog), October 29, 2021. https://voxeu.org/article/zombie-lending-and-policy-traps.

Adalet McGowan, Müge, Dan Andrews, and Valentine Millot. 2018. "The Walking Dead? Zombie Firms and Productivity Performance in OECD Countries." *Economic Policy* 33 (96): 685–736.

Aiyar, Shekhar, Wolfgang Bergthaler, Jose M. Garrido, Anna Ilyina, Andreas Jobst, Kenneth H. Kang, Dmitriy Kovtun, Yan Liu, Dermot Monaghan, and Marina Moretti. 2015. "A Strategy for Resolving Europe's Problem Loans." IMF Staff Discussion Note SDN/15/19, International Monetary Fund, Washington, DC.

Andrews, Dan, and Filippos Petroulakis. 2019. "Breaking the Shackles: Zombie Firms, Weak Banks, and Depressed Restructuring in Europe." ECB Working Paper 2240, European Central Bank, Frankfurt.

Anginer, Deniz, Ata Can Bertay, Robert Cull, Asli Demirgüç-Kunt, and Davide S. Mare. 2021. "Bank Capital Regulation and Risk after the Global Financial Crisis." *Journal of Financial Stability*. Published ahead of print, May 17, 2021. https://doi.org/10.1016/j.jfs.2021.100891.

Ari, Anil, Sophia Chen, and Lev Ratnovski. 2021. "The Dynamics of Non-performing Loans during Banking Crises: A New Database with Post-COVID-19 Implications."

Journal of Banking and Finance. Published ahead of print, April 27, 2021. https://doi.org/10.1016/j.jbankfin.2021.106140.

Awad, Rachid, Caio Ferreira, Aldona Jociene, and Luc Riedweg. 2020. "Restriction of Banks' Capital Distribution during the COVID-19 Pandemic (Dividends, Share Buybacks, and Bonuses)." Special Series on COVID-19, Monetary and Capital Markets Department, International Monetary Fund, Washington, DC.

Balgova, Maria, Michel Nies, and Alexander Plekhanov. 2016. "The Economic Impact of Reducing Non-performing Loans." EBRD Working Paper 193, European Bank for Reconstruction and Development, London.

Banerjee, Ryan Niladri, and Boris Hofmann. 2018. "The Rise of Zombie Firms: Causes and Consequences." *BIS Quarterly Review* (September 23): 67–78.

Barth, James R., Daniel E. Nolle, Triphon Phumiwasana, and Glenn Yago. 2003. "A Cross-Country Analysis of the Bank Supervisory Framework and Bank Performance." *Financial Markets, Institutions, and Instruments* 12 (2): 67–120.

Baudino, Patrizia, Jacopo Orlandi, and Raihan Zamil. 2018. "The Identification and Measurement of Non-performing Assets: A Cross-Country Comparison." FSI Insights 7 (April 10), Financial Stability Institute, Bank for International Settlements, Basel, Switzerland. https://www.bis.org/fsi/publ/insights7.htm.

Baudino, Patrizia, Carlos Sánchez, and Ruth Walters. 2021. "Institutional Arrangements for Bank Resolution." FSI Insights 32 (May), Financial Stability Institute, Bank for International Settlements, Basel, Switzerland.

Baudino, Patrizia, and Hyuncheol Yun. 2017. "Resolution of Non-performing Loans: Policy Options." FSI Insights on Policy Implementation 3 (October), Financial Stability Institute, Bank for International Settlements, Basel, Switzerland.

Bauze, Karlis. 2019. "Non-performing Loan Write-Offs: Practices in the CESEE Region." Policy Brief, World Bank, Washington, DC.

BCBS (Basel Committee on Banking Supervision). 2012. "Core Principles for Effective Banking Supervision." BCBS, Bank for International Settlements, Basel, Switzerland. https://www.bis.org/publ/bcbs230.htm.

BCBS (Basel Committee on Banking Supervision). 2016. "Guidelines: Prudential Treatment of Problem Assets; Definitions of Non-performing Exposures and Forbearance." BCBS, Bank for International Settlements, Basel, Switzerland. https://www.bis.org/bcbs/publ/d403.htm.

BCBS (Basel Committee on Banking Supervision). 2020. "Measures to Reflect the Impact of Covid-19." BCBS, Bank for International Settlements, Basel, Switzerland. https://www.bis.org/bcbs/publ/d498.pdf.

BCBS (Basel Committee on Banking Supervision). 2021. "Climate-Related Risk: Drivers and Their Transmission Channels." BCBS, Bank for International Settlements, Basel, Switzerland.

Ben-David, Itzhak, Ajay A. Palvia, and René M. Stulz. 2019. "Do Distressed Banks Really Gamble for Resurrection?" NBER Working Paper 25794, National Bureau of Economic Research, Cambridge, MA.

Bertay, Ata Can, Asli Demirgüç-Kunt, and Harry Huizinga. 2015. "Bank Ownership and Credit over the Business Cycle: Is Lending by State Banks Less Procyclical?" *Journal of Banking and Finance* 50 (January): 326–39.

Blattner, Laura, Luísa Farinha, and Francisca Rebelo. 2019. "When Losses Turn into Loans: The Cost of Undercapitalized Banks." ECB Working Paper 2228, European Central Bank, Frankfurt.

BNM (Bank Negara Malaysia, Central Bank of Malaysia). 2021. "FSR: Financial Stability Review, Second Half 2020." BNM, Kuala Lumpur. https://www.bnm.gov.my/documents/20124/3026574/fsr2020h2_en_book.pdf.

BNR (National Bank of Rwanda). 2021. *Monetary and Financial Stability Statement.* Kigali, Rwanda: BNR. https://www.bnr.rw/fileadmin/user_upload/Monetary_Policy_and_Financial_Stability_Statement_Feb_21_Booklet.pdf.

Bonaccorsi di Patti, Emilia, and Anil Kashyap. 2017. "Which Banks Recover from Large Adverse Shocks?" NBER Working Paper 23654, National Bureau of Economic Research, Cambridge, MA.

Bonfim, Diana, Geraldo Cerqueiro, Hans Degryse, and Steven Ongena. 2020. "On-Site Inspecting Zombie Lending." SFI Research Paper 20-16, Swiss Finance Institute, Zürich.

BoT (Bank of Tanzania). 2018. "Measures to Increase Credit to Private Sector and Contain Non-performing Loans." BoT Circular Fa. 178/461/01/02, BoT, Dodoma, Tanzania.

Brei, Michael, Leonardo Gambacorta, and Goetz von Peter. 2013. "Rescue Packages and Bank Lending." *Journal of Banking and Finance* 37 (2): 490–505.

Brierley, Peter. 2009. "The UK Special Resolution Regime for Failing Banks in an International Context." Bank of England Financial Stability Paper 5, Bank of England, London.

Caballero, Ricardo J., Takeo Hoshi, and Anil K. Kashyap. 2008. "Zombie Lending and Depressed Restructuring in Japan." *American Economic Review* 98 (5): 1943–77.

Caruso, Ezio, Katia D'Hulster, Tatsiana Kliatskova, and Juan Ortiz. 2021. "Accounting Provisioning under the Expected Credit Loss Framework: IFRS 9 in Emerging Markets and Developing Economies; A Set of Policy Recommendations." Finance: Equitable Growth, Finance, and Institutions Insight Series, World Bank, Washington, DC. https://openknowledge.worldbank.org/handle/10986/35373.

Cerra, Valerie, and Sweta Chaman Saxena. 2008. "Growth Dynamics: The Myth of Economic Recovery." *American Economic Review* 98 (1): 439–57.

Cerruti, Caroline, and Ruth Neyens. 2016. *Public Asset Management Companies: A Toolkit.* World Bank Study Series. Washington, DC: World Bank.

Chopra, Yakshup, Krishnamurthy Subramanian, and Prasanna L Tantri. 2021. "Bank Cleanups, Capitalization, and Lending: Evidence from India." *Review of Financial Studies* 34 (9): 4132–76.

Claessens, Stijn, Ceyla Pazarbasioglu, Luc Laeven, Marc C. Dobler, Fabian Valencia, Oana Nedelescu, and Katharine Seal. 2011. "Crisis Management and Resolution: Early Lessons from the Financial Crisis." IMF Staff

Discussion Note SDN/11/05, International Monetary Fund, Washington, DC.

Cucinelli, Doriana. 2015. "The Impact of Non-performing Loans on Bank Lending Behavior: Evidence from the Italian Banking Sector." *Eurasian Journal of Business and Economics* 8 (16): 59–71.

Cull, Robert, María Soledad Martínez Pería, and Jeanne Verrier. 2018. "Bank Ownership: Trends and Implications." Policy Research Working Paper 8297, World Bank, Washington, DC.

Dell'Ariccia, Giovanni, Enrica Detragiache, and Raghuram Rajan. 2008. "The Real Effect of Banking Crises." *Journal of Financial Intermediation* 17 (1): 89–112.

DeYoung, Robert, Anne Gron, Gökhan Torna, and Andrew Winton. 2015. "Risk Overhang and Loan Portfolio Decisions: Small Business Loan Supply before and during the Financial Crisis." *Journal of Finance* 70 (6): 2451–88.

D'Hulster, Katia, Valeria Salomao Garcia, and Raquel Letelier. 2014. "Loan Classification and Provisioning: Current Practices in 26 ECA Countries; Overview Paper." FinSAC Working Paper, Financial Sector Advisory Center, World Bank, Vienna. https://openknowledge .worldbank.org/handle/10986/21109.

Dijkman, Miquel, and Valeria Salomao Garcia. 2020. "Borrower Relief Measures in ECA Region." FinSAC Policy Note, Financial Sector Advisory Center and the Financial Stability and Integrity Unit, Finance, Competitiveness, and Innovation Global Practice, World Bank, Vienna. https://thedocs.worldbank.org/en/doc/99370158 8092073659-0130022020/original/BorrowerRelief MeasuresNoteforECA.pdf.

Dijkman, Miquel, and Eva Gutierrez. 2019. "Establishing a Fit-for-Purpose Banking Law in Uzbekistan." *Private Sector Development* (blog), December 3, 2019. https://blogs .worldbank.org/psd/establishing-fit-purpose-banking -law-uzbekistan.

Diwan, Ishac, and Dani Rodrik. 1992. "Debt Reduction, Adjustment Lending, and Burden Sharing." NBER Working Paper 4007, National Bureau of Economic Research, Cambridge, MA.

Dobler, Marc C., Marina Moretti, and Alvaro Piris. 2020. "Managing Systemic Banking Crises: New Lessons and Lessons Relearned." MCM Departmental Paper 20/05, Monetary and Capital Markets Department, International Monetary Fund, Washington, DC.

Dordevic, Ljubica, Caio Ferreira, Moses Kitonga, and Katharine Seal. 2021. "Strengthening Bank Regulation and Supervision: National Progress and Gaps." MCM Departmental Paper 21/05, Monetary and Capital Markets Department, International Monetary Fund, Washington, DC.

Dursun-de Neef, H. Özlem, and Alexander Schandlbauer. 2021. "COVID-19 and Lending Responses of European Banks." *Journal of Banking and Finance 2021.* Published ahead of print, July 2, 2021. https://doi.org/10.1016/j .jbankfin.2021.106236.

EBA (European Banking Authority). 2018. *Final Report: Guidelines on Management of Non-performing and Forborne Exposures.* Document EBA/GL/2018/06. London: EBA. https://www.eba.europa.eu/regulation-and

policy/credit-risk/guidelines-on-management-of-non -performing-and-forborne-exposures.

EBCI (European Bank Coordination Initiative). 2012. "Working Group on NPLs in Central, Eastern, and South-eastern Europe." EBCI, International Monetary Fund, Washington, DC. https://www.imf.org/external/region /eur/pdf/2012/030112.pdf.

ECB (European Central Bank). 2014. *Aggregate Report on the Comprehensive Assessment.* Frankfurt: ECB. https://www.bankingsupervision.europa.eu/ecb/pub /pdf/aggregatereportonthecomprehensiveassessment 201410.en.pdf?68911b281b9d831540bb474c334437e7.

ECB (European Central Bank). 2016. *Financial Stability Review.* Frankfurt: ECB. https://www.ecb.europa.eu /pub/pdf/fsr/financialstabilityreview201611.en.pdf.

ECB (European Central Bank). 2017. *Guidance to Banks on Non-performing Loans.* Frankfurt: ECB. https://www .bankingsupervision.europa.eu/ecb/pub/pdf/guidance _on_npl.en.pdf.

Ehrentraud, Johannes, and Raihan Zamil. 2020. "Prudential Response to Debt under Covid-19: The Supervisory Challenges." FSI Brief 10, Financial Stability Institute, Bank for International Settlements, Basel, Switzerland.

Experian. 2020. "White Paper: 2020 State of Alternative Credit Data." Experian, Costa Mesa, CA. http://images .go.experian.com/Web/ExperianInformationSolutions Inc/%7Be5c60202-67a3-4b0e-a757698e6300e1ed%7D _P_2020StateofAltCreditData-WP.pdf.

Eyraud, Luc, Irina Bunda, Jehann Jack, Tarak Jardak, Rasmané Ouedraogo, Zhangrui Wang, and Torsten Wezel. 2021. "Resolving Nonperforming Loans in Sub-Saharan Africa in the Aftermath of the COVID-19 Crisis." Departmental Paper DP/2021/014, African Department, International Monetary Fund, Washington, DC.

Feyen, Erik H. B., Tatiana Alonso Gispert, Tatsiana Kliatskova, and Davide S. Mare. 2021. "Financial Sector Policy Response to COVID-19 in Emerging Markets and Developing Economies." *Journal of Banking and Finance.* Published ahead of print, May 21, 2021. https://doi .org/10.1016/j.jbankfin.2021.106184.

Feyen, Erik H. B., and Davide S. Mare. 2021. "Assessing Banking Sector Vulnerabilities in EMDEs: A Basic Reverse Stress Testing Approach." Working paper, World Bank, Washington, DC.

FSB (Financial Stability Board). 2014. "Key Attributes of Effective Resolution Regimes for Financial Institutions." FSB, Basel, Switzerland. https://www.fsb.org/wp -content/uploads/r_141015.pdf.

FSB (Financial Stability Board). 2015. "Principles on Loss-Absorbing and Recapitalisation Capacity of G-SIBs in Resolution: Total Loss-Absorbing Capacity (TLAC) Term Sheet." FSB, Basel, Switzerland. https://www .fsb.org/wp-content/uploads/TLAC-Principles-and -Term-Sheet-for-publicationfinal.pdf.

FSB (Financial Stability Board). 2020a. "COVID-19 Pandemic: Financial Stability Implications and Policy Measures Taken." FSB, Basel, Switzerland. https://www.fsb .org/wpcontent/uploads/P150720-2.pdf.

FSB (Financial Stability Board). 2020b. "2020 Resolution Report: 'Be Prepared.'" FSB, Basel, Switzerland. https:// www.fsb.org/wp-content/uploads/P181120.pdf.

FSB (Financial Stability Board). 2021. "COVID-19 Support Measures: Extending, Amending, and Ending." FSB, Basel, Switzerland. https://www.fsb.org/wp-content /uploads/P060421-2.pdf.

Gaston, Ellen, and In Won Song. 2014. "Supervisory Roles in Loan Loss Provisioning in Countries Implementing IFRS." IMF Working Paper WP/14/170, International Monetary Fund, Washington, DC.

Giannetti, Mariassunta, and Andrei Simonov. 2013. "On the Real Effects of Bank Bailouts: Micro Evidence from Japan." *American Economic Journal: Macroeconomics* 5 (1): 135–67.

Granja, João, and Sara Moreira. 2021. "Product Innovation and Credit Market Disruptions." Paper presented at Faculty of Economics, Cambridge–Institute for New Economic Thinking, and Centre for Macroeconomics Virtual Mini-Conference, "From Firms to the Aggregate Economy: The Role of Financial Frictions," University of Cambridge, Cambridge, UK, March 2, 2021.

Gutierrez, Joaquin, Dermot Monaghan, and Alvaro Piris. 2019. "The Role of Bank Diagnostics in IMF-Supported Programs." Technical Notes and Manuals 2019/04, International Monetary Fund, Washington, DC.

HKMA (Hong Kong Monetary Authority) and ASTRI (Hong Kong Applied Science and Technology Research Institute). 2020. *Alternative Credit Scoring of Micro-, Small, and Medium-Sized Enterprises.* Hong Kong SAR, China: HKMA and ASTRI. https://www.hkma.gov.hk/media /eng/doc/key-functions/financial-infrastructure /alternative_credit_scoring.pdf.

Hohl, Stefan, Maria Cynthia Sison, Tomas Stastny, and Raihan Zamil. 2018. "The Basel Framework in 100 Jurisdictions: Implementation Status and Proportionality Practices." FSI Insights on Policy Implementation 11, Financial Stability Institute, Bank for International Settlements, Basel, Switzerland.

Homar, Timotej. 2016. "Bank Recapitalizations and Lending: A Little Is Not Enough." ESRB Working Paper 16, European Systemic Risk Board, Frankfurt.

Homar, Timotej, and Sweder J. G. van Wijnbergen. 2017. "Bank Recapitalization and Economic Recovery after Financial Crises." *Journal of Financial Intermediation* 32 (October): 16–28.

IADI (International Association of Deposit Insurers). 2014. "IADI Core Principles for Effective Deposit Insurance Systems." IADI, Bank for International Settlements, Basel, Switzerland. https://www.iadi.org/en/assets/File /Core%20Principles/cprevised2014nov.pdf.

IMF (International Monetary Fund). 2019. "Ghana: Selected Issues Paper." IMF Country Report 19/368, IMF, Washington, DC. https://www.imf.org/en /Publications/CR/Issues/2019/12/18/Ghana-Selected -Issues-Paper-48884.

IMF (International Monetary Fund). 2020. *Global Financial Stability Report: Bridge to Recovery.* Washington, DC: IMF.

IMF (International Monetary Fund). 2021. "Ghana: Staff Report for the 2021 Article IV Consultation." IMF Country Report 2021/165, IMF, Washington, DC. https:// www.imf.org/en/Publications/CR/Issues/2021/07/23 /Ghana-2021Article-IV-Consultation-Press-Release -Staff-Report-and-Statement-by-the-462570.

IMF (International Monetary Fund) and World Bank. 2020. "COVID-19: The Regulatory and Supervisory Implications for the Banking Sector." Staff Position Note 2020/001, IMF, Washington, DC.

Jordà, Òscar, Moritz Schularick, and Alan M. Taylor. 2013. "When Credit Bites Back." *Journal of Money, Credit, and Banking* 45 (s2): 3–28.

Kongsamut, Piyabha, Dermot Monaghan, and Luc Riedweg. 2021. "Unwinding COVID-19 Policy Interventions for Banking Systems." Special Series on COVID-19, Monetary and Capital Markets Department, International Monetary Fund, Washington, DC.

Kulkarni, Nirupama, S. K. Ritadhi, Siddharth Vij, and Katherine P. Waldock. 2021. "Unearthing Zombies." Economics Discussion Paper 59, Ashoka University, Sonepat, Haryana, India.

Levy Yeyati, Eduardo, Alejandro Micco, and Ugo Panizza. 2007. "A Reappraisal of State-Owned Banks." *Economía* 7 (2): 209–47.

Lindgren, Carl-Johan, Tomás J. T. Baliño, Charles Enoch, Anne-Marie Gulde, Marc Quintyn, and Leslie Teo. 1999. "Financial Sector Crisis and Restructuring: Lessons from Asia." Occasional Paper 188, International Monetary Fund, Washington, DC. https://www.imf.org /external/pubs/ft/op/opfinsec/index.htm.

Medas, Paulo, and Elif Ture. 2020. "Public Banks' Support to Households and Firms." Special Series on Fiscal Policies to Respond to COVID-19, Fiscal Affairs, International Monetary Fund, Washington, DC.

Müller, Karsten, and Emil Verner. 2021. "Credit Allocation and Macroeconomic Fluctuations." Paper presented at Federal Reserve Bank of Cleveland and the Office of Financial Research Virtual Conference, "Financial Stability: Planning for Surprises, Learning from Crises," November 17–19, 2021.

NBS (National Bank of Serbia). 2015. *Annual Financial Stability Report, 2015.* Belgrade, Serbia: NBS. https://nbs .rs/export/sites/NBS_site/documents-eng/publikacije /fs/fsr_2015.pdf.

NBS (National Bank of Serbia). 2021. "Quarterly Review of the Dynamics of Financial Stability Indicators for the Republic of Serbia: Third Quarter 2021." https://www .nbs.rs/export/sites/NBS_site/documents-eng /finansijska-stabilnost/pregled_grafikona_e.pdf.

Nolte, Jan Philipp, and David Hoelscher. 2020. "Using the FSB Key Attributes to Design Bank Resolution Frameworks for Non-FSB Members: Proportionality and Implementation Challenges." Working paper, Finance, Competitiveness, and Innovation Insight: Financial Stability and Integrity Series, World Bank, Washington, DC.

Panizza, Ugo. 2021. "State-Owned Commercial Banks." CEPR Discussion Paper DP16259, Centre for Economic Policy Research, London.

Peek, Joe, and Eric S. Rosengren. 2005. "Unnatural Selection: Perverse Incentives and the Misallocation of Credit in Japan." *American Economic Review* 95 (4): 1144–66.

RBI (Reserve Bank of India). 2016. "RBI Releases June 2016 Financial Stability Report." Press release, June 28, 2016.

https://rbi.org.in/Scripts/BS_PressReleaseDisplay .aspx?prid=37342.

Reinhart, Carmen M., and Kenneth S. Rogoff. 2009a. "The Aftermath of Financial Crises." *American Economic Review* 99 (2): 466–72.

Reinhart, Carmen M., and Kenneth S. Rogoff. 2009b. *This Time Is Different: Eight Centuries of Financial Folly.* Princeton, NJ: Princeton University Press.

Rochet, Jean-Charles. 1992. "Capital Requirements and the Behaviour of Commercial Banks." *European Economic Review* 36 (5): 1137–70.

Sanglap, Ranina. 2021. "Indian Central Bank Takes Steps to Dampen NPL Formation amid COVID-19 Resurgence." *Banking* (blog), May 9, 2021. https://www .spglobal.com/marketintelligence/en/news-insights /latest-news-headlines/indian-central-bank-takes-steps -to-dampen-npl-formation-amid-covid-19-resurgence -63881838.

Schivardi, Fabiano, Enrico Sette, and Guido Tabellini. 2021. "Credit Misallocation during the European Financial Crisis." *Economic Journal.* Published ahead of print, April 29, 2021. https://doi.org/10.1093/ej/ueab039.

Schwert, Michael. 2018. "Bank Capital and Lending Relationships." *Journal of Finance* 73 (2): 787–830. https:// doi.org/10.1111/jofi.12604.

Tan, Yuyan, Yiping Huang, and Wing Thye Woo. 2016. "Zombie Firms and the Crowding-Out of Private Investment in China." *Asian Economic Paper* 15 (3): 32–55.

Villanueva, Joann. 2021. "Banks' NPL Ratio to Remain in Single Digit until 2022: Diokno." Philippine News Agency, September 22, 2021. https://www.pna.gov.ph /articles/1154356.

World Bank. 2012. *Global Financial Development Report 2013: Rethinking the Role of the State in Finance.* Washington, DC: World Bank.

World Bank. 2016. *A Toolkit for Out-of-Court Workouts.* Washington, DC: World Bank.

World Bank. 2018. *Global Financial Development Report 2017/2018: Bankers without Borders.* Washington, DC: World Bank.

World Bank. 2020a. "COVID-19 and Non-performing Loan Resolution in the Europe and Central Asia Region: Lessons Learned from the Global Financial Crisis for the Pandemic." FinSAC Policy Note, Financial Sector Advisory Center, World Bank, Vienna. https://pubdocs .worldbank.org/en/460131608647127680/FinSAC -COVID-19-and-NPL-Policy-NoteDec2020.pdf.

World Bank. 2020b. *Global Financial Development Report 2019/2020: Bank Regulation and Supervision a Decade after the Global Financial Crisis.* Washington, DC: World Bank. https://www.worldbank.org/en/publication/gfdr /report.

World Bank. 2021. "How Insolvency and Creditor-Debtor Regimes Can Help Address Nonperforming Loans." Equitable Growth, Finance, and Institutions Note– Finance, World Bank, Washington, DC.

World Bank and BoS (Bank of Slovenia). 2017. "Handbook for Effective Management and Workout of MSME NPLs." World Bank, Ljubljana, Slovenia. https://www .bsi.si/en/publications/other-publications/handbook -for-msme-npl-management-andworkout.

Spotlight 2.1

Strengthening the regulation and supervision of microfinance institutions

Low-income households and micro-, small, and medium enterprises (MSMEs) in emerging economies often rely on microfinance institutions (MFIs) instead of conventional banks for financial services. The microfinance sector consists of a diverse group of regulated and unregulated financial service providers.[1]

Microfinance institutions are often the sole providers of financial services to vulnerable segments of a population. They play a critical role in local economies, household resilience, and women's financial inclusion. One source suggests that up to 80 percent of MFI borrowers in emerging economies are female, and 65 percent are located in rural areas.[2] MFIs rarely become large enough to threaten the stability of the financial system when they are in financial distress. But because many MSMEs and low-income households, including very poor, hard-to-reach populations, depend on MFIs as a source of credit and as a custodian of their financial assets, the safety and soundness of the microfinance sector are critical for this population.

Effects of the pandemic on MFIs and the policy and regulatory responses

MSMEs and low-income households were affected disproportionately by the COVID-19 (coronavirus) pandemic and the ensuing containment measures. Many MFI clients, suffering significant income losses, were unable to pay loan installments. Meanwhile, some clients had no way to make payments in person during lockdowns and lacked digital payment alternatives. Moratoria were introduced to give MFI clients breathing room, while avoiding steep increases in capital buffers for MFIs, which would constrain lending.[3] At the same time, credit moratoria delayed borrower payments, which meant MFIs had less liquidity. However, this problem was to some extent mitigated by a slowdown in new disbursements on the back of weakening demand. On the whole, then, these liquidity pressures were short-lived.

Policy makers and regulators responded to the pandemic with support measures, which varied across countries and markets. Although unregulated nongovernmental organizations only benefited from broader policy measures such as fiscal support, regulated MFIs received support similar to that offered to commercial banks:[4]

- *Relief for MFI clients*, such as mandated credit moratoria or permission for MFIs to offer credit moratoria, with or without prior consent of customers; easing of loan restructuring requirements; and protection of borrowers' credit histories.
- *Relief for MFIs, lending support, and capital conservation*, such as direct liquidity support for MFIs or indirect support via creditor banks (for example, guarantee schemes); temporary changes in prudential standards, including reduction of collateral, provisioning, and risk-weighted capital requirements for small and medium enterprises (SMEs) or microfinance loans; reduction of the capital adequacy ratio, reserve requirement, liquidity ratio, leverage ratio, and minimum paid up capital; deferment or suspension of supervisory activities (MFIs have been subject to enhanced reporting of priority data); and suspension of discretionary payments (such as dividends) aimed at conserving capital.

The general thrust of these measures was to boost the sector's resilience and avoid liquidity and capital constraints that would limit MFI lending. But the measures did not always achieve those goals because support measures largely mirrored those for conventional banks and were not customized for the distinct features of microfinance portfolios[5]

and the realities of microfinance clients.[6] In some instances, measures arrived too late in view of the short-term nature of microfinance loans and the early impacts of the pandemic on low-income customers and MSMEs. Similarly, some central bank liquidity facilities that targeted MFIs imposed eligibility or collateral requirements that could not be met by MFIs.

The credit moratoria also raised consumer protection issues that may resurface as prudential challenges in the future. In many cases, missing or inadequate regulatory guidance for the use of moratoria saddled borrowers with additional debt burdens through fees and compounded interest that they did not always understand. In addition, when moratoria were lifted some deferred payments came due as a lump-sum payment that borrowers struggled to repay.[7] Some MFIs were also unprepared to follow up with each borrower and process a sudden increase in requests for loan restructuring. This led to blanket moratoria with automatic opt-ins without borrower consent and without considering the potential negative effects on borrowers, including on their credit history. Furthermore, in some cases weaknesses in internal controls led to the embezzlement of unsolicited loan disbursements by MFI staff. Finally, there was a spike in disbursements of high-cost, short-term loans by lightly regulated or unregulated lenders—loans sought by low-income clients who were unable to meet their need for immediate cash by borrowing from regulated MFIs.

The limited data and anecdotal evidence available indicate that at the onset of the pandemic there was a short-lived but dramatic drop in loan repayments and disbursements. Disbursements were made only to the best clients, or in some cases were halted altogether. Subsequently, in July 2020 reported NPLs began to increase as broad-based credit moratoria were phased out or replaced with more targeted borrower support measures (that often provided MFIs with greater discretion in

Figure S2.1.1 Credit risk ratio and restructured portfolio ratio, by size of microfinance institution and World Bank region, 2019 and 2020

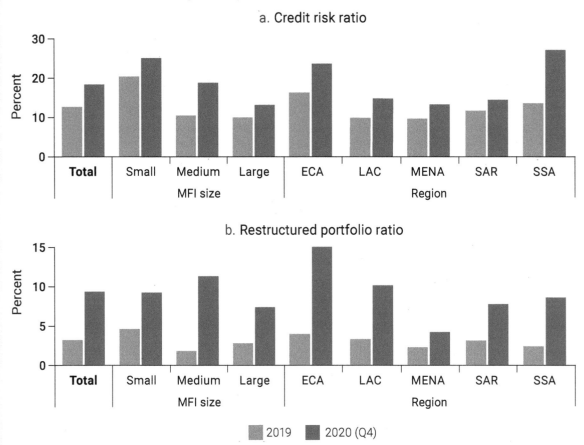

a. Credit risk ratio

b. Restructured portfolio ratio

2019 2020 (Q4)

Source: CGAP and MFR 2021. Data from MicroFinanza Rating, Atlas (dashboard), https://www.atlasdata.org/; Consultative Group to Assist the Poor, CGAP Global Pulse Survey of Microfinance Institutions (dashboard), https://www.cgap.org/pulse.
Note: Panel a: 2019 data, 375 microfinance institutions (MFIs); 2020 (Q4) data, 152 MFIs. Panel b: 2019 data, 457 MFIs; 2020 (Q4) data, 158 MFIs. The sample includes only MFIs that entered the pandemic with an above-average portfolio-at-risk 30 ratio (PAR 30—loans overdue more than 30 days) of more than 8.5 percent. The credit risk ratio is calculated as the mean of the sum of write-offs, restructured loans, and PAR 30, all divided by the average gross outstanding portfolio. ECA = Europe and Central Asia; LAC = Latin America and the Caribbean; MENA = Middle East and North Africa; SAR = South Asia Region; SSA = Sub-Saharan Africa.

terms of debtor selection and types of support measures offered).[8] The combination of slowing disbursements, rising provisioning expenditures, and ongoing fixed operational expenditures (including salaries) translated into pressures on profitability.

Figure S2.1.1 compares the credit risk ratio (panel a) and the restructured portfolio ratio (panel b) for 2019 with that for the fourth quarter of 2020 by size of MFI and by World Bank region. As economies reopened, MFIs and their clients opted for

loan restructuring or new disbursements rather than moratoria extensions. The portion of the MFI portfolio under moratoria declined from over 90 percent in March/April 2020 to around 20 percent by December 2020.[9] Although MFIs have so far weathered the pandemic better than initially expected, the situation is still fluid, and pressures on asset quality—which so far have been relatively stable—may increase as moratoria are fully lifted and restructured loans begin coming due. This may happen in the context of the continuing global impact of the pandemic and a generally uncertain economic outlook.

Regulation and supervision of MFIs

During the pandemic, the prospect of growing pressure on asset quality and solvency put a spotlight on the long-standing weaknesses in microfinance regulation and supervision. For example, large nonprofit MFIs, including deposit-takers, do not always fall within the regulatory perimeter, and they are not required to transform into companies whose ownership is organized via shares. Moreover, regulatory, resolution, and consumer protection frameworks in emerging economies are often inadequate and accompanied by underresourced supervisory functions that lack microfinance expertise and reliable data. Some of these weaknesses are rooted in the origins and structure of the microfinance sector, which is often challenging to regulate and supervise because of the sheer number of entities, their legal status, often remote locations, and underdeveloped information systems. Reforms have been overdue, and it is now time to prioritize the reform of microfinance regulation, beginning by widening the regulatory perimeter; strengthening regulatory, resolution, and consumer protection frameworks;[10] and improving supervisory capacity and data collection systems. There are also important lessons to learn from the pandemic on how to be better prepared for the next crisis by tailoring response measures such as credit moratoria to the specific needs of MFIs and their clients.

Notes

1. CGAP (2020c).
2. Convergences (2018).
3. CGAP (2020b).
4. CGAP and MFR (2021); Dias (2021).
5. BCBS (2016).
6. Dias (2021).
7. CGAP (2020a); Dias (2021).
8. CGAP and Symbiotics (2020).
9. CGAP and Symbiotics (2020).
10. A recent example is a consultative document released by the Reserve Bank of India in June 2021, which advocates harmonizing microfinance regulation for all regulated entities (RBI 2021). It also proposes revising the definition of microfinance loans and the limits applicable to such loans.

References

BCBS (Basel Committee on Banking Supervision). 2016. "Guidelines: Prudential Treatment of Problem Assets; Definitions of Non-performing Exposures and Forbearance." BCBS, Bank for International Settlements, Basel, Switzerland. https://www.bis.org/bcbs/publ/d403.htm.

CGAP (Consultative Group to Assist the Poor). 2020a. "Debt Relief in the Pandemic: Lessons from India, Peru, and Uganda." COVID-19 Briefing: Insights for Inclusive Finance, CGAP, Washington, DC. https://www.cgap.org/sites/default/files/publications/2020_12_COVID_Briefing_Debt_Relief.pdf.

CGAP (Consultative Group to Assist the Poor). 2020b. "Microfinance in the COVID-19 Crisis: A Framework for Regulatory Responses." COVID-19 Briefing: Insights for Inclusive Finance, CGAP, Washington, DC. https://www.cgap.org/sites/default/files/publications/2020_06_COVID_Briefing_Framework_Regulatory_Response.pdf.

CGAP (Consultative Group to Assist the Poor). 2020c. "Typology of Microfinance Providers (MFPs)." COVID-19 Briefing, CGAP, Washington, DC. https://www.cgap.org/sites/default/files/research_documents/2020_06_Typology_Microfinance_Providers.pdf.

CGAP (Consultative Group to Assist the Poor) and MFR (MicroFinanza Rating). 2021. "COVID-19 Impact on Financial Service Providers." Presentation at virtual meeting, World Bank, Washington, DC, June 14, 2021.

CGAP (Consultative Group to Assist the Poor) and Symbiotics. 2020. "MFIs on the Rebound, but Will It Last?" COVID-19 Briefing: Snapshot, MFIs during the Crisis, CGAP, Washington, DC. https://www.cgap.org/sites/default/files/2020-11/11-2020-COVID19-Briefing-Snapshot-MFIs-During-the-Crisis.pdf.

Convergences. 2018. *Microfinance Barometer 2019*. Paris: Convergences. https://www.convergences.org/wp-content/uploads/2019/09/Microfinance-Barometer-2019_web-1.pdf.

Dias, Denise. 2021. "Regulatory Flexibility during the Pandemic: Emerging Lessons." With contributions of Loretta Michaels. Center for Financial Inclusion, Cambridge, MA. https://www.centerforfinancialinclusion.org/regulatory-flexibility-during-the-pandemic-emerging-lessons.

RBI (Reserve Bank of India). 2021. "Consultative Document on Regulation of Microfinance." RBI, Mumbai. https://www.rbi.org.in/Scripts/PublicationsView.aspx?id=20377.

3 Restructuring firm and household debt

The COVID-19–induced economic crisis and the temporary government measures intended to protect firms and households from bankruptcy have created unprecedented opacity about the financial health of households and businesses. Some borrowers are temporarily short on liquid assets, while others are facing longer-term structural difficulties and should exit the market. The challenge, then, is sorting the illiquid from the insolvent. Historically, court-led bankruptcy systems have performed this sorting function, and so these systems are scrutinized in times of financial crisis. Effective insolvency systems can help to quickly resolve high levels of debt distress to prevent collapse of the financial sector without relying on costlier forms of policy intervention. Reforms to strengthen bankruptcy systems also improve the underlying economic conditions and so are critical to an equitable recovery. This chapter lays out a blueprint for bankruptcy reforms that will help governments manage high levels of debt distress while laying the groundwork for economic recovery.

Policy Priorities

Countries can mitigate the risk of an onslaught of insolvent households and businesses by investing in four policy reforms:

- **Strengthening formal insolvency mechanisms** so that the rules that define the rights and behaviors of debtors and creditors are in place, giving each an incentive to negotiate and come to an agreement, whether in court or out of court.

- **Facilitating alternative dispute resolution systems such as conciliation and mediation** to enable faster and cheaper resolution of disputes than in the formal court system, but with some of the rigor that courts provide.

- **Establishing accessible and inexpensive in-court and out-of-court debt resolution procedures for micro-, small, and medium enterprises** to facilitate the recapitalization of viable but illiquid firms and the swift, efficient market exit of nonviable firms. Rules designed for small entities can help resolve their debts more quickly and cheaply with less burden on the judicial system than requiring the same rules regardless of firm size.

- **Promoting debt forgiveness and discharge of natural person debtors** so that solo entrepreneurs and individuals unable to pay their debts—through no fault of their own—can be discharged of those debts and more quickly move on from them, avoiding the stigma and loss of productivity that come from long-term debt distress.

Introduction

Building on chapter 2 on financial institutions, this chapter looks at the consumers of finance—households and firms—and especially at the insolvency systems countries can use in facilitating an equitable recovery from the COVID-19 (coronavirus) economic crisis. Those systems—debt enforcement laws and their institutional framework—are essential to achieving recovery. The reforms highlighted in this chapter, informed by the World Bank's "Principles for Effective Insolvency and Creditor/Debtor Regimes" and the "Legislative Guide on Insolvency Law" issued by the United Nations Commission on International Trade Law (UNCITRAL),[1] focus on mechanisms for restructuring or discharging debt.

Effective debt resolution, which these reforms facilitate, can contribute to economic growth and contain the wider economic impact of business distress. In addition to establishing fairness for debtors by providing a pathway out of perpetual indebtedness, well-functioning insolvency systems can spur future innovation and economic growth by freeing up capital for lending to new and productive enterprises. To deliver on this potential, insolvency systems have to find an effective balance between the need, on the one hand, to address individual instances of overindebtedness and, on the other, to discourage borrowers from engaging in unnecessary risk-taking.

Why should anyone care about insolvency systems?

Financial crises typically draw attention to insolvency systems because they are an effective way to manage and reduce high rates of nonperforming loans (NPLs).[2] However, this ex post argument for strong insolvency systems is accompanied by an ex ante justification for pursuing insolvency reforms as well.[3] Improvements in insolvency systems are associated with greater access to credit,[4] improved creditor recovery, strengthened job preservation,[5] higher productivity,[6] and lower failure rates for small businesses.[7] Cost-reducing reforms can also create the right conditions for nonviable firms to file for liquidation,[8] which can help resolve the problem of so-called zombie firms, discussed shortly. In short, the rationale for reforms to strengthen insolvency frameworks in the COVID-19 era is a mix of crisis management and recovery planning.

This chapter highlights the positive benefits of insolvency systems (a primer on those systems appears in box 3.1). But it is also important to recognize the risks of maintaining the status quo for those countries lacking sound insolvency systems. One characteristic of inadequate insolvency frameworks is the lengthy processes that can reduce the returns to creditors because of the costs of recovery proceedings

Box 3.1 A short primer on the insolvency process

Despite differences in insolvency frameworks across countries, most involve a contractual relationship between a firm or individual (the debtor) and one or more creditors. This relationship can be for the provision of goods and services (such as utilities or suppliers), labor (such as employees), or debt financing (such as lenders). In most jurisdictions, a debtor will be insolvent under the law if it is unable to meet one or more of its contractual obligations in the ordinary course of business or if the total of the debtor's assets is less than the total of its liabilities. If a debtor company becomes insolvent under the law, the debtor or the creditor (in some jurisdictions) can seek a court order declaring that the company is to cease operations and its assets are to be sold to repay, to the extent

(Box continues next page)

Box 3.1 **A short primer on the insolvency process** *(continued)*

possible, what creditors are owed (also known as liquidation).

An alternative to liquidation is restructuring a company's affairs so it can continue to operate and meet its debt obligations (or meet altered obligations to which the creditors agree or are required to accept). Restructuring typically occurs in circumstances in which the alternative is liquidation, and it can occur either before or after court liquidation is sought. Identification of the assets and obligations of the debtor is required for both liquidation and restructuring to determine how to proceed.

Liquidation and restructuring are collective processes. They are designed to address a situation in which a debtor is no longer able to pay its creditors. Both liquidation and restructuring provide a mechanism for the equitable treatment of all creditors—that is, they avoid a race to the bottom in which individual creditors seek to enforce their own contractual rights.[a]

These processes vary across countries. They may be implemented by an insolvency practitioner, who is tasked with administering such formal insolvency procedures. Depending on the jurisdiction, the insolvency practitioner may operate under a license granted by their country's insolvency authority.

The outcomes of liquidation and restructuring are different. In liquidation, the business is eventually deregistered. In restructuring, the ultimate aim is for the business to resume normal operations. Components of restructuring can include debt forgiveness, debt rescheduling, debt equity conversions, or sale of the business (or parts of it) as a going concern. Failed restructuring can ultimately result in liquidation.

Three additional mechanisms can augment a typical insolvency framework. First, early warning tools can detect or predict a borrower's inability to repay its debts before that inability arises. Second, credit reporting frameworks serve as a classification system for borrowers' inability to meet their debt obligations. They are most relevant in the period after default, but before engaging the court. Third, out-of-court workout options can prevent liquidation using varying degrees of court or noncourt supervision. They can be instituted at any time between failure to pay and liquidation, with some technical limitations on what can be negotiated once the court is involved.

Figure B3.1.1 depicts the key elements of the insolvency process in a timeline format.

Figure B3.1.1 **Insolvency process timeline**

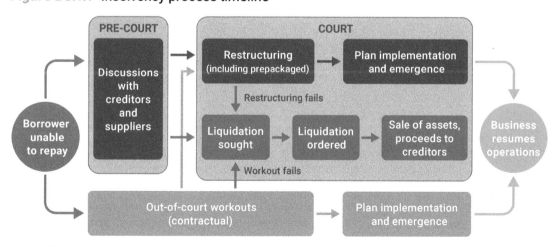

Source: WDR 2022 team.

a. IMF (1999).

and deterioration of the value of underlying assets. Long processes also delay the redeployment of capital tied up in nonviable firms to viable businesses and productive sectors.

Nonviable zombie firms[9] generate enough income to repay interest on outstanding debts but not enough to repay the outstanding debt balance. They drain productivity from the economy by absorbing resources that would produce better returns if they were used to finance healthier businesses.[10] The relationship between insolvency systems and zombie firms is supported by empirical findings that higher barriers to restructuring are associated with "zombie congestion" in high-turnover industries and with a lower ability to attract capital.[11] Effective insolvency systems reduce such barriers.

Restructuring and forcing the market exit of zombie firms have significant political economy dimensions. Most important are the jobs lost by the employees of restructured or liquidated companies. Complicating matters further, in the present crisis it is very difficult to distinguish between liquid and illiquid firms because even healthy firms have experienced a temporary collapse in liquidity.[12] The COVID-19 emergency government measures aimed at preventing widespread business collapse have made this identification process even murkier.

This difficulty was of little consequence in the short term because propping up both zombie firms and viable firms likely produced economic benefits in the form of continued employment for workers at zombie firms at a time when new job opportunities were severely limited. However, over the longer term government measures that inhibit the exit of zombie firms should be removed, while recognizing that these actions may create other challenges. For example, simplifying the liquidation or restructuring process for nonviable companies may produce rapid job losses in certain sectors, even as it creates higher returns for creditors and releases more value into the economy. At scale, however, delaying liquidation or restructuring of zombie firms because of fears of job losses may be counterproductive. Actual job losses may also be less than feared: empirical evidence suggests that zombie firms tend to use loans to build up cash reserves instead of contributing to economic activity through hiring or spending.[13]

The absence of effective insolvency frameworks especially hurts small businesses and individuals. Without a working framework for restructuring debts, businesses experiencing a temporary inability to repay their loans are more likely to have to exit the market.[14] Sole proprietors in countries that subject the proprietors to personal bankruptcy regimes may face the threat of a lifetime of debt because of the unavailability of discharge (cancellation of debt).[15] Small and medium enterprises (SMEs), particularly unincorporated enterprises where the line between individual and business is blurred,[16] are inherently more vulnerable to insolvency because of their informality, low operating margins, and constrained access to credit (see spotlight 3.1 for a discussion of the microfinance institutions overcoming this constraint). SMEs are widespread in emerging economies, where the challenges of inadequate insolvency regimes are more pronounced.[17]

Countries that lack effective bankruptcy frameworks have limited options for dealing with high NPL levels other than blunt public intervention. Governments may be forced to turn to borrower bailouts (in which the cost is borne by the taxpayer, insulating creditors) or bail-ins (in which the cost is borne by the creditor, insulating debtors and the taxpayer).[18] For some industries or in some circumstances, these approaches may be desirable,[19] but they come with substantial risks.

Studies of borrower bailouts suggest that the short-term benefits of debt relief come with long-term costs. In particular, future borrowers may be more likely to engage in a strategic default in the belief that they will not have to repay, and creditors may, in turn, respond by restricting access to credit. Although some studies have found that debt relief programs can have positive welfare effects and lead to positive outcomes in certain cases,[20] research indicates that, overall, the risk of future strategic loan default rises, especially among previously "good" borrowers, and there are no improvements in real outcomes.[21]

A study of debt relief in India in the wake of the global financial crisis found a subsequent increase in strategic default and a decrease in new lending to the sectors that were bailed out.[22] Another study of a mortgage modification program for delinquent borrowers in the United States revealed that announcement of the program was followed immediately by a 10 percent relative increase in delinquencies, predominantly attributable to new delinquencies among borrowers otherwise deemed least likely to default.[23] Other studies showed the same—that previously "good," or nondistressed, borrowers were more likely to strategically default or take longer to repay their loans after a bailout.[24] Risks emerge for the political economy of credit as well. In India, defaults were found to be sensitive to the electoral cycle, and the pattern was magnified after the bailout.[25] Furthermore, borrowers who are angrier about the economic situation, who trust banks less, and who want to see more banking regulation are more likely to default strategically. Borrowers are more willing to default as knowledge of others defaulting and media coverage of the same become more widespread.[26]

Ad hoc bailouts, as opposed to those conducted systematically, put governments in the position of picking winners—a skill they usually lack. The problems are compounded for emerging economies because there is less budget flexibility for bailouts.[27] The moral hazard risk may be exacerbated in jurisdictions in which declaring bankruptcy is not a viable alternative or even an option in the current legal framework.[28] Bail-ins, by contrast, are likely to increase the risk of financial sector collapse and may result in reduced future lending.[29]

International best practice, empirical research, and lessons from previous high-profile financial crises point to four critical areas for legal reform of insolvency: (1) strengthen formal insolvency mechanisms; (2) facilitate alternative dispute resolution systems such as conciliation and mediation; (3) establish accessible, inexpensive liquidation, in-court, and out-of-court procedures for micro-, small, and medium enterprises (MSMEs);[30] and (4) promote debt forgiveness and discharge of natural person debtors. The remaining sections of this chapter address these four areas and elaborate on how to manage the expected increases in nonperforming loans in a way that enables an efficient and effective recovery.

Strengthening formal insolvency mechanisms

A strong formal insolvency law regime is critical to the successful functioning of an insolvency system with both formal and informal options. Strong formal regimes have default rules and boundaries within which creditors and debtors can mediate or otherwise negotiate debt outside, but "in the shadow" of, formal insolvency law.[31] Participants in out-of-court processes know how their case would be treated in the in-court system and behave accordingly. Furthermore, if out-of-court bargaining fails, participants have recourse to the formal system. A strong formal system thus creates the right incentives and defines the rights and behaviors needed to make both in-court and out-of-court workouts orderly, which, in turn, spurs innovation and economic growth, as articulated in the introduction to this chapter.

Both debtors and creditors should have incentives to engage with the insolvency system and participate in good-faith negotiations. For creditors, the key incentives of a strong insolvency system include the possibility of negotiating an out-of-court debt restructuring plan that may yield a greater return than a forced liquidation. Effective insolvency systems also enable creditors to feel secure in their rights. Thus rather than resort to a unilateral approach, they are willing to coordinate with other creditors in the expectation that coordination will maximize returns.

A strong insolvency regime creates incentives to negotiate a debt restructuring plan in good faith. Creditors may make concessions, and the plan may open a path to the continued operation and turnaround of the indebted business. In regimes in which management loses control of the business once the company enters administration, debtor companies may prefer to negotiate out of court to avoid losing control of their business. If the court system provides an avenue for creditor recourse, debtors are also less likely to misbehave by using out-of-court processes to stall or defer repayment.

For these reasons, functioning insolvency laws underpin the reforms recommended in this chapter. No one-size-fits-all model will work in all jurisdictions and all circumstances. However, strong formal insolvency systems exhibit the following characteristics: (1) predictable creditor priority rules; (2) timely resolution of insolvency proceedings; and (3) strong, accessible bankruptcy expertise among private practitioners and government officials.

These three characteristics warrant particular attention because they are versatile—they can be implemented or improved within the multitude of extant frameworks worldwide—and there is empirical support to suggest they can improve the efficiency of insolvency regimes. These characteristics are generally achieved by writing formal legal requirements into legislation, combined with the ongoing efforts of adequately resourced institutions. For example, strict court deadlines written into an insolvency law to speed up the insolvency process may not work if there are not enough judges to hear cases within the specified time frame. These characteristics are an important part of the World Bank's "Principles for Effective Insolvency and Creditor/Debtor Regimes" and will be especially important in navigating the post–COVID-19 recovery.

Role of the judiciary in the insolvency process

A country typically relies on its judicial system to play a critical role in the insolvency process because of the legal and procedural complexity of the issues and the need to balance the interests of debtors, creditors (including employees), and the public at large. Even in well-functioning judicial systems, the time between an application for liquidation and the final distribution of funds to creditors can take years, particularly for large companies with complex affairs. For example, in Australia insolvency proceedings launched in 1991 for one set of companies were finally resolved in 2020. The main trial was held between July 2003 and September 2006, consuming 404 days of court time. The 26,430-page judgment was drafted over two years.[32]

Clearly, then, insolvencies can place heavy demands on court resources and time. Improving the legal capacity to manage insolvency is therefore critical to economic recovery. A sudden rise in NPLs is likely to strain even the most sophisticated, well-resourced, and well-structured judiciary[33] because insolvency court cases require technical specialization and expertise.[34] Without reforms to simplify and scale the process, judiciaries are likely to experience a case backlog, resulting in further delays.

Countries cannot afford the delay. Longer court cases can reduce the value of assets and the ultimate recovery rate for creditors. Systemically, low recovery rates for creditors reduce the availability of credit within an economy and raise its cost.[35] Weak enforcement, or the perception of weak enforcement, that may arise from backlogs can lead to late payments. They, in turn, can create further insolvencies for businesses connected within supply chains.[36]

Characteristics of strong insolvency frameworks

1. Predictable creditor priority rules

Insolvency systems should provide clear, predictable rules of priority when there are competing claims for or interests in the same assets.[37] Such rules facilitate an orderly process if a debtor is unable to repay its debts, and they increase the appeal of a jurisdiction where investors have greater certainty about what will happen if the debtor fails to repay. Clear priority rules also benefit other aspects of insolvency frameworks. In particular, for out-of-court resolution to work effectively in the shadow of the law, parties must know their rights and how their claims would be treated if they go to court.

Jurisdictions differ widely in their priority rules, in the balance between debtor and creditor rights, and in the domestic policy choices and frameworks that underpin different approaches. For example, some jurisdictions treat employee entitlements as having no priority in the order of repayment, whereas others give employees the highest priority. These matters are important policy and political choices for governments that may be influenced by other factors such as the existence of social safety nets for particular groups. Some frameworks give secured creditors absolute priority, while others give creditors that provide an illiquid business with fresh financing higher priority than preexisting creditors.[38]

Notwithstanding these variations, predictability can play an important stabilizing role in credit markets. A clear priority order that remains the same before and after the onset of insolvency proceedings increases predictability and fairness, which can, in turn, increase the availability and lower the cost of credit. On the other hand, the absence of clarity and predictability decreases the availability and increases the cost of credit because creditors factor the uncertainty into their decision-making or restrict their lending within a jurisdiction. If the law is not clear and predictable (such as on the relative position of creditors), parties may also exploit the court system. For example, creditors may unilaterally seek liquidation of a viable business, and debtors may seek to delay debt repayment or stall on relinquishing control of their business. In the 1994 Mexican tequila crisis, systemic financial sector weaknesses, including those in the bankruptcy law, prolonged and frustrated repeated government efforts to stabilize and reduce NPLs. Ultimately, from a high of 30–45 percent in 2002, NPL rates only began to decline meaningfully one year after comprehensive insolvency reforms were adopted. Around the same time, domestic credit began to rise again as a share of the gross domestic product (GDP) after having bottomed out at 12 percent in 2001 (see online annex 3A).[39]

2. Timely resolution

Reducing the amount of time needed to satisfy creditors after the filing for insolvency in court is a common target for reform because of the benefits of moving faster.[40] Timely resolution of insolvency proceedings correlates strongly with higher returns to all creditors[41] and allows the rapid redeployment of capital from unproductive to productive enterprises.[42] In this way, timely resolution creates a positive feedback loop that motivates all actors to engage in out-of-court workouts, confident that, should the situation escalate, in-court options are available and efficient.

One method commonly used by governments to resolve insolvency proceedings is the imposition of time limits for some stages in the process. Many jurisdictions temporarily extended these time limits in the context of COVID-19 either through legislation or through a more lenient approach in the courts. For example, Australia extended the response time to a bankruptcy notice from 21 days to six months.[43] In Mauritius in November 2020, the Supreme Court granted the administrators of Air Mauritius a long extension (seven months) to hold a watershed meeting.[44] Extensions like these should be phased out as the recovery continues to prevent the perpetuation of zombie firms and facilitate the reallocation of capital from nonviable to viable firms (see chapter 1).

Divergent views among creditors are another source of delay. These can be managed with measures that (with a court order) allow restructuring agreements to proceed without the support of all creditors. In a "cramdown," the majority of a creditor class binds the minority in that class. In a "cross-class cramdown," a majority in a creditor class binds a minority in other creditor classes. The United States has cramdown mechanisms in place,[45] and they were recently introduced in the United Kingdom.[46] Momentum is growing for their introduction in other jurisdictions as well[47]—in some cases unrelated to the COVID-19 pandemic.

Institutional capacity reforms can also speed up the insolvency process by clearing backlogs and increasing efficiency within the courts. For example, in Indonesia a judicial reform program enacted in the aftermath of the Asian financial crisis helped to reduce the time needed to conclude SME insolvency from 72 months in 2004 to 13 months in 2012.[48] Among other reforms, responsibility for administration of the courts was transferred from the executive to the judicial branch; a centralized unit was established for judicial training and development; and commercial court judges with jurisdiction over insolvency cases received insolvency-specific training. Similarly, reforms to Chile's insolvency law in 2014 included a requirement for insolvency law training for civil judges dealing with insolvency proceedings. As a result, the time to resolve insolvency dropped from 3.2 years in 2014 to 2 years in 2018. The improvements in various metrics in India also demonstrate the value of institutional reforms like these, which are especially important to address the anticipated increase in judicial caseloads described earlier in this chapter. Ongoing research and experimentation by the World Bank's Data and Evidence for Justice Reform (DE JURE) project have pointed to the potential for improving the efficiency of judicial decision-making through the use of data-based performance metrics (see online annex 3B).[49]

3. Expertise in bankruptcy

Expert practitioners, judges, and regulators are key to the success of well-designed insolvency legislation. Insolvency is a technical field at the intersection of law, finance, and policy. The availability of workable valuation estimates of a business and its property is fundamental for avoiding a sell-off, if reorganization is intended. For judges, insolvency presents complex legal and factual matrixes. Countries attempting to develop these sorts of capacities should strive to develop sustainable institutional capacity, including through ongoing training. Also critical are systems to oversee and regulate private bankruptcy professionals, particularly in a crisis, when the opportunities for bankruptcy fraud and abuse of power are greater.

With this in mind, many economies have embarked on reforms to bolster the capacity of their judiciaries. Some have sought insolvency-specific reforms, while others have aimed to boost capacity generically (which will nonetheless have benefits in the insolvency space). In Brazil, the National Justice Council introduced standardized procedures for judicial reorganization proceedings during the COVID-19 pandemic.[50] Spain announced its intention to create 100 additional judicial units within three years.[51] Similarly, many countries have pursued or are pursuing judicial capacity-building programs in collaboration with the World Bank Group. These training programs educate judges about insolvency law, as well as about practical aspects of their work such as case management and drafting judgments. Digitalization is also increasing. For example, Nigeria has announced measures to deploy digital facilities to enable taking evidence and alternative dispute-resolution filing.[52]

Beyond technical capacity, an effective insolvency regime requires stakeholder commitment. In the aftermath of the 1997 Asian financial crisis, the impact of insolvency reforms was limited by a "culture of non-payment" that, according to a report by the Organisation for Economic Co-operation and Development (OECD), prevailed in the affected countries.[53] That culture emerged because borrowers rarely faced consequences when they failed to repay their loans. To prevent this type of situation, countries must embed specific rules in their broader legal, economic, political, and social contexts, and insolvency judges and practitioners must have access to the training needed to abide by and enforce the rules correctly.

The institutional framework for insolvency includes courts and enforcement agencies, collateral registry and credit reporting systems, insolvency regulators, and insolvency practitioners. It requires judges able to interpret the law and manage caseloads. It also requires professionals (liquidators, administrators, receivers, conservators, and legal advisers) who have the technical ability to discharge their obligations to the court effectively.[54] In many cases, these bankruptcy professionals play a critical role in an efficient bankruptcy system. In many countries, they can be a key determinant of the speed of a reorganization. The presence of professionals with skills in these areas will increase the efficacy of the reforms discussed in the balance of this chapter because they will provide the solid formal legal foundation needed to facilitate out-of-court resolution of creditor-debtor disputes. Box 3.2 describes the comprehensive efforts in India to strengthen its institutional insolvency framework.

In 2016, India overhauled its business and personal insolvency law framework, the Insolvency and Bankruptcy Code 2016 (IBC). It was then updated in 2018, 2019, 2020, and 2021.[a] The consolidated national law is designed to address the fragmentation of the previous regime, which made it difficult for firms and individuals to understand their rights. Prior to the overhaul, there were different rules for the rescue or rehabilitation of industrial companies and other businesses,[b] different recovery powers for financial institutions and other creditors,[c] and different rules for personal insolvency that varied by region.[d] As a result of this patchwork of arrangements, many different court jurisdictions heard insolvency proceedings. And the time needed to conclude insolvency was, on average, 4.3 years,[e] which allowed debtors to avoid repaying or restructuring debts for long periods without consequences.[f]

In addition to the changes in the legal framework,[g] the 2016 reforms took significant steps toward establishing insolvency expertise and specialization within the judiciary and the insolvency profession and redressing the issues just described. The IBC established the Insolvency and Bankruptcy Board of India (IBBI) to administer the law as well as to accredit and supervise insolvency professionals. The National Company Law Tribunal was designated the sole court with jurisdiction over first-instance corporate insolvency proceedings.[h] Meanwhile, the number of registered insolvency professionals steadily expanded, from 1,812 at the end of 2018 to 3,309 at the end of 2020.[i]

Early evidence suggests that the reforms have had numerous positive effects. The overall recovery rate for creditors increased from $.27 on the dollar before reforms to $.72 on the dollar in 2020, and the time needed to settle insolvency more than halved in that period, from 4.3 years to 1.6 years. Case backlog remains an issue (figure B3.2.1) and is the subject of an ongoing reform effort.[j]

Figure B3.2.1 **Insolvency backlog in India, 2018–20**

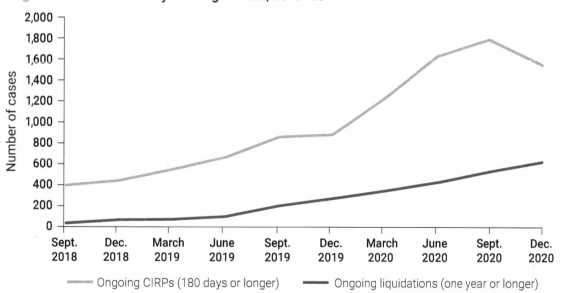

Source: Insolvency and Bankruptcy Board of India, *Quarterly Newsletter*, various, https://www.ibbi.gov.in/publication?title=quarterly&date=.

Note: Corporate Insolvency Resolution Process (CIRP) arrangements are meant to be finalized within 180 days.

(Box continues next page)

In response to COVID-19, India temporarily amended the business and personal insolvency law. Most significantly, it suspended creditors' ability to initiate insolvency proceedings on the basis of defaults arising between March 25, 2020, and March 24, 2021.[k] It also raised the minimum default requirement for the purposes of corporate insolvency to ₹1 crore (10 million rupees) from Rs 1 lakh (to about $130,000 from about $1,300).[l] In April 2021, the government permanently amended the IBC to include a framework for insolvency for MSMEs, which may help prevent a further backlog and delays by easing the demand for the Corporate Insolvency Resolution Process (CIRP), a restructuring framework.[m]

a. Insolvency and Bankruptcy Code (Amendment) Ordinance(s), 2018, 2019, 2020, and 2021.
b. The Sick Industrial Companies (Special Provisions) Act (SICA) 1985 governed industrial companies.
c. Recovery of Debt Due to Banks and Financial Institutions Act (RDDBFI) 1993.
d. The two laws were the Presidency Towns Insolvency Act 1909 and the Provincial Insolvency Act 1920.
e. World Bank (2014a).
f. BLRC (2015).
g. For further analysis of these changes, see World Bank (2020, 54).
h. And for appeals, the National Company Law Appellate Tribunal and subsequently the Supreme Court of India.
i. IBBI (2020).
j. Shikha and Shahi (2021).
k. Insolvency and Bankruptcy Code (Amendment) Ordinance, 2021.
l. PIB (2020).
m. Amendments are carried out through the Insolvency and Bankruptcy Code (Amendment) Ordinance, 2021. See PIB (2021).

Early warning tools

Systems for detecting and responding to potential insolvencies before they arise are important to strengthen insolvency frameworks. The earlier a debtor perceives financial difficulties, the higher is the probability of avoiding insolvency.[55] Similarly, if the viability of a business is permanently impaired, the liquidation process will be more orderly and efficient the earlier it begins. For these reasons, policy makers are increasingly aware of the importance of alerting businesses to upcoming troubles, especially in the European Union after the introduction of the Restructuring Directive in 2019.[56]

An early warning tool (EWT) is a means of helping businesses detect financial difficulties so they can be addressed proactively. Within this broad definition, EWTs may take many different forms, ranging from purely internal control systems involving corporate bodies to external control systems that rely on the intervention of third-party experts.

The French alert procedure,[57] which relies on the workers' council and corporate auditors to alert the debtor's managers of upcoming difficulties, is a well-known example of an internal control system. Of external systems, the Danish approach is among the most developed, leveraging an algorithm run by the Danish Business Authority that detects companies potentially at risk. At-risk companies are then referred to a network of restructuring consultants who advise the debtor.

Until recently, EWTs were typically designed to alert creditors and public authorities about the upcoming distress of corporate and special debtors. However, EWTs now focus on debtors to enable them to take early action. Although this tool is aimed at serving all debtors that engage in economic activities, EWTs are likely to be particularly useful for SMEs because those facing financial difficulties often do not have the resources they need to cope with high restructuring costs, such as advisers who can prevent or mitigate the effects of insolvency.

Strong insolvency frameworks in the context of COVID-19 recovery

In addition to the financial measures adopted to staunch the worst of the damage from the COVID-19 economic crisis, many governments undertook temporary legal changes in their insolvency frameworks. According to a joint World Bank/INSOL International survey spanning both advanced and emerging economies, 67 of the 69 surveyed economies enacted some insolvency reforms in 2020.[58] The purpose of the reforms was to "flatten the curve" of insolvencies by creating breathing room for businesses, individuals, and financial institutions and preventing widespread economic collapse.

The most common reforms were relaxing debt repayment requirements (80 percent); placing moratoria on the initiation of insolvency proceedings by creditors (43 percent); and altering or temporarily suspending the obligations of directors and firm managers to enter insolvency proceedings in circumstances in which they ordinarily would be required to do so (30 percent). Relaxed debt repayment requirements included measures addressing borrowers' diminished ability to make payments, such as moratoria on or extensions of loan repayment terms (about 34 percent); measures addressing the effects of nonpayment, such as prohibiting the acceleration of contractual terms (about 55 percent); suspension of judicial proceedings (about 28 percent); and suspension of the execution of certain debtor-owned assets (about 4 percent).

In 2021, the World Bank designed a survey to identify the characteristics of corporate debt restructuring frameworks, as well as the types of insolvency-related COVID-19 emergency measures that jurisdictions had introduced.[59] The World Bank team worked with INSOL International and the International Association of Insolvency Regulators to distribute the survey.[60] Experienced insolvency professionals in 135 economies were contacted, and at least three independent contributors were contacted in 100 jurisdictions. Responses were forthcoming from 114 economies, including multiple responses from 71 percent of those economies. The survey found that OECD economies introduced measures to stymie debtor (57 percent) or creditor (54 percent) bankruptcy filings more frequently than non-OECD economies (24 percent and 17 percent, respectively). By contrast, debt repayment emergency measures (that is, those contract modification measures addressing either the prospects of repayment or the effects of nonpayment) as well as suspension of judicial procedures were more evenly distributed.[61] This finding is consistent with the fact that advanced economies tend to have more robust insolvency systems and insolvency usage.

Most of the insolvency-related emergency measures introduced after the onset of the pandemic included sunset clauses determining the timing for winding them down. Although many of these measures were extended (and they may be further extended or even reintroduced), a clear picture has emerged of their duration. Debt repayment measures, preventing the crystallization of insolvency, were estimated to have the longest duration—on average, 451 days or about 15 months.[62] Three-quarters of economies wound down debt repayment measures within 600 days, though in one country a measure was set to last 1,035 days. Suspension of judicial procedures measures was much shorter-lived—on average, 273 days. Three-quarters of the economies studied halted these measures in just over 400 days. As for measures to increase barriers to creditor-initiated insolvency filings, they lasted 384 days, on average, with three-quarters of the economies winding down these measures within 550 days. Finally, measures to avoid forcing debtors to file for bankruptcy lasted, on average, 324 days, with three-quarters of the economies drawing these measures to a close in just under 500 days. All in all, only a

Figure 3.1 Share of enterprises in arrears or expecting to fall into arrears within six months, selected countries, May–September 2020

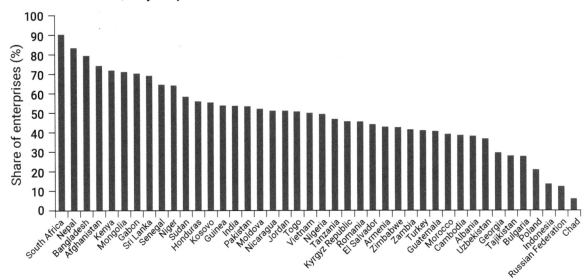

Source: Apedo-Amah et al. 2020, based on World Bank, COVID-19 Business Pulse Survey Dashboard, 2020–21 data, https://www.worldbank.org/en/data/interactive/2021/01/19/covid-19-business-pulse-survey-dashboard.
Note: The figure presents percentages for countries surveyed by the World Bank.

few of the insolvency-related emergency measures introduced in the context of COVID-19 were expected to remain in place at the end of 2021.

As governments ease short-term support measures, experts expect to see an increase in COVID-19–related business and personal insolvencies stemming in no small part from widespread business distress (see figure 3.1). The International Monetary Fund (IMF), the Bank for International Settlements, and others predicted that beginning in 2020 business insolvencies would exceed pre–COVID-19 levels by 20–35 percent.[63]

Facilitating alternative dispute resolution systems such as conciliation and mediation

Alternative dispute resolution (ADR) systems will be an essential mechanism for economies seeking to emerge stronger after the COVID-19 pandemic. Effective ADR frameworks allow quicker and cheaper resolution of disputes than the formal court system, while retaining some of the rigor that courts provide.[64] ADR in the insolvency context involves direct engagement between debtor and creditors to come to a resolution about an outstanding debt. ADR is typically, but not necessarily, overseen by a third party, and any resolution is contractually binding. ADR can be initiated voluntarily by the parties or at the order of a court. Third-party mediators ideally facilitate, as opposed to actively participate in, the resolution of intercreditor differences.[65]

One of several structural obstacles to effective ADR deployment in the insolvency context is the challenge of convincing multiple parties with varied interests to agree on a resolution that is consistent with the obligations of the parties under the broader insolvency law. Before the pandemic, many countries had already introduced or were in the process of introducing schemes that sought to facilitate ADR systems that addressed these challenges (see online annex 3C). Ideally, this trend will continue in the near to medium term—a possibility that underlies the guidance offered in this section.

Aristotle would likely have found ADR preferable to in-court proceedings because "an arbitrator goes by the equity of a case, a judge by the strict law."[66] There is growing evidence that ADR can be cheaper, quicker, and more satisfactory than court proceedings.[67] In the insolvency context, out-of-court resolution of debt disputes has the added advantage of occurring confidentially, which allows participants to avoid harm from public knowledge of debt distress, including constraints on capital and supply chains.[68] Although the data on the efficacy of ADR in the context of insolvency are limited, a 2012 pilot program in the District Court of Amsterdam found that over 70 percent of cases resulted in successful solutions at greater speed and less cost when measured against the alternative—litigation.[69]

An oft-cited example of a jurisdiction with a successful insolvency ADR regime is the United Kingdom. The "London approach," a nonlegislative set of cultural norms and principles fostered by the Reserve Bank,[70] guides the manner in which creditors voluntarily and collectively approach debtor distress. It does not require a third-party mediator or a conciliator. The London approach has four key tenets: (1) creditors keep existing facilities in place and do not rush to appoint receivers; (2) reliable financial information about the debtor exists and is shared among creditors; (3) creditors work collectively to resolve the issue; and (4) the burden of debtor concessions is shared equally among creditors.[71]

Because of its informal, confidential nature, limited empirical evidence is available on the merits of the London approach. It requires significant creditor buy-in and cohesion. However, these may be lacking in jurisdictions without the requisite trust in debtors or the underlying system to enforce legal rights. For example, creditors from multiple jurisdictions may be unable or unwilling to attempt a coherent approach to the problem. Or they may be willing to make concessions only if other creditors make equivalent concessions. Thus creditors unwilling to make concessions can frustrate the process.[72]

The challenge of creditor cohesion has been addressed in some jurisdictions by mechanisms that allow, in certain circumstances, for the courts to approve (and bind creditors to) restructuring plans negotiated outside of court. The French conciliation approach consists of a two-part model toward this end. In the informal method (*mandat ad hoc*), the court appoints a representative to mediate a nonbinding resolution of the debt distress. In the semiformal method (*conciliation*), the court approves and makes binding the output of mediation.[73] In practice, debtors tend to begin within the *mandat ad hoc* framework and then proceed to *conciliation* to obtain court approval of the restructuring agreement.[74]

Several advanced economies have included variations on this model (court endorsement of out-of-court negotiations) in their COVID-19 reforms. Germany has introduced a new conciliation scheme (Stabilization and Restructuring Framework) in which the debtor can apply for a court-appointed mediator ("restructuring facilitator") to assist in negotiations with creditors for up to three months. After successful mediation, the court can confirm the agreement, which protects the participants from avoidance or liability claims.[75] The Netherlands has introduced reforms that enable debtors to offer their creditors restructuring plans outside of the formal bankruptcy procedure. If approved by a court, these plans can bind unwilling creditors (including secured creditors) to a restructuring arrangement in a cross-class cramdown.[76]

Another way of managing the problem of creditor cohesion is use of an intercreditor agreement—a contract among creditors—that sets the general rules for approaching restructuring, while allowing flexibility for individual restructuring. A recent example of this approach is Turkey's updated Framework Agreements on Financial Restructuring. Such an approach, which is in effect a co-regulatory model subject to the oversight of the regulator with a more limited role for the courts, may be attractive in jurisdictions with fewer court systems.

Poland's experience demonstrates how the adoption of out-of-court restructuring can quickly take the heat out of widespread and rising NPL levels and lay the foundation for future economic health by putting banks on a firmer footing to extend new credit. As part of a larger effort in the early 1990s to establish a market-based economy, Poland adopted the Act on Financial Restructuring of Enterprises and Banks.[77] In effect until 1996, this legal framework for insolvency was intended to supplement formal bankruptcy and liquidation proceedings when the state-owned national bank was split into nine commercial banks—a step that revealed high levels of nonperforming loans in the banks' portfolios.[78] The act empowered financial institutions to design and implement a process for restructuring enterprises through which they brokered conciliation agreements with debtors and divested NPLs on the secondary market.[79] The banks received an influx of capital to facilitate the restructuring process.[80]

By mid-1995, about 85 percent of the conciliation agreements had been finalized.[81] Common features of the agreements included debt write-offs or extensions of the payment period, more favorable terms for small creditors, and debt-for-equity swaps (in about one-third of cases). Less than 1 percent of borrowers were required to make immediate partial payments. Meanwhile, the more viable firms (23 percent) went into conciliation, while the financially weaker firms went into liquidation or court bankruptcy.

The firms that entered bank conciliation accounted for 46 percent of the debt owed at the end of 1991, reflecting the unequal distribution of debt within the economy. Overall, thanks to the Polish conciliation scheme the NPL rates of bank portfolios fell rapidly, from 31 percent in 1993 to 9 percent in 1996.[82] Loans were written down or swapped without widespread debt forgiveness,[83] leaving banks in a better position to extend new loans on market-oriented terms.

Despite these improvements, the increase in conciliation and restructuring alone failed to address the underlying problems of firm mismanagement and unprofitability. Restructuring plans did not require changes in management or operational restructuring, and less than half of firms committed to asset sales or reduction of staff. As a result, during the first two years of implementation businesses subject to conciliation saw their average operating profit decline, and few were privatized. Because MSMEs were excluded from the conciliation scheme (the threshold debt level was high, and the cost was substantial), they struggled to access credit over the course of the recovery.[84] Thus, although the adoption of legal frameworks to facilitate ADR can contribute significantly to the swift resolution of NPLs, regulators should push for workout agreements to include commitments that put businesses on a path to viability, lest they merely prolong or defer the underlying economic challenges.

Establishing accessible and inexpensive in-court and out-of-court debt resolution procedures for MSMEs

MSMEs play a critical role in economic growth and employment, particularly in emerging economies, but they have been the enterprises hardest-hit by the COVID-19 pandemic. They are more vulnerable than large enterprises to debt distress and less equipped to seek recourse in either the debt market or the legal system. It is therefore not surprising that they have shorter survival times (figure 3.2).[85] Post–COVID-19 insolvency reforms should therefore address the specific needs of MSMEs to facilitate the recapitalization of viable but illiquid firms and the swift but least painful market exit of nonviable firms. This is particularly important in emerging economies, where MSMEs represent a large proportion of total firms.[86]

Figure 3.2 Enterprise ability to survive a drop in sales, selected countries

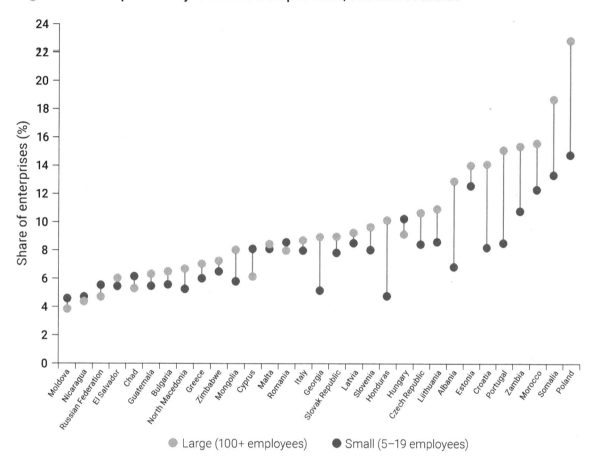

Source: World Bank, COVID-19 Business Pulse Survey Dashboard, 2020–21 data, https://www.worldbank.org/en/data/interactive/2021/01/19/covid-19-business-pulse-survey-dashboard.

Why MSME procedures matter

The World Bank's Business Pulse Survey, conducted on a rolling basis of enterprises in 50 countries, has revealed the outsize impact of the COVID-19 pandemic on MSMEs, especially microenterprises. From June to September 2020, of the firms reporting they were in arrears or expecting to be in arrears within six months, 48 percent were MSMEs (including 53 percent of microenterprises within that group), compared with only 36 percent of large enterprises (figure 3.3). Furthermore, 83 percent of MSMEs (including 84 percent of microenterprises within that group) reported lower monthly sales than in the previous year, compared with 73 percent of large enterprises (figure 3.4).

Most insolvency frameworks subject MSMEs and large companies to the same rules and processes.[87] Complexity, length, and cost are obstacles to the use of these frameworks by MSMEs.[88] In the circumstances, insolvency can be "a luxury that many MSMEs cannot afford."[89] This is a critical factor in why small enterprises are more likely than large enterprises to become zombie firms. Financially distressed small businesses with limited or no prospects for future rehabilitation continue to operate because the obstacles to liquidation are too high. Targeted insolvency frameworks could help them, while also facilitating access to credit for viable MSMEs.[90]

Figure 3.3 Share of enterprises in arrears or expecting to be in arrears within six months, June–September 2020

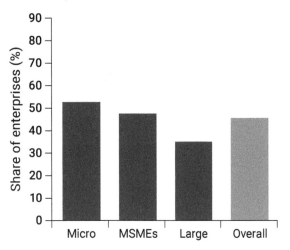

Source: World Bank, COVID-19 Business Pulse Survey Dashboard, https://www.worldbank.org/en/data/interactive /2021/01/19/covid-19-business-pulse-survey-dashboard.
Note: MSMEs = micro-, small, and medium enterprises.

Figure 3.4 Share of enterprises with lower monthly sales than in the previous year, June–September 2020

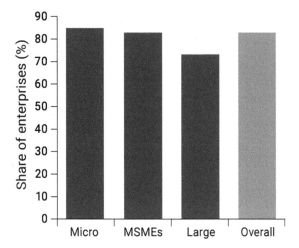

Source: World Bank, COVID-19 Business Pulse Survey Dashboard, https://www.worldbank.org/en/data/interactive /2021/01/19/covid-19-business-pulse-survey-dashboard.
Note: MSMEs = micro-, small, and medium enterprises.

Lessons learned from MSME insolvency reform during the Asian financial crisis

In the late 1990s and early 2000s, firms in Southeast Asia experienced widespread debt distress. In fact, NPL rates exceeded 40 percent in some jurisdictions (see figure 3.5). MSMEs were unable to obtain credit or were subjected to high interest rates. In Indonesia, the number of MSMEs fell by about 7 percent between 1997 and 1998 and did not return to their former level until 2000.[91] In Thailand, in 1998 a greater proportion of MSMEs (55 percent) than large enterprises (45 percent) experienced a reduction in employees.[92]

Figure 3.5 Nonperforming loans, selected Asian countries, 1998–2005

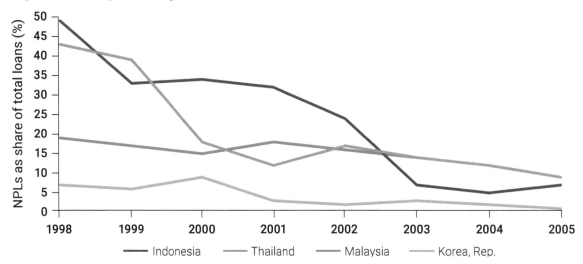

Source: Lee and Rosenkranz 2019.
Note: NPLs = nonperforming loans.

In response, countries adopted various reform measures (see online annex 3D). Of countries in Southeast Asia, Thailand's reforms resulted in the most rapid reduction in NPL rates, but there was a long tail: rates remained above 10 percent until 2005, and only 48 percent of NPLs in Thailand were resolved by mid-2003. By contrast, 77 percent of the debt referred to Malaysia's Corporate Debt Restructuring Committee was resolved by that time. In the Republic of Korea, by mid-2003 restructuring agreements were reached for about 80 percent of registered cases representing about 95 percent of total (corporate) debt. Thailand did the least to address restructuring, and it did not enforce any changes in management. Its approach can be attributed to deficiencies in the formal insolvency framework and the lack of political will to force change in large companies.[93] Echoing the experience in Poland, in Thailand the absence of substantive restructuring of large companies likely delayed resolution.

Reforms to facilitate MSME insolvency proceedings

As noted earlier, in 2017 the World Bank published a comprehensive review of MSMEs and insolvency frameworks, setting out the characteristics and requirements.[94] The 2021 "Principles for Effective Insolvency and Creditor/Debtor Regimes" and an updated version of the UNCITRAL "Legislative Guide on Insolvency Law" (see online annex 3E) together provide a series of principles and recommendations on insolvency frameworks aimed at assisting MSMEs with insolvency. Drawing on those sources, table 3.1 sets out some priority areas of reform in the context of COVID-19 recovery. It is important to note that the World Bank's "Principles" and UNCITRAL's "Guide" include significant flexibility in how a MSME insolvency framework can be achieved.

Even before the onset of the pandemic, some jurisdictions implemented reforms tailored to MSMEs. For example, in February 2020 Myanmar implemented a MSME-specific insolvency regime that included a business rescue framework under a debtor-in-possession model. In the United States, the 2019 Small Business Reorganization Act introduced a distinct insolvency framework for small enterprises. Meanwhile, the Lao People's Democratic Republic's December 2019 Enterprise Rehabilitation and Bankruptcy Law contains provisions for small enterprises.[95]

The COVID-19 crisis spurred other jurisdictions to follow suit with temporary reforms. For example, Colombia introduced a temporary fast-track restructuring framework administered by the Chamber of Commerce for MSMEs.[96] Similarly, in December 2020 Singapore introduced a temporary Simplified Insolvency Program that lowers the proportion of creditors required to approve an MSME insolvency plan,[97] which expired on July 28, 2021.[98] The United States temporarily raised the debt threshold for business restructuring (thereby increasing the accessibility of more heavily indebted businesses to restructuring) and implemented other temporary insolvency reforms. These changes were initially set to expire in 2021, but were extended to 2022.[99] Addressing obstacles to creditor recovery, New Zealand introduced the COVID-19 Response Legislation Act 2020, which put in place a business debt hibernation scheme,[100] and Spain extended the duty of administrators to request the declaration of bankruptcy, while also increasing the standard of the liquidity test.[101]

Other jurisdictions have implemented longer-term reforms in response to COVID-19. These reforms are aimed at simplifying and demystifying the bankruptcy process for small businesses. In terms of simplification, legislation pending in Chile will streamline liquidation and reorganization proceedings for small businesses.[102] And in January 2021, the United Kingdom introduced a simplified process for restructuring and liquidating small businesses. As for demystification, in 2021 Australia introduced permanent reforms that create a role for a "small business restructuring practitioner" to advise and guide MSME debtors through the various stages of restructuring: development of the plan, approval by creditors, and implementation.[103] Also in 2021, Greece implemented a simplified electronic scheme for small

Table 3.1 Principles for adapting insolvency frameworks for MSMEs

Principle	Rationale
Lower or remove documentation requirements	Inadequate record keeping can mean MSMEs, especially microenterprises, are unable to provide the required pre-filing documentation such as audited historic financial records.[a]
Keep the debtor in control of the business	Although it can increase the risk that debtors dispose of assets in a manner adverse to the creditor's interests, a debtor-in-control model makes more sense in the context of MSMEs because the owner/manager is more likely to be indispensable to the continued operation of the business. Australia, India, and the Republic of Korea are examples of jurisdictions in which MSME debtors maintain control of their business.[b]
Ensure supervision by an insolvency/restructuring practitioner	An experienced, knowledgeable practitioner could ascertain business viability faster and more affordably than a court.
Simplify plan approval mechanisms and subsidize the costs of engaging facilitators/insolvency practitioners	Measures like this are appropriate in the context of COVID-19 recovery, although policy makers should be aware of the trade-offs involved in facilitating restructuring approval at the expense of minority creditor rights. Alternative measures such as reducing the formalities involved in obtaining court approval (also part of the Singapore reforms described earlier) may be a more neutral way of simplifying restructuring plans.
Simplify procedures for the liquidation of businesses	Some jurisdictions implemented temporary fast-track liquidation schemes that removed procedural steps and evidentiary burdens and operated on a faster timetable.[c] Many of these temporary measures have since expired, revealing the need for more permanent reforms specific to small businesses, such as the removal of procedural steps, shortening time frames, and easing evidentiary burdens.
Provide access to fresh financing (including debt-to-equity financing)	Debt-to-equity financing allows MSMEs to continue operating without incurring more debt. It also gives creditors greater visibility into business operations.[d] Increased visibility may help reduce the extent to which creditors, lacking positive information, seek to liquidate viable businesses.[e] International best practice is for fresh financers to be given priority over the existing unsecured creditors, but not over secured creditors[f] because regimes that protect the absolute priority of claims increase the confidence of secured creditors.[g]
Ensure minimal or no use of the courts	Using scarce resources on court proceedings for MSMEs is inefficient. Providing ways to resolve insolvency outside court can have a large impact on managing large volumes of insolvent firms.

Sources: United Nations Commission on International Trade Law (UNCITRAL), UNCITRAL Legislative Guide on Insolvency Law (dashboard), https://uncitral.un.org/en/texts/insolvency/legislativeguides/insolvency_law; World Bank 2021c.

Note: MSMEs = micro-, small-, and medium enterprises.

a. World Bank (2017).

b. For Australia, see, for example, Corporations Amendment (Corporate Insolvency Reforms) Act 2020 (Cth); Frydenberg (2020). For India, see, for example, Sen (2020). A case study on this aspect of Korea's insolvency law appears in World Bank (2017). In India, the Pre-Packaged Insolvency Resolution Process for MSMEs, which keeps the debtors in possession, is an option only for the creditors. The main Corporate Insolvency Resolution Process, with creditor in possession, remains an alternative.

c. For example, in September 2020 the Australian government introduced a temporary new liquidation framework designed to allow insolvent MSMEs to exit the market quickly and cheaply.

d. Empirical evidence suggests that, for creditors lending to small enterprises, lack of information contributes to a greater likelihood they will seek liquidation, or it may raise credit costs. See Cook, Pandit, and Milman (2001).

e. Information asymmetry about MSMEs (that is, when creditors do not know as much as debtors about the debtors' operations) can affect the decision-making of creditors. See ICCR (2014).

f. Adalet McGowan and Andrews (2016).

g. Armour et al. (2015); Djankov (2009).

business insolvency that places a degree of responsibility with a trustee, reducing the burden on the courts. Another category of reform is India's Insolvency and Bankruptcy Code (Amendment) Ordinance, 2021, which introduces a prepackaged insolvency resolution process for MSMEs.

Promoting debt forgiveness and discharge of natural person debtors

This section addresses the bankruptcy of natural person debtors—that is, individual entrepreneurs or just individual debtors. Because the pandemic has devastated many people's livelihoods through no fault of their own, debt forgiveness and discharge, as well as reputational protections, are critical tools in the COVID-19 recovery. The law and the courts should aim to quickly resolve no-income, no-asset cases and provide a discharge and fresh start for all natural person debtors.

Despite the potential benefits of personal bankruptcy frameworks, a significant proportion of emerging economies have none. In 2011, a World Bank survey of 25 advanced and 33 emerging economies found that 48 percent of emerging economies lacked a legal framework for the discharge or cancellation of an insolvent individual's debt, compared with 12 percent of advanced economies. Of the emerging economies, 51 percent lacked a legal framework for the restructuring of individual debt obligations, compared with 20 percent of advanced economies.[104]

Personal bankruptcy frameworks can benefit individual debtors both in their capacity as consumers and producers and in their ownership of unincorporated businesses because there is no legal separation between owners and their businesses. Personal bankruptcy laws, and particularly a pathway to discharge, are important for MSMEs, which are often financed at least in part by debt that has been personally guaranteed by the entrepreneur.[105] Comparable global data are limited on the share of personal bankruptcies resulting from business debt, partly because of the different ways in which business debt and nonbusiness debt are classified. However, statistics published by the Australian personal insolvency regulator suggest that between July 2019 and October 2021 about one in four personal bankruptcies was of a sole trader, partner in a partnership, or company officer.[106]

Personal bankruptcy laws provide an orderly framework for repaying or discharging the debts of individual debtors. This framework is especially helpful in periods of high levels of personal insolvency because the lack of a credible alternative to recover a debt often drives creditors to pursue piecemeal approaches. Those approaches can result in the unnecessary destruction of value stemming from court filing fees, enforcement costs, and the lost opportunity costs of a negotiated pathway to solvency and repayment.[107] Piecemeal approaches also clog the courts and impose avoidable hardships on debtors, including the loss of domicile and the stigma of ongoing debt collection.

Reforms of personal bankruptcy frameworks in response to COVID-19 have been minimal. One reform includes a framework for bankruptcy for natural persons in China's Shenzhen Special Economic Zone. The first of its kind in China, the framework provides for a three-year probationary period during which the bankrupt person's spending is subject to supervision before debts are discharged.[108] Temporary reforms enacted in Australia increase the threshold for the value of debts outstanding required to commence bankruptcy proceedings and facilitate the use of personal insolvency agreements for debt resolution.[109]

In addition to personal insolvency reforms, many countries have reformed their legal frameworks for dealing with the insolvency of MSMEs. To the extent that these reforms also apply to the owners of unincorporated businesses and address their personal liability for business debt, they fall into the category of personal insolvency reforms because they provide a pathway out of overindebtedness for individuals, including through discharge.[110]

A principal purpose of a personal insolvency regime is to rehabilitate insolvent debtors and restore their economic capacity.[111] In circumstances in which there is no prospect of repayment (or the societal cost of enforcing repayment outweighs the value of the repayment), there is no benefit to enforcement for creditors. However, the extent to which policy makers can and will allow debt forgiveness is a political decision and will depend on the context.

Excessive filing costs can deter debtors from filing for personal insolvency.[112] These obstacles should be removed for low-income and asset debtors. Examples of jurisdictions with frameworks to alleviate filing costs for low-income and asset debtors are Ireland, New Zealand, Scotland, and the United Kingdom (and Wales).[113] Regimes can target these procedures at those who are genuinely unable to meet their obligations. Digitalization also holds some promise as a means of lowering costs and increasing accessibility. In October 2020, Australia introduced a digital bankruptcy application process for personal bankruptcy.[114]

Another avenue for the protection of individual debtors is credit reporting frameworks. Many jurisdictions responded to the COVID-19 crisis by temporarily altering credit reporting frameworks to limit the long-term reputational harm to debtors temporarily unable to meet their debt obligations as a result of the pandemic. Crises tend to lower the credit scores of affected borrowers. A study of the impact of natural disasters on the financial health of US residents in affected regions found that credit scores declined by as much as 22 points.[115]

Forbearance programs to temporarily pause or reduce installments for a limited time were used in the COVID-19 pandemic by 57 percent of the 65 countries surveyed by the International Committee on Credit Reporting.[116] During the forbearance period—often three or six months and in some places up to a year—accounts were "frozen/paused" so that clients were reported as current even if payments were reduced or suspended. To reflect the forbearance programs, credit reporting bureaus implemented or used existing special reporting codes to flag the type of facilities affected by COVID-19.

In the United States, the CARES Act provided for 180 days of forbearance for federally backed loans, and credit providers were encouraged to consider their own programs for similar modification.[117] The main credit reporting agencies adjusted their algorithms to ensure that accounts affected by the COVID-19 pandemic were not negatively impacted. Kenya, Malaysia, and Greece took a more direct approach by barring the submission of negative credit data for a period of six months, nine months, and the pandemic period, respectively. During the prescribed period, credit bureaus did not include delinquency data on the credit report and scores. Four countries—Denmark, the Netherlands, Norway, and Tanzania—did not implement any specific measures to protect borrowers, which was largely consistent with the health policy positions of these countries during the pandemic. In the absence of any relief, delinquencies affected the borrowers' credit report and score in the ordinary manner.

Policies suspending adverse reporting on borrowers during a grace period should be phased out with an eye toward maintaining the integrity of the credit reporting system. In the absence of complete information, credit providers lack a full view of borrowers, and they may adopt a cautious lending approach that is counterproductive to the recovery. Suppression of data also introduces operational challenges. In the absence of data, TransUnion estimates that when full file information reporting resumed in Kenya, 12 percent of borrowers shifted to a high-risk score, reflecting increasing delinquencies.[118] In addition, banks' requests for credit bureau reports declined from 3.1 million a month in March 2020 to a low of 1.6 million in June 2020, but recovered to 3.6 million in December 2020.[119]

Conclusion

Debt is critical to prosperity and progress, but the complexity of the problems that arise when debtors cannot meet their obligations requires sophisticated legal and institutional frameworks. This is true in ordinary times, but the challenges are amplified when many debtors cannot meet their obligations within a short stretch of time. Inaction or mismanagement in such circumstances can lead to substantial economic harm. The reforms advocated in this chapter are directed at strengthening courts so they can continue to function in a period of high nonperforming loans, capture the value of debt for economic recovery in the form of new investment, and provide individual debtors with a degree of protection.

Notes

1. In the aftermath of the 2007–09 global financial crisis, the Financial Stability Board created in 2011 the Insolvency and Creditor Rights Standard (ICR Standard) and designated it as one of its key standards for sound financial systems (FSB 2011). The unified global standard for insolvency is represented by two international instruments: the World Bank's "Principles for Effective Insolvency and Creditor/Debtor Regimes," first published in 2001 and periodically revised (World Bank 2021c), and UNCITRAL's "Legislative Guide on Insolvency Law," which was first adopted in 2004, with new "parts" added over time. See UNCITRAL Legislative Guide on Insolvency Law (dashboard), United Nations Commission on International Trade Law, Vienna, https://uncitral.un.org/en/texts/insolvency/legislativeguides/insolvency_law. The ICR Standard informs the findings in this Report because it is integral to helping countries further develop such systems.
2. Terminology in this area can be confusing because different terms are used to describe similar processes in different jurisdictions. In this chapter, the terms *insolvency* and *bankruptcy* are used interchangeably to describe both liquidation and restructuring. *Restructuring* can refer to both formal and informal (out-of-court) processes to reorganize a firm's operations, finances, or both.
3. Consolo, Malfa, and Pierluigi (2018); D'Apice, Fiordelisi, and Puopolo (2021).
4. Araujo, Ferreira, and Funchal (2013).
5. Fonseca and Van Doornik (2020).
6. Lim and Hahn (2003); Neira (2017).
7. See Acharya and Subramanian (2009); Araujo, Ferreira, and Funchal (2013); Dewaelheyns and Van Hulle (2010); Gamboa-Cavazos and Schneider (2007).
8. Giné and Love (2006).
9. Zombie firms are firms unable to cover debt servicing costs from current profits over an extended period.
10. Andrews, Adalet McGowan, and Millot (2017); Banerjee and Hofmann (2018).
11. Menezes and van Zwieten (forthcoming).
12. Laeven, Schepens, and Schnabel (2020).
13. Acharya et al. (2019).
14. Menezes and van Zwieten (forthcoming).
15. Menezes and van Zwieten (forthcoming).
16. The issue of quantifying informal MSMEs is considered by Stein, Ardiç, and Hommes (2013) and International Finance Corporation, MSME Finance Gap (dashboard), SME Finance Forum, https://www.smefinanceforum.org/data-sites/msme-finance-gap.

17. World Bank (2017).
18. van Zwieten, Eidenmüller, and Sussman (2020).
19. Casey (2021).
20. Agarwal et al. (2017); Bolton and Rosenthal (2002); Mukherjee, Subramanian, and Tantri (2018).
21. Alston (1984); De and Tantri (2014); Guiso, Sapienza, and Zingales (2013); Kanz (2016); Mayer et al. (2014); Rucker and Alston (1987).
22. Giné and Kanz (2018).
23. Mayer et al. (2014).
24. See De and Tantri (2014); Mukherjee, Subramanian, and Tantri (2018).
25. Giné and Kanz (2018).
26. Guiso, Sapienza, and Zingales (2013).
27. G30 (2020, 3, 30).
28. Ayotte and Skeel (2010).
29. Calomiris, Klingebiel, and Laeven (2004).
30. Cirmizi, Klapper, and Uttamchandani (2012); World Bank (2021b, 2021c, 2022).
31. World Bank (2021c).
32. The case is *Bell Group (UK) Holdings Limited (In Liquidation)* [2020] WASC 347.
33. Laryea (2010).
34. This was identified as a particular challenge in responding to the Asian financial crisis. See OECD (2001).
35. Jappelli, Pagano, and Bianco (2005); Menezes and van Zwieten (forthcoming).
36. Esposito, Lanau, and Pompe (2014).
37. World Bank (2021c).
38. More in-depth comparative analysis is available in Adalet McGowan and Andrews (2016).
39. Chapter 3 annexes can be found at http://bit.do/WDR2022-Chapter-3-Annexes.
40. See, for example, Gadgil, Ronald, and Vyakaranam (2019).
41. See Menezes and van Zwieten (forthcoming).
42. Menezes and van Zwieten (forthcoming).
43. This measure, now ended, is summarized in AFSA (2021).
44. Air Mauritius (2020). A watershed meeting describes the turning point at which critical decisions are made about the future of an insolvent business—in particular, whether it will undergo restructuring or proceed to liquidation.
45. Via confirmation of a restructuring plan under Chapter 11 of the Bankruptcy Code (§ 1129).
46. Corporate Insolvency and Governance Act 2020.
47. Harris (2017).
48. World Bank (2019b).

49. This program is led by the World Bank's Development Impact Evaluation (DIME) team. See World Bank (2019a).
50. INSOL International and World Bank (2021a).
51. INSOL International and World Bank (2021d).
52. INSOL International and World Bank (2021c).
53. OECD (2003).
54. A regulatory framework for professional insolvency practitioners is a key component. Many countries—such as Australia, Brazil, Canada, China, Japan, Mexico, the Republic of Korea, the Russian Federation, and the United Kingdom—have facilitated the development of an insolvency practitioner profession whose members manage the economic and operational aspects of a proceeding. Practitioners are subject to strict qualification, training, monitoring, and licensing or registration requirements.
55. See, among others, EC (2011).
56. Directive 2019/1023 on Restructuring and Insolvency.
57. Procedure is applicable to the largest companies only (société anonyme). See Article L234-1 of the French Commercial Code.
58. World Bank (2021a).
59. Menezes and Muro (forthcoming).
60. INSOL International is a worldwide federation of national associations of accountants and lawyers who specialize in turnaround and insolvency. It has over 10,500 members. For more information, see https://www.insol.org/. For information on the International Association of Insolvency Regulators, see https://www.insolvencyreg.org/.
61. INSOL International, International Association of Insolvency Regulators, and World Bank (forthcoming).
62. In constructing these estimates, it was assumed that all measures were introduced on March 1, 2020.
63. See Allianz Research (2020); Banerjee, Cornelli, and Zakrajšek (2020).
64. World Bank (2022).
65. World Bank (2021c).
66. Part 13, Aristotle ([350 BCE]).
67. A review of the empirical evidence of alternative dispute resolution in civil law, family law, and workplace law is available in Veen (2014).
68. Cutler and Summers (1988).
69. Boon et al. (2019).
70. Armour and Deakin (2001).
71. Kent (1993).
72. Lucarelli and Forestieri (2017).
73. Kastrinou (2016).
74. Lucarelli and Forestieri (2017).
75. Madaus (2020).
76. Act on Court Confirmation of Extrajudicial Restructuring Plans.
77. Lipton and Sachs (1990).
78. Bogdanowicz-Bindert (1997).
79. Montes-Negret and Papi (1997).
80. Bogdanowicz-Bindert (1997).
81. Pomerleano and Shaw (2005).
82. Palinksi (1999), cited by Hersic (2007).
83. Pomerleano and Shaw (2005).
84. Montes-Negret and Papi (1997).
85. The survival rates of MSMEs may also be shorter than those of large firms when sales fall off because they are not well managed or have less liquidity.
86. The World Bank's 2017 "Report on the Treatment of MSME Insolvency" is a comprehensive review of the economic importance of MSMEs, their particular needs and challenges, and the insolvency reforms recommended for addressing these challenges.
87. Gurrea-Martínez (2021).
88. World Bank (2017).
89. Gurrea-Martínez (2021, 4).
90. World Bank (2018).
91. Tambunan (2018).
92. Bakiewicz (2005).
93. Mako (2005).
94. World Bank (2017).
95. For a more comprehensive review of such reforms, see Gurrea-Martínez (2021).
96. Decreto Legislativo 560 de 2020, https://dapre.presidencia.gov.co/normativa/normativa/DECRETO%20560%20DEL%2015%20DE%20ABRIL%20DE%202020.pdf.
97. Insolvency, Restructuring and Dissolution (Amendment) Act 2020.
98. Ministry of Law, Singapore (2021).
99. For a summary of the CARES Act and COVID-19 Bankruptcy Relief Extension Act, see ABI (2021).
100. COVID-19 Response Legislation Act 2020.
101. INSOL International and World Bank (2021d).
102. INSOL International and World Bank (2021b).
103. Corporations Amendment (Corporate Insolvency Reforms) Act 2020 (Cth). See Frydenberg (2020).
104. World Bank (2014b).
105. World Bank (2017).
106. The share is 8,889 of 34,339 personal bankruptcies. See Australian Financial Security Authority, Quarterly Personal Insolvency Statistics (dashboard), https://www.afsa.gov.au/about-us/statistics/quarterly-personal-insolvency-statistics.
107. IMF (1999); World Bank (2014b).
108. Reuters (2020).
109. Attorney-General's Department (2021).
110. For more detailed consideration of the blurred lines between personal and corporate insolvency frameworks, see Spooner (2019).
111. World Bank (2014b).
112. Heuer (2020).
113. Respectively, "Debt Relief Notice," "No Asset Procedure," "Minimal Asset Process," and "Debt Relief Order."
114. AFSA (2021).
115. Data from the International Committee on Credit Reporting, which conducted a survey in 65 countries in September and October 2020 on COVID-19 credit support programs; see ICCR (2020).
116. ICCR (2020).
117. Forbes and Sparkes (2020).
118. TransUnion presentation at the 2021 Kenya CIS Virtual Conference. See CIS Kenya (2021).
119. Central Bank of Kenya presentation at the 2021 Kenya CIS Virtual Conference. See CIS Kenya (2021).

References

ABI (American Bankruptcy Institute). 2021. "President Biden Signs COVID-19 Bankruptcy Relief Extension Act into Law." Press release, March 29, 2021. https://www.abi.org/newsroom/press-releases/president-biden-signs-covid-19-bankruptcy-relief-extension-act-into-law.

Acharya, Viral V., Tim Eisert, Christian Eufinger, and Christian W. Hirsch. 2019. "Whatever It Takes: The Real Effects of Unconventional Monetary Policy." *Review of Financial Studies* 32 (9): 3366–411.

Acharya, Viral V., and Krishnamurthy V. Subramanian. 2009. "Bankruptcy Codes and Innovation." *Review of Financial Studies* 22 (12): 4949–88.

Adalet McGowan, Müge, and Dan Andrews. 2016. "Insolvency Regimes and Productivity Growth: A Framework for Analysis." OECD Economics Department Working Paper 1309, ECO/WKP(2016)33, Organisation for Economic Co-operation and Development, Paris.

AFSA (Australian Financial Security Authority). 2021. "Temporary Debt Relief Measures Ended on 1 January 2021." *News*, January 4, 2021. https://www.afsa.gov.au/about-us/newsroom/temporary-debt-relief-measures-ended-1-january-2021.

Agarwal, Sumit, Gene Amromin, Itzhak Ben-David, Souphala Chomsisengphet, Tomasz Piskorski, and Amit Seru. 2017. "Policy Intervention in Debt Renegotiation: Evidence from the Home Affordable Modification Program." *Journal of Political Economy* 125 (3): 654–712.

Air Mauritius. 2020. "Air Mauritius Ltd (Administrators Appointed)." News release, November 16, 2020. https://www.stockexchangeofmauritius.com/media/5182/17112020aml1.pdf.

Allianz Research. 2020. "Calm before the Storm: Covid-19 and the Business Insolvency Time Bomb." Allianz Research, Munich. https://www.eulerhermes.com/en_global/news-insights/economic-insights/Calm-before-the-storm-Covid19-and-the-business-insolvency-time-bomb.html.

Alston, Lee J. 1984. "Farm Foreclosure Moratorium Legislation: A Lesson from the Past." *American Economic Review* 74 (3): 445–57.

Andrews, Dan, Müge Adalet McGowan, and Valentine Millot. 2017. "Confronting the Zombies: Policies for Productivity Revival." OECD Economic Policy Paper 21, Organisation for Economic Co-operation and Development, Paris.

Apedo-Amah, Marie Christine, Besart Avdiu, Xavier Cirera, Marcio Cruz, Elwyn Davies, Arti Grover, Leonardo Iacovone, et al. 2020. "Unmasking the Impact of COVID-19 on Businesses: Firm Level Evidence from across the World." Policy Research Working Paper 9434, World Bank, Washington, DC.

Araujo, Aloisio P., Rafael V. X. Ferreira, and Bruno Funchal. 2013. "The Brazilian Bankruptcy Law Experience." *Journal of Corporate Finance* 18 (4): 994–1004.

Aristotle (c. 350 BCE). *Rhetoric*. Translated by W. Rhys Roberts. Internet Classics Archive. Cambridge, MA: Massachusetts Institute of Technology. http://classics.mit.edu/Aristotle/rhetoric.mb.txt.

Armour, John, and Simon F. Deakin. 2001. "Norms in Private Bankruptcy: The 'London Approach' to the Resolution of Financial Distress." *Journal of Corporate Law Studies* 1 (1): 21–51.

Armour, John, Antonia Menezes, Mahesh Uttamchandani, and Kristen van Zwieten. 2015. "How Do Creditor Rights Matter for Debt Finance? A Review of Critical Evidence." In *Research Handbook on Secured Financing in Commercial Transactions*, edited by Frederique Dahan, 3–25. Research Handbooks in Financial Law Series. London: European Bank for Reconstruction and Development; Cheltenham, UK: Edward Elgar.

Attorney-General's Department. 2021. "The Bankruptcy System and the Impacts of Coronavirus." Attorney-General's Department, Barton, Australia. https://www.ag.gov.au/sites/default/files/2021-01/discussion-paper-bankruptcy-system-and-the-impact-of-coronavirus.pdf.

Ayotte, Kenneth M., and David Arthur Skeel, Jr. 2010. "Bankruptcy or Bailouts?" *Journal of Corporation Law* 35 (3): 469–98.

Bakiewicz, Anna. 2005. "Small and Medium Enterprises in Thailand: Following the Leader." *Asia and Pacific Studies* 2 (January): 131–51.

Banerjee, Ryan Niladri, Giulio Cornelli, and Egon Zakrajšek. 2020. "The Outlook for Business Bankruptcies." *BIS Bulletin* 30 (October 9), Bank for International Settlements, Basel, Switzerland.

Banerjee, Ryan Niladri, and Boris Hofmann. 2018. "The Rise of Zombie Firms: Causes and Consequences." *BIS Quarterly Review* (September 23): 67–78.

BLRC (Bankruptcy Law Reforms Committee, Government of India). 2015. *Rationale and Design.* Vol. 1, *The Report of the Bankruptcy Law Reforms Committee*. New Delhi: BLRC, Government of India. https://ibbi.gov.in/BLRC ReportVol1_04112015.pdf.

Bogdanowicz-Bindert, Christine A. 1997. "How Polish Banks Beat Bad Debt." *Wall Street Journal*, April 15, 1997. https://www.wsj.com/articles/SB861044025355211500.

Bolton, Patrick, and Howard Rosenthal. 2002. "Political Intervention in Debt Contracts." *Journal of Political Economy* 110 (5): 1103–34.

Boon, Gert-Jan, Maciek Bednarski, Carlotte Dessauvagie, and Milan Pastoors. 2019. "The Mediator in Insolvency Law: Exploring New Terrain." *Leiden Law Blog*, July 30, 2019. https://www.leidenlawblog.nl/articles/the-mediator-in-insolvency-law-exploring-new-terrain.

Calomiris, Charles, Daniela Klingebiel, and Luc Laeven. 2004. "A Taxonomy of Financial Crisis Resolution Mechanisms: Cross-Country Experience." Policy Research Working Paper 3379, World Bank, Washington, DC.

Casey, Anthony J. 2021. "Bankruptcy and Bailouts, Subsidies and Stimulus: The Government Toolset for Responding to Market Distress." ECGI Working Paper 578/2021, European Corporate Governance Institute, Brussels.

Cirmizi, Elena, Leora Klapper, and Mahesh Uttamchandani. 2012. "The Challenges of Bankruptcy Reform." *World Bank Research Observer* 27 (2): 185–203.

CIS Kenya (Credit Information Sharing Association of Kenya). 2021. "Conference Report: Enhancing Resilience of the CIS Framework in the Face of Crisis; Kenya CIS Virtual Conference 2021." CIS Kenya, Kenya School of Monetary Studies, Ruaraka, Nairobi. https://ciskenya.co.ke/wp-content/files/2021/06/Post-Conference-Report-2021-31-03-2021.pdf.

Consolo, Agostino, Federica Malfa, and Beatrice Pierluigi. 2018. "Insolvency Frameworks and Private Debt: An Empirical Investigation." ECB Working Paper 2189, European Central Bank, Frankfurt.

Cook, Gary A. S., Naresh R. Pandit, and David Milman. 2001. "Formal Rehabilitation Procedures and Insolvent Firms: Empirical Evidence on the British Company Voluntary Arrangement Procedure." Small Business Economics 17 (4): 255–71.

Cutler, David M., and Lawrence H. Summers. 1988. "The Costs of Conflict Resolution and Financial Distress: Evidence from the Texaco-Pennzoil Litigation." RAND Journal of Economics 19 (2): 157–72.

D'Apice, Vincenzo, Franco Fiordelisi, and Giovanni Walter Puopolo. 2021. "Lending Quality and Contracts Enforcement Reforms." SSRN Electronic Journal, February 17, 2021. https://papers.ssrn.com/sol3/papers.cfm?abstract_id=3786050.

De, Sankar, and Prasanna L. Tantri. 2014. "Borrowing Culture and Debt Relief: Evidence from a Policy Experiment." Paper presented at Asian Finance Association's AsianFA 2014 Conference, Bali, Indonesia, June 24–27, 2014.

Dewaelheyns, Nico, and Cynthia Van Hulle. 2010. "Internal Capital Markets and Capital Structure: Bank versus Internal Debt." European Financial Management 16 (3): 345–73.

Djankov, Simeon. 2009. "Bankruptcy Regimes during Financial Distress." Working Paper 50332, World Bank, Washington, DC.

EC (European Commission). 2011. Business Dynamics: Start-Ups, Business Transfers, and Bankruptcy, Final Report. Brussels: Entrepreneurship Unit, Directorate-General for Enterprise and Industry, EC.

Esposito, Gianluca, Sergi Lanau, and Sebastiaan Pompe. 2014. "Judicial System Reform in Italy: A Key to Growth." IMF Working Paper WP/14/32, International Monetary Fund, Washington, DC.

Fonseca, Julia, and Bernadus Van Doornik. 2020. "Financial Development and Labor Market Outcomes: Evidence from Brazil." Working Paper 532, Research Department, Central Bank of Brazil, Brasília.

Forbes, Brian M., and Robert W. Sparkes, III. 2020. "COVID-19: Credit Reporting in the Age of COVID-19." National Law Review 11 (252). https://www.natlawreview.com/article/covid-19-credit-reporting-age-covid-19.

Frydenberg, Josh. 2020. "Australia's Landmark New Rescue and Liquidation Processes for SMEs." Communication, September 24, 2020, Norton Rose Fulbright, Sydney. https://www.nortonrosefulbright.com/-/media/files/nrf/nrfweb/knowledge-pdfs/australias-landmark-new-rescue-and-liquidation-processes-for-smes.pdf?la=en-au&revision.

FSB (Financial Stability Board). 2011. "Insolvency and Creditor Rights Standard." January 20, 2011. https://www.fsb.org/2011/01/cos_051201/.

G30 (Group of Thirty). 2020. "Reviving and Restructuring the Corporate Sector Post-COVID: Designing Public Policy Interventions." G30, Washington, DC.

Gadgil, Shon, Bindu Ronald, and Lasya Vyakaranam. 2019. "Timely Resolution of Cases under the Insolvency and Bankruptcy Code." Journal of Critical Reviews 6 (6): 156–67.

Gamboa-Cavazos, Mario, and Frank Schneider. 2007. "Bankruptcy as a Legal Process." Working paper, Department of Economics, Harvard University, Cambridge, MA.

Giné, Xavier, and Martin Kanz. 2018. "The Economic Effects of a Borrower Bailout: Evidence from an Emerging Market." Review of Financial Studies 31 (5): 1752–83.

Giné, Xavier, and Inessa Love. 2006. "Do Reorganization Costs Matter for Efficiency? Evidence from a Bankruptcy Reform in Colombia." Policy Research Working Paper 3970, World Bank, Washington, DC.

Guiso, Luigi, Paola Sapienza, and Luigi Zingales. 2013. "The Determinants of Attitudes toward Strategic Default on Mortgages." Journal of Finance 68 (4): 1473–1515.

Gurrea-Martínez, Aurelio. 2021. "Implementing an Insolvency Framework for Micro and Small Firms." International Insolvency Review 30 (S1): S46–S66.

Harris, Jason. 2017. "Class Warfare in Debt Restructuring: Does Australia Need Cross-Class Cram Down for Creditors' Schemes of Arrangement?" University of Queensland Law Journal 36 (1): 73–97.

Hersic, Ladislav. 2007. "The Effects of Foreign Entry in Banking Sectors of Transitional Economies: The Case of Slovakia." PhD diss., Business School, University of Leeds, Leeds, UK. http://etheses.whiterose.ac.uk/244/1/uk_bl_ethos_485968.pdf.

Heuer, Jan-Ocko. 2020. "Hurdles to Debt Relief for 'No Income No Assets' Debtors in Germany: A Case Study of Failed Consumer Bankruptcy Law Reforms." International Insolvency Review 29 (S1): S44–S76.

IBBI (Insolvency and Bankruptcy Board of India). 2020. "Pre-packaged Insolvency Resolution." IBBI Quarterly 17 (October–December), IBBI, New Delhi. https://www.ibbi.gov.in/uploads/publication/9c804e45a2741e109a6cab56f48a140b.pdf.

ICCR (International Committee on Credit Reporting). 2014. "Facilitating SME Financing through Improved Credit Reporting." Financial Infrastructure Series: Credit Reporting Policy and Research, World Bank, Washington, DC.

ICCR (International Committee on Credit Reporting). 2020. "Treatment of COVID Credit Support Programs." PowerPoint presentation, November 24, World Bank, Washington, DC.

IMF (International Monetary Fund). 1999. Orderly and Effective Insolvency Procedures: Key Issues. Washington, DC: Legal Department, IMF.

INSOL International, International Association of Insolvency Regulators, and World Bank. Forthcoming. "Global Perspectives on COVID-19 Insolvency Emergency Measures." World Bank, Washington, DC.

INSOL International and World Bank. 2021a. "Brazil." Global Guide: Measures Adopted to Support Distressed Businesses through the COVID-19 Crisis, INSOL International, London; World Bank, Washington, DC. https://insol.azureedge.net/cmsstorage/insol/media/documents_files/covidguide/30%20april%20updates/brazil-sa-signed-off-28-april-2021.pdf.

INSOL International and World Bank. 2021b. "Chile." Global Guide: Measures Adopted to Support Distressed Businesses through the COVID-19 Crisis, INSOL International, London; World Bank, Washington, DC. https://insol.azureedge.net/cmsstorage/insol/media/documents_files/covidguide/30%20april%20updates/chile_final.pdf.

INSOL International and World Bank. 2021c. "Nigeria." Global Guide: Measures Adopted to Support Distressed Businesses through the COVID-19 Crisis, INSOL International, London; World Bank, Washington, DC. https://insol.azureedge.net/cmsstorage/insol/media/documents_files/covidguide/30%20april%20updates/nigeria-v3-12-may2021-final.pdf.

INSOL International and World Bank. 2021d. "Spain." Global Guide: Measures Adopted to Support Distressed Businesses through the COVID-19 Crisis, INSOL International, London; World Bank, Washington, DC. https://insol.azureedge.net/cmsstorage/insol/media/documents_files/covidguide/30%20april%20updates/spain_v2-final.pdf.

Jappelli, Tullio, Marco Pagano, and Magda Bianco. 2005. "Courts and Banks: Effects of Judicial Enforcement on Credit Markets." *Journal of Money, Credit, and Banking* 37 (2): 223–44.

Kanz, Martin. 2016. "What Does Debt Relief Do for Development? Evidence from India's Bailout for Rural Households." *American Economic Journal: Applied Economics* 8 (4): 66–99.

Kastrinou, Alexandra. 2016. "Comparative Analysis of the Informal, Pre-insolvency Procedures of the UK and France." *International Insolvency Review* 25 (2): 99–118.

Kent, Pen. 1993. "The London Approach." *Quarterly Bulletin* Q1 (March 1): 110–15, Bank of England, London.

Laeven, Luc, Glenn Schepens, and Isabel Schnabel. 2020. "Zombification in Europe in Times of Pandemic." VoxEU.org, October 11, 2020. https://voxeu.org/article/zombification-europe-times-pandemic.

Laryea, Thomas. 2010. "Approaches to Corporate Debt Restructuring in the Wake of Financial Crises." IMF Staff Position Note SPN/10/02, International Monetary Fund, Washington, DC.

Lee, Junkyu, and Peter Rosenkranz. 2019. "Nonperforming Loans in Asia: Determinants and Macrofinancial Linkages." ADB Economics Working Paper 574, Asian Development Bank, Manila.

Lim, Youngjae, and Chin Hee Hahn. 2003. "Bankruptcy Policy Reform and Total Factor Productivity Dynamics in Korea: Evidence from Macro Data." NBER Working Paper 9810, National Bureau of Economic Research, Cambridge, MA.

Lipton, David, and Jeffrey D. Sachs. 1990. "Creating a Market Economy in Eastern Europe: The Case of Poland." *Brookings Papers on Economic Activity* 1990, 1: 75–147, Brookings Institution, Washington, DC.

Lucarelli, Paola, and Ilaria Forestieri. 2017. "The Three Targets of Insolvency Mediation: Dispute Resolution, Agreement Facilitation, Corporate Distress Management." *TDM: Transnational Dispute Management* 4 (2017). https://www.transnational-dispute-management.com/article.asp?key=2494.

Madaus, Stephan. 2020. "A Giant Leap for German Restructuring Law? The New Draft Law for Preventive Restructuring Procedures in Germany." *BLB, Business Law Blog*, October 26, 2020. https://www.law.ox.ac.uk/business-law-blog/blog/2020/10/giant-leap-german-restructuring-law-new-draft-law-preventive.

Mako, William P. 2005. "Emerging-Market and Crisis Applications for Out-of-Court Workouts: Lessons from East Asia, 1998–2001." In *Corporate Restructuring: Lessons from Experience*, edited by Michael Pomerleano and William Shaw, 99–125. Washington, DC: World Bank.

Mayer, Christopher, Edward Morrison, Tomasz Piskorski, and Arpit Gupta. 2014. "Mortgage Modification and Strategic Behavior: Evidence from a Legal Settlement with Countrywide." *American Economic Review* 104 (9): 2830–57.

Menezes, Antonia, and Sergio Muro. Forthcoming. "Addressing Insolvency Risk through Corporate Debt Restructuring Frameworks." World Bank, Washington, DC.

Menezes, Antonia, and Kristin van Zwieten. Forthcoming. "Insolvency." Viewpoint: Public Policy for the Private Sector, Trade and Competitiveness Global Practice, Note, World Bank, Washington, DC.

Ministry of Law, Singapore. 2021. "Financially Distressed Micro and Small Companies May Apply for Simplified Insolvency Programme from 29 January 2021." Press release, January 28, 2021. https://www.mlaw.gov.sg/news/press-releases/simplified-insolvency-programme-commences.

Montes-Negret, Fernando, and Luca Papi. 1997. "The Polish Experience with Bank and Enterprise Restructuring." Policy Research Working Paper 1705, World Bank, Washington, DC.

Mukherjee, Saptarshi, Krishnamurthy Subramanian, and Prasanna Tantri. 2018. "Borrowers' Distress and Debt Relief: Evidence from a Natural Experiment." *Journal of Law and Economics* 61 (4): 607–35.

Neira, Julian. 2017. "Bankruptcy and Cross-Country Differences in Productivity." *Journal of Economic Behavior and Organization* 157 (January): 359–81.

OECD (Organisation for Economic Co-operation and Development). 2001. "Insolvency Reforms in Asia: An Assessment of the Implementation Process and the Role of Judiciary." Synthesis Note, Forum for Asian Insolvency Reform, Bali, Indonesia, February 7–8, 2001. https://www.oecd.org/daf/ca/corporategovernanceprinciples/1873992.pdf.

OECD (Organisation for Economic Co-operation and Development). 2003. "Informal Workouts, Restructuring, and the Future of Asian Insolvency Reform: Proceedings from the Second Forum for Asian Insolvency Reform (December 2002)." Centre for Co-operation with

Non-Members, OECD, Paris. oecd.org/corporate/ca
/corporategovernanceprinciples/16211282.pdf.

Palinksi, A. 1999. "Evaluation of Bank Debt Restructuring in
1992–98 for Selected Polish Banks." *Bank and Credit* 12,
National Bank of Poland, Warsaw.

PIB (Press Information Bureau, India). 2020. "Finance Minister Announces Several Relief Measures Relating to
Statutory and Regulatory Compliance Matters across
Sectors in View of COVID-19 Outbreak." Press Release
1607942, March 24, 2020. https://ibbi.gov.in/uploads
/press/50277513bcc7d94092ce4ee2b6591aad.pdf.

PIB (Press Information Bureau, India). 2021. "President
Promulgates Insolvency and Bankruptcy Code (Amend-
ment) Ordinance, 2021." Annexure 1, "Amendments
Carried Out through the Insolvency and Bankruptcy
Code (Amendment) Ordinance, 2021." Press Release
1710161, April 7, 2021. https://pib.gov.in/PressRelese
Detail.aspx?PRID=1710161.

Pomerleano, Michael, and William Shaw, eds. 2005. *Corporate Restructuring: Lessons from Experience.* Washington, DC: World Bank.

Reuters. 2020. "Shenzhen Drafts China's First Personal
Bankruptcy Laws as Virus Pressures Economy." *Emerging
Markets*, June 4, 2020. https://www.reuters.com/article
/us-china-economy-bankruptcy-idUSKBN23B1EG.

Rucker, Randal R., and Lee J. Alston. 1987. "Farm Failures
and Government Intervention: A Case Study of the
1930's." *American Economic Review* 77 (4): 724–30.

Sen, Oitihjya. 2020. "Introducing a Special Framework for
Resolving Insolvency of MSMEs." *Vidhi Legal Policy*
(blog), October 23, 2020. https://vidhilegalpolicy.in
/blog/introducing-a-special-framework-for-resolving
-insolvency-of-msmes/.

Shikha, Neeti, and Urvashi Shahi. 2021. "Assessment of
Corporate Insolvency and Resolution Timeline." IBBI
Research Initiative, RP-01/2021, Insolvency and Bankruptcy Board of India, New Delhi. https://www.ibbi.gov
.in/uploads/publication/2021-02-12-154823-p3xwo
-8b78d9548a60a756e4c71d49368def03.pdf.

Spooner, Joseph. 2019. *Bankruptcy: The Case for Relief in
an Economy of Debt.* International Corporate Law and
Financial Market Regulation Series. Cambridge, UK:
Cambridge University Press.

Stein, Peer, Oya Pinar Ardiç, and Martin Hommes. 2013.
"Closing the Credit Gap for Formal and Informal Micro,
Small, and Medium Enterprises." IFC Access to Finance,
Advisory Services, International Finance Corporation,
Washington, DC.

Tambunan, Tulus T. H. 2018. "The Impact of the Economic
Crisis on Micro, Small, and Medium Enterprises and
Their Crisis Mitigation Measures in Southeast Asia with
Reference to Indonesia." *Asia and the Pacific Policy
Studies* 6 (1): 19–39.

van Zwieten, Kristin, Horst Eidenmüller, and Orsen Sussman. 2020. "Bail-Outs and Bail-Ins Are Better Than
Bankruptcy: A Comparative Assessment of Public Policy Responses to COVID-19 Distress." ECGI Working
Paper 535/2020, European Corporate Governance Institute, Brussels.

Veen, Sarah Vander. 2014. "A Case for Mediation: The
Cost-Effectiveness of Civil, Family, and Workplace
Mediation." Mediate BC: Dispute Resolution and Design,
Vancouver, BC, Canada. https://www.mediatebc.com
/sites/default/files/The-Case-for-Mediation-min.pdf.

World Bank. 2014a. *Doing Business 2015: Going Beyond
Efficiency.* Washington, DC: World Bank. https://www
.doingbusiness.org/en/reports/global-reports/doing
-business-2015.

World Bank. 2014b. *Report on the Treatment of the Insolvency of Natural Persons.* Report No. ACS6818. Washington, DC: Working Group on the Treatment of the
Insolvency of Natural Persons, Insolvency and Creditor/
Debtor Regimes Task Force, World Bank.

World Bank. 2017. "Report on the Treatment of MSME Insolvency." Working Group on the Treatment of MSME Insolvency, Insolvency and Creditor/Debtor Regimes Task
Force, World Bank, Washington, DC.

World Bank. 2018. "Improving Access to Finance for
SMEs: Opportunities through Credit Reporting,
Secured Lending, and Insolvency Practices." Doing
Business, World Bank, Washington, DC. https://www
.doingbusiness.org/en/reports/thematic-reports
/improving-access-to-finance-for-smes.

World Bank. 2019a. "Data and Evidence for Justice
Reform (DE JURE)." i2i DIME Brief (November), Development Impact Evaluation, World Bank, Washington,
DC. https://thedocs.worldbank.org/en/doc/77121157
5476485169-0090022019/render/DEJURENov2019
.pdf.

World Bank. 2019b. "Enforcing Contracts and Resolving Insolvency: Training and Efficiency in the Judicial
System." In *Doing Business 2019: Training for Reform*,
53–60. Washington, DC: World Bank. https://www
.doingbusiness.org/content/dam/doingBusiness
/media/Annual-Reports/English/DB2019-report_web
-version.pdf.

World Bank. 2020. *Doing Business 2020: Comparing Business Regulation in 190 Economies.* Washington, DC:
World Bank. https://openknowledge.worldbank.org
/bitstream/handle/10986/32436/9781464814402
.pdf?sequence=24&isAllowed=y.

World Bank. 2021a. "The Calm before the Storm: Early Evidence on Business Insolvency Filings after the Onset of
COVID-19." COVID-19 Notes, Finance Series (February
25), World Bank, Washington, DC.

World Bank. 2021b. "How Insolvency and Creditor-Debtor
Regimes Can Help Address Nonperforming Loans."
Equitable Growth, Finance, and Institutions Note–
Finance, World Bank, Washington, DC.

World Bank. 2021c. "Principles for Effective Insolvency and
Creditor/Debtor Regimes." World Bank, Washington, DC.

World Bank. 2022. *A Toolkit for Corporate Workouts.* Washington, DC: World Bank. https://documents1.worldbank
.org/curated/en/982181642007438817/pdf/A-Toolkit
-for-Corporate-Workouts.pdf.

Spotlight 3.1

Supporting microfinance to sustain small businesses

M icro, small, and medium enterprises (MSMEs) and the informal sector will play a critical role in the long-term recovery from the COVID-19 (coronavirus) crisis. In low- and middle-income countries, small firms are vital for job creation, economic growth, provision of goods and services, and poverty alleviation. Formal and informal MSMEs make up over 90 percent of all firms and account, on average, for 60–70 percent of total employment and 50 percent of GDP worldwide.[1] Yet despite their important economic role, these businesses struggle to access formal financial services. About 130 million, or 41 percent, of formal MSMEs in low- and middle-income countries faced credit constraints before the COVID-19 pandemic, and the MSME finance gap (the difference between current supply and potential demand, which can potentially be addressed by financial institutions) was estimated at $5 trillion.[2] The demand for finance from informal enterprises was an estimated $2.8 trillion, equivalent to 11 percent of GDP in these countries.

Policies to support the continuity of financial services to MSMEs and the informal sector and protect these clients through restructuring processes are essential to avoid a delayed recovery. Although microfinance institutions (MFIs) are often small and may seem unimportant in balance sheet terms, they serve a segment of an economy that is macroeconomically significant. MFIs typically have detailed operational knowledge of local business conditions and the skills and abilities of individual entrepreneurs, which enables them to direct funds from recapitalized institutions to productive lending opportunities. Globally, the formal microfinance sector provides over 140 million low-income clients with credit and savings services.[3]

The sector's reach is much larger when nongovernmental organizations (NGOs), cooperatives, and informal savings and loan groups are included. In 2018 the global microfinance sector oversaw $124 billion in outstanding loans and $80 billion in savings. Specialized microfinance investors had a $17 billion portfolio in MFIs.[4]

The state of MFIs during COVID-19 and the policy response

During the pandemic, several governments took important steps to protect MFIs when borrowers began to default on their loans. The differences between MFIs and conventional banking institutions required a tailored approach. Whereas most banks rely on asset-based lending, MFIs maintain close relationships with their clients to assess and ensure each client's willingness and ability to repay. Microfinance lending is typically high-touch, with frequent, even weekly, in-person meetings with borrowers. But such meetings became difficult, if not impossible, under lockdowns. Moreover, MFI balance sheets are highly granular and may consist of hundreds of thousands of borrowers with relatively small short-term loans. Thus the sheer volume and varying circumstances of individual borrowers can make blanket moratoria on loans and formal loan rescheduling difficult to organize and implement—and borrowers may not even want them. Finally, with their links to the informal sector and their deep knowledge of local economies and communities, MFIs are important channels for payments (such as government-to-person transfers) that regulators and policy makers can leverage to support recovery.

As the lockdowns and decline in economic activity precipitated by the COVID-19 pandemic took hold, experts anticipated that MFIs would face swift deterioration of their performance metrics, especially liquidity and asset quality. But based on a global assessment of MFIs in July 2021,[5] the overall impacts of the pandemic on MFI balance sheets seem to have been mixed based on MFI characteristics, government assistance, and specific market dynamics, among other things (also see spotlight 2.1 on MFIs). Key factors in MFI resilience during the pandemic are national government and regulatory responses (box S3.1.1), the nature and type of institution (such as whether deposit-taking or credit only), the prepandemic financial and operational strength of individual institutions (box S3.1.2), and how individual

Box S3.1.1 How Pakistani MFIs and regulators managed the crisis

As the economic crisis arising from the COVID-19 pandemic unfolded in Pakistan, MFI operations became severely restricted, and some MFIs were forced to close temporarily. Many MFIs acted quickly, however, to initiate business continuity plans to ensure the health and safety of staff and clients and work around lockdowns. Digital financial services and branchless banking surged. In the first year of the pandemic, the number of active branchless banking accounts increased by 53.7 percent, from 27.7 million to 42.6 million.[a] Meanwhile, from March 2020 to March 2021 regulators enacted a debt moratorium to ease the financial crunch on borrowers caused by lockdowns and the decline in economic activity. In addition, nonbank microfinance companies (NBMFCs) were shielded by federal guidelines asking commercial banks and other lenders to MFIs, such as the Pakistan Microfinance Investment Company, to reschedule wholesale lending to the sector. Anecdotal reports also suggest that handshake agreements with other MFI lenders to extend repayment terms, as well as the continued availability of wholesale funding for creditworthy MFIs, helped buoy the sector.

Overall, these measures appear to have averted a liquidity crisis among Pakistan's MFIs in the short term, particularly those regulated, deposit-taking, and digitally enabled.[b] Indeed, during 2020 loans totaling approximately $635 million in the sector were deferred or rescheduled. Some MFIs even experienced an increase in business. Microfinance banks (MFBs) saw a net increase in deposits in 2020 of 29 percent, and gross loan portfolios increased from $1.97 billion to $2.02 billion during 2020.[c] However, results were mixed across the sector. The largest MFBs

(Box continues next page)

saw growth continue, while the smaller players, including the vast majority of NBMFCs, saw declines in their portfolios and asset quality. By the end of 2020, many Pakistani MFIs had temporarily suspended their lending operations, and the demand for credit declined slightly as people suffered income losses.[d]

Whether some consolidation and solvency support, particularly for smaller institutions, are needed in the sector remains to be seen. Going forward, it will be important to distinguish viable MFIs from those likely to fail. MFIs, especially those unable to restart lending and return to prepandemic levels of growth, may find that their weaker balance sheets no longer meet prudential requirements once temporary regulatory forbearance is lifted. Recapitalization of institutions focused on MSME lending, especially MFIs, may be necessary and critical to restoring the viability of private sector MSMEs. The government's Kamyab Pakistan Programme, rolled out in September 2021 to provide subsidized or interest-free loans to SMEs and agricultural workers, could also have mixed impacts on the stability and future growth potential of the microfinance sector by distorting the price of credit and increasing the moral hazard of strategic future default.

a. Compare the relevant data in SBP (2020) and SBP (2021).
b. A study of 31 economies found that firms with an online presence were more likely to stay in business during the pandemic than those with no online presence, suggesting that digital technology helps small firms innovate and adapt to changing market conditions (Muzi et al. 2021).
c. See Basharat, Sheikh, and Fatima (2021).
d. The number of active borrowers in Pakistan dropped from 7.25 million to 7 million.

Box S3.1.2 **Case study: A compounded crisis in Lebanon**

The Lebanese economy entered a recession in 2019, pressured by fiscal and trade balance deficits, declining capital inflows, and dwindling foreign exchange reserves. Acute political and financial crises ensued, leading to a run on banks, default by the government on debt obligations, and a proliferation of exchange rates in a historically dollarized market. Alongside the COVID-19 pandemic and the catastrophic explosion at the Port of Beirut, the compounded political and financial crises have had devastating effects on MFIs and their clients.

A survey conducted by the Consultative Group to Assist the Poor (CGAP) and the Lebanese Micro-Finance Association of almost 1,000 microfinance borrowers in Lebanon found that their situation deteriorated sharply between mid-2019 and the last quarter of 2020. Half of the respondents had stopped working or had a less stable income. Entrepreneurs, who account for the majority of MFI clients, saw a 94 percent decrease in sales and faced challenges arising from exchange rate fluctuations and loss of customers. Fifty percent of those employed experienced salary

(Box continues next page)

cuts, and 20 percent lost their jobs. Women, who make up half of borrowers and are generally self-employed, were the most affected, with three times as many women as men reporting they had stopped working, and most saying they had to handle family care alone during the pandemic.

Purchasing power declined dramatically in Lebanon from mid-2019 to mid-2020 as the pound's exchange rate deteriorated and inflation rose. In mid-2019, spending by a typical borrower's household was more than $1,000 a month for 4.5 members, or $7.90 per person per day. A year later, inflation-adjusted spending had dropped by more than half, to $3.40, indicating that the 35 percent real contraction in GDP had hit the poorest more severely. With curtailed income, 40 percent of microfinance clients were no longer able to meet their basic needs. Sixty percent cut consumption, including of meat or fruit; 50 percent of households were forced to tap into savings; and 43 percent sold movable assets, primarily gold. In the face of impoverished clients and lower levels of economic activity, MFIs saw their nonperforming loans (NPLs) rise from 2 percent in mid-2019 to over 20 percent in 2020.[a]

In 2019, prior to the crisis, the microfinance sector had roughly 1,000 staff members and an aggregate outreach of about 150,000 clients for a loan portfolio of $220 million. However, activity rates dropped as the crisis deepened, and the sector began downsizing. By 2021, portfolios stood at $150 million for some 100,000 loans. But NPLs in the newly disbursed portfolio were still manageable at 8–10 percent.

Nonetheless, the financial crisis exposed some of Lebanon's large top-tier MFIs—representing 75 percent of the market—to potential solvency issues stemming from their significant assets, liabilities, and currency mismatches. On the liabilities side, because of the previous ease of borrowing from foreign lenders, MFIs had accumulated outstanding foreign debt totaling $80 million, but capital controls imposed by local banks on external transfers prevented them from servicing it. On the assets side, MFIs' loan values fell to about 10 percent of precrisis values as the exchange rate depreciated, including the US dollar–denominated loans that clients were repaying in pounds at the officially pegged rate. The future value of MFIs' $45 million in local deposits is uncertain. They could be written off in whole or in part, stretched out, or mandatorily converted into local currency, depending on how the banking sector is restructured. These MFIs are at a de facto standstill with their creditors. Clearly recapitalization, together with debt restructuring and relief, will be needed. Left unaddressed, this need could result in less access to finance, with disproportionate impacts on a significant portion of low-income borrowers in a context of rising poverty and unemployment.

Source: Chehade (2021).

a. CGAP, Lebanese Micro-Finance Association, and Consultation and Research Institute (2020).

MFIs responded as market conditions changed. Borrower profiles undoubtedly play a role in MFI experiences as well. For example, World Bank phone surveys in Sub-Saharan Africa suggest that, although female-led MSMEs experienced a greater drop in sales than male-led firms between March and July 2020, they did not face greater problems in repaying their loans.[6] Meanwhile, a survey of 225 microfinance institutions of different sizes and in different regions in the early months of the pandemic found that although liquidity problems among MFIs were not severer than they were prior to COVID-19, small MFIs were nearly twice as likely as medium-size ones to face liquidity constraints.[7] In Latin America and the Caribbean and Sub-Saharan Africa, problems were worse than in other regions. However, by the first quarter of 2021 liquidity problems were receding. As for asset quality, in the early months of the pandemic there was a spike in restructured portfolios and portfolio-at-risk levels. A year later, a strong recovery was under way in all regions except Africa, where portfolio growth rates remained negative.[8]

Looking ahead

As moratoria are lifted, questions linger about the asset quality of MFI portfolios. Questions also remain about the ongoing solvency of the smaller MFIs that do not take deposits, especially those that at the onset of the pandemic had weak financial positions, including limited capital buffers. Identifying those MFIs viable in the new environment will be a challenge. A restructuring and consolidation exercise could effectively clean up the sector by closing or consolidating weak and poorly governed institutions. Past MFI crises have demonstrated that out-of-court restructuring or workout processes and the use of distressed asset facilities that specialize at the sector level are the best practice. In addition, markets for distressed assets could enable microfinance providers to better manage their balance sheets by shedding nonperforming assets to focus on building sound portfolios of productive loans. However, success in exercising these options is not guaranteed: distressed MFI loan assets are typically difficult to collect because of the inherent characteristics of microlending, which involves uncollateralized, high-touch loans, often based on the relationship between the MFI agent and the borrower. Furthermore, distressed asset purchases are especially risky in the microlending context because of the relatively large numbers of loans involved and the associated due

diligence requirements, which are rendered even more complex and uncertain in the context of government support such as loan moratoria.

Nonetheless, policy makers should pursue measures that support the provision of financial services to MSMEs and the informal sector. Encouraging the emergence of markets for secured transactions and better credit information sharing could enable a broader range of funding and lending instruments and help manage MFI lending risks going forward. Digital transformation of MFI operations and service delivery should also be encouraged—successful MFIs will draw on new technologies for better risk management, develop new business models that leverage their infrastructure and client positioning, and offer products that are more accessible to the informal sector and micro and small businesses. A lesson from the Lebanese experience is that it may be prudent for future microfinance models to limit currency risks. There, blended finance options could be explored to allow renewed investments by development finance institutions and microfinance investment vehicles, but all of them require, first and foremost, macroeconomic stabilization.

Notes

1. For more information on MSMEs in emerging economies, see Department of Economic and Social Affairs, United Nations, "Micro-, Small, and Medium-Sized Enterprises (MSMEs)," https://sdgs.un.org/topics/capacity-development/msmes; World Bank, "Small and Medium Enterprises (SMEs) Finance," https://www.worldbank.org/en/topic/smefinance.
2. For more information on the MSME finance gap, see the International Finance Corporation, IFC MSME Finance Gap database (updated October 2018), https://www.smefinanceforum.org/data-sites/msme-finance-gap, and the associated report (IFC 2017).
3. Convergences (2018).
4. Symbiotics (2019).
5. CGAP and Symbiotics (2021).
6. IFC (2021).
7. Spaggiari (2021).
8. CGAP (2021).

References

Basharat, Ali, Zeenoor Sohail Sheikh, and Tehreem Fatima. 2021. "Pakistan Microfinance Review 2020." Draft, Pakistan Microfinance Network, Islamabad. https://www.cgap.org/sites/default/files/datasets/2021_07_COVID_MFI_Symbiotics.pdf.

CGAP (Consultative Group to Assist the Poor). 2021. "Microfinance Solvency and COVID-19: A Call for Coordination." COVID-19 Briefing: Insights for Inclusive Finance (September), CGAP, Washington, DC. https://www.cgap.org/research/covid-19-briefing/microfinance-solvency-and-covid-19-call-coordination.

CGAP (Consultative Group to Assist the Poor), Lebanese Micro-Finance Association, and Consultation and Research Institute. 2020. "Impact of Economic and COVID-19 Crises on Microcredit Borrowers." Slide Deck, November 26, CGAP, Washington, DC. https://www.findevgateway.org/slide-deck/2020/11/impact-economic-and-covid-19-crises-microcredit-borrowers.

CGAP (Consultative Group to Assist the Poor) and Symbiotics. 2021. "Global Microfinance Recovery Continues, Especially in Africa, but Pandemic's Long-Term Impact Remains Uncertain." COVID-19 Briefing, Snapshot: MFIs during the Crisis (July), CGAP, Washington, DC; Symbiotics Group, Geneva. https://www.findevgateway.org/paper/2021/07/global-microfinance-recovery-continues-especially-africa-pandemics-long-term-impact.

Chehade, Nadine. 2021. "Preserving Decades of Development: A Plea for Lebanon." CGAP (blog), February 10, 2021. https://www.cgap.org/blog/preserving-decades-development-plea-lebanon.

Convergences. 2018. *Microfinance Barometer 2019*. Paris: Convergences. https://www.convergences.org/wp-content/uploads/2019/09/Microfinance-Barometer-2019_web-1.pdf.

IFC (International Finance Corporation). 2017. "MSME Finance Gap: Assessment of the Shortfalls and Opportunities in Financing Micro, Small, and Medium Enterprises in Emerging Markets." IFC, Washington, DC.

IFC (International Finance Corporation). 2021. "COVID-19 and Women-Led MSMEs in Sub-Saharan Africa: Examining the Impact, Responses, and Solutions." IFC, Washington, DC. https://www.ifc.org/wps/wcm/connect/industry_ext_content/ifc_external_corporate_site/financial+institutions/resources/covid19-and-women-led-firms-in-africa.

Muzi, Silvia, Filip Jolevski, Kohei Ueda, and Domenico Viganola. 2021. "Productivity and Firm Exit during the COVID-19 Crisis: Cross-Country Evidence." Policy Research Working Paper 9671, World Bank, Washington, DC.

SBP (State Bank of Pakistan). 2020. "Branchless Banking Statistics (Jan–Mar 2020)." Agricultural Credit and Microfinance Department, SBP, Karachi, Pakistan. https://www.sbp.org.pk/acd/branchless/Stats/BBSQtr-Jan-Mar-2020.pdf.

SBP (State Bank of Pakistan). 2021. "Branchless Banking Statistics (Jan–Mar 2021)." Agricultural Credit and Microfinance Department, SBP, Karachi, Pakistan. https://www.sbp.org.pk/acd/branchless/Stats/BBSQtr-Jan-Mar-2021.pdf.

Spaggiari, Lucia. 2021. "COVID-19 and Microfinance: What the Data Says About Risk in the Sector." CGAP (blog), September 29, 2021. https://www.cgap.org/blog/covid-19-and-microfinance-what-data-says-about-risk-sector.

Symbiotics. 2019. "2019 Symbiotics MIV Survey: Market Data and Peer Group Analysis." 13th ed. Symbiotics Group, Geneva. https://symbioticsgroup.com/wp-content/uploads/2020/02/symbiotics-symbiotics-2019-miv-survey.pdf.

Lending during the recovery and beyond

The ongoing impact of the COVID-19 crisis on business performance and household incomes could inhibit new lending because of increased credit risk. Risk can be mitigated by better visibility into borrower viability and improved recourse in the event of default. Reassessing credit models to take into account the "new normal," as well as innovations in digital finance that leverage alternative data and tailor loans to the borrower and the lending environment, can help keep credit flowing. Regulatory frameworks that enable innovation can support credit in the recovery while ensuring consumer and market protections.

Policy Priorities

Mitigating the environment of uncertainty and the lack of transparency that are making the traditional approaches to measuring risk less effective calls for the following measures:

- **Creating an enabling environment to leverage alternative data.** Lenders should look to adapt underwriting approaches, with support from supervisory model validation and regulatory frameworks that open access to data while ensuring privacy and consumer protection.

- **Embracing innovations in product design and embedded finance** that tailor loans to customer and market conditions or link credit to underlying business transactions to increase visibility and improve recourse.

- **Providing well-tuned guarantee programs** where needed to bridge the gap between lenders' risk aversion and the role of credit as a driver of an equitable recovery.

- **Advancing the regulatory framework and financial infrastructure** to support innovation; adjust the regulatory perimeter; provide clear, effective, and enforceable consumer and market protections; and facilitate digital payments, information exchange, and asset registration.

Introduction

Previous chapters focused on the actions countries can take to reduce damage to the financial sector if long-term, widespread income losses stemming from the COVID-19 (coronavirus) pandemic force borrowers to default on their debt. For the economy, however, the risks associated with past loans are not the only concern. A separate challenge is the ability of financial service providers to continue extending credit to fuel the recovery. As countries embark on the road to recovery and policy makers wind down the exceptional fiscal and other policy support measures put in place to help the economy through the pandemic, it is paramount that businesses and households have adequate access to credit to withstand economic uncertainty, invest in opportunities, and take part in the recovery.

The onset of the pandemic extensively disrupted economies worldwide. Lockdowns, business interruptions and closures, and job losses in the real sector (the activities associated with goods and services) were reflected almost immediately in the financial sector by a tightening of lending conditions. Bank supervisors and lenders worried that the crisis would rapidly translate into loan losses and cash withdrawals by the public.

As discussed in chapter 1, unprecedented government intervention and regulatory forbearance to mitigate the impacts of the crisis have so far helped banks maintain capital levels and liquidity. Yet the ongoing impacts of the crisis on business performance and household incomes, as well as the expected rise in nonperforming loans (NPLs) and tightening of monetary policies, will create challenges for new lending. Continued economic disruptions and uncertainty will increase credit risk, reduce visibility into borrower viability, and diminish the realizable value of traditional sources of recourse in the event of default. Reporting practices around loan moratoria and debt restructuring further cloud visibility into the actual credit performance of certain customers.

In this environment of heightened risk and continued uncertainty, finance providers need to adapt credit models and product offerings if they are to continue lending. Ways of doing this include making changes in product design—the terms and lengths (tenors) of loans—as well as integrating new types of data into credit models. These adaptations will benefit from the continuing adoption of new technologies and digital channels supporting payments, credit information, and secured transactions. A silver lining of the pandemic is that it accelerated digital adoption in the economy as a whole, as well as among finance providers and borrowers, thereby laying the foundation for better credit analysis and monitoring, greater product diversity, and a broader range of credit providers.

Financial service providers, infrastructure providers, governments, and the regulatory community can all help advance the adoption of solutions to facilitate access to credit during the recovery. This chapter describes approaches available to finance providers for adjusting their operations and products to continue lending. It also describes the role of governments, regulators, and financial infrastructure in helping the credit market adapt to the new environment—such as by integrating new data and business models—and in countering market tendencies to limit credit to larger firms and better-off borrowers. As credit conditions improve, markets that have been able to roll out these solutions and restrain a "flight to quality" will be in a better position to tackle long-standing credit gaps and foster financial inclusion.

Examples in this chapter illustrate how financial service providers have delivered credit to underserved customers and entrepreneurs during the pandemic by mitigating risk through product design, or by integrating new technologies or improved data models for credit underwriting and servicing. Innovations in channels, products, and processes have enabled the expansion of lending to riskier and previously underserved segments. Although these innovations will be pivotal to achieving additional visibility and recourse in the pandemic context, even for previously well-served segments, the rollout of certain products, business models, and data may not be feasible in all markets. Their adoption will require thoughtful consideration of systemic and institutional factors as well as consumer protection.

The borrowers referred to in this chapter include the small and medium businesses that make up the majority of enterprises providing jobs in most emerging economies,[1] as well as households and micro-entrepreneurs. These groups find it challenging to access formal credit even when the economy is sound and growing, and all have been significantly affected by the pandemic. Nonetheless, the credit needs of small businesses differ from those of microentrepreneurs, for example, and they are often served by different financial services providers, offering different solutions.

Solving the COVID-19 risk puzzle: Risk visibility and recourse

Beyond its profound impacts on the credit risk of households and businesses, the pandemic significantly impaired the visibility that lenders have into a borrower's capacity and willingness to repay a loan, and it limited lenders' options for recourse in the increasingly likely event of a default. Policy responses to help alleviate the impacts of the pandemic reduced near-term risks, but further reduced visibility into and certainty about the underlying viability of borrowers. The protracted effects of the pandemic on the economy and the financial sector may over time affect the liquidity and capital of finance providers, diminishing even more their willingness and ability to take on risk.

A lender's decision to extend credit and the associated terms reflect the amount of risk the lender is willing to take based on estimates of both the borrower's probability of default and the anticipated loss in the event of a default. The ability to assess the likelihood of repayment depends on the available information about the borrower and the context of the loan (visibility), whereas estimates of loss in case of default are based on the market for collateral or the enforceability of guarantees (recourse).

As noted in earlier chapters, the pandemic and associated lockdowns had a profound impact on economic activity, affecting borrowers (businesses and households) directly and increasing credit risk. For some sectors and businesses, the impact was transitory and it diminished as lockdowns were lifted. For others, the effects will last longer. For example, in Rwanda business sectors that rely on in-person work (such as construction and accommodation and food) were more affected by the lockdowns than sectors that could transition some of their activities to remote working. Once lockdowns were lifted, however, construction quickly recovered well above precrisis levels, but for the accommodation and food sector, where face-to-face interactions with customers are necessary, the crisis dragged on.[2] When lenders confront uncertain conditions, they typically respond by tightening credit standards and reducing credit supply, shifting to safer assets. If lenders lack solid information with which to assess risks, they reduce credit not only to insolvent businesses and households, but also to everyone else because they are not able to distinguish between the two groups.

Although uncertainty has always been part of lender business models, before the pandemic finance providers were better able to determine a borrower's ability and willingness to repay and the probability of default by taking into account credit and payment histories, income, or assets; nonfinancial information (such as home address, relevant sector of the borrower's business, and length of banking relationship) that can act as a proxy for income; the purpose of the loan (home loans or loans for business equipment have a different risk profile than loans for consumption or working capital); and the time horizon for the loan (visibility tends to be higher over shorter time horizons). For business loans, lenders would rely on heuristics and models to take into account sector or demographic norms (such as typical inventory turns or balance sheet ratios for a given industry).

The significant structural break caused by the crisis diminished, however, the value of past data and heuristics. Traditional credit data sources are largely backward-looking. But with so many sectors, businesses, and individual incomes disrupted, past performance is no longer as strong an indicator of future performance. Typical reporting delays by lenders and infrequent updates of credit registries and credit bureau data are a challenge in the rapidly evolving pandemic. Even for sectors that might be expected to recover, lenders might not have the timely relevant information needed to accurately determine whether an existing or prospective borrower would still have the income and ability to navigate the new economic environment.

Even the more qualitative relationship-based methods that lenders typically use to smooth lending over an economic cycle were compromised. Loan officer visits were limited or delayed by lockdowns and social distancing.[3] Lenders had difficulty meeting new clients, verifying customer identity, and evaluating a borrower's business operations on site, and they curtailed the in-person collections and group meetings central to many microfinance business models. These and other operational challenges were particularly acute earlier in the crisis. Many of these challenges have since been overcome through the use of digital tools, but operational constraints continue to be a factor in many markets.

The unprecedented level of policy interventions—including government transfers, debt moratoria, loan reschedulings, and suspension of NPL classifications—further clouded lender visibility by reducing the usefulness of financial data and credit information as predictors of a borrower's ability to repay. Lenders must be able to distinguish whether a borrower's business is sustainably recovering due to sound fundamentals or is dependent on government support of the business or its customers. Even relatively recent data can be misleading.[4] Positive cash flows or increases in account balances resulting from government support programs do not indicate longer-term viability. Eventual winding down of that support could later affect ability to repay.

Thus policy interventions that stabilized markets may have, paradoxically, made it more difficult in some cases for lenders to extend the credit needed to resume growth. Along with these challenges around visibility, the pandemic has also affected the traditional forms of recourse that limit lenders' losses in the event of default. Having recourse also dissuades borrowers from defaulting in the first place. Typical forms of recourse are collateral and personal guarantees, and both play multiple roles. Lenders use collateral to (1) assess a borrower's financial condition; (2) motivate repayment because a borrower would want to avoid losing the asset; and (3) offset losses in the event of default by seizing and selling the collateral. Personal guarantees signal that the borrower has reputable relationships that the lender can call on to repay a loan in the event the borrower defaults; this is both an indicator of financial standing and a loss mitigant in the event of default. Guarantees also formalize an element of social pressure to motivate repayment. Providing collateral or personal guarantees has long been a challenge for micro-, small-, and medium enterprises (MSMEs) and households in emerging economies. Group guarantees as part of microfinance lending are an attempt to fill that gap for individual microentrepreneurs. Guarantees from government or development finance institutions are another form of recourse, and these may be made more available to MSMEs under some programs. Less traditional forms of recourse—such as automatic repayments, liens on future digital receipts and cash flows, and exclusion from marketplace platforms in case of default on a loan from the platform—can be incorporated into MSME and consumer lending, particularly in the embedded finance models discussed later in this chapter. The bankruptcy and resolution frameworks described in previous chapters can influence how effectively and efficiently lenders can use certain types of recourse.

Recourse options during the pandemic were reduced by moratoria, and the value of traditional forms of collateral was altered. Will a commercial building losing tenants (due to the pandemic) be as valuable as it was with full occupancy? If many restaurants are going out of business, what is the resale value of a commercial oven? Beyond the theoretical value of an asset, will a bank be able to realize that value during a period of economic uncertainty? Monetary policy and moratoria temporarily forestalled defaults and liquidations, supporting asset prices. Implemented over long periods, however, debt moratoria, rent holidays, and credit guarantees can have the unintended effects of heightening volatility and further eroding collateral asset values. The lifting of moratoria and government support measures could provoke further post-default liquidations, triggering fire sales of assets.[5] These factors have reduced not only the degree to which lenders can rely on traditional forms of recourse, but also their ability to project the value of that recourse.

Reacting to the combined effects of higher credit risk in the economy, low visibility, and reduced recourse, lenders have tightened credit standards and reduced the amount of new credit available to support the recovery.[6] A review of quarterly central bank surveys on credit conditions from both emerging and advanced economies finds that the majority of economies have experienced several quarters of tightening credit standards since the onset of the crisis. Figure 4.1 presents the quarterly net change in credit conditions relative to previous quarters for a sample of 38 countries, as reported in the central bank or monetary authority surveys of credit conditions in those countries. March 2020 onward saw a sharp increase in the share of countries whose financial service providers tightened credit standards compared with the previous quarter. Although the pace of tightening appears to have slowed in 2021 with lenders across many countries beginning to ease credit conditions, the data suggest that for many of the countries surveyed credit standards remain substantially tighter than their prepandemic levels.

Figure 4.1 **Quarterly trends in credit conditions, by country income group, 2018–21**

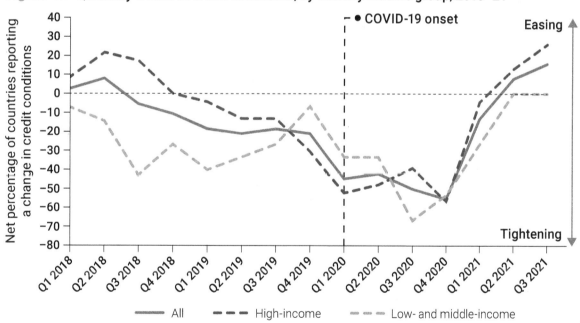

Source: WDR 2022 team calculations, based on data from survey reports by the central banks of 38 countries published or accessed as of December 15, 2021: Albania, Argentina, Austria, Belgium, Canada, Chile, Cyprus, Czech Republic, Estonia, France, Germany, Ghana, Greece, Hungary, India, Indonesia, Ireland, Italy, Japan, Latvia, Lithuania, Mexico, the Netherlands, North Macedonia, the Philippines, Poland, Portugal, Romania, the Russian Federation, Serbia, Spain, Thailand, Turkey, Uganda, Ukraine, the United Kingdom, the United States, and Zambia.

Note: The figure shows the net percentage of countries in which banks reported a change in overall credit conditions in quarterly central bank loan officer or credit condition surveys. The net percentage is the difference between the share of countries that report an overall easing in credit conditions and the share of countries that report an overall tightening of credit conditions relative to the previous quarter. A negative net percentage value indicates an overall tightening of credit conditions in the sample of countries covered. For Chile, Japan, Mexico, Poland, Russia, the United States, and Zambia, the overall credit conditions are estimated from an index of reported credit conditions in business and consumer segments.

Reduced credit in the context of crises is particularly challenging for MSMEs and other segments of the economy such as women and informal entrepreneurs who even before the crisis were viewed by financial institutions as riskier and more challenging to serve.[7] These businesses tend to be more thinly capitalized, have fewer assets and little excess liquidity, and be relatively undiversified in terms of product markets and customer base. The systemic, negative, real sector shock of the pandemic interrupted revenue streams of the segments already viewed as riskier.[8] Because of this differential impact on their customer base, specialized lenders, including credit unions, savings banks, microfinance institutions (MFIs), and other nonbank financial institutions that focus on MSMEs and underserved households, faced operational and fundraising challenges that affected their ability to deliver credit. In addition, access to short-term trade finance was a challenge for small and medium enterprises (SMEs) during the COVID-19 pandemic as costs and application rejection rates increased.[9] The International Chamber of Commerce reported that banks either retrenched from segments perceived as high risk such as SMEs or hiked prices for short-term trade financing for them.[10]

Many lenders lack the capacity to mitigate effectively the new risks introduced by the COVID-19 crisis and have responded by limiting credit to all but the lowest-risk borrowers. If financial markets continue this trend, they could unleash a vicious cycle (see figure 1.2 in chapter 1). In such a cycle, the widespread reduction in credit to MSMEs forces more of them out of business before they can recover and drive growth, with follow-on impacts on the households whose members are employed by or otherwise depend on these businesses for income, products, or services.[11] Business failures can have a domino effect, with the first failures pushing upstream companies out of business because of the reduced demand for their products or services. Over time, accelerating business failures increase the bad debt burden on lenders and reduce their capital and capacity to lend, as well as their willingness to take risk. Movement in this direction would cut government tax revenue while at the same time increasing the need for fiscal support for households, firms, and potentially financial institutions in need of bailouts.

Markets in which lenders are able to manage and mitigate the risk of new lending to meet the financing needs of businesses and households despite the heightened uncertainty could unleash a virtuous cycle, supporting the efforts of small and large businesses and households to restart spending and to invest in the economic recovery. For example, a small shop may be solvent and viable but need additional working capital to replace spoiled inventory and cover costs until retail activity recovers. Or a manufacturer may need to invest in raw materials and production well before it receives income from sales. For households, credit could help them maintain consumption—such as paying fees for school or childcare—or meet financial emergencies before their income has fully recovered, with benefits for the broader economy through spending. Improved prospects for businesses and households have a positive impact on the income and capital of the lenders serving them, further increasing lenders' capacity to lend and their risk appetite.

Regulators have a central role in supporting a virtuous cycle by encouraging the financial sector's efforts to adapt while monitoring financial stability. Recovery of economic activity and spending can raise tax revenue and allow governments to shift their focus from broad-based fiscal support programs to targeted ones to support those parts of the economy hardest-hit by the crisis and to lower the risk associated with longer-term investments to support job creation and a sustainable recovery. Finally, as economic conditions stabilize in the recovery, lenders that have successfully adapted to the "new normal" may become better able to extend longer-term financing to support capital investments by MSMEs and to reach low-income households and informal businesses previously excluded by the financial sector, thereby further reducing the need for government intervention.

To prevent onset of the vicious cycle and unleash a virtuous one, lenders will have to embrace tools that allow them to overcome the visibility and recourse challenges affecting their ability to measure and manage risk.

Improving risk mitigation

This section highlights strategies that lenders can adopt to manage or mitigate risk so they can provide financially viable borrowers with credit in an environment of heightened risk and uncertainty. Digitalization, which accelerated during the pandemic, can facilitate the feasibility and adoption of many of these strategies.

To continue to lend through the pandemic and the recovery, finance providers need new approaches to measuring risk, as well as new approaches to product design, both of which can improve visibility and strengthen recourse in order to balance risk. Lenders can start by reassessing their existing sector and borrower scoring models and updating them where possible based on information on economic activity by sector or geography. Most lenders have by now recognized that there has been a structural break, and both business models and financial models need to be retuned. Supervisors can help ensure this is done in a timely fashion and that any approvals needed to adapt underwriting and collection procedures or deploy updates of risk models are expedited.

Some banks have assessed the impact of lockdowns by characterizing the risk for each industry-geography intersection.[12] Banco Pichincha in Ecuador personalized repayment terms and adapted its financial and nonfinancial services to support borrowers and continue lending, while Konfío in Mexico took time to adapt its credit algorithms before resuming its growth. 4G Capital in Kenya piloted mobile surveys to seek to incorporate a measure of borrower financial stress in its credit underwriting.[13] Lenders can also improve the data and analytics they use for risk modeling, adjust product mix and design, and incorporate risk-sharing facilities where available. These approaches, and their potential impacts on visibility, recourse, and credit risk to the lender are outlined in figure 4.2.

Figure 4.2 Impacts of selected risk mitigation strategies on visibility, recourse, and risk

	Improve visibility	Strengthen recourse	Reduce risk
Risk measurement			
Alternative data	●	○	○
Enhanced analytics	●	○	○
Product choice and design			
Loan tenor	●	○	○
Secured credit	◑	◑	○
Embedded finance	●	◑	◑
Supply chain finance	◔	◔	◑
Insuring risk			
Credit guarantees	○	●	●

Source: WDR 2022 team.

Note: Shaded circles indicate the increasing relevance of each solution for the respective challenge, from not applicable (○) to degrees of relevance (◔◑●) to highly relevant (●).

Policy makers can also help by establishing the infrastructure and regulatory environment needed to support new approaches to visibility and recourse and to encourage innovation and the growth of new players with diverse business models and risk appetites. For riskier sectors and segments, governments may also have to continue deploying risk mitigation instruments, such as well-calibrated credit guarantees, to support access to finance. Targeted liquidity or income support schemes may continue to be required for those in need for whom borrowing is not appropriate.

Alternative data

Although the pandemic reduced lenders' visibility into credit risk, they are not without options. Alternative data sources can inform risk assessments and allow lenders to fill pandemic-related information gaps. As risk and uncertainty decline, these approaches can also be used to extend credit to underserved segments that were informationally opaque even before the pandemic.

The term *alternative data* refers to information not included in traditional credit reports, which focus on outstanding loans and repayment history. For example, a wide range of transactional data are available from financial service providers, mobile network operators and other utilities, traditional businesses and online platforms, and governments. These data include bank deposits and withdrawals, mobile money use, airtime top-ups and utilities payments, payroll, rent, taxes, supply orders and deliveries, sales orders, invoices, and business receipts. Nonfinancial data from social media footprints, psychometrics, online behavior, and telecommunications usage, including top-up and calling patterns, contacts, and global positioning system (GPS) data, can supplement transactional data.[14] These data have been found to provide information that is at least as predictive as that held by credit bureaus. Many of these data are considered "big data"—that is, data produced by digital channels and characterized by high volume, variety, and velocity.[15]

One study found that in Germany credit scoring models based on digital footprints were better at predicting creditworthiness than credit bureau scores. The two assessments can complement each other for greater sensitivity.[16] A study of loan data from a large fintech lender in India showed that use of mobile and social footprints can improve risk assessments for individuals with credit scores and be an effective indicator for individuals who lack credit bureau records.[17] Research from South America found similar results from the use of call data records to predict credit repayment outcomes for individuals lacking a credit history.[18] Meanwhile, a US study found that transaction data can be used to create risk profiles capable of serving individuals otherwise excluded or charged higher interest rates.[19] Finally, research from China found that the use of big data to assess the probability of default led to increased credit access for borrowers who otherwise would have remained unbanked or who would have been required to pledge collateral to access financing.[20]

Alternative data can also help lenders to update sector and business assessments (see box 4.1). Because some industries have been more (and some less) directly affected by the pandemic, standard market reports are no longer as accurate. Retuning existing models is an important first step to improving risk assessments, although the scale and depth of the crisis will likely continue to require lenders to update or reset benchmarking data over time.

Despite the opportunity presented by the growing abundance of alternative and big data, several challenges are posed by issues of availability, validation, and interpretation in underwriting. Availability is affected by a prospective borrower's use of the services and platforms that generate and hold alternative data. These platforms are often owned and controlled by private third parties, and so lenders must secure access to the data. For example, although a bank may have payment transaction data, the mobile operator collects call records, and the electric company has utility billing and payment records.

Lenders may collect some data directly from the borrower's phone, which raises privacy concerns about, for example, other people's data that may reside in the borrower's contacts list and text message records. Some prospective borrowers may have documents such as bills or payment records containing these data, but these can be hard to assemble and validate. In some markets, credit registries and bureaus, as well as new fintech data companies, are beginning to collect and validate this information (see box 4.8 later in this chapter). Data privacy and open banking frameworks are increasingly seeking to vest ownership and control of data in data subjects,[21] enabling those subjects to grant permission to third parties—including lenders—to access their data. The 2021 *World Development Report* discusses issues related to accessibility and intellectual property of this type of private intent data.[22]

In addition to accessing and validating new data, lenders need ways to confirm its interpretation as credit-relevant and incorporate it into underwriting models, while ensuring fairness and validity.

Box 4.1 Case study: Adaptive underwriting in Mexico

Konfío is a Mexican technology-based company seeking to boost the growth of underserved micro-, small, and medium enterprises (MSMEs) by way of an array of offerings, including financial services, payment solutions, and business tools. Through its digital lending platform, Konfío provides these MSMEs with the working capital funds they are unable to borrow from banks, often because they lack the collateral and credit history that banks require.[a]

Konfío, which launched operations in 2014, uses the data generated by MSMEs to meet government-established electronic invoicing requirements in its underwriting. Konfío developed an algorithm that supplements traditional financial history with electronic invoicing data, as well as data on a firm's network and digitally acquired information from payroll and annual statements. The company employs technology and machine learning to integrate these forms of alternative data in its underwriting and automate much of the traditional manual MSME credit scoring and underwriting process.

After the first measures to contain the spread of the COVID-19 virus were enacted in Mexico in March 2020, MSMEs' access to finance significantly deteriorated.[b] Faced with heightened portfolio risk and great uncertainty, lenders tightened loan requirements and reduced lending to MSMEs. A national survey of Mexico's businesses found that as recently as February 2021 a large share of MSMEs previously served by banks were suffering challenges in accessing financing.[c]

Konfío also reduced lending in the first months of the crisis in response to tightening credit standards and a drop in loan applications. It adapted its credit algorithm to integrate data on the impacts of COVID-19 containment measures across industry subsectors. The result was a new index to inform portfolio collection strategies, loan renewals, and new loan originations. Konfío's leadership believes that approach enabled them to limit portfolio delinquencies and to recalibrate credit underwriting to identify lower-risk MSMEs. As demand for credit among MSMEs picked up, Konfío was able to resume lending to both existing and first-time clients. In August 2020, Konfío began to rapidly grow its new loan bookings. Indeed, it achieved records in both the number and volume of monthly loans disbursed as of February 2021 (figure B4.1.1).

As economic conditions and outlook evolve, Konfío continues to track business performance by industry and economic activity to continually recalibrate how it classifies performing versus underperforming industries. By dynamically adapting its credit policies, Konfío has been able to gradually expand its coverage. The company claims that as of July 2021 it was serving more than 90 percent of the industries and regions in Mexico.

(Box continues next page)

Box 4.1 **Case study: Adaptive underwriting in Mexico** *(continued)*

Figure B4.1.1 **Growth in loan disbursements by Konfío, 2019–21**

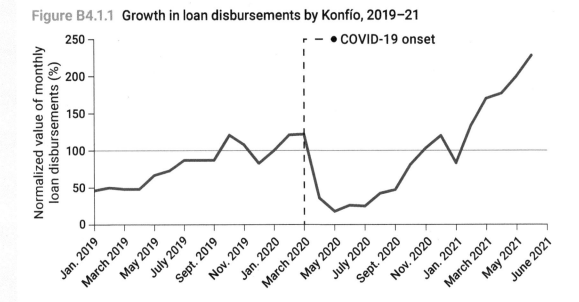

Source: Konfío, proprietary portfolio data, 2021.

Note: The figure shows the ratio between the value of monthly loan disbursements and that for January 2020.

a. IFC (2017b).

b. National Institute of Statistics and Geography (Instituto Nacional de Estadística y Geografía), ECOVID-IE (Survey on the Economic Impact Generated by COVID-19 on Enterprises) (dashboard), Aguascalientes, Mexico, http://en.www.inegi.org .mx/programas/ecovidie/. This survey on the impact of COVID-19 on businesses in Mexico found that as of April 2020, 12 percent of MSMEs had suffered a reduction in access to financial services.

c. ECOVID-IE. As of February 2021, 8 percent of MSMEs still suffered from lower access to finance. An earlier economic census by Mexico's National Institute of Statistics and Geography found that access to finance is historically limited for MSMEs in Mexico. In 2019, an estimated 11.4 percent of microenterprises (0–10 employees) and 25.7 percent of small and medium enterprises (11–250 employees) had access to finance (INEGI 2020).

Regulators typically require lenders to ensure the *explicability* of their credit scoring models and algorithms and of the data they use.[23] This is particularly important in the use of nontraditional data to predict creditworthiness. Reliance on such data can lead to unintended biases due to the differential availability or use of some of the data sources. The sheer newness of complex algorithms may be a factor as well (see box 4.2). The widespread use of alternative data, which depends on a customer having access to utilities, mobile money, smartphones, e-commerce or social media platforms, or other data generators, could result in "digital redlining"—that is, the exclusion of individuals whose activities, location, or socioeconomic situation are data-poor. For example, alternative data such as the operating system used by a borrower's smartphone, the timing and location of a loan application, or device data on mobile phone top-ups and e-commerce activity, can indicate asset ownership and the regularity of behavior and cash flows.[24] In some markets, however, they may also map to the protected characteristics[25] of potential borrowers or exclude borrowers who do not have smartphones.

Box 4.2 Credit and algorithmic biases

How will credit risk modeling innovations such as machine learning and alternative data affect the distribution of credit? Who can access credit, and at what cost? Gender bias and discrimination in face-to-face loan officer decision-making are well documented.[a] As the COVID-19 crisis accelerates the adoption of machine learning and big data, there is potential to reduce the historical biases on gender and race stemming from human discretion in lending decisions. On the other hand, new types of discrimination through algorithms and biases in programming and data could be introduced.[b] The emerging academic literature on the topic paints a nuanced picture of whether these new sources of bias reduce or exacerbate the overall level of discrimination in financial services.[c]

A study from Pakistan of 5,500 digital loan applications compared outcomes of submissions randomly assigned for review by loan officers or by a machine learning algorithm. The study found that the algorithm achieved a 21 percent reduction in loan defaults while serving a similar share of female and ethnic minority group borrowers.[d]

However, when the gender of the applicants was revealed in the data, loan officers exhibited a positive bias, approving 22 percent more applications from women than those based on an anonymized review, without leading to an increase in defaults. When the algorithm was exposed to gender information, it was better able to predict defaults than loan officers, but it approved 16–21 percent fewer applications from women than when it was fed anonymized data.

A study that examined data on over 9 million loans from the US mortgage market found that moving from "traditional" statistical models to machine learning models improved the accuracy of default predictions, leading to an overall reduction in default risk for the median borrower.[e] However, as shown in figure B4.2.1, the benefits from the new technology are not distributed equally across groups in society. The researchers in this case concluded that gains from new technology are skewed in favor of racial groups who already have better access to credit, while disadvantaged groups are less likely to benefit. The study also found that

Figure B4.2.1 Share of borrowers who appear more creditworthy when using a machine learning model than when using traditional statistical methods

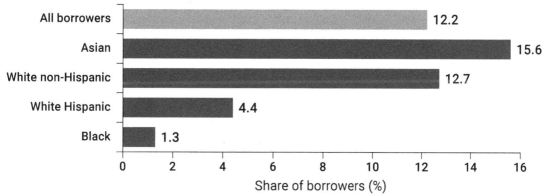

Source: WDR 2022 team, adapted from Fuster et al. (2021).

Note: The figure shows the share of borrowers assigned a lower risk of default as lenders move from traditional predictive technology (a "Logit" classifier) to machine learning technology (a "Random Forest" classifier) in the US mortgage market.

(Box continues next page)

Box 4.2 **Credit and algorithmic biases** *(continued)*

both the improved predictive power from machine learning models and its unequal outcomes stem from the ability of this new technology to learn how nonlinear combinations of characteristics predict default.

These studies indicate that, although machine learning algorithms appear to be more efficient than other methods in assessing credit risk, in some contexts artificial intelligence may lead to undesirable biases. The results from the Pakistan study are consistent with nondiscrimination laws, which typically do not allow lending decisions to be based on personal characteristics.[f] The results of the US mortgage study suggest that in a different context algorithms may use available borrower characteristics (such as income, credit score, or collateral value) to implicitly proxy for a borrower's race or gender, effectively (though not always intentionally) sidestepping fair lending regulations. Legal scholars, economists, and computer scientists have debated how the texts of fair lending laws could need to be adjusted to take into account the realities of data-driven lending and prevent intended or unintended discrimination.[g]

a. Montoya et al. (2020).
b. World Bank (2021c).
c. Morse and Pence (2020).
d. Kisat (2021).
e. Fuster et al. (2021).
f. For a more detailed discussion of potential biased and discriminatory outcomes, see World Bank (2021a, 2021c).
g. Bartlett et al. (2020); Gillis and Spiess (2019); Yang and Dobbie (2020).

Enhanced analytics for underwriting

Just as important as the data used to measure and assess creditworthiness are the models that lenders use to analyze that data. Conventional statistical models, which are based on multivariate regression analysis and similar tools, can be adapted to incorporate a wide range of data. Yet it is difficult to adapt them quickly and dynamically in fluid situations such as the one sparked by the COVID-19 pandemic. Even if the overall form of the models is maintained, retuning the parameters requires a period of data measurement under the new conditions to validate predictive capacity. If typical monthly or quarterly data were used, by the time the impact of one wave of the pandemic has been incorporated, many markets could be in another wave, with potentially different sectoral impacts. Although subject to many of the same constraints related to data access and validation, machine learning (ML) models can more easily integrate real-time, high-frequency data and adapt to changing economic situations. Because ML models continually adapt to changes in data, they can tune and retune as a situation evolves, with potentially higher predictive capacity over time than traditional multivariate models and analyses.[26]

The benefits of alternative data, artificial intelligence (AI), and ML for improving visibility in credit underwriting have become increasingly well understood by financial institutions, but the barriers to adoption—technical, operational, and regulatory—can be significant.[27] On the technical side, legacy systems often lack the capacity and flexibility to support the data processing and analysis requirements of AI applications. Effectively employing AI therefore requires significant investments in platform modernization, as well as investments in the AI models themselves. It also requires access to expert data scientists and software development engineers, who are in short supply in both emerging and advanced economies.[28] On the operational side, adoption of AI technology by the leading financial institutions is steadily increasing, yet an industry survey estimated that, going into the pandemic, just 25 percent of financial sector firms relied on ML to detect fraud or support underwriting and risk management.[29] Increasingly, software-as-a-service solutions as well as integrations with specialized technology allow for modular offerings and subscription models that are reducing barriers to entry and time to market for incumbent finance providers. In the regulatory realm, slow supervisory approvals may delay adoption of underwriting innovations by financial service providers. Lack of adequate or clear regulations on data usage, privacy, and permitted credit information sharing could prevent financial institutions from taking full advantage of the data available to them.[30]

Alternative lenders with operating models designed to leverage technology for process automation and to incorporate alternative data in credit underwriting grew rapidly in the years prior to the pandemic. COVID-19 demonstrated that these lenders could also withstand a major shock.[31] The business models of alternative lenders vary widely, as do the size and economic status of the borrowers they target. The range of business models includes crowdfunding and marketplace platforms; mobile phone lenders that access transaction and mobile phone data; lending to MSMEs based on invoices, payment flows, or order information from suppliers; and personal loans based on regular salary or remittance income.[32] Many of these business models target formalized small businesses and middle-income to affluent individuals. However, some alternative lending models specifically focus on microloans and microleases to individuals or working capital for informal businesses and MSMEs. Although it is too early to conclude that during the pandemic alternative lenders as a whole demonstrated greater resilience than traditional financial services providers, the case studies in this chapter on Konfío (box 4.1) and MYbank (box 4.6) show that these models can adapt to a new normal for a tier of borrowers that otherwise would find it difficult to access credit.

Scaling up the use of alternative data and AI to enable equitable access to finance during the pandemic recovery will require investments not just by alternative, digital-first lenders, but also by traditional banks and other financial service providers, including those that serve lower-income households and microenterprises. Meanwhile, alternative finance businesses serve too few customers relative to the scale of finance likely to be needed to drive the recovery in most markets. More specifically, alternative finance providers represent less than 1 percent of credit flows worldwide. Lending by fintech and technology companies in 2019 was estimated to be 5.8 percent of the stock of credit in Kenya, 2 percent in China, 1.1 percent in Indonesia, and less than 1 percent of overall credit to the private sector in other major markets.[33] Incumbent financial institutions, by contrast, have the capital, size, and client relationships to supply credit to drive a broader recovery in their economies. It will be imperative that they overcome any cultural and capacity constraints and regulatory frictions that limit their ability to innovate to both support the recovery from the pandemic and compete longer term with new technology-driven lenders.

Two areas needing attention in the near term to ensure that innovations in the use of data and analytics—and, indeed, all of the technological advances discussed in this chapter—are truly beneficial are consumer protection and cybersecurity. Globally, supervisors listed cybersecurity (78 percent) and consumer protection (27 percent) among the top three growing risk areas related to the use of financial technology emerging during the pandemic because of the accelerated transition to digital services and remote interactions.[34]

A significant risk from which consumers need protection is cybercrime. Surveys of users of digital financial services in Kenya and Nigeria found that over 50 percent of respondents reportedly experienced fraud or attempted fraud when using a financial service since the onset of COVID-19.[35] Meanwhile, cybersecurity breaches increased by an average of 15 percent for fintech firms during the pandemic.[36] Recent reports from the G20/OECD Task Force on Financial Consumer Protection (FCP) and the World Bank provide extensive policy guidance on FCP in the digital age.[37]

Consumer protection guidelines must also ensure that digital financial service providers deliver products appropriate for a given customer. Financial literacy levels among households and MSMEs remain low.[38] The proliferation of digital finance has outpaced the financial literacy of many consumers, as well as their ability to use credit wisely. Mobile lending apps in Kenya and Tanzania provide just one example.[39] Because the use of new data can reveal borrowers' willingness and ability to pay, those data can be exploited to bring prices in line with what lower-income segments can afford. These data can also be used for predatory pricing. Although the price discrimination enabled by AI-powered models is a form of economic efficiency, it can lead to unfair outcomes for riskier or less financially literate borrowers.[40]

Digital technologies can play a role in helping to address this challenge. Consumer advocates can use technology channels to deliver simple, actionable, accessible, and personalized financial education, especially to youth. Many governments delivered financial education messages through digital channels during the pandemic. Innovations such as personalized financial counseling and behavioral nudges related to financial goals can also strengthen financial consumer protection.[41] Technology, and social media in particular, can also be used to achieve a more robust redress mechanism for consumers.[42] Although digital delivery of financial education promotes financial resilience in several ways, it requires basic digital skills and access to information infrastructure (such as a smartphone and broadband/ internet). Lack of connectivity may exclude the households most in need of financial literacy support.[43]

Substantial evidence is emerging of a lasting "digital dividend" of the pandemic related to the adoption of digital channels for the delivery of and access to financial services (see box 4.3). However, many of the access gaps that existed before the crisis persist, risking a further deepening of financial and economic exclusion for those segments of the population that lack mobile phones or internet access. As discussed in detail in the 2021 *World Development Report,* countries will be limited in their ability to adapt many of the innovative mitigation strategies without investing in digital infrastructure and supportive regulatory frameworks.[44]

Box 4.3 The COVID-19 digital shock

The pandemic created near-immediate challenges for financial service providers across all facets of their operations. The most immediate impact was on physical branch operations, which in several countries closed to protect clients and staff. Although banks were often considered essential services and so were exempted from lockdowns, the microfinance institutions (MFIs) and mobile money agents that act as front-line providers of financial services to low-income and rural customers did not always receive similar dispensations. Within a matter of weeks, institutions had to combine on-site activities with remote work to keep operations running and ensure staff safety.[a] Remote working operations of financial institutions in emerging economies were significantly limited by deficiencies in internet access and systems.[b]

Digital payments and mobile and internet banking helped financial institutions continue to serve customers during lockdowns.[c] In many countries, this was a massive transition because most financial transactions used cash prior to the pandemic.[d] The first wave of lockdowns spurred a spike in downloads of digital banking apps.[e] A study of 71 countries estimated that the pandemic led to an increase of 21–26 percent in the rate of daily downloads of finance-related mobile applications from the countries' first confirmed COVID-19 cases through December 2020.[f]

Likewise, mobility restrictions fueled a surge in the adoption of digital payments.[g] In Indonesia, the value of e-money transactions grew about 39 percent between 2019 and 2020.[h] In India, the monthly volume of digital payments as of November 2021

(Box continues next page)

Box 4.3 **The COVID-19 digital shock** *(continued)*

was 57 percent higher compared to the year before.[i] A survey in Pakistan found that active mobile money users increased from 8 percent of adults in February–March 2020 to 14 percent by the end of the year.[j] These new banking behaviors resulted in several challenges for financial institutions. In India, for example, repeated service outages led the Reserve Bank of India to ask one of the country's largest commercial banks to temporarily halt the rollout of new digital financial services.[k]

The growth in digital financial services spurred by COVID-19 was in many ways built on a foundation laid well before the pandemic. The share of adults who made or received a digital payment grew from 32 percent in 2013 to 44 percent in 2017.[l] In Sub-Saharan Africa, the number of mobile money accounts surpassed 500 million in 2020.[m] In several emerging economies during the pandemic, an initial drop in digital payments concurrent with a decline in economic activity was followed by a rapid recovery and growth of digital payments and electronic transactions that surpassed previous levels. For example, data for the first semester of 2021 from Colombia's Superintendencia Financiera show that the number of monetary transactions conducted through a mobile phone doubled, replacing ATMs as the most common transaction channel.[n]

The uptake of digital platforms did not occur evenly across or within countries. Figure B4.3.1 shows how the adoption of digital channels among businesses was greater in middle-income countries, albeit with significant differences across markets. Some of the larger markets and markets that already had a certain percentage of connected residents saw the highest growth in the share of businesses that adopted or increased use of digital channels during the pandemic. By contrast, in low-income countries and markets with low internet penetration, the impact of the pandemic on the use of digital channels among businesses was also lower.[o] Surveys conducted in 2020 also found that firm size influenced digital adoption: as many

as 44 percent of large enterprises reported that they adopted or increased use of digital channels for their business, compared with just 27 percent of microenterprises.[p]

Women and rural residents have less access to the key enablers of financial access, such as mobile connectivity and accepted forms of identification (ID), than men or urban dwellers. A GSMA report estimates that 234 million fewer women than men use mobile internet.[q] Continued lack of connectivity or ID risks entrenching precrisis financial exclusion. Surveys in Pakistan revealed that gains in mobile money adoption in 2020 were concentrated among urban and financially literate groups.[r]

Beyond payments, financial service providers had to ensure the continuity of a wide range of operations, from account opening to loan underwriting and loan collections. Prior to the pandemic, the majority of financial institutions relied fully or in part on face-to-face engagement of their staff with clients. A survey of International Finance Corporation (IFC) financial institution clients on the early impacts of COVID-19 found that over 60 percent of respondents indicated that the crisis had led them to introduce or prioritize the digitalization of internal operations or the rollout of digital channels.[s] Technology and digital channels can significantly lower operating costs for lenders and enable them to sustainably offer small-value loans and products, reach underserved segments, and maintain viable operations through the crisis.[t]

Among MFIs, adoption of technology and digital financial services has been slower historically. However, anecdotal evidence indicates that institutions were better able to maintain operational resilience and support access to financial services if they had invested in back-office automation and digital channels prior to the pandemic. For example, Bancamía, one of the largest MFIs in Colombia, played a central role in the government's digital cash transfer programs.[u] The institution also leveraged its agent network and mobile banking services and accelerated the rollout of a process automation initiative

(Box continues next page)

Box 4.3 **The COVID-19 digital shock** *(continued)*

Figure B4.3.1 Impact of the COVID-19 pandemic on adoption of technology by businesses, by country income group

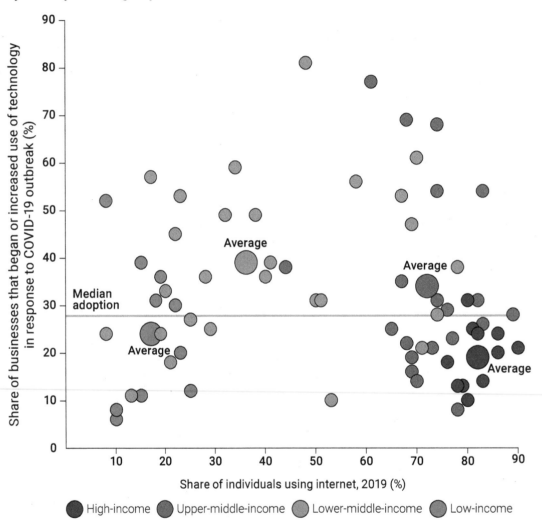

Source: WDR 2022 team, based on International Telecommunication Union, Statistics (database), https://www.itu.int/en/ITU-D/Statistics/Pages/stat/default.aspx; World Bank, COVID-19 Business Pulse Survey Dashboard, https://www.world bank.org/en/data/interactive/2021/01/19/covid-19-business-pulse-survey-dashboard; World Bank, Enterprise Surveys (database), https://www.enterprisesurveys.org/.

Note: The figure shows, by country income group, the share of firms that started using or increased the use of internet, online social media, specialized apps, or digital platforms, or invested in any new equipment, software, or digital solution in response to the COVID-19 outbreak. The vertical axis indicates the percentage of firms in low- and middle-income countries that adopted or increased use of digital channels after the onset of COVID-19. The horizontal axis indicates the percentage of individuals within a country using the internet by the end of 2019, or the most recent value before then.

(Box continues next page)

Box 4.3 **The COVID-19 digital shock** *(continued)*

to facilitate remote work for part of its back-office staff. Likewise, LAPO Microfinance Bank in Nigeria was able to rely on its agent network to continue to provide basic services to customers during an early lockdown that required it to stop branch operations. As Nigeria eased restrictions, the microfinance bank continued to rapidly scale up its agent network, more than doubling transaction volumes over precrisis levels by August 2020.[v]

a. See International Monetary Fund, Policy Responses to COVID-19: Policy Tracker (dashboard), https://www.imf.org/en /Topics/imf-and-covid19/Policy-Responses-to-COVID-19.
b. Garrote Sanchez et al. (2021).
c. Klapper and Miller (2021).
d. McKinsey (2020).
e. Koetsier (2020).
f. Fu and Mishra (2020).
g. Auer et al. (2020).
h. Crisanto (2021).
i. RBI (2021b).
j. Ghosh (2020); Karandaaz (2021).
k. The temporary ban issued on new digital initiatives to safeguard consumer protection and systemic stability was partially lifted in August 2021, allowing the concerned bank to issue new credit cards.
l. World Bank, Global Findex Database 2017 (Global Financial Inclusion Database), https://globalfindex.worldbank.org/.
m. GSMA (2021b).
n. SFC (2021).
o. Apedo-Amah et al. (2020); World Bank, COVID-19 Business Pulse Survey Dashboard, https://www.worldbank.org/en /data/interactive/2021/01/19/covid-19-business-pulse-survey-dashboard.
p. Adian et al. (2020).
q. GSMA (2021a).
r. Khan and Jaffar (2021).
s. IFC (2021).
t. Pazarbasioglu et al. (2020).
u. Banca de las Oportunidades (2020).
v. Froeling, Garcia Vargas, and Savonitto (2021).

Product choice and design

In addition to improving data and analytics, lenders can manage the heightened credit risk environment of the pandemic by focusing on credit products and product features that offer higher levels of visibility and recourse. For example, shorter-term loans require less information to gauge a borrower's ability and willingness to repay than loans with longer tenors. A projection of the next year's income and risks may not be necessary if a loan's duration is only one month, and yet a one-year projection would offer inadequate visibility for a three-year unsecured loan. Alternatively, a loan secured by inventory may not require as much visibility into future cash flows. This logic applies to personal lending as well. For example, a mortgage has different terms and longer tenor than an unsecured loan because recourse to the property reduces both the probability of default and loss in the event of a default. Lending products linked to other revenue-generating activities may provide greater visibility of the borrowers and enable credit losses to be offset by other revenue streams, thereby increasing the ability of lenders to assume credit risk.

Loan tenor

Matching the exposure period of a loan to the time frame over which the lender has visibility into the borrower's prospects is an age-old way to manage credit risk. During the COVID-19 recovery, lenders may reduce tenors for new loans to avoid having to predict longer-term economic outcomes. The challenge with shorter-term loans is that the costs of origination and servicing are essentially fixed, which reduces the potential profit from the loan. Digital technologies can reduce these costs by automating credit underwriting, monitoring, and collection and by using low-cost digital disbursement and repayment processes, making short-term loans to digitally connected MSMEs and households more viable.

Digital loans offered through mobile phones are one example of short-tenor loans that have grown rapidly in emerging economies (box 4.4). Research from Kenya found that access to these products increases household resilience in the face of economic shocks.[45] On the other hand, concerns have arisen about the cost, transparency, and consumer risks of these types of loans.[46] However, if these loans are appropriately designed and regulated, they have the potential to help unbanked customers build or rebuild credit history and gain access to more formal, larger, and longer-term loans.

Well-known products such as installment plans and point-of-sale financing are additional lending approaches that mitigate credit risk through short tenors and ongoing reviews of borrower risk. Installment plans allow borrowers who do not have enough cash to buy a product outright to divide a

---

Box 4.4 Case study: Mobile money overdrafts in Kenya

In Kenya, the migration of payments, savings, lending, and investment to digital channels predates the COVID-19 pandemic. By 2019, 79 percent of adults had a mobile money account, and nearly 60 percent of micro- and small enterprises used mobile money for business transactions.[a] Short-term digital loans had also become mainstream: survey data indicate that 14 percent of adults borrowed digitally in 2019, compared with the 9 percent of adults who had access to traditional sources of bank and nonbank credit.[b]

The number and types of digital lenders and the products they offer range from bank loans disbursed into mobile money accounts (such as M-Shwari) to digital loan apps (such as Tala, Branch) that were mostly unregulated until December 2021.[c] These products typically allow customers to conveniently access short-term, low-value credit from their phones. The lenders manage risk by analyzing alternative data and limiting exposure through low-value loans that can be easily renewed. These credit products have proven useful to many borrowers but raise concerns about transparency, appropriateness, high rates of default, and overindebtedness.[d] Emerging research suggests that they can be an important tool for smoothing consumption and financial management.[e] According to survey data, during the pandemic entrepreneurs and households across Kenya found it challenging to access traditional bank and nonbank credit, while digital credit continued to be used widely to support short-term liquidity and smooth consumption, complementing social networks and informal risk coping channels.[f]

During the crisis, lenders tightened credit standards significantly on both digital and traditional products in response to increased uncertainty.[g] New regulations issued in April 2020 introduced a moratorium on loan repayments and set a minimum threshold for negative reports to credit bureaus for both.[h] As a result, disbursements for the two largest digital term loan products fell significantly (a 41 percent year-on-year decrease as of

(Box continues next page)

Box 4.4 **Case study: Mobile money overdrafts in Kenya** *(continued)*

March 2021) stemming both from a reduction in demand and from lenders rejecting applications for smaller-value loans and focusing on a smaller pool of lower-risk borrowers.[i] Digital loan apps saw the largest decline in use, from 8.3 percent of adults in 2019 to 2.1 percent in 2021, according to the 2021 FinAccess Household Survey.[j]

By contrast, Fuliza M-PESA, the mobile money overdraft facility launched in 2019 by Safaricom, in partnership with NCBA Bank Kenya and KCB Bank Kenya, grew rapidly (figure B4.4.1). The Fuliza M-PESA overdraft facility saw its number of daily active users more than double, from 0.7 million to 1.7 million between April 2020 and September 2021, and the disbursement value grew by 62 percent year-on-year.[k] The 2021 FinAccess Survey results indicate that 18.3 percent of adult respondents used Fuliza in the last 12 months.[l] By allowing mobile money account holders to complete payments or execute transfers even without sufficient balance in their accounts, the Fuliza facility effectively functions as low-value, short-term credit, most commonly used for household expenses, emergencies, and business expenses.[m] The overdraft is

Figure B4.4.1 Growth of merchant payments and mobile money overdrafts in Kenya, 2019–21

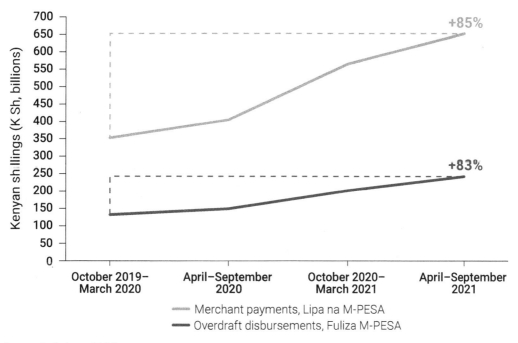

Source: Safaricom 2021b.

Note: The value of payments for goods and services through the Lipa na M-PESA platform grew from K Sh 353 billion ($3.4 billion) in October 2019–March 2020 to K Sh 653 billion ($5.9 billion) in April–September 2021. The value of overdraft disbursements grew from K Sh 132.4 billion ($1.3 billion) in October 2019–March 2020 to K Sh 242.6 ($2.2 billion) in April–September 2021.

(Box continues next page)

Box 4.4 **Case study: Mobile money overdrafts in Kenya** *(continued)*

automatically credited back when payments or cash arrive in the borrower's mobile money account. These product features offer lenders more visibility and recourse than a term loan product, allowing lenders to continue providing liquidity to Fuliza users through the crisis.

Together with government policies that temporarily removed transfer fees for low-value mobile payments, the overdraft product is likely to have been an important factor in the doubling of digital payments processed in Kenya in 2021.[n] Fuliza gave account holders much-needed flexibility to execute digital payments to merchants—including through the Lipa na M-PESA merchant payment service—and business transactions in a context of heightened uncertainty and payment delays. Although the growth of the Fuliza overdraft product has democratized access to low-value credit, including for low-income consumers,[o] concerns about transparency,[p] the cost of these short-term digital products, and the risk they pose to consumers suggest a need for careful oversight.

a. CBK (2019, 2021c).
b. For a more detailed review of the Kenyan credit market in 2019, see Gubbins (2019).
c. CBK (2021b).
d. Burlando, Kuhn, and Prina (2021); Izaguirre, Kaffenberger, and Mazer (2018). A study in Mexico found evidence that delaying digital loan disbursements can significantly reduce default rates, suggesting that easy access to loans may lead to significant impulse and temptation buying.
e. Bharadwaj and Suri (2020).
f. Blackmon, Mazer, and Warren (2021); FSD Kenya (2021).
g. CBK (2020a, 2020b, 2021a). Credit officer surveys show a progressive tightening of credit standards for households and personal loans starting in March 2020.
h. CBK (2020c).
i. Safaricom (2021a).
j. CBK, KNBS, and FSD Kenya (2021). The report attributes the decline in usage of digital loan apps to competition from formal digital credit products (including Fuliza), unfair debt collection practices, the impact of new regulation prohibiting listing of small-value loan borrowers to credit bureaus, and anticipated regulation by the CBK.
k. Safaricom (2021b).
l. CBK, KNBS, and FSD Kenya (2021).
m. Putnam, Mazer, and Blackmon (2021).
n. Safaricom (2021a). Total Fuliza M-PESA transaction value grew 58.2 percent year-to-year, while the volume of Fuliza M-PESA transactions grew 29.8 percent year-to-year as of March 2021. The Fuliza M-PESA ecosystem saw increased activity as customers took advantage of no fees on Lipa na M-PESA transactions below K Sh 1,000 (approximately $9).
o. CBK, KNBS, and FSD Kenya (2021) identifies Fuliza as the likely driver of the increase in adoption of formal credit products regulated and supervised by the Central Bank among lower-income segments of the population.
p. For a discussion on transparency of overdraft accounts, see Sule et al. (2018).

purchase into smaller payments that are collected over time. Installment loans can be used for household purchases as well as for the machinery or equipment needed for a small business. These lending products have a long history, with many examples of positive uses, as well as some abuses by bad actors.

Data from Poland's credit bureau (figure 4.3) show that, although demand for consumer loans fell in the months following the outbreak of the pandemic, lenders reacted by significantly tightening credit conditions for consumer cash loans, leading to a significant reduction in loan approval rates. For installment products, which typically offer more visibility to lenders, approval rates fell only slightly and rapidly returned to precrisis levels.

Figure 4.3 Impact of the COVID-19 pandemic on consumers' loan approval rates, by product type, Poland, 2019–21

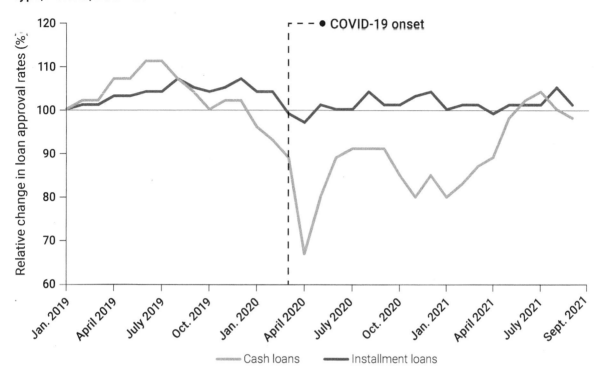

Source: Biuro Informacji Kredytowej S.A. (Credit Information Bureau) analysis based on proprietary data.

Note: The figure shows for Poland the relative change in approval rates for cash and installment consumer loan products from January 2019 to September 2021, compared with their respective approval rates as of January 2019. Approval rates are defined as the share of customers who applied for a cash or installment loan during a two-week period and were granted the respective loan product by any Polish lender.

Short-term financing is not appropriate for all borrowers. For example, a short-term loan, even with rollovers, may not be suitable for long-term projects or capital investments. Short-duration credit terms can, however, help lenders improve visibility on certain informationally opaque borrowers and open the door to subsequent longer-term financing.

Secured credit

Another approach to mitigating risk is through product configurations that improve recourse. Traditional recourse options are limited for many borrowers in emerging economies because real estate is the preferred collateral for most banks, and many small firms and individuals do not own property. As a result, loan applications from small firms are frequently rejected for lack of collateral, according to World Bank Enterprise Surveys data.[47] Because the pandemic introduced uncertainty around the value of collateral, financial institutions increased collateral requirements, making it harder to obtain financing, even for those who do have qualifying assets. In quarterly surveys of credit conditions in Mexico, for example, firms reported a progressive increase in bank collateral requirements through June 2021.[48] Other forms of recourse more common for lower-income borrowers, such as personal guarantees and the reputational sanctions characteristic of group microfinance lending models, may also have been affected by the pandemic. For example, social distancing prevented group meetings.

Widening the range of assets accepted as collateral could enable lenders to find effective means of recourse where hard collateral is not available, allowing them to better manage the risk of extending credit through the pandemic and the recovery. Movable assets account for roughly 78 percent of enterprise capital stock in emerging economies, and yet many lack modern, secured transaction regimes that would permit the use of movable assets as collateral.[49] The modernization of legal frameworks for secured transactions and the introduction of movable asset collateral registries create new options to mitigate credit risk. Technology, including digital ledgers, can be implemented to facilitate the design and implementation of collateral registries, as well as for the creation and transfer of digital assets to be used as collateral.[50] A study found that collateral registries for movable assets effectively address information asymmetries and foster access to finance. In countries that introduced registries, the number of firms with access to finance increased by an average of 10 percentage points, interest rates declined, and tenors lengthened, with stronger impacts on smaller and younger firms.[51]

Asset-based lending can thus reduce the risk of default and create the conditions for lenders to provide larger loans and serve borrowers with no previous credit history. A study in Kenya found that farmers who were offered an asset-backed, small down payment loan to purchase water tanks were much more likely to make the investment than farmers offered a standard collateralized loan—and the repayment rates were comparable.[52] Another study in Pakistan found that hire purchase agreements—a type of leasing contract—motivated an MFI to finance business assets worth several times its prevailing borrowing limit, while maintaining low default rates and offering flexible repayment options. The asset-based finance contracts had significant and persistent effects on the resilience and growth of the microenterprises, as well as on corresponding household wealth, compared with the MFI's traditional loan products.[53]

Another type of asset-based, flexible leasing contract known as pay-as-you-go (PAYGo) had been emerging as an effective product for small asset financing prior to the pandemic, and it has shown resilience through the crisis. The product was originally developed to enable households to finance solar home systems, but it has also been used for the purchase of two-wheel transport and appliances.[54] Some PAYGo providers incorporate innovative forms of recourse, such as a remote "lockout" that makes the asset unusable for nonperforming borrowers (see box 4.5).

Box 4.5 Case study: Pay-as-you-go home solar systems

An estimated 590 million people in Africa live without access to electricity. COVID-19 deepened this challenge, in part because some governments redirected limited resources from energy subsidies to funding for emergency response measures.[a] The impact of lockdown measures on household budgets, as well as on the operations and supply chains of solar energy providers, also contributed to an 18 percent fall in off-grid solar lighting sales in 2020.[b] In a challenging year for off-grid energy, however, pay-as-you-go (PAYGo) financing models swiftly recovered, proving to be an accessible, resilient way to support access to electricity for households and microentrepreneurs.

PAYGo is a form of asset-based financing that relies on mobile technology to offer flexible financing

(Box continues next page)

Box 4.5 Case study: Pay-as-you-go home solar systems *(continued)*

for small asset purchases such as solar home systems and consumer electronics. Low-income consumers who lack credit histories or collateral are able to acquire these types of assets with a relatively small down payment.[c] For solar home systems, borrowers also enter into a contract, typically ranging from one to three years, to buy credits for daily, weekly, or monthly energy usage. By purchasing credits, borrowers pay down the loan interest and principal. When credits run out, the system automatically shuts off until the user tops up the balance. Embedding loan repayments in a fee-for-service model (akin to buying mobile phone airtime) is a flexible form of financing that allows clients to reduce or pause payments in the event of a shock. The lockout technology likewise reduces the risk for providers that would have no recourse in the event of default other than to repossess the asset—an expensive option. Although the lockout technology does not necessarily reduce loss in the event of default, it encourages borrowers to behave in a way that reduces the probability of default.

According to industry data, PAYGo solar companies have been able to weather the COVID-19 crisis relatively well (figure B4.5.1). Cash sales for solar systems through June 2021 were well below those for previous years, whereas sales through PAYGo contracts recovered and continue to grow. Performance data on 20 PAYGo providers found some signs of distress, including an increase in write-offs and receivables at risk. But many performance measures remained consistent with pre–COVID-19 metrics.[d]

The resilience of the PAYGo market can be attributed to a few factors. Most fundamentally, electricity is a basic need, and therefore some governments gave solar companies essential business status, like that given to the traditional power sector. High demand also helped buffer the effects of the pandemic. Many PAYGo companies reported record sales during the early months of COVID-19,

Figure B4.5.1 Volume of off-grid lighting products sold as cash products and via PAYGo, 2018–21

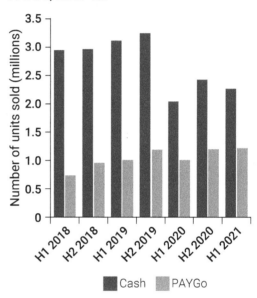

Source: GOGLA 2021.

Note: Products are classified as cash when sold in a single transaction (including products purchased via tenders) or as PAYGo when the customer pays for the product in installments over time or pays for use of the product as a service. H1 and H2 refer to the first and second halves of the fiscal year, respectively. PAYGo = pay-as-you-go.

which may indicate that consumers facing lockdowns anticipated the need for reliable electricity at home and so took advantage of the PAYGo model to acquire it at low initial costs. They were then able to use (and pay for) the asset only when they needed it.

Finally, a field experiment in Uganda demonstrated the viability of PAYGo asset-secured financing models beyond their initial use to acquire the solar home systems. The study found that the lockout technology can enable lenders to leverage

(Box continues next page)

LENDING DURING THE RECOVERY AND BEYOND | **177**

Box 4.5 **Case study: Pay-as-you-go home solar systems** *(continued)*

the solar asset as collateral to secure other types of household finance—in this case, school loans. The fact that the lender could temporarily disable the flow of energy to solar home systems led to a 19 percentage point reduction in default rates compared with default rates for uncollateralized loans. Researchers concluded that the recourse provided by the asset lockout feature led to a reduction in adverse selection and moral hazard among borrowers.[e]

a. IEA (2020).
b. GOGLA (2021).
c. This is typically a lease-to-own contract with down payments lower than 20 percent of the value of the asset.
d. The PAYGo COVID Impact Monitor, an initiative by the Consultative Group to Assist the Poor (CGAP), Global Off-Grid Lighting Association (GOGLA), and International Finance Corporation (IFC) under the PAYGo PERFORM program, collected data from 20 companies to gauge the effect of COVID-19 on the sector. See Global Off-Grid Lighting Association, "PAYGo COVID Impact Monitor (PCIM)," Amsterdam, https://www.gogla.org/sites/default/files/overview_paygo_covid_impact_monitor_17082020.pdf.
e. Gertler, Green, and Wolfram (2021).

Embedded finance

Where data on a borrower's credit history are no longer reliable and visibility into future economic activity is limited, linking lending directly to an underlying economic activity is a powerful way for lenders to mitigate credit risk. Contextual finance provides credit in the context of another transaction, such as the payment of a utility bill or the purchase of an appliance or business inventory. The category of embedded or contextualized finance[55] includes a wide range of products and credit underwriting modalities, which typically combine features that lead to greater visibility and recourse in the context of a monitorable transaction or a broader relationship with the borrower.

When lending in the context of another transaction, lenders typically have access to a range of current data on the borrower, the other parties involved, the use of funds, and the timing of the underlying economic activity. Lending in the context of supply and distribution chains, for example, has a long history dating back to early trade and commerce between regular counterparties. In increasingly digitalized economies, lenders connected to or integrated with a marketplace or a transaction platform can combine contextual information about the current transaction with historical, high-frequency transaction data to further improve visibility.

Embedding credit in another transaction motivates borrowers to repay the loan, as doing so helps maintain the ability to engage in future transactions with that counterparty. Embedded lending may also have recourse through a lien on future cash flows between the parties, or it may benefit from the effect of automated payments on delinquencies.[56] Merchant cash advances, which are based on patterns of credit and debit card receipts, are one example of automated payments. These loans are typically repaid as a percentage of daily or weekly receipts directly from the account through which the merchant's card payment receipts flow.

Providing finance in the context of another transaction may also motivate lenders to take on more risk than they would in the context of a stand-alone loan. For example, a seller might offer credit to a buyer that lacks collateral because the seller is willing to bear the risk in order to make the sale. Merchant working capital provided by an online marketplace platform allows the merchants to do more business on the platform, generating more revenue for the marketplace. Buy now, pay later (BNPL) products are an example of lending in which sellers bear all or some of the costs and risks of providing credit to their customers in order to increase sales.[57]

Although embedded finance is not new, innovative uses and larger scale are now possible in the context of digitally enabled economic activity. The disaggregation and reconfiguring of financial services by fintech innovators have lowered the barriers to entry for nonbanks. Likewise, technology platforms are enabling embedded financial products to scale by inserting them directly into the workflows of an inventory order, invoicing process, crop planting, or e-commerce transaction.[58] This insertion can lead to significant cost efficiencies in customer acquisition and loan processing. Loans may be offered directly by the platform (or other business counterpart), or they may be originated and serviced by the platform using its customer information and transaction processes, but funded by a third-party financial institution.

The surge in digital adoption during the pandemic created opportunities to turn to digital channels and platforms to extend credit to consumers and businesses. The major e-commerce platforms are increasingly offering embedded financing to merchants selling on their marketplaces. These platforms use data about their sellers—including their sales, revenue, and returns history—to underwrite working capital loans. Platform providers with a wealth of data have been shown to have better visibility into credit risk than traditional lenders.[59] Some e-commerce marketplaces such as Amazon, Mercado Libre, and Alibaba lend directly or through subsidiaries (box 4.6). Others, such as Hepsiburada, Jumia, Lazada, and Shopee, provide data to third-party banks and accredited finance providers that offer loans via the marketplace. The loans may be disbursed and collected by the platform or by a partner financial institution.[60]

Box 4.6 Case study: Doubling down on MSE finance throughout the pandemic

MYbank, an online bank serving mostly micro- and small enterprises (MSEs) in China, continued to grow throughout the COVID-19 pandemic, nearly doubling its reach from 21 million MSEs in 2019 to 40 million MSEs as of June 2021.[a] MYbank has expanded its customer base beyond e-commerce merchants, reaching millions of offline merchants, rural and agricultural customers, and supply chain MSEs, among others. MYbank was able to accomplish this expansion by using its unique data partnerships and digital business model to adjust its underwriting models during the pandemic. MYbank also broadened its reach by partnering with other banks to offer MYbank's adaptable scoring and risk management through them. Approximately 80 percent of MYbank's MSE clients had fewer than 10 employees, and most had limited or no access to finance from banks.[b] An analysis of over 40,000 MSE clients of MYbank found a positive association between access to working capital financing during the early months of the pandemic and higher sales revenue. The average loan size was ¥38,000 (less than $6,000) with an average term of about 12 months.[c]

MYbank leverages channel integration with Alibaba Group e-commerce platforms and Alipay to serve e-commerce customers. Alipay offers electronic payments and a broader range of digital financial services to more than 1 billion customers and 80 million MSEs across China. MYbank's credit underwriting uses machine learning techniques to integrate payments and transaction data, as well as other user information from these platforms to inform its risk profiles.[d] Such techniques not only enable more accurate risk assessments, but also reduce the risk of excessive lending. As of June 2021, MYbank's nonperforming loan ratio was 1.52 percent. Research has found that smaller businesses and enterprises in less-developed cities benefit the

(Box continues next page)

Box 4.6 **Case study: Doubling down on MSE finance through the pandemic** *(continued)*

most from big tech lenders because proprietary data allow these lenders to compensate for the lack of traditional data from credit assessment.[e] Although MYbank is a stand-alone bank, its ability to rely on e-commerce and payments platforms allows it to better assess the customer's ability to repay (visibility), as well as take advantage of recourse features such as automatic loan payments from the client's Alipay account.

China's economy improved faster than many other markets during the second half of 2020, but the impact of the COVID-19 crisis on Chinese firms was severe. A survey on the early impact of the pandemic revealed that more than half of the Chinese MSE respondents expected their income to fall by 50 percent in the first quarter of 2020.[f] As of June 2021, an index of MSE operations indicated that smaller businesses had not yet returned to prepandemic levels.[g] MYbank was able to use real-time business transaction information to adjust its credit underwriting models and strategy to continue to lend to these customers and expand its reach in China. MYbank made nearly 100 changes

in its model in the first quarter of 2020 and continues to adjust its underwriting through regular sectoral analysis and client updates.

One of MYbank's responses to the COVID-19 crisis was initiating in March 2020 a partnership with the All-China Federation of Industry and Commerce to collaborate with over 100 banks to offer a jointly financed and administered loan product.[h] Through this partnership, banks were able to provide access to finance for MSEs by leveraging MYbank's loan processing facility and its transaction data. Each bank followed its in-house credit policies using MYbank's updated sector-level and firm-level assessments to provide additional risk mitigation. MYbank's role in providing MSEs with access to credit during the pandemic using alternative forms of data is consistent with earlier research on 2 million Chinese firms that received credit from MYbank and from traditional banks between 2017 and 2019.[i] In the study, researchers found MYbank's underwriting to be less dependent on the financial cycle than that of traditional lenders and therefore potentially less affected by a negative shock.

a. *Businesswire* (2021).
b. Sun et al. (2021).
c. Sun et al. (2021).
d. Gambacorta et al. (2020).
e. Huang et al. (2020).
f. Sun et al. (2021).
g. PSBC (2021).
h. *China Banking News* (2020).
i. Gambacorta et al. (2020).

Embedded finance opportunities can be found across many types of digital platforms. Kobo360 is an African e-logistics platform for truck drivers and small-fleet operators in Ghana, Kenya, Nigeria, Togo, and Uganda. Because Kobo360 has insight into the portion of a truck operator's cash flow that stems from bookings through the platform, it can offer participating operators working capital financing. The platform underwrites loans using proprietary data on the trip and income history of the driver or company, as well as on supply, demand, and bookings. Because payments for trips booked on the platform flow through Kobo360's systems, the company can automate loan repayments.[61] Moreover, because drivers rely on Kobo360 for future trip bookings and income, they would be more likely to prioritize repayment of a loan to the platform relative to other expenses.

Supply chain finance

Supply chain finance shares many of the features of embedded finance in terms of its ability to mitigate risk by linking credit to a commercial interaction. By tying short-term credit exposures to the movement of goods or inventories in the context of an established relationship between supply chain participants, supply chain finance improves visibility into the borrower's probability of default.[62] Even though credit in a supply chain transaction is typically unsecured, lenders gain recourse from the fact that transactions take place within a network that includes anchor buyers or distributors on whom the borrower depends for business. These relationships within a supply chain mitigate risk, improve efficiency, and lower the cost of providing finance.

Larger corporate buyers or distributors often provide their value chains with financing. For example, buyers may decide to pay their suppliers faster to support their working capital and operations, or sellers and distributors may allow downstream MSMEs to pay later or in installments. This form of supply chain finance depends on the liquidity of these corporate anchors and their willingness to take on the risk of providing—and typically subsidizing—credit to ensure the viability of their value chains. As the pandemic broke out, many corporate anchors sought to support the liquidity of their suppliers and distributors.[63] For example, 10 global fast-moving consumer goods (FMCGs) manufacturers increased their own use of working capital during the first half of 2020, largely to support their commercial counterparties. [64] To protect the liquidity of their distributors, seven of the 10 FMCGs manufacturers on-lent working capital by extending receivable payment terms. The same corporate anchors reduced accounts payable by around 10 percent, thereby channeling working capital to suppliers. The anchors increased their outstanding debt by 13 percent (approximately $45 billion) from the end of 2019 to the second quarter of 2020, effectively intermediating between the capital markets and their value chains to take on credit risk that banks or other lenders may not have been willing to assume.

Not all anchors are willing or able to take on the balance sheet volumes and risks involved in extending financing to their suppliers and distributors. Supply chain finance programs that involve a third-party financial institution (such as factoring or reverse factoring programs) can be very effective in reducing risk and supporting access to finance for suppliers.[65] Lenders in these programs—embedded between a corporate buyer and its suppliers, often SMEs—use invoice data to gain visibility into the future cash flows of the borrowing suppliers. In some programs, the lender may have additional recourse to the buyer that established the program. Hepsiburada, a Turkish e-commerce platform, facilitates financing for merchants and suppliers both directly and by enabling bank lending through an internal platform that submits a supplier's or merchant's invoices to the lending bank as evidence of receivables.[66] Supply chain finance can be less risky than a standard (unsecured) working capital line even when the lender is not a direct participant in the supply chain. Through the pandemic, the supplier finance program of the International Finance Corporation (IFC) saw greater growth and borrower uptake (see box 4.7).

Digitalization has significantly reduced the operating costs of supply chain accounts.[67] Digital technologies enable supply chain partners and lenders to automate processes and lessen the burden of documenting receivables, tracking amounts due, and collecting payments. Advances in the use of digital technologies in both commerce and finance are enabling supply chain finance programs to scale up and serve more businesses with a broader range of loan sizes, including smaller loans that were previously uneconomical to service.

In Latin America, Citibank announced in October 2020 its partnership with PepsiCo and the fintech Amigo PAQ to digitalize payments and offer small shops working capital lines of credit. The partners underwrote, monitored, and collected payment for a portfolio of small loans to thousands of *tienditas*. By the end of 2020, the partnership was serving more than 4,000 SMEs in Peru, with ongoing operations

Box 4.7 The supply chain finance response to the pandemic

The pandemic profoundly disrupted international trade and domestic supply chains. Faced with a sudden drop in revenue and greater uncertainty about future cash flows and operations, many buyers sought to reduce inventory by delaying or canceling orders. They also sought to preserve liquidity by extending their payment terms with suppliers. The suppliers, for their part, were also concerned about preserving liquidity and attempted to provide discounts for early payments in an attempt to cash in receivables. Despite these efforts, many struggled to remain viable. On average, the crisis led to an immediate increase in working capital requirements for firms, driven by the reduction in revenue and the increase in accounts receivables and inventory.[a]

During the pandemic, the trade finance programs of the International Finance Corporation (IFC) saw a surge in interest from suppliers driven by these factors. For example, IFC's Global Trade Supplier Finance (GTSF) Program, which provides short-term financing to suppliers that sell to large domestic buyers or export to international buyers, saw total commitments rise from $1.2 billion in the

year ending June 2019 to just over $2 billion in the year ending June 2021. Sixty-five percent of this volume was disbursed to suppliers based in six lower-middle-income countries: Bangladesh, Cambodia, Honduras, Pakistan, Sri Lanka, and Vietnam.

The increase stemmed from the growth in volume financed by existing suppliers in the program, some of which had previously used bank finance that became less available during the crisis, and by new anchor buyers that joined in 2020 to broaden the availability of finance to their suppliers. For example, a GTSF anchor buyer in the automotive industry—one of the sectors most affected by the pandemic—saw 300 percent growth in the number of its suppliers that joined the program and more than 10 times the volume financed. Overall, the number of suppliers actively participating in IFC's GTSF Program surged 230 percent between the year ending June 2019 and the year ending June 2021. This activity suggests the value during the pandemic of a program enabling buyers to help their suppliers access finance, thereby stabilizing the buyers' supply chains.

a. PwC (2021a, 2021b).

in Mexico and Guatemala.[68] The size and number of these loans would not have been feasible if the end-to-end processes had not been digitalized.[69] As digital order, inventory, and payment systems become more widely used and the track records of smaller borrowers and supply chain instruments are established, the receivables assets can be bundled and transferred, so funding could move from corporate balance sheets to bank balance sheets, the capital markets, or to other investment vehicles. Such developments would create new options for the external finance of downstream payables.[70]

Insuring credit risk and catalyzing long-term investments

This chapter has highlighted examples of lenders adopting innovative and often tech-enabled approaches to improving visibility and recourse so they can continue and even increase lending. Achieving the right mix of risk management approaches is challenging in a high-risk and rapidly changing context. For that reason, credit guarantees (CGs) have been, and will continue to be, a useful tool for motivating lenders to continue offering credit during high-risk periods.

By having recourse to a guarantor when a borrower defaults, lenders are able to significantly reduce their losses. Guarantors are often government agencies or public institutions, but mutual guarantee systems are available in some markets, especially in Europe. Private trade credit insurance also plays an important role in global markets and particularly trade finance. Public development banks and development finance institutions also play an important role in promoting lending to MSMEs, other productive sectors, and areas of policy priority.[71]

Credit guarantee schemes have been a central pandemic response by governments in advanced and several emerging economies. In 2020, public credit guarantee schemes amounted to an estimated 2 percent of global gross domestic product (GDP).[72] Evidence from some countries such as Spain that embraced CGs during the COVID-19 crisis indicates that CGs have improved MSMEs' access to finance and have imposed a smaller fiscal burden relative to government-backed grants or direct lending.[73] A recent study of the impact of COVID-19 on SME failures estimates that loans backed by government guarantees can be more effective and efficient than cash grants for limiting bankruptcy rates and returning trends to precrisis levels.[74] Furthermore, guarantees played a crucial role in supporting the access of SMEs to trade finance products. A survey of member countries of the Organisation for Economic Co-operation and Development (OECD) found that commercial banks and trade credit insurance providers displayed a diminished appetite for risk, while government-supported export credit agencies saw a significant increase in applications and volume.[75]

As economies reduce the use of broad fiscal and monetary support measures, guarantors may have to continue supporting lenders where credit risk remains high and visibility and recourse remain limited. Because CGs play a role in balancing the risk equation for lenders even during normal times, they could be among the last fiscal measures to be reduced or withdrawn, possibly playing an even bigger role than before the crisis. In addition to reducing the risk of financing MSMEs and sectors especially affected by the crisis, guarantee programs can be adjusted to reduce lenders' risk of providing longer-term financing to support investments by businesses in adapting to their new economic reality as well as to de-risk financing to emerging areas and sectors with the potential to support a sustainable, inclusive recovery.

In the transition from pandemic response to economic recovery, guarantors should, however, adjust CG program parameters gradually and in sync with the unwinding of fiscal support measures. Many of these adjustments may require tightening the program design to ensure that only firms that are well run yet need support benefit from guarantees.[76] Like cash grants and loans by state-owned banks, CGs can potentially misallocate resources to weak "zombie firms," or to strong firms that do not need the CG to survive. A recent analysis concludes that the more common resource misallocation is use of guarantees for firms that did not need them (thus tying up limited capital).[77]

Digital technologies can enable the collection and analysis of data to facilitate timely performance assessments of CGs and ensure transparent reporting. As the economy recovers, stricter screening should aim to exclude zombie firms and reduce the portion of each loan that is guaranteed to motivate strong underwriting practices by loan originators and maintain program sustainability to reduce the fiscal burden. To direct resources toward smaller enterprises, governments could lower the size cap for eligible borrowers. An appropriately priced guarantee premium could help discourage lenders from overusing guarantees; guarantors should revise pricing as economic conditions improve. (For more on the design and execution of effective credit guarantees, see spotlight 4.1.)

Beyond insuring against credit risk, development banks, as well as regional and international financial institutions, will continue to play an important role in the recovery by providing long-term finance and support for capacity development and digital transformation. That role could include catalyzing private lending that can produce positive long-term returns, such as adapting to climate change or shifting to low carbon business models. It could also include reaching those underserved parts of the economy (such as women and their businesses, minorities, rural areas, and migrants) at risk of being excluded from the economic recovery because of lack of access to finance.

The experience of Banco Pichincha (BP), the largest commercial bank in Ecuador, illustrates how technical assistance and funding from development finance institutions can help financial institutions achieve their strategic objectives despite the crisis. In 2017, BP, with the support of IFC and other institutions, significantly expanded its MSME portfolio and tackled the country's large gender gap in access to finance.[78] It did so by addressing biases in credit review and customizing credit products for women entrepreneurs. BP entered the pandemic having doubled its portfolio of women entrepreneurs. As the pandemic unfolded, the bank continued to focus on women entrepreneurs, adapting its financial and nonfinancial services offerings to continue growing its portfolio. Between March 2020 and August 2021, BP's MSME loan portfolio grew by 16 percent, with over 50 percent of new loans disbursed to MSMEs owned by women.[79]

Policies to enable access to credit and address risks

Approaches to restoring credit growth involve adapting or innovating ways in which finance providers manage risk. Product features and existing approaches to risk modeling can be adapted to the pandemic economy, while other measures to improve visibility and recourse may depend on digital channels and tools. Many of the solutions supporting new lending in this context will be technology-driven. Policy makers should therefore consider taking measures to facilitate such innovations in business models and products, including by supporting the participation of new types of credit providers in the market and by enabling use of new types of data and analytics. Upgrades in financial infrastructure can further foster access to finance and support resilience in credit markets. However, financial innovation may also pose new risks to businesses and consumers, as well as to financial stability and integrity (see online annex 4A[80]). Addressing these risks requires adequate oversight by regulators. In fact, in many countries legacy financial sector regulatory and supervisory frameworks and approaches need to be updated.[81] This section reviews some of the policies that may help foster innovation and access to credit while minimizing risks to consumers and the financial sector.

Facilitating innovation through new providers, products, and uses of data and analytics

The digital transformation of finance is enabling the atomization of services, the recombination of value chains, and the participation of nontraditional providers.[82] These advances can contribute to greater efficiency, more diverse and inclusive markets, and the expanded availability of credit. New entrants, from challenger banks to fintech lenders, can improve the range of products and the appetite for risk in a market that includes banks, MFIs, supply chain finance providers, and others. Regulatory and supervisory frameworks can support healthy innovation by allowing diverse lenders with modern business models to participate in the market.

The entry of new financial service providers may require adjustments in the regulatory perimeter. Digital credit providers, for example, offer products similar to those provided by regulated banks, but may not be subject to oversight by the financial regulator because of the current definitions of regulated activities or institutions.[83] For example, in Kenya between 2016 and 2019, the providers of app-based, short-term, small-value loans operated outside of the regulatory perimeter. During those years, use of these products expanded from 0.6 percent to 8.3 percent of adults and resulted in instances of irresponsible lending.[84] This is one example of a new provider playing an important role that should be encouraged, but also overseen within an expanded regulatory perimeter.[85] Regulators worldwide are developing capacity and assessing their approaches to regulating institutions and activities to accommodate the entry of new providers on a level playing field, while ensuring soundness, financial integrity, consumer protection, and inclusion.

Rapid innovation and shifts to new providers and infrastructure can pose risks to stability.[86] Some promising approaches to managing these risks include expanding the regulatory perimeter, deploying differentiated licensing requirements proportionate to the risks presented by a product or provider, and introducing activity-based regulation. New guidance is also emerging from the global standard-setting bodies.[87]

The need for well-designed regulatory and supervisory frameworks applies not just to new entrants, but also to all providers to encourage sound experimentation with new channels, products, and processes. Regulatory or supervisory restrictions could impede revisions of risk models to adapt to sectoral shifts and new economic conditions, as well as the adoption of new technologies, products, and processes needed to adapt to changing postpandemic markets. There is scope to provide more latitude for experimentation and innovation without sacrificing institutional or systemic soundness, such as by allowing innovative products or business models to be deployed within a given risk envelope or exposure limit. For example, in 2018 the Bank of Thailand indicated a move from specific product reviews to umbrella approvals covering a range of related products or setting exposure thresholds.[88]

New regulatory approaches to spur innovation will naturally require that regulators build their own internal capacity to understand new technologies and monitor the market to ensure that experimentation is consistent with the broader goals of a stable, productive financial sector. Regulatory innovation hubs and sandboxes can help regulators be digitally informed and narrow the gap between regulation and financial innovation. A survey of regulators in 2020 found that 16 percent had introduced regulatory sandbox initiatives, while about 36 percent had accelerated deployment during the pandemic.[89]

Supervision technologies (suptech) can also enable supervisory agencies to monitor a broader and more complex financial sector more efficiently.[90] Just as financial service providers are reaping gains from technology, regulators and supervisors can embrace technology to improve market surveillance, enforce market conduct and consumer protection standards, and better respond to complaints. During the pandemic, many supervisors either accelerated or introduced new suptech initiatives.[91] Technology can also lower the cost to collect and analyze data for regulators, to identify potential discrimination in lending practices, and to inform policy design. The example of Chile[92] indicates that consideration can be given to producing anonymized gender disaggregated data for the financial sector, with the goal of capturing differential developments in borrowing and credit risk, identifying potential discrimination in lending practices, and informing market and policy efforts to close the gender gap in credit access.

The bigger role of data, coupled with advanced analytics enabled by machine learning and AI, also requires new regulatory and supervisory policies. Financial institutions will provide some of the data used to measure risk during and after the pandemic. Other data will come from third parties such as credit bureaus, utilities, employers, and government databases. Data governance frameworks will be critical for defining the rules around data ownership and use. For example, a rights-based data governance framework can enable data sharing while protecting against misuse.[93] Fair lending frameworks should encompass algorithmic accountability and transparency to reduce the chances that bias becomes hardwired into AI-based decision models (see box 4.2 earlier in the chapter). Several jurisdictions are crafting policies for algorithmic transparency and accountability.[94] Regulation should address the ownership of and access to data, protection of data (including cybersecurity), and potential bias in data analysis.

Adoption of emerging technologies such as cryptocurrency and decentralized finance will also require new regulatory frameworks. Cryptocurrency and blockchain technologies do not appear to be positioned to play a significant role in access to credit during the near-term pandemic recovery. But applications such as remittances and central bank digital currencies are being deployed, and the underlying distributed ledger technology could have applications in capital markets and credit markets and as foundational infrastructure for permissioned sharing of validated data such as identity or credit history. These technologies bear monitoring from financial regulatory and market conduct perspectives, with the goals of supporting sound innovation in financing and equal access to digital solutions. Authorities, the private sector, and development institutions need to work together to address technology gaps, enhance digital literacy, and ensure adequate transparency and management of cyber risks.

Operationalizing advances in technology, new products, alternative data, and data protection frameworks requires infrastructure that protects data subjects from breaches and cybercrime. Regulators will therefore have to strengthen their capacity to address cyber risks, enhance international coordination, and implement guidance and evolving best practices on operational resilience from international standard-setting bodies.[95] Efforts by regulators to address data governance, fair lending, and cybersecurity will not only enable lenders to develop and deploy innovative approaches to lending, but also improve the transparency, equity, and consumer protection needed to create trust and drive responsible adoption.

Improving financial sector infrastructure

Financial infrastructure comprises the legal and regulatory frameworks and public and private sector institutions and practices that support the efficient and sound functioning of the financial systems. This infrastructure must also keep pace with digitalization to support the evolving needs of lenders.

Digital identity, an important element of financial infrastructure, can enable broader access to finance while maintaining system integrity. A recent study revealed that 49 percent of surveyed regulators implemented measures related to eKYC (electronic Know Your Customer) and digital identity during the pandemic. Examples include digital contracts and signatures to support access to and resilience of financial services.[96]

Payment systems are another key element of financial infrastructure. The physical infrastructure used by clearinghouses and switches, as well as the soft infrastructure of rules and practices on participation, origination, recission rights, and finality, must be modernized to cope with the digital transformation of finance and the shift away from cash accelerated by the pandemic.

Credit infrastructure includes the hard infrastructure of asset registry systems and credit bureau databases and the soft infrastructure of laws and institutions designed to support efficient and responsible allocation of credit in the economy. Together, they reduce lending costs and frictions and facilitate access to credit.[97] For the data-driven innovations discussed in this chapter to be broadly usable, lenders must be able to access and integrate a wider range of data into their underwriting models. Credit bureaus such as Creditinfo, CRIF, Dun & Bradstreet, Experian, and TransUnion are working toward expanding access by leveraging technology to incorporate alternative data to enrich their data sets (see box 4.8). Regulators must also update their credit information-sharing regimes to guarantee the safe use of alternative data.[98] Credit information system regulations that guide credit bureaus and registries should ensure that nontraditional lenders also have access and report their credit exposures because a gap in reporting by any set of lenders renders the credit information system less valuable to everyone. The People's Bank of China, for example, granted alternative lenders access to its credit registry.[99]

Another form of infrastructure that can facilitate access to credit during and after the pandemic is the laws and registries that allow lenders to accept innovative forms of collateral, such as movable

Box 4.8 Case study: Use of alternative data by credit bureaus during the pandemic

The COVID-19 pandemic accelerated efforts by credit reporting service providers (CRSPs), such as credit bureaus, to integrate alternative data into credit reports to help address the limitation of historical repayment data and inform credit underwriting decisions through the crisis.

As governments provided direct financial support, regulatory authorities implemented moratoria, and credit bureaus adopted adjusted technical reporting codes, traditional credit data became less useful to inform risk assessments. Some of these measures would tend to result in "false positives"— that is, borrowers with the ability to service existing debt and apparently qualified to borrow further, despite their underlying viability being compromised by job loss or permanent business closure. Other measures exacerbated "false negatives"— that is, borrowers who otherwise would be able to meet debt obligations but were flagged as ineligible because of the short-term impacts of the COVID-19 crisis on their ability to meet loan obligations. For example, in South Africa the rate of false negatives increased from its precrisis level of 1.5 percent of credit applicants to 8 percent in October 2020.[a]

To address this gap in usability of traditional data, many CRSPs accelerated efforts to incorporate alternative data into their scoring.[b] Alternative data typically increase the precision of credit score models,[c] especially during periods of stress.[d] The crisis also gave lenders and policy makers new incentives to integrate these new models and overcome the risk management and regulatory barriers that had stifled adoption of third-party scoring innovation (the most popular third-party scoring model used in 2020 was based on data from before the 2007–09 global financial crisis).[e]

The three main US credit bureaus have launched partnerships with data aggregators to supplement traditional credit scores with consumer permissioned data on positive repayment behavior.[f] For example, Experian reported that as of March 2021 nearly 7 million consumers in the United States and the United Kingdom had connected to its Experian Boost service. Launched in 2019, the service allows customers to authorize Experian to access real-time payments data from customers' utility, telecom, and streaming service providers. The credit bureau reported that by adding real-time alternative data, the majority of Experian Boost users improved their credit score—for example, 22 percent of users with "poor" credit ratings were shifted to a "fair" score band.[g]

Meanwhile, the data analytics company FICO and three consumer reporting agencies (Equifax, TransUnion, and Experian) launched products in the summer of 2020 incorporating analytics and sector data for users who are experiencing financial distress from the pandemic or have benefited from moratoria. Similar products were launched across the world, including in Croatia,[h] the Baltics, and Iceland.[i]

a. Experian (2021).
b. GPFI (2018).
c. Djeundje et al. (2021).
d. Gambacorta et al. (2019).
e. FinRegLab (2020).
f. FinRegLab (2020).
g. Gambacorta et al. (2019).
h. Fina (2021). The COVID Score developed by the Financial Agency of Croatia (Fina) is an input in the process used to evaluate applications by businesses and income-generating professions for government support. The Fina COVID Score evaluates the impact of the pandemic on a business, assesses the results of previous government support, and estimates whether there will be any need for additional financing. The score has seven risk elements, including business, industry, staffing levels and ability to meet salary payments, and credit risk.
i. Creditinfo (2021). Launched by Creditinfo, the COVID-19 Impact Score is a synthetic score designed to help identify companies hardest-hit by the COVID-19 crisis and likely to soon have solvency problems. The score incorporates data on supply chain, health, and proximity to industries most affected, such as tourism.

assets and receivables. For example, Pakistan launched an electronic registry in 2020 to enable financial institutions to register rights in movable assets (machinery, furniture, inventory, accounts receivable, and digital assets) and accept these as collateral for loans. The launch was particularly timely considering the urgent need for credit by low-income households and MSMEs arising from the pandemic.[100] Collateral registries must adhere to harmonized requirements for secured transaction law and prudential regulation, specifically capital and loan-loss provisioning requirements.[101] Product- or sector-specific digital platforms can complement this core infrastructure by accepting security in the form of assets such as invoices and warehouse receipts.[102] An example is Mexico's Nafinet invoice financing platform.

Finally, digital infrastructure in the form of reliable fixed and mobile telephony and data services underpins the functioning of digital economies and all noncash financial services. Gaps in coverage and high costs continue to exclude significant portions of the population of emerging economies. Likewise, disruptions of information and communications technology, the communications network, and energy supplies can be a serious source of operational risk to financial service providers. Policy makers should ensure that core telecommunications and energy infrastructure is robust and that competitive markets produce adequate capacity, fault tolerance, and redundancy.

The systems on which financial services delivery depends have also become more complex because technology has enabled the atomization of service components and the reconfiguration of what had been internalized processes owned by distinct service providers.[103] One example of the consequences of these dependencies is the widespread internet outage in February 2021 that affected Fiserv, a major financial services technology outsourcer. That outage resulted in interruptions in payment acceptance at many businesses across the United States.[104] In another example, a hardware failure in June 2018 disrupted the Visa network in Europe, halting digital payments across the continent.[105] The growing adoption of digital financial services, coupled with the concentration of infrastructure in large payment networks and cloud computing platforms, will make even rare events more damaging. Financial regulators must set minimum standards for risk management and operational reliability that cover outsourcing and partnership arrangements. Individual regulators are increasingly doing this, as are standard-setting bodies.[106]

Increasing collaboration among regulators

Digitalization has increased the cross-border and cross-sector dimensions of financial services. A country's regulator defines when a foreign provider can offer services to domestic customers and what services it can provide, but compliance relies on cooperation across jurisdictions. The digital transformation of finance also brings multiple domestic regulators into play. A digital finance provider or product may fall within the jurisdictions of telecommunications, information, data, consumer protection, competition, and other regulators. Regulators need to establish modes of collaboration both within and across borders and within and across regulatory domains.[107] In Bangladesh, for example, the Central Bank and the Telecommunications Regulatory Commission are part of a multistakeholder consultative committee on Unstructured Supplementary Service Data (USSD) communications, a key enabler of mobile money.[108] A coordinated regulatory approach can narrow disparities between regulatory frameworks and anticipate new risks.

The growth of alternative lenders, including fintechs, big techs, and other embedded finance providers, has the potential to change the market structure of the financial sector, with implications for competition as well as consumer protection.[109] Digital technology and new entrants in the credit market can foster competition, increase innovation and efficiency, and challenge incumbents.[110] On the other hand, economies of scale and scope in data and network effects can compound the existing scale advantages of incumbents' capital and customer bases. Crossover big tech platforms may provide additional competition in financial services, bringing their own scale advantages, but market abuses by some big tech companies are already a concern in their core product areas. Financial regulators must work with competition authorities as well as consumer protection entities to monitor and prevent anticompetitive or abusive practices as the sector evolves in each market.

Open access to customer data and financial infrastructure could reduce the tendency toward market concentration, particularly as data and credit infrastructure become critical factors for lending in the COVID-19 crisis recovery. By leveling the playing field, open data frameworks can empower smaller players and increase contestability and competition. However, open access to personal and financial data is technically difficult to implement securely. A proliferation of entities involved in providing a single service could reduce accountability for service quality and data use and leave consumers wondering who is responsible when a transaction fails or fraud occurs. Although data portability can increase bank lending, the effects on consumer welfare can be nuanced.[111] Efforts to spur competition through open banking[112] need to move in tandem with cybersecurity, privacy protections, consumer financial education, and an analysis of market dynamics.

Conclusion

The ability of credit markets to reach and serve businesses and households—including micro- and small businesses and low-income households—will be central to an equitable recovery. To effectively support the recovery, lenders will have to adjust their credit models and product portfolios to improve visibility and recourse in a way that manages heightened risks and counters the impacts of the pandemic. Digitalization of economic activities and adoption of financial technology can enable development of the solutions and product innovations needed.

Governments and regulators should support sound innovations in financing, particularly those for MSMEs and vulnerable segments; facilitate upgrades in data-driven underwriting; encourage product diversification; and enable the entry of innovative lenders such as fintechs into the market. Maximizing the benefits of innovation in the financial sector will require modernizing regulatory and supervisory approaches, along with financial infrastructure. Collaboration among regulators will become increasingly important as financial activities cut across sectors and the powerful advantages of scale and scope in networks, data, and capital lead to greater provider concentration.

Although credit markets can effectively support MSMEs and households in the recovery, governments may need to continue to help balance the risks and returns for lenders serving the most affected segments and sectors of the economy. In addition to enabling markets through the measures outlined above, some credit markets may benefit from well-targeted guarantee schemes.

The solutions and policy recommendations discussed in this chapter are aimed primarily at countering a reluctance to lend in the context of the heightened risk and uncertainty of the pandemic and ensuring adequate access to finance to allow even the more affected households and entrepreneurs to take part in the recovery. These measures can also serve as the foundation for more efficient and resilient credit markets that can address structural constraints, progressively reduce long-standing gaps in access to finance, and foster responsible financial inclusion.

Notes

1. Ayyagari, Demirgüç-Kunt, and Maksimovic (2011).
2. Byrne et al. (2021).
3. Berger et al. (2021) found that relationship clients of some US financial institutions were more negatively affected by loan contract terms than other borrowers.
4. Haughwout et al. (2021).
5. Shleifer and Vishny (2011).
6. Bodovski et al. (2021).
7. Wagner and Winkler (2013); Wehinger (2014).
8. Apedo-Amah et al. (2020).
9. OECD (2021d).
10. ICC (2020).
11. Gourinchas et al. (2021b).
12. Koulouridi et al. (2020).
13. Simanowitz, Hennessy-Barrett, and Izaguirre (2021).
14. World Bank (2019b).
15. Some definitions of big data add a fourth "v"—veracity. It is a characteristic needed so that the data are truly useful. See Lukoianova and Rubin (2014). Some add a fifth "v"—value (BBVA 2020).
16. Berg et al. (2020).
17. Agarwal et al. (2020).
18. Björkegren and Grissen (2020).
19. Jagtiani and Lemieux (2018).
20. Gambacorta et al. (2020).
21. A data subject is a person who can be identified directly or indirectly through personal data identifiers.
22. World Bank (2021c). Parlour, Rajan, and Zhu (2020) examine the impacts of financial technology (fintech) competition in the payments market, concluding that, although payment innovations promote financial inclusion, they may lead to ambiguous effects on consumer welfare.
23. Ostmann and Dorobantu (2021).
24. Berg et al. (2020); Hurley and Adebayo (2017).
25. Personal characteristics are regulated by legislation seeking to prevent discrimination or bias. Although these characteristics may vary by legislation, commonly regulated characteristics include gender, familial status, race, disability, religion or belief, and sexual orientation.
26. Leo, Sharma, and Maddulety (2019); Ostmann and Dorobantu (2021).
27. Feyen et al. (2021).
28. IFC (2020a).
29. McKinsey (2019).
30. Alonso-Gispert et al. (2022).
31. Ziegler et al. (2021).
32. For a comprehensive review, see Teima et al. (forthcoming).
33. Cornelli et al. (2020).
34. World Bank and CCAF (2020).
35. Blackmon, Mazer, and Warren (2021).
36. World Bank and CCAF (2020).
37. OECD (2018, 2021b); World Bank (2017, 2021a).
38. OECD (2021c).
39. Izaguirre, Kaffenberger, and Mazer (2018).
40. Calvano et al. (2020) find that AI/ML techniques can encourage collusive behavior.
41. Carpena et al. (2017).
42. Garz et al. (2021).
43. OECD (2021a).
44. World Bank (2021c).
45. Bharadwaj and Suri (2020).
46. Gwer (2019); Melzer (2011); Morse (2011); Skiba and Tobacman (2019).
47. Fan, Nguyên, and Qian (2020).
48. Banco de México (2021).
49. World Bank (2019c).
50. World Bank (2020a).
51. Love, Martínez Pería, and Singh (2016).
52. Jack et al. (2016).
53. Bari et al. (2021).
54. GOGLA (2021); Waldron (2016).
55. Feyen et al. (2021).
56. Automation of payments is a behavioral strategy to overcome inattention. See Moulton et al. (2014).
57. Buy now, pay later (BNPL) products—an e-commerce version of point-of-sale financing—experienced a surge in adoption, fueled by the growth in e-commerce and digital payments during the pandemic. See Alfonso et al. (2021).
58. Feyen et al. (2021).
59. Gambacorta et al. (2019).
60. World Bank (2020c).
61. Amosun and Unger (2020); Maylie (2020).
62. IFC (2019).
63. Caniato, Moretto, and Rice (2020).
64. Dunbar and Singh (2020).
65. For a review, see IFC (2019).
66. SEC (2021).
67. IFC (2017a, 2020c).
68. Perú21 (2021).
69. Citigroup (2020).
70. See Meki, Quinn, and Roll (2021) for another example of how technology can enable product innovations that allow anchors to sustainably take on more risk to improve the performance of a last-mile distribution network leading to higher profits for microdistributors and a substantial increase in sales for the anchors.
71. See Xu, Marodon, and Ru (2021) for an effort to map development banks worldwide.
72. Calice (2020).
73. Corredera-Catalán, di Pietro, and Trujillo-Ponce (2021).
74. Gourinchas et al. (2021a).
75. OECD (2021d).
76. World Bank and FIRST Initiative (2015).
77. Gourinchas et al. (2021a).
78. Ecuador has one of the largest gender gaps in access to finance in Latin America. Men are twice as likely as women to borrow from a financial institution or use a credit card, and they are nearly 40 percent more likely than women to have a savings account. See BCE (2020) and World Bank, Global Findex Database 2017 (Global Financial Inclusion Database), https://global findex.worldbank.org/.
79. Banco Pichincha (2021).
80. Annex 4A can be found at http://bit.do/WDR2022-Chapter-4-Annex.
81. Alonso-Gispert et al. (2022); IMF and World Bank (2018); World Bank (2021c).
82. Feyen et al. (2021).

83. World Bank (2021a).
84. CBK (2019).
85. CBK (2021b). Since December 2021, an amendment to the Central Bank of Kenya Act has provided the financial sector regulator with the power to license and oversee app-based lenders.
86. Feyen et al. (2021).
87. Alonso-Gispert et al. (2022).
88. IMF (2019).
89. World Bank and CCAF (2020).
90. Broeders and Prenio (2018); di Castri et al. (2019).
91. World Bank (2021b); World Bank and CCAF (2020).
92. Data2x (2016).
93. World Bank (2021c).
94. European Parliament (2019). For example, the European Parliamentary Research Service put forward four policy elements: (1) awareness-raising: education, watchdogs, and whistleblowers; (2) accountability in public sector use of algorithmic decision-making; (3) regulatory oversight and legal liability; and (4) global coordination for algorithmic governance.
95. Major elements include BCBS (2021); BIS and IOSCO (2016); FSB (2018, 2020); and G-7 (2016).
96. World Bank and CCAF (2020).
97. Pazarbasioglu et al. (2020).
98. World Bank (2019a, 2020b).
99. Pazarbasioglu et al. (2020).
100. Ruch (2020).
101. IFC (2020b).
102. Pazarbasioglu et al. (2020).
103. Feyen et al. (2021).
104. Dailey and Taylor (2021). Fiserv serves about 6 percent of the merchant acquiring market.
105. Togoh and Topping (2018).
106. For example, see IOSCO (2020); MAS (2018); OJK (2017a, 2017b); and RBI (2021a), paragraph 17 and annex VI.
107. Alonso-Gispert et al. (2022).
108. Plaitakis, Wills, and Church (2016).
109. Feyen et al. (2021).
110. Claessens (2009).
111. Parlour, Rajan, and Zhu (2020).
112. He, Huang, and Zhou (2020) highlight that although open banking favors new entrants in the credit market, it may under certain conditions negatively affect borrowers because of its impact on market dynamics and because of its signaling effect on borrowers, who may decide to opt out from sharing data.

References

Adian, Ikmal, Djeneba Doumbia, Neil Gregory, Alexandros Ragoussis, Aarti Reddy, and Jonathan Timmis. 2020. "Small and Medium Enterprises in the Pandemic: Impact, Responses, and the Role of Development Finance." Policy Research Working Paper 9414, World Bank, Washington, DC.

Agarwal, Sumit, Shashwat Alok, Pulak Ghosh, and Sudip Gupta. 2020. "Financial Inclusion and Alternate Credit Scoring for the Millennials: Role of Big Data and Machine Learning in Fintech." Paper presented at Cambridge Centre for Alternative Finance's "Fifth Annual Conference on Alternative Finance," Judge Business School, University of Cambridge, Cambridge, UK, June 29–July 1, 2020.

Alfonso, Viviana, Codruta Boar, Jon Frost, Leonardo Gambacorta, and Jing Liu. 2021. "E-commerce in the Pandemic and Beyond." *BIS Bulletin* 36, Bank for International Settlements, Basel, Switzerland.

Alonso-Gispert, Tatiana, Pierre-Laurent Chatain, Karl Driessen, Danilo Queiroz Palermo, and Ariadne Plaitakis. 2022. "Regulation and Supervision of Fintech: Considerations for EMDE Policymakers." Technical Note, Future of Finance Report, World Bank, Washington, DC.

Amosun, Adedoyin, and Deborah Unger. 2020. "Keeping African Goods Moving." *Thought Leaders*, August 26, 2020. https://www.strategy-business.com/article/Keeping-African-goods-moving.

Apedo-Amah, Marie Christine, Besart Avdiu, Xavier Cirera, Marcio Cruz, Elwyn Davies, Arti Grover, Leonardo Iacovone, et al. 2020. "Unmasking the Impact of COVID-19 on Businesses: Firm Level Evidence from across the World." Policy Research Working Paper 9434, World Bank, Washington, DC.

Auer, Raphael, Jon Frost, Thomas Lammer, Tara Rice, and Amber Wadsworth. 2020. "Inclusive Payments for the Post-Pandemic World." SUERF Policy Note 193, European Money and Finance Forum, Vienna. https://www.suerf.org/policynotes/16645/inclusive-payments-for-the-post-pandemic-world.

Ayyagari, Meghana, Asli Demirgüç-Kunt, and Vojislav Maksimovic. 2011. "Small vs. Young Firms across the World: Contribution to Employment, Job Creation, and Growth." Policy Research Working Paper 5631, World Bank, Washington, DC.

Banca de las Oportunidades. 2020. "Reporte de Inclusión Financiera: Primer Semestre, 2020" [Financial inclusion report: First semester, 2020]. Departamento Nacional de Planeación and Banca de las Oportunidades, Bogotá, Colombia. https://bancadelasoportunidades.gov.co/sites/default/files/2020-10/BDO_Reporte%20Semestral_0.pdf.

Banco de México. 2021. "Evolución del Financiamiento a las Empresas durante el Trimestre Abril–Junio de 2021" [Quarterly trends in financing to companies during the quarter April–June 2021]. Press release, August 19, 2021. https://www.banxico.org.mx/publicaciones-y-prensa/evolucion-trimestral-del-financiamiento-a-las-empr/%7BF3F3AFEC9-A775-BC0B-1640-5950FAAE46E3%7D.pdf.

Banco Pichincha. 2021. MSME Business Update, September 2021. Banco Pichincha, Quito, Pichincha, Ecuador.

Bari, Faisal, Kashif Malik, Muhammad Meki, and Simon Quinn. 2021. "Asset-Based Microfinance for Microenterprises: Evidence from Pakistan." CEPR Discussion Paper DP15768, Centre for Economic Policy Research, London.

Bartlett, Robert P., III, Adair Morse, Nancy Wallace, and Richard Stanton. 2020. "Algorithmic Accountability: A Legal and Economic Framework." *Berkeley Technology*

Law Journal, Haas School of Business, University of California, Berkeley.

BBVA (Banco Bilbao Vizcayza Argentaria). 2020. "The Five V's of Big Data." *Big Data*, May 26, 2020. https://www .bbva.com/en/five-vs-big-data/.

BCBS (Basel Committee on Banking Supervision). 2021. "Principles for Operational Resilience." BCBS, Bank for International Settlements, Basel, Switzerland. https:// www.bis.org/bcbs/publ/d516.pdf.

BCE (Banco Central de Ecuador). 2020. "Estrategia Nacional de Inclusión Financiera 2020–2024." BCE, Quito, Ecuador. http://rfd.org.ec/docs/comunicacion/Documento ENIF/ENIF-BCE-2021.pdf.

Berg, Tobias, Valentin Burg, Ana Gombović, and Manju Puri. 2020. "On the Rise of the Fin Techs: Credit Scoring Using Digital Footprints." *Review of Financial Studies* 33 (7): 2845–97.

Berger, Allen N., Christa H. S. Bouwman, Lars Norden, Raluca A. Roman, Gregory F. Udell, and Teng Wang. 2021. "Is a Friend in Need a Friend Indeed? How Relationship Borrowers Fare during the COVID-19 Crisis." Research Department Working Paper WP 21-13, Federal Reserve Bank of Philadelphia, Philadelphia, PA.

Bharadwaj, Prashant, and Tavneet Suri. 2020. "Improving Financial Inclusion through Digital Savings and Credit." *AEA Papers and Proceedings* 110 (May): 584–88.

BIS (Bank for International Settlements) and IOSCO (International Organization of Securities Commissions). 2016. "Guidance on Cyber Resilience for Financial Market Infrastructures." Committee on Payments and Market Infrastructures, Board of the International Organization of Securities Commissions, BIS, Basel, Switzerland. https://www.bis.org/cpmi/publ/d146.pdf.

Björkegren, Daniel, and Darrell Grissen. 2020. "Behavior Revealed in Mobile Phone Usage Predicts Credit Repayment." *World Bank Economic Review* 34 (3): 618–34.

Blackmon, William, Rafe Mazer, and Shana Warren. 2021. "Kenya Consumer Protection in Digital Finance Survey Report." Innovations for Poverty Action, New Haven, CT. https://www.poverty-action.org/publication/kenya -consumer-protection-digital-finance-survey-report.

Bodovski, David, Hannah Firestone, Seung Jung Lee, and Viktors Stebunovs. 2021. "Bank Lending Conditions during the Pandemic." *FEDS Notes*, October 15, Board of Governors of the Federal Reserve System, Washington, DC. https://doi.org/10.17016/2380-7172.3000.

Broeders, Dirk, and Jermy Prenio. 2018. "Innovative Technology in Financial Supervision (SupTech): The Experience of Early Users." *FSI Insights on Policy Implementation* 9 (July), Financial Stability Institute, Bank for International Settlements, Basel, Switzerland. https://www .bis.org/fsi/publ/insights9.htm.

Burlando, Alfredo, Michael A. Kuhn, and Silvia Prina. 2021. "Too Fast, Too Furious? Digital Credit Delivery Speed and Repayment Rates." CEGA Working Paper WPS-151, Center for Effective Global Action, University of California, Berkeley. https://doi.org/10.26085/C32P49.

Businesswire. 2021. "MYbank's Use of Digital Technology Leads to Record Growth in Rural Clients." *Businesswire*, June 23, 2021. https://www.businesswire.com/news /home/20210623005998/en/MYbank%E2%80%99s -Use-of-Digital-Technology-Leads-to-Record-Growth -in-Rural-Clients.

Byrne, Kieran, Saahil Karpe, Florence Kondylis, Megan Lang, and John Loeser. 2021. "Sectoral Heterogeneity in the Covid-19 Recovery: Evidence from Rwanda." In *Shaping Africa's Post-Covid Recovery*, edited by Rabah Arezki, Simeon Djankov, and Ugo Panizza. London: CEPR Press. https://voxeu.org/content/shaping -africa-s-post-covid-recovery.

Calice, Pietro. 2020. "Boosting Credit: Public Guarantees Can Help Mitigate Risk during COVID-19." *Private Sector Development Blog*, May 28, 2020. https://blogs .worldbank.org/psd/boosting-credit-public-guarantees -can-help-mitigate-risk-during-covid-19.

Calvano, Emilio, Giacomo Calzolari, Vincenzo Denicolò, and Sergio Pastorello. 2020. "Artificial Intelligence, Algorithmic Pricing, and Collusion." *American Economic Review* 110 (10): 3267–97.

Caniato, Federico, Antonella Moretto, and James B. Rice, Jr. 2020. "A Financial Crisis Is Looming for Smaller Suppliers." *Harvard Business Review*, August 6, 2020. https://hbr.org/2020/08/a-financial-crisis-is-looming -for-smaller-suppliers.

Carpena, Fenella, Shawn Cole, Jeremy Shapiro, and Bilal Zia. 2017. "The ABCs of Financial Education: Experimental Evidence on Attitudes, Behavior, and Cognitive Biases." *Finance and PSD Impact: The Lessons from DECFP Impact Evaluations* 40 (February), World Bank, Washington, DC. https://openknowledge.worldbank.org /handle/10986/26068.

CBK (Central Bank of Kenya). 2019. "2019 FinAccess Household Survey." CBK, Kenya National Bureau of Statistics, and Financial Sector Deepening Kenya, Nairobi. https://www.centralbank.go.ke/wp-content/uploads /2019/04/2019-FinAcces-Report.pdf.

CBK (Central Bank of Kenya). 2020a. "Commercial Banks' Credit Officer Survey December 2020." CBK, Nairobi, Kenya. https://www.centralbank.go.ke/2021/02/01 /credit-officer-survey-report-december-2020/.

CBK (Central Bank of Kenya). 2020b. "Commercial Banks' Credit Officer Survey June 2020." CBK, Nairobi. https:// www.centralbank.go.ke/2020/12/18/credit-officer -survey-report-2020/.

CBK (Central Bank of Kenya). 2020c. "Publication of the Credit Reference Bureau Regulations, 2020 and Additional Measures on Credit Information Sharing." Press release, April 14, 2020. https://www.centralbank.go .ke/uploads/press_releases/850440997_Press%20 Release%20-%20Credit%20Reference%20Bureau%20 Regulations%20-%20April%202020.pdf.

CBK (Central Bank of Kenya). 2021a. "Credit Officer Survey, March 31, 2021." CBK, Nairobi. https://www.centralbank .go.ke/2021/05/05/credit-officer-survey-report -march-2021/.

CBK (Central Bank of Kenya). 2021b. "Enactment of the Law to Regulate Digital Lenders and Issuance of the Corresponding Draft Regulations for Public Comment." Press release, December 23, 2021. https://www.centralbank .go.ke/2021/12/23/enactment-of-the-law-to-regulate -digital-lenders-and-issuance-of-the-corresponding -draft-regulations-for-public-comment/.

CBK (Central Bank of Kenya). 2021c. "FinAccess MSE Covid-19 Tracker Survey." CBK, Nairobi. https://www.centralbank.go.ke/2021/06/23/finaccess-mse-covid-19-tracker-survey-report/.

CBK (Central Bank of Kenya), KNBS (Kenya National Bureau of Statistics), and FSD Kenya (Financial Sector Deepening Kenya). 2021. "FinAccess Household Survey—December 2021." FSD Kenya, Narobi. https://www.fsdkenya.org/blogs-publications/publications/finaccess-household-surveys/.

China Banking News. 2020. "100 Chinese Banks Sign Up for MYbank's 'Non-Contact' Micro-Loan Plan to Help Mitigate Coronvirus Impacts." Fintech, March 8, 2020. https://www.chinabankingnews.com/2020/03/08/100-chinese-banks-sign-up-for-mybanks-non-contact-micro-loan-plan-to-help-mitigate-coronavirus-impacts/.

Citigroup. 2020. "Citibanamex, PepsiCo, and Amigo PAQ Expand Digital Financial Inclusion for Underbanked Retailers through CoDi." Press release, October 26, 2020. https://www.citigroup.com/citi/news/2020/201030b.htm.

Claessens, Stijn. 2009. "Competition in the Financial Sector: Overview of Competition Policies." *World Bank Research Observer* 24 (1): 83–118. https://doi.org/10.1093/wbro/lkp004.

Cornelli, Giulio, Jon Frost, Leonardo Gambacorta, Raghavendra Rau, Robert Wardrop, and Tania Ziegler. 2020. "Fintech and Big Tech Credit: A New Database." BIS Working Paper 887, Monetary and Economic Department, Bank for International Settlements, Basel, Switzerland.

Corredera-Catalán, Félix, Filippo di Pietro, and Antonio Trujillo-Ponce. 2021. "Post-COVID-19 SME Financing Constraints and the Credit Guarantee Scheme Solution in Spain." *Journal of Banking Regulation* 22 (3): 250–60. https://doi.org/10.1057/s41261-021-00143-7.

Creditinfo. 2021. "The Creditinfo Global Impact Score." Creditinfo, Prague, Czech Republic. https://chronicle.creditinfo.com/2020/09/15/players-in-baltic-markets-latvia-estonia-and-iceland-measure-risk-better-benefitting-from-covid-19-impact-score-developed-by-creditinfo.

Crisanto, Janine Marie. 2021. "Indonesia E-wallet Transaction to Reach $18.5 Billion in 2021 amid Fierce Competition." *Asian Banker*, April 9, 2021. https://www.theasianbanker.com/updates-and-articles/big-tech-platforms-heat-up-competition-in-indonesias-digital-payments-landscape.

Dailey, Natasha, and Kate Taylor. 2021. "Customers Are Reporting Credit-Card Payment Crashes at Restaurants and Stores across the US, Including Chick-fil-A and Ikea." *Business Insider*, February 26, 2021. https://www.businessinsider.com/credit-card-payments-system-outage-stores-restaurants-chick-fil-a-2021-2.

Data2x. 2016. "Catalyzing Inclusive Financial Systems: Chile's Commitment to Women's Data." Case study. Data2x, Washington, DC. https://data2x.org/wp-content/uploads/2019/05/Chile-Case-study_English_Final.pdf.

di Castri, Simone, Stefan Hohl, Arend Kulenkampff, and Jermy Prenio. 2019. "The SupTech Generations." *FSI Insights on Policy Implementation* 19 (October),

Financial Stability Institute, Bank for International Settlements, Basel, Switzerland. https://www.bis.org/fsi/publ/insights19.htm.

Djeundje, Viani B., Jonathan Crook, Raffaella Calabresea, and Mona Hamid. 2021. "Enhancing Credit Scoring with Alternative Data." *Expert Streams with Applications* 163 (January): 113766. https://doi.org/10.1016/j.eswa.2020.113766.

Dunbar, Nicholas, and Manpreet Singh. 2020. "Consumer Goods Giants Grow Inventory, Extend Receivables amid Covid-19 Shift." *Eurofinance*, September 1, 2020. https://www.eurofinance.com/news/consumer-goods-giants-grow-inventory-extend-receivables-amid-covid-19-shift/.

European Parliament. 2019. *A Governance Framework for Algorithmic Accountability and Transparency*. Brussels: Panel for the Future of Science and Technology, Scientific Foresight Unit, European Parliamentary Research Service, European Union. https://www.europarl.europa.eu/RegData/etudes/STUD/2019/624262/EPRS_STU(2019)624262_EN.pdf.

Experian. 2021. "The Impact of COVID-19 on Business: The State of Business Credit in South Africa." Webinar, January 20, 2021, Experian, Dublin.

Fan, Yuting, Hà Minh Nguyên, and Rong Qian. 2020. "Collateralized Borrowing around the World: Insights from the World Bank Enterprise Surveys." *International Journal of Finance and Economics*. Published ahead of print, September 29, 2020. https://doi.org/10.1002/ijfe.2279.

Feyen, Erik H. B., Jon Frost, Leonardo Gambacorta, Harish Natarajan, and Matthew Saal. 2021. "Fintech and the Digital Transformation of Financial Services: Implications for Market Structure and Public Policy." BIS Paper 117, Monetary and Economic Department, Bank for International Settlements, Basel, Switzerland.

Fina (Financial Agency, Croatia). 2021. "E-relief Application Point and COVID Score." Fina, Zagreb, Croatia. https://www.fina.hr/en/e-relief-application-point-and-covid-score#covid-score.

FinRegLab. 2020. "Data Diversification in Credit Underwriting." Research Brief, FinRegLab, Washington, DC. https://finreglab.org/data-diversification-in-credit-underwriting/.

Froeling, Maarten, Angela Garcia Vargas, and Beniamino Savonitto. 2021. "LAPO Agent Banking: Increased Reach and Client Diversity." International Finance Corporation, Washington, DC. https://www.ifc.org/wps/wcm/connect/5eae1f1d-ad47-41db-93c9-eebd858b07e7/LAPO+Agent+Banking-+Increased+reached+and+client+diversity.pdf?MOD=AJPERES&CVID=nyyOk5M.

FSB (Financial Stability Board). 2018. "Implementation and Effects of the G20 Financial Regulatory Reforms." Fourth Annual Report, FSB, Basel, Switzerland. https://www.fsb.org/2018/11/implementation-and-effects-of-the-g20-financial-regulatory-reforms-fourth-annual-report/.

FSB (Financial Stability Board). 2020. "Effective Practices for Cyber Incident Response and Recovery: Final Report." FSB, Basel, Switzerland. https://www.fsb.org/2020/10/effective-practices-for-cyber-incident-response-and-recovery-final-report/.

FSD Kenya (Financial Sector Deepening Kenya). 2021. "State of the Economy: Focus on Digitisation and the Impact of COVID-19 on MSEs." FSD Kenya, Nairobi. https://www.fsdkenya.org/wp-content/uploads/2021/06/State-of-the-Economy-Q1-2021.pdf.

Fu, Jonathan, and Mrinal Mishra. 2020. "Fintech in the Time of COVID-19: Trust and Technological Adoption during Crises." Swiss Finance Institute Research Paper 20–38, Swiss Finance Institute; Department of Banking and Finance, University of Zurich, Zurich, Switzerland.

Fuster, Andreas, Paul Goldsmith-Pinkham, Tarun Ramadorai, and Ansgar Walther. 2021. "Predictably Unequal: The Effects of Machine Learning on Credit Markets." *Journal of Finance*. Published ahead of print, October 28, 2021.

G-7 (Group of Seven). 2016. "G7 Fundamental Elements of Cybersecurity for the Financial Sector." European Commission, Brussels. https://ec.europa.eu/info/publications/g7-fundamental-elements-cybersecurity-financial-sector_en.

Gambacorta, Leonardo, Yiping Huang, Zhenhua Li, Han Qiu, and Shu Chen. 2020. "Data vs Collateral." BIS Working Paper 881, Monetary and Economic Department, Bank for International Settlements, Basel, Switzerland.

Gambacorta, Leonardo, Yiping Huang, Han Qiu, and Jingyi Wang. 2019. "How Do Machine Learning and Non-Traditional Data Affect Credit Scoring? New Evidence from a Chinese Fintech Firm." BIS Working Paper 834, Monetary and Economic Department, Bank for International Settlements, Basel, Switzerland.

Garrote Sanchez, Daniel, Nicolas Gomez Parra, Caglar Ozden, Bob Rijkers, Mariana Viollaz, and Hernan Winkler. 2021. "Who on Earth Can Work from Home?" *World Bank Research Observer* 36 (1): 67–100.

Garz, Seth, Xavier Giné, Dean Karlan, Rafe Mazer, Caitlin Sanford, and Jonathan Zinman. 2021. "Consumer Protection for Financial Inclusion in Low- and Middle-Income Countries: Bridging Regulator and Academic Perspectives." *Annual Review of Financial Economics* 13 (November): 219–46.

Gertler, Paul, Brett Green, and Catherine Wolfram. 2021. "Digital Collateral." NBER Working Paper 28724, National Bureau of Economic Research, Cambridge, MA.

Ghosh, Suvashree. 2020. "HDFC Bank Experiences Net Banking Snags Day after RBI Curbs." *Bloomberg*, December 4, 2020. https://www.bloombergquint.com/business/hdfc-bank-experiences-net-banking-snags-day-after-rbi-curbs.

Gillis, Talia B., and Jann L. Spiess. 2019. "Big Data and Discrimination." *University of Chicago Law Review* 86 (2): 4.

GOGLA (Global Off-Grid Lighting Association). 2021. *Global Off-Grid Solar Market Report: Semi-Annual Sales and Impact Data*. Public Report, January–June 2021. Amsterdam: GOGLA. https://www.gogla.org/global-off-grid-solar-market-report.

Gourinchas, Pierre-Olivier, Şebnem Kalemli-Özcan, Veronika Penciakova, and Nick Sander. 2021a. "COVID-19 and SME Failures." NBER Working Paper 27877, National Bureau of Economic Research, Cambridge, MA.

Gourinchas, Pierre-Olivier, Şebnem Kalemli-Özcan, Veronika Penciakova, and Nick Sander. 2021b. "COVID-19 and SMEs: A 2021 'Time Bomb.'" NBER Working Paper 28418, National Bureau of Economic Research, Cambridge, MA.

GPFI (Global Partnership for Financial Inclusion). 2018. "Use of Alternative Data to Enhance Credit Reporting to Enable Access to Digital Financial Services by Individuals and SMEs Operating in the Informal Economy." Guidance Note, G20 Global Partnership for Financial Inclusion, World Bank, Washington DC. https://www.gpfi.org/publications/guidance-note-use-alternative-data-enhance-credit-reporting-enable-access-digital-financial-services.

GSMA (GSM Association). 2020. "The State of Mobile Internet Connectivity 2020." GSMA, London. https://www.gsma.com/r/wp-content/uploads/2020/09/GSMA-State-of-Mobile-Internet-Connectivity-Report-2020.pdf.

GSMA (GSM Association). 2021a. "The Mobile Gender Gap Report 2021." GSMA, London. https://www.gsma.com/r/gender-gap/.

GSMA (GSM Association). 2021b. "State of the Industry Report on Mobile Money 2021." GSMA, London. https://www.gsma.com/mobilefordevelopment/wp-content/uploads/2021/03/GSMA_State-of-the-Industry-Report-on-Mobile-Money-2021_Full-report.pdf.

Gubbins, Paul. 2019. "Digital Credit in Kenya: Facts and Figures from FinAccess 2019." Focus Note (December), Financial Sector Deepening Kenya, Nairobi. https://fsdkenya.org/wp-content/uploads/2020/07/Focus-Note-Digital-Credit-in-Kenya_Updated.pdf.

Gwer, Francis. 2019. "Digital Credit Audit Report: Evaluating the Conduct and Practice of Digital Lending in Kenya." With Jack Odero and Edoardo Totolo. Digital Credit Audit Report (September), Financial Sector Deepening Kenya, Nairobi. https://www.fsdkenya.org/research-and-publications/digital-credit-audit-report-evaluating-the-conduct-and-practice-of-digital-lending-in-kenya/.

Haughwout, A., D. Lee, J. Scally, and W. van der Klaauw. 2021. "What's Next for Forborne Borrowers?" *Liberty Street Economics*, May 19, 2021, Federal Reserve Bank of New York. https://libertystreeteconomics.newyorkfed.org/2021/05/whats-next-for-forborne-borrowers/.

He, Zhiguo, Jing Huang, and Jidong Zhou. 2020. "Open Banking: Credit Market Competition When Borrowers Own the Data." NBER Working Paper 28118, National Bureau of Economic Research, Cambridge, MA.

Huang, Yiping, Longmei Zhang, Zhenhua Li, Han Qiu, Tao Sun, and Xue Wang. 2020. "Fintech Credit Risk Assessment for SMEs: Evidence from China." IMF Working Paper WP/20/193, International Monetary Fund, Washington, DC. https://www.imf.org/en/Publications/WP/Issues/2020/09/25/Fintech-Credit-Risk-Assessment-for-SMEs-Evidence-from-China-49742.

Hurley, Mikella, and Julius Adebayo. 2017. "Credit Scoring in the Era of Big Data." *Yale Journal of Law and Technology* 18 (1): 148–216.

ICC (International Chamber of Commerce). 2020. "Priming Trade Finance to Safeguard SMEs and Power a Resilient Recovery from COVID-19." Memo to G20 Governments, Central Banks, and International Financial Institutions, ICC, Paris. https://iccwbo.org/content/uploads/sites/3/2020/11/memo-g20-recommendations-smes.pdf.

IEA (International Energy Agency). 2020. "The Covid-19 Crisis Is Reversing Progress on Energy Access in Africa." *IEA*, November 20, 2020. https://www.iea.org/articles/the-covid-19-crisis-is-reversing-progress-on-energy-access-in-africa.

IFC (International Finance Corporation). 2017a. "Beyond Fintech: Leveraging Blockchain for More Sustainable and Inclusive Supply Chains." EMCompass Note 45, IFC, Washington, DC.

IFC (International Finance Corporation). 2017b. "MSME Finance Gap: Assessment of the Shortfalls and Opportunities in Financing Micro, Small, and Medium Enterprises in Emerging Markets." IFC, Washington, DC.

IFC (International Finance Corporation). 2019. "Supply Chain Finance Knowledge Guide." Financial Institutions Group, IFC, Washington, DC.

IFC (International Finance Corporation). 2020a. *Artificial Intelligence in Emerging Markets: Opportunities, Trends, and Emerging Business Models*. Washington, DC: IFC.

IFC (International Finance Corporation). 2020b. "Coordinating Prudential Regulation and Secured Transactions Frameworks: A Primer." IFC, Washington, DC.

IFC (International Finance Corporation). 2020c. *Handbook: Technology and Digitization in Supply Chain Finance*. Washington, DC: IFC.

IFC (International Finance Corporation). 2021. "The Early Impact of COVID-19 on Financial Institutions: Insights from a Survey of IFC Financial Institution Clients." IFC, Washington, DC. https://www.ifc.org/wps/wcm/connect/587d57c6-74dd-4efb-90cc-5dec218fd00e/Covid-19+Impact+on+FI+Survey+2020+-+5-11-2021_FINAL+REVIEW.pdf?MOD=AJPERES&CVID=nBz3kgr.

IMF (International Monetary Fund). 2019. *Thailand: Financial System Stability Assessment*. IMF Country Report 19/308. Washington, DC: IMF.

IMF (International Monetary Fund) and World Bank. 2018. "The Bali Fintech Agenda." IMF Policy Paper, IMF, Washington, DC. https://www.imf.org/en/Publications/Policy-Papers/Issues/2018/10/11/pp101118-bali-fintech-agenda.

INEGI (National Institute of Statistics and Geography). 2020. "Economic Censuses 2019." Press release. https://www.inegi.org.mx/contenidos/saladeprensa/boletines/2020/OtrTemEcon/CenEconResDef2019_Nal.pdf.

IOSCO (International Organization of Securities Commissions). 2020. "Principles on Outsourcing: Consultation Report." IOSCO, Madrid. https://www.iosco.org/library/pubdocs/pdf/IOSCOPD654.pdf.

Izaguirre, Juan Carlos, Michelle Kaffenberger, and Rafe Mazer. 2018. "It's Time to Slow Digital Credit's Growth in East Africa." *Digital Credit: Borrower Experiences and Emerging Risks* (blog), September 25, 2018. https://www.cgap.org/blog/its-time-slow-digital-credits-growth-east-africa.

Jack, William, Michael R. Kremer, Joost de Laat, and Tavneet Suri. 2016. "Borrowing Requirements, Credit Access, and Adverse Selection: Evidence from Kenya." NBER Working Paper 22686, National Bureau of Economic Research, Cambridge, MA.

Jagtiani, Julapa A., and Catharine M. Lemieux. 2018. "Do Fintech Lenders Penetrate Areas That Are Underserved by Traditional Banks?" *Journal of Economics and Business* 100 (November–December): 43–54.

Karandaaz. 2021. "Mobile Money Adoption Increased during Pandemic by 4%: Karandaaz Survey on COVID-19's Impact on Financial Behavior." Karandaaz press release, May 18, 2021.

Khan, Imran, and Karrar Hussain Jaffar. 2021. "Searching for the Binding Constraint to Digital Financial Inclusion in Pakistan: A Decision Tree Approach." CGD Policy Paper 218, Center for Global Development, Washington, DC. https://pmic.pk/wp-content/uploads/2021/09/pakistan-decision-tree.pdf.

Kisat, Faizaan. 2021. "Loan Officers, Algorithms, and Credit Outcomes: Experimental Evidence from Pakistan." Job Market Paper, Department of Economics, Princeton University, Princeton, NJ.

Klapper, Leora, and Margaret Miller. 2021. "The Impact of COVID-19 on Digital Financial Inclusion." Global Partnership for Financial Inclusion and World Bank, Washington, DC. https://www.gpfi.org/sites/gpfi/files/sites/default/files/5_WB%20Report_The%20impact%20of%20COVID-19%20on%20digital%20financial%20inclusion.pdf.

Koetsier, John. 2020. "Banking on Mobile Up 35–85% Thanks to Coronavirus (After 1 Trillion App Opens in 2019)." *Editors' Pick* (blog), April 15, 2020. https://www.forbes.com/sites/johnkoetsier/2020/04/15/report-35-85-fintech-growth-on-mobile-thanks-to-coronavirus-after-1-trillion-app-opens-in-2019/?sh=d12c9ec759a0.

Koulouridi, Efstathia, Sameer Kumar, Luis Nario, Theo Pepanides, and Marco Vettori. 2020. "Managing and Monitoring Credit Risk after the COVID-19 Pandemic." *Our Insights* (blog), July 31, 2020. https://www.mckinsey.com/business-functions/risk/our-insights/managing-and-monitoring-credit-risk-after-the-covid-19-pandemic.

Leo, Martin, Suneel Sharma, and K. Maddulety. 2019. "Machine Learning in Banking Risk Management: A Literature Review." *Risks* 7 (1): 29.

Love, Inessa, María Soledad Martínez Pería, and Sandeep Singh. 2016. "Collateral Registries for Movable Assets: Does Their Introduction Spur Firms' Access to Bank Financing?" *Journal of Financial Services Research* 49 (1): 1–37.

Lukoianova, Tatiana, and Victoria L. Rubin. 2014. "Veracity Roadmap: Is Big Data Objective, Truthful, and Credible?" Advances in Classification Research Online 24 (1): 4–15. https://doi.org/10.7152/acro.v24i1.14671.

MAS (Monetary Authority of Singapore). 2018. "Guidelines on Outsourcing." MAS, Singapore. https://www.mas.gov.sg/regulation/guidelines/guidelines-on-outsourcing.

Maylie, Devon. 2020. "Unsung Heroes: Truckers Keep Delivering, Thanks to Online Platform." *IFC Insights*, March 2020. https://www.ifc.org/wps/wcm/connect/news_ext_content/ifc_external_corporate_site/news+and+events/news/insights/unsung-heroes-truckers.

McKinsey. 2019. "Global AI Survey: AI Proves Its Worth but Few Scale Impact." McKinsey Analytics, McKinsey and Company. https://www.mckinsey.com/featured-insights/artificial-intelligence/global-ai-survey-ai-proves-its-worth-but-few-scale-impact.

McKinsey. 2020. "The 2020 McKinsey Global Payments Report." Global Banking Practice, McKinsey and Company.

Meki, Muhammad, Simon Quinn, and Kate Roll. 2021. "Mutuality and the Potential of Microequity: Credit with Performance-Contingent Repayment for Gig Workers." In *Putting Purpose into Practice: The Economics of Mutuality*. Oxford, UK: Oxford University Press.

Melzer, Brian T. 2011. "The Real Costs of Credit Access: Evidence from the Payday Lending Market." *Quarterly Journal of Economics* 126 (1): 517–55.

Montoya, Ana María, Eric Parrado, Alex Solís, and Raimundo Undurraga. 2020. "Bad Taste: Gender Discrimination in the Consumer Credit Market." IDB Working Paper IDB-WP-1053, Department of Research and Chief Economist, Inter-American Development Bank, Washington, DC.

Morse, Adair. 2011. "Payday Lenders: Heroes or Villains?" *Journal of Financial Economics* 102 (1): 28–44.

Morse, Adair, and Karen Pence. 2020. "Technological Innovation and Discrimination in Household Finance." NBER Working Paper 26739, National Bureau of Economic Research, Cambridge, MA.

Moulton, Stephanie, J. Michael Collins, Cäzilia Loibl, and Anya Samek. 2014. "Effects of Monitoring on Mortgage Delinquency: Evidence from a Randomized Field Study." *Journal of Policy Analysis and Management* 34 (1): 184–207.

OECD (Organisation for Economic Co-operation and Development). 2018. "G20/OECD Policy Guidance: Financial Consumer Protection Approaches in the Digital Age." OECD, Paris. https://www.oecd.org/finance/G20-OECD-Policy-Guidance-Financial-Consumer-Protection-Digital-Age-2018.pdf.

OECD (Organisation for Economic Co-operation and Development). 2021a. "Digital Delivery of Financial Education: Design and Practice." OECD, Paris. https://www.oecd.org/financial/education/Digital-delivery-of-financial-education-design-and-practice.pdf.

OECD (Organisation for Economic Co-operation and Development). 2021b. "Lessons Learnt and Effective Approaches to Protect Consumers and Support Financial Inclusion in the Context of COVID-19." G20/OECD Report. OECD, Paris. https://www.oecd.org/daf/fin/financial-education/g20-oecd-report-on-financial-consumer-protection-and-financial-inclusion-in-the-context-of-covid-19.htm.

OECD (Organisation for Economic Co-operation and Development). 2021c. "Navigating the Storm: MSMEs' Financial and Digital Competencies in COVID-19 Times." G20/OECD-INFE report. OECD, Paris. https://www.oecd.org/financial/education/navigating-the-storm-msmes-financial-anddigital-competencies-in-covid-19-times.htm.

OECD (Organisation for Economic Co-operation and Development). 2021d. "Trade Finance in the COVID Era: Current and Future Challenges." OECD Policy Responses to Coronavirus (COVID-19), OECD, Paris. https://www.oecd.org/coronavirus/policy-responses/trade-finance-in-the-covid-era-current-and-future-challenges-79daca94/.

OJK (Financial Services Authority of Indonesia). 2017a. "Financial Services Authority Circular Number 18/SEOJK.02/2017 Regarding Information Technology Risk Management and Management in Information Technology-Based Lending." [In Indonesian]. https://www.ojk.go.id/id/regulasi/otoritas-jasa-keuangan/surat-edaran-ojk-dan-dewan-komisioner/Documents/Pages/SEOJK-Tata-Kelola-dan-Manajemen-Risiko-Teknologi-Informasi-pada-Layanan-Pinjam-Meminjam-Uang-Berbasis-Teknologi-Informasi/SAL%20SEOJK%2018%20FINTECH.pdf.

OJK (Financial Services Authority of Indonesia). 2017b. "OJK Issues Regulation on IT-Based Lending Services." Press Release SP 01/DKNS/OJK/I/2017, January 10, 2017. https://www.ojk.go.id/en/berita-dan-kegiatan/siaran-pers/Documents/Pages/Press-Release-OJK-Issues-Regulation-on-It-Based-Lending-Services/SIARAN%20PERS%20POJK%20%20%20FIntech-ENGLISH.pdf.

Ostmann, Florian, and Cosmina Dorobantu. 2021. "AI in Financial Services." Alan Turing Institute, London. https://www.turing.ac.uk/research/publications/ai-financial-services.

Parlour, Christine A., Uday Rajan, and Haoxiang Zhu. 2020. "When FinTech Competes for Payment Flows." Working paper, Haas School of Business, University of California, Berkeley.

Pazarbasioglu, Ceyla, Alfonso Garcia Mora, Mahesh Uttamchandani, Harish Natarajan, Erik H. B. Feyen, and Mathew Saal. 2020. "Digital Financial Services." World Bank, Washington, DC. https://pubdocs.worldbank.org/en/230281588169110691/Digital-Financial-Services.pdf.

Perú21. 2021. "More Than 4 thousand Winemakers Will Benefit through 'Amigo PAQ.' " *Economy*, February 3, 2021. https://peru21.pe/economia/emprendedor-mas-de-4-mil-bodegueros-se-beneficiaran-a-traves-de-amigo-paq-pepsico-cbc-citi-pos-movil-prestamos-noticia/.

Plaitakis, Ariadne, Thomas Kirk Wills, and Bryan Church. 2016. "Regional: Promoting Remittance for Development Finance" and "Digital Payment Systems, Mobile Money Services, and Agent Banking: Bangladesh, Nepal, and Sri Lanka." ADB Technical Assistance Consultant's Report, Asian Development Bank, Manila. https://www.adb.org/sites/default/files/project-document/195971/48190-001-tacr.pdf.

PSBC (Postal Savings Bank of China). 2021. "Release of the Economic Daily–PSBC Small and Micro-Sized Enterprise Operating Index Report of June 2021." PSBC, Beijing. https://www.psbc.com/en/products_and_services/corporate/samseoi/202107/t20210713_108141.html.

Putnam, Daniel, Rafe Mazer, and William Blackmon. 2021. "Report on the Competition Authority of Kenya Digital Credit Market Inquiry." Competition Authority of Kenya and Innovations for Poverty Action, Nairobi. https://www.poverty-action.org/publication/competition-authority-kenya-digital-credit-market-inquiry.

PwC (PricewaterhouseCoopers). 2021a. "Keep Your Capital Working to Recover from the Crisis." Working Capital Report 2021, DACH and Benelux Regions, PwC, Bielefeld, Germany. https://www.pwc.nl/nl/assets /documents/pwc-working-capital-report-2021.pdf.

PwC (PricewaterhouseCoopers). 2021b. "Working Capital Study 20/21: From Recovery to Growth in the Face of Supply Chain Instability." PwC, London. https://www .pwc.co.uk/services/business-restructuring/insights /working-capital-study.html.

RBI (Reserve Bank of India). 2021a. "Master Directions, Non-Banking Financial Company: Peer to Peer Lending Platform (Reserve Bank) Directions, 2017 (Updated as on October 05, 2021)." RBI, Mumbai. https://www.rbi .org.in/Scripts/NotificationUser.aspx?Id=11137.

RBI (Reserve Bank of India). 2021b. "Payment System Indicators—November 2021." https://rbidocs.rbi.org.in /rdocs/PSI/PDFs/PAYMENTNOVEMBER2021105 57582EEF946AB8DBA2A8442DA8DDF.PDF.

Ruch, Madigan. 2020. "MicroCapital Brief: Pakistan Launches Electronic Registry of Movable Assets, with Support from IFC." *MicroCapital*, May 20, 2020. https://www.microcapital.org/microcapital-brief -pakistan-launches-electronic-registry-of-movable -assets-with-support-from-ifc/.

Safaricom. 2021a. "Results Booklet for the Year Ended 31st March 2021." Safaricom PLC, Nairobi, Kenya. https:// www.safaricom.co.ke/images/Downloads/FY21 ResultsBooklet13May2021.pdf.

Safaricom. 2021b. "Safaricom PLC Results Booklet for the Six Months Period Ended 30th September 2021." Safaricom PLC, Nairobi, Kenya. https://www.safaricom .co.ke/images/Downloads/Resources_Downloads/H1 _FY22/HY22_Results_Booklet_9_November_2021.pdf.

SEC (United States Securities and Exchange Commission). 2021. *Hepsiburada*. SEC Form F-1, Registration 333 (May 28). Washington, DC: SEC. https://hepsiburada .gcs-web.com/static-files/5ed9bceb-386a-4712-9507 -0406097902af?auth_token=df23ffe8-8292-49b7 -99e5-21225fac63b4.

SFC (Superintendencia Financiera de Colombia). 2021. "Informe de Operaciones: Segundo Semestre 2020." SFC, Bogotá, Colombia.

Shleifer, Andrei, and Robert W. Vishny. 2011. "Fire Sales in Finance and Macroeconomics." *Journal of Economic Perspectives* 25 (1): 29–48.

Simanowitz, Anton, Genevieve Hennessy-Barrett, and Juan Carlos Izaguirre. 2021. "Is It Possible to Estimate Financial Stress before It Harms Borrowers?" *CGAP* (blog), October 11, 2021. https://www.cgap.org /blog/it-possible-estimate-financial-stress-it-harms -borrowers.

Skiba, Paige Marta, and Jeremy Tobacman. 2019. "Do Payday Loans Cause Bankruptcy?" *Journal of Law and Economics* 62 (3): 485–519.

Sule, Alan, Mehmet Cemalcilar, Dean Karlan, and Jonathan Zinman. 2018. "Unshrouding: Evidence from Bank Overdrafts in Turkey." *Journal of Finance* 73 (2): 481–522.

Sun, Tao, Alan Feng, Yiyao Wang, and Chun Chang. 2021. "Digital Banking Support to Small Businesses amid COVID-19: Evidence from China." Global Financial Stability Note 2021/02, Monetary and Capital Markets, International Monetary Fund, Washington, DC. https:// imf.org/-/media/Files/Publications/gfs-notes/2021 /English/GSNEA2021002.ashx.

Taylor, David. 2021. "Mobile Money 1 Year into a Pandemic: A Shift away from Cash towards a Cash-Lite Economy." *Blog*, September 30, 2021. https://www.fsdkenya.org /blogs-publications/mobile-money-1-year-into-a -pandemic-a-shift-away-from-cash-towards-a-cash -lite-economy/.

Teima, Ghada O., Ivor Istuk, Luis Maldonado, Miguel Soriano, and John S. Wilson. Forthcoming. "Fintech and SME Finance: Expanding Responsible Access." Technical Note, Future of Finance Report, World Bank, Washington, DC.

Togoh, Isabel, and Alexandra Topping. 2018. "Visa Outage: Payment Chaos after Card Network Crashes; As It Happened." *Guardian*, June 1, 2018. https://www.the guardian.com/world/live/2018/jun/01/visa-outage -payment-chaos-after-card-network-crashes-live -updates.

Wagner, Charlotte, and Adalbert Winkler. 2013. "The Vulnerability of Microfinance to Financial Turmoil: Evidence from the Global Financial Crisis." *World Development* 51 (November): 71–90.

Waldron, Daniel. 2016. "Tugende: Analog Credit on Digital Wheels." Consultative Group to Assist the Poor, Washington, DC. https://www.cgap.org/blog/tugende -analog-credit-digital-wheels.

Wehinger, Gert. 2014. "SMEs and the Credit Crunch." *Financial Market Trends* 2013 (2): 115–48.

World Bank. 2017. *Good Practices for Financial Consumer Protection, 2017 edition.* Washington, DC: World Bank.

World Bank. 2019a. "Cybersecurity in Credit Reporting Guidelines." World Bank, Washington, DC. https://the docs.worldbank.org/en/doc/735641585870130697 -0130022020/original/Cybersecurityincreditreporting guidelinefinal.pdf.

World Bank. 2019b. "Disruptive Technologies in the Credit Information Sharing Industry: Developments and Implications." Fintech Note 3, Finance, Competitiveness, and Innovation Global Practice, World Bank, Washington, DC. http://documents.worldbank.org/curated/en /587611557814694439/Disruptive-Technologies-in-the -Credit-Information-Sharing-Industry-Developments -and-Implications.

World Bank. 2019c. *Secured Transactions, Collateral Registries, and Movable Asset-Based Financing.* Knowledge Guide. Washington, DC: World Bank.

World Bank. 2020a. "Collateral Registry, Secured Transactions Law and Practice." Distributed Ledger Technology and Secured Transactions: Legal, Regulatory, and Technological Perspectives; Guidance Notes Series, Note 1, World Bank, Washington, DC.

World Bank. 2020b. "Credit Bureau Licensing and Supervision: A Primer." World Bank, Washington, DC.

World Bank. 2020c. "Embedding Digital Finance in E-commerce Platforms during the COVID-19 Pandemic." Discussion note, World Bank, Washington, DC.

World Bank. 2021a. "Consumer Risks in Fintech: New Manifestations of Consumer Risks and Emerging Regulatory

Approaches." Policy research paper, Finance, Competitiveness, and Innovation Group Practice, World Bank, Washington, DC.

World Bank. 2021b. "The Next Wave of Suptech Innovation: Suptech Solutions for Market Conduct Supervision." Technical note, World Bank, Washington, DC.

World Bank. 2021c. *World Development Report 2021: Data for Better Lives*. Washington, DC: World Bank.

World Bank and CCAF (Cambridge Centre for Alternative Finance). 2020. "The Global Covid-19 FinTech Regulatory Rapid Assessment Report." World Bank, Washington, DC; CCAF, Judge Business School, University of Cambridge, Cambridge, UK. https://www.jbs.cam .ac.uk/faculty-research/centres/alternative-finance /publications/2020-global-covid-19-fintech-regulatory -rapid-assessment-study/.

World Bank and FIRST Initiative. 2015. "Principles for Public Credit Guarantee Schemes for SMEs." World Bank, Washington, DC. https://www.worldbank.org/en/topic /financialsector/publication/principles-for-public -credit-guarantee-schemes-cgss-for-smes.

Xu, Jiajun, Régis Marodon, and Xinshun Ru. 2021. "Mapping 500+ Development Banks: Qualification Criteria, Stylized Facts, and Development Trends." New Structural Development Financing Research Report 2, Institute of New Structural Economics at Peking University, Beijing. https://www.nse.pku.edu.cn/dfidatabase/database reports/517163.htm.

Yang, Crystal S., and Will Dobbie. 2020. "Equal Protection under Algorithms: A New Statistical and Legal Framework." *Michigan Law Review* 119 (2): 291–395.

Ziegler, Tania, Rotem Shneor, Karsten Wenzlaff, Krishnamurthy Suresh, Felipe Ferri de Camargo Paes, Leyla Mammadova, Charles Wanga, et al. 2021. *The 2nd Global Alternative Finance Market Benchmarking Report*. Cambridge, UK: Cambridge Centre for Alternative Finance, Judge Business School, University of Cambridge.

Spotlight 4.1

Public credit guarantee schemes

Public credit guarantee schemes (PCGSs) are a policy tool used widely by governments to ease access to finance for firms—especially small and medium enterprises (SMEs)—while limiting the burden on public finances. Akin to an insurance product, a PCGS provides a guarantee on a loan to a firm by covering a portion of the default risk of the loan. In the case of default by a firm, the lender recovers the value of the guarantee. The lender is also usually obligated to proceed with the collection of the loan and share the proceeds with the guarantor. Guarantees are usually provided for a fee covered by the firm, the lender, or both.

PCGSs, typically operated by an independent company, a development finance institution, or a government agency, are used to alleviate the constraints facing SMEs in accessing finance.[1] Lenders are usually reluctant to extend credit to firms that do not have the necessary amount and type of assets that could serve as collateral for the loan. Moreover, SMEs, especially small and young companies, have a limited credit history and opaque financial statements. Sometimes, they are unable to prepare bankable business plans. As a result, many SMEs with economically viable projects cannot obtain the necessary financing from the formal financial sector.

In use by many countries since the beginning of the twentieth century, PCGSs experienced unprecedented growth in the aftermath of the 2007–09 global financial crisis, when they were widely embraced to stimulate the flow of countercyclical finance to small businesses. Thanks in part to that experience, during the COVID-19 (coronavirus) crisis more than 40 countries, especially advanced economies and emerging markets, relied on PCGSs to support firms' financing needs arising from pandemic-induced shocks.[2]

The expansion of PCGSs triggered demand for good practices in their design, execution, and evaluation. An effective, efficient PCGS is one that maximizes outreach (the number of firms served) and additionality (among other things, its intended outcomes in terms of additional credit mobilized, improved terms and conditions, and jobs created), while maintaining financial sustainability. Against this background, in 2015 the World Bank, in partnership with international associations of PCGSs and lenders and with the support of the FIRST Initiative, developed a set of high-level principles to guide the operations of PCGSs.[3]

The principles recommend adoption of a set of legal, regulatory, governance, and risk management arrangements. They also include operational conduct rules for PCGSs, which are expected to lead to better outcomes for beneficiary firms. The principles draw from the sound practices of PCGSs implemented in jurisdictions such as Chile and the European Union. The principles are also aligned with the practices of those PCGSs whose financial and economic impacts have been positively evaluated.[4] Although the principles have been widely adopted across countries, some gaps remain.[5]

The unprecedented economic distress caused by the pandemic and the need to act swiftly to preserve economic stability have necessitated in many cases a departure from the principles, especially those on the legal and institutional framework, risk-sharing, and pricing. Although the vast majority of jurisdictions already had a legal and institutional framework in place to issue guarantees, especially in Europe, Latin America, and parts of Asia, changes have been made to adapt PCGSs to the unique circumstances created by the pandemic, such as in Colombia. Some credit guarantee programs have been used to target specific sectors or marginalized communities for credit. For example, Burkina Faso has a specific program that targets small businesses owned by women. In some countries such as South Africa that had no PCGS, it has been established. There have also been adjustments to credit guarantee schemes, such as extensions to loan tenors so borrowers have more time to make payments and increases in the coverage ratio of the guarantee to expand eligibility. However, some countries such as Argentina have raised the coverage rate of the guarantee up to 100 percent, especially for the most vulnerable borrowers, thereby increasing the risk of moral hazard. In several cases (such as in Italy), fees have been capped or waived altogether, decoupling pricing from risk.

These design features of PCGSs have involved difficult trade-offs, with important implications for the reach of the guarantee programs, the risk of "zombification" of economies, the size and type of the contingent liability for governments, and the impacts on financial sectors.[6] Although in the midst of a pandemic PCGSs should ideally target viable but temporarily illiquid firms, in practice distinguishing viable from unviable businesses is difficult, especially when information is scarce. In view of the massive uncertainty, many governments have opted instead to include large segments of sectors and firms. This strategy has ensured wider reach and speed, but it will have unintended consequences for long-term growth if it ends up zombifying parts of the economy, especially where complemented by loan moratoria and where zombie firms were proliferating even before the pandemic.[7]

The design of a PCGS also has a bearing on the fiscal risk assumed by a government. The state bears a contingent liability in all countries, and yet the type of exposure may depend not only on the size of the scheme but also on how it is implemented.[8] The contingent liability is direct when the guarantees are issued and administered by the central government, such as in Belgium, and indirect when the guarantees are channeled through public independent entities, such as in Morocco. In some cases, the contingent liability is supplemented by funds channeled to the public financial institution, such as in Chile. Finally, PCGS design features can impose costs on the financial sector. Loose credit requirements and ultra-low interest rates may eventually propel a rise in nonperforming loans once moratoria and suspension of classification criteria are lifted.

It is too early for an impact assessment of the unprecedented use of PCGSs in the context of the COVID-19 crisis, but several governments have promised robust ex post evaluations, especially because of suspicions of significant fraud.[9] Yet some preliminary conclusions are emerging: at least in the European context, where PCGSs have been designed without too much consideration for fiscal capacity, use of the schemes was positively correlated with the drop in economic activity, and demand for guarantees plateaued in mid-2020 after an initial burst.[10] As economies have entered the rebound if not recovery phase, the challenge for governments will be to shift their focus from protection to reallocation of capital and labor in a context of high corporate leverage and more limited fiscal resources. In such an environment, PCGSs could still play an important role in facilitating the flow of finance to the productive sector, and yet their design will have to adapt to that role to remain relevant and effective.

Countries relying on PCGSs will have to pursue at least three strategic and operational changes to support the process of resource reallocation.[11] First, because PCGSs will have to confront a wave of borrower defaults, at least in jurisdictions where the government has not directly underwritten the COVID-19–related risk, it may be necessary to maximize recovery for the exposures to nonviable firms and to convert into equity or quasi-equity instruments the exposures to viable businesses. Second, PCGSs will have to return to "normal" to minimize moral hazard, phasing out the exceptional design features implemented during the COVID-19 crisis. Such a return implies adopting the highest standards of risk management and more targeted eligibility criteria. It also implies developing new products such as equity guarantees to help firms rebalance their capital structure. Finally, PCGSs could play a pivotal role in redirecting financial flows toward low-carbon activities, thereby supporting the green recovery. That would imply a redesign of PCGSs' mandate, corporate governance and risk management framework, eligibility criteria, and product range.

Notes

1. Credit guarantee schemes can also be private, and in many economies they are run by private companies, cooperatives, or consortia of firms. However, they are often financially supported, directly or indirectly, by the public sector.
2. OECD (2021).
3. World Bank and FIRST Initiative (2015).
4. See OECD (2016) for a review of the literature.
5. Calice (2016).
6. Anderson, Papadia, and Véron (2021).
7. Banerjee and Hofmann (2020).
8. Emre et al. (2020).
9. Thomas and Morris (2020).
10. Anderson, Papadia, and Véron (2021).
11. Calice (2021).

References

Anderson, Julia, Francesco Papadia, and Nicolas Véron. 2021. "COVID-19 Credit-Support Programmes in Europe's Five Largest Economies." Working Paper 03/2021, Bruegel, Brussels.

Banerjee, Ryan, and Boris Hofmann. 2020. "Corporate Zombies: Anatomy and Life Cycle." BIS Working Paper 882, Monetary and Economic Department, Bank for International Settlements, Basel, Switzerland.

Calice, Pietro. 2016. "Assessing Implementation of the Principles for Public Credit Guarantees for SMEs: A Global Survey." Policy Research Working Paper 7753, World Bank, Washington, DC.

Calice, Pietro. 2021. "From Protection to Reallocation: Public Credit Guarantee Schemes in the Post-Pandemic World." Private Sector Development (blog), January 21, 2021. https://blogs.worldbank.org/psd/protection-reallocation-public-credit-guarantee-schemes-post-pandemic-world.

Emre, Ender, Alessandro Gullo, Cristina Müller, Mia Pineda, Mario Tamez, and Karla Vasquez. 2020. "Legal Considerations on Public Guarantees Schemes Adopted in Response to the COVID-19 Crisis." Special Series on COVID-19, IMF Legal Department, International Monetary Fund, Washington, DC.

OECD (Organisation for Economic Co-operation and Development). 2016. "Evaluating Costs and Benefits of Policy Interventions to Facilitate SME Access to Credit: Lessons from a Literature Review." Document DAF/CMF(2016)17, Committee on Financial Markets, Directorate for Financial and Enterprise Affairs, OECD, Paris.

OECD (Organisation for Economic Co-operation and Development). 2021. "One Year of SME and Entrepreneurship Policy Responses to COVID-19: Lessons Learned to 'Build Back Better.'" OECD Policy Responses to Coronavirus (COVID-19), OECD, Paris. https://www.oecd.org/coronavirus/policy-responses/one-year-of-sme-and-entrepreneurship-policy-responses-to-covid-19-lessons-learned-to-build-back-better-9a230220/#boxsection-d1e30.

Thomas, Daniel, and Stephen Morris. 2020. "'A Giant Bonfire of Taxpayers' Money': Fraud and the UK Pandemic Loan Scheme." Financial Fraud (blog), December 20, 2020. https://www.ft.com/content/41d5fe0a-7b46-4dd7-96e3-710977dff81c.

World Bank and FIRST Initiative. 2015. "Principles for Public Credit Guarantee Schemes for SMEs." World Bank, Washington, DC. https://www.worldbank.org/en/topic/financialsector/publication/principles-for-public-credit-guarantee-schemes-cgss-for-smes.

Managing sovereign debt

Governments around the world mobilized enormous resources to pay for the COVID-19 pandemic response. Many emerging economies, already heavily indebted at the outset of the crisis, took on additional debt to support households and firms. During 2020, this led to an increase in the total debt burden for low- and middle-income countries of 9 percentage points of gross domestic product (GDP), compared with an average annual increase of 1.9 percentage points over the previous decade. Managing and reducing elevated levels of sovereign debt improve the ability of governments to continue providing support through the recovery, especially to low-income households and small businesses, which is key to ensure an equitable recovery. However, coordination between debtors and creditors has become more difficult than in previous crises because of the greater number of creditors and the higher participation of commercial and nontraditional creditors in the market for sovereign debt.

Policy Priorities

Governments can take proactive policy approaches to mitigating the risks posed by high levels of sovereign debt to an equitable recovery:

- **Governments at high risk of debt distress can pursue proactive debt management approaches** with creditors through, for example, debt reprofiling, which replaces existing debts with new debt with a different currency or maturity profile.

- **Governments in debt distress must coordinate with creditors to restructure debt.** Effective restructuring requires the prompt and comprehensive recognition of debts, coordination with and among creditors, and a medium-term plan of reforms needed to achieve debt sustainability.

- **Governments and their creditors can benefit from improvements in sovereign debt transparency,** which requires comprehensive disclosure of claims against the government and terms of the contracts that govern the debt.

- **Contractual innovations can help overcome coordination problems and speed up the resolution of unsustainable debts,** but they are not a universal cure.

- **Well-developed tax policy and investments in tax administration can support debt sustainability in the longer run** by increasing the government's ability to mobilize revenue.

Introduction

The impacts of the COVID-19 (coronavirus) crisis on sovereign debt are unusual in the speed and global synchronicity of the surge in debt levels. If the economic recovery from the pandemic is delayed or falters, the buildup of sovereign debt will threaten debt sustainability in many emerging economies, and could produce longer-term economic and social consequences that look very similar to those of debt crises in the past.

Many emerging economies entered the pandemic with record levels of sovereign debt,[1] and they took on additional debt to pay for programs aimed at limiting the economic and human costs of the pandemic. This was a practical choice driven by limited options: increasing taxes in a struggling economy is not viable, and reducing other public spending is, in most cases, not sufficient to cover the magnitude of additional financing needs. The resulting debt burdens will have to be managed carefully to prevent them from becoming a drag on the economic recovery.

Managing and reducing elevated levels of sovereign debt is crucial to ensure a strong and equitable recovery. Sovereign debt crises are costly for sustained growth. One study finds that every year a country remains in default reduces its GDP growth by 1–1.5 percentage points.[2] High levels of sovereign debt also have significant social costs. They reduce the government's ability to spend on social safety nets and public goods such as education and public health, which can worsen inequality and human development outcomes. When debt sustainability problems are not resolved, they tend to worsen over time because the choices of each government constrain the options of future governments as more revenue is directed to debt service. Sovereign debt crises also frequently coincide with other types of economic crises—such as financial sector crises, rising inflation, and output collapses—that have far-reaching negative consequences for poverty and inequality.[3]

Importantly, debt dynamics, financing opportunities, and options to manage debt differ significantly between emerging and advanced economies.[4] For example, advanced economies tend to have better market access and financing options. They are also able to rely more heavily on domestic borrowing, and many can issue debt in their own currency and at different maturities, which facilitates borrowing and debt management. There are also important differences in the ability of advanced and emerging economies to service debts. Many observers have noted that since the 2007–09 global financial crisis, economic growth globally has remained above the effective interest rates on sovereign debt, thereby keeping debt service burdens manageable.[5] However, this observation masks important differences across countries. Although interest payments in advanced economies have been trending lower in recent years and account, on average, for only around 1 percent of GDP, the cost of interest payments for emerging economies has been rising steadily, and reached nearly 8 percent of GDP in 2020.[6]

This chapter examines the impact of the COVID-19 crisis on sovereign debt. It documents the sharp increase in sovereign debt stemming from the crisis and charts the options available to policy makers to manage dramatically increased debt burdens, while differentiating between countries based on characteristics such as market access and income levels.[7] Learning from past experience is essential to inform the policies governments will need to adopt to address debt sustainability concerns as the immediate effects of the COVID-19 pandemic begin to recede. To this end, this chapter highlights the importance of addressing debt sustainability problems promptly and proactively, as well as the substantial economic and social costs of delayed action.

The impact of COVID-19 on sovereign debt

The COVID-19 crisis led to a dramatic increase in sovereign debt, with average total debt burdens among low- and middle-income countries increasing by roughly 9 percent of GDP during 2020, compared with an average of 1.9 percent of GDP per year over the previous decade.[8]

This increase in debt burdens has serious implications, especially for low-income countries, whose financial position had already been deteriorating before the pandemic. Between 2019 and 2020, the average domestic and external debt stock of low-income and lower-middle-income countries increased by roughly 7 percent of GDP (figure 5.1). Over the same time period, the average debt stock of countries eligible for the Group of Twenty (G20) Debt Service Suspension Initiative (DSSI) increased from 50 to 57 percent of GDP. By 2019, half of the countries in this group were in debt distress—that is, unable to meet their financial obligations to creditors—or at high risk of debt distress (figure 5.2).[9] This trend accelerated after the onset of the pandemic and was poised to accelerate further with the expiration of DSSI in December 2021.[10]

Sovereign debt burdens are unlikely to decrease in the near future because they are the combined result of large fiscal support programs necessary to mitigate the worst effects of the pandemic and the contemporaneous collapse in government revenue due to the global slowdown in economic activity. Tax revenue as a share of GDP, for example, declined in 96 of the 133 low- and middle-income countries in 2020.[11] The costs of the pandemic are far exceeding the amount of money countries can easily shift from other areas of their budgets; countries that have access to credit markets have taken on new debt to finance emergency expenditures.

The prospect of a slow recovery places further pressure on government budgets, even as the immediate effects of the pandemic subside. During an economic crisis, governments can and often do function as the lender of last resort for firms and households, which means that private debts can quickly become public debts in a large, protracted economic crisis. When an economic crisis threatens the survival of economically important sectors and firms, governments have often taken on significant additional debt to stabilize those sectors or firms. Some of the debt-financed stimulus programs implemented during the COVID-19 crisis are examples of how governments step in to absorb economic risks when the private and financial sectors are unable to do so. If successful, the stimulus should result in economic growth and the deleveraging of private borrowers. However, such a solution comes at the cost of higher public debt burdens.[12]

Figure 5.1 **General government gross debt, by country income group, 2010–20**

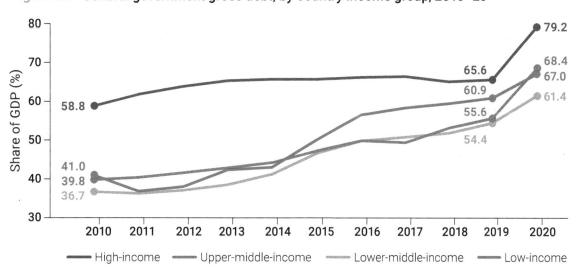

Source: WDR 2022 team, using data from World Bank, World Development Indicators (database), https://datatopics.world bank.org/world-development-indicators/; International Monetary Fund, World Economic Outlook Database: Download WEO Data, April 2021 Edition (dashboard), https://www.imf.org/en/Publications/WEO/weo-database/2021/April.
Note: The figure shows the general public debt stock as a share of the gross domestic product (GDP) by World Bank income classification.

Figure 5.2 **Level of risk of external debt distress, low-income countries, 2011–21**

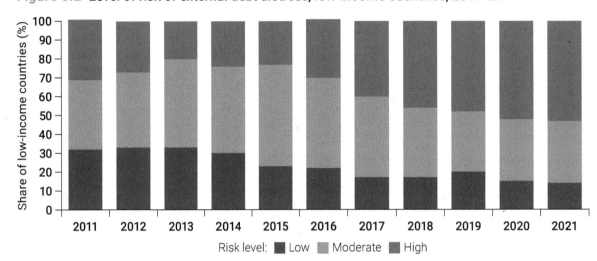

Source: World Bank and International Monetary Fund, Joint World Bank–International Monetary Fund LIC DSF Database (Debt Sustainability Framework for Low-Income Countries), June 2021 data, https://www.worldbank.org/en/programs /debt-toolkit/dsf.

Note: The figure shows the risk of debt distress among low-income countries on which a debt sustainability analysis (DSA) has been run. As of June 2021, this information was available on 66 of the 73 countries eligible to participate in the G20 Debt Service Suspension Initiative (DSSI). The latest available risk rating has been extrapolated pending a new DSA. If more than one DSA exist for one country in a calendar year, the most recent rating is used. The 2021 ratings are as of June 30, 2021. The high-risk category includes countries assessed to be in debt distress. For the DSA, see International Monetary Fund, DSA LIC (Debt Sustainability Analysis Low-Income Countries) (dashboard), https://www.imf.org/en /publications/dsa. For the DSSI, see World Bank, DSSI (COVID 19: Debt Service Suspension Initiative) (dashboard), https://www.worldbank.org/en/topic/debt/brief/covid-19-debt-service-suspension-initiative.

In countries where state-owned banks and state-owned enterprises (SOEs) are an important part of the economy, governments are more directly exposed to the risks of a prolonged economic downturn. Significant contingent liabilities might materialize if, for example, systemically relevant financial institutions or SOEs need to be rescued by the government. When such contingent liabilities arise, they often lead to a significant deterioration of the government's financial position that may require new borrowing.[13] In past crises, the cost of bank bailouts, for example, has totaled as much as 40 percent of GDP.[14] Between 2017 and 2020, Ghana's ailing energy and financial sectors required a cleanup that added an estimated 7 percent of GDP to its debt stock.[15] In 2018, Angola faced downward pressure on its sovereign credit ratings after the government had to make an unexpected, one-off support payment of $8 billion (7 percent of GDP) to the national oil company.[16] Similarly, Indonesia had to bail out its largest utility company in 1998 during the country's financial crisis at a cost of 4 percent of GDP.

In emerging economies, government finances may come under additional pressure from developments in the global economy. In the COVID-19 pandemic, unequal access to vaccines, among other factors, will likely lead the economic recovery to proceed faster in advanced economies than in the rest of the world. As the United States and Europe phase out their unprecedented monetary stimulus programs, global interest rates are bound to increase. This could have outsize effects on borrowing costs for emerging economies and make it more difficult for governments and private enterprises to refinance their debt. The normalization of monetary policy in high-income countries may also spur capital outflows from emerging markets, exert pressure on exchange rates, and aggravate debt sustainability concerns.

A high-risk scenario is one in which a large share of the global population remains unvaccinated or one in which mutations render the existing vaccines less effective. This would delay the recovery of incomes and government revenue, and yet governments will need to maintain spending to cope with the consequences of the pandemic and protect households and firms from further economic disruptions.

Meanwhile, elevated levels of sovereign debt can also weaken the recovery, through their impact on the financial sector. Many governments have financed their COVID-19 response by issuing new domestic debt that is held predominantly by domestic financial institutions. While this helped governments mobilize resources for the crisis response, it exposes financial institutions to sovereign risk as the financial position of the government deteriorates. This, in turn, reduces the ability of the financial sector to issue new credit and support economic growth. High levels of sovereign debt, particularly in the relatively shallow domestic markets of many emerging economies, can also dampen economic activity by leading to higher interest rates and affecting the prices firms and households pay for financing.

High levels of sovereign debt also affect the private sector directly, such as through the government's inability to provide ongoing support in a prolonged recession or economic setbacks during the recovery. Governments that are near or in debt distress do not have room to provide even temporary fiscal support to firms and households. Moreover, an increase in the risk of debt distress typically leads to a downgrade in the sovereign credit rating, which sets off self-fulfilling dynamics because the downgrade itself deteriorates macroeconomic fundamentals and the access to capital by private firms.[17]

Finally, it is important to note that the COVID-19 pandemic is a "crisis within a crisis." Countries may face additional pressure on government finances from other economic disruptions, some stemming from the risks posed by climate change. Policy makers will need to confront these risks by mobilizing fiscal resources to combat the effects of climate change.

The human costs of debt crises

Managing and resolving elevated levels of sovereign debt are essential to ensuring an equitable recovery from the COVID-19 crisis. Long-lasting debt distress has far-reaching negative consequences for the economy and population. These consequences are typically borne disproportionately by vulnerable populations, low-income households, and small businesses, and tend to worsen pre-existing poverty and inequality.

Sovereign debt crises affect human development in many ways because they rarely occur as an isolated event and often are only one component of a conglomerate crisis affecting multiple sectors of the economy.[18] Debt distress or default often coincide with a myriad of economic problems that may include output collapses, financial crises, currency crashes, and high inflation, which disproportionately affect the poor. Though the initial crisis trigger and order of events may differ, conglomerate crises have larger economic and human costs than crises confined to one sector of an economy. Because the COVID-19 pandemic simultaneously weakened private sector, financial sector, and government balance sheets (and weakened the ability of governments to mitigate spillover risks), many countries are at risk of experiencing these types of mutually reinforcing crises in the aftermath of the pandemic.

Evidence shows that sovereign debt crises are often associated with large output collapses that have significant human costs.[19] Data on economic crises during the 1980s and 1990s, for example, indicate that the number of people living in poverty increased by as much as 25 percent during large contractions in output.[20] Not surprisingly, aggregate economic shocks that weaken the government's ability to provide public goods, such as health care and education, are also associated with a deterioration in human development and social indicators.[21] On this point, there is significant heterogeneity between advanced and emerging economies. In advanced economies, where households can draw on insurance mechanisms that do not necessarily depend on current government spending, health and education outcomes are considerably less affected during crises. However, in emerging economies they deteriorate rapidly—for example, a 10 percent decline in GDP is associated with an increase of 1.5 child deaths per 1,000 live births.[22] Identifying and resolving debt sustainability problems can restore the government's ability to invest in public goods and reverse these trends, as the case study of Rwanda in box 5.1 illustrates.

Sovereign debt crises also often go hand in hand with high inflation and sharp exchange rate depreciations, disproportionately burdening the poor. Low-income households spend a higher share of their income on basic goods, whose price increases with inflation. They are also more likely to rely on wage

Box 5.1 Case study: Debt relief to create space for social spending in Rwanda

In 1996, the World Bank and International Monetary Fund (IMF) launched the Heavily Indebted Poor Countries (HIPC) Initiative to ensure that low-income countries do not face unmanageable debt burdens. In 2005, HIPC was complemented by the Multilateral Debt Relief Initiative (MDRI), which also includes the African Development Bank. In 2007, the Inter-American Development Bank joined this initiative. Together, these initiatives provided 38 countries with debt relief totaling over $100 billion. Rwanda is one of those countries.

The main rationale underlying the HIPC and related initiatives was that debt service obligations made it difficult for low-income countries to meet poverty reduction–related expenditures, including social spending and investment in infrastructure. The target of these initiatives was low-income countries facing unsustainable public debt that could not be solved through a traditional debt restructuring. To be eligible for HIPC relief, countries needed to commit to developing and implementing a poverty reduction strategy.

Notwithstanding the goals of the initiatives, the economic literature on debt relief (without broader reforms) is inconclusive about its impact on economic outcomes. Establishing the impacts in practice is difficult. Although high levels of debt may constrain economic development, it is also plausible that the same factors that lead to worse economic outcomes (such as conflict and weak institutions) are responsible for high levels of debt in the first place. Nonetheless, some studies find that decreases in debt service resulting from the HIPC Initiative were accompanied by increases in poverty-reducing expenditures, such as on basic health care, primary education, basic sanitation, and HIV/AIDS programs.[a] Furthermore, debt service

decreases were associated with better outcomes, such as lower infant mortality rates, that were linked to increases in social expenditures.[b] However, other contributions to the literature find little evidence of debt relief affecting the level or composition of public spending, growth, investment rates, or the quality of policies and institutions.[c]

Rwanda was one of the countries that used the HIPC Initiative successfully. It received full debt relief from the HIPC Initiative in April 2005 (completion point). Over the next four years, Rwanda increased its poverty-reducing expenditures by almost 50 percent, compared with an average of 3 percent for the remaining HIPCs that reached a completion point (see figure B5.1.1). Furthermore, over the previous four years Rwanda also substantially increased its expenditures on poverty reduction—expenditures that were tracked as one of the conditions for obtaining full debt relief. Among other things, Rwanda reformed and operated primary teacher training centers and implemented health plans to reduce mortality from malaria, as well as infant and maternal mortality.[d]

Since the HIPC Initiative completion point, Rwanda has made important progress toward increasing its gross domestic product (GDP) per capita and reducing extreme poverty. GDP per capita almost doubled, from $465 in 2005 to $849 in 2020, and the share of people living in poverty, defined as those living at most on $1.90 a day, fell from 69 percent of the population in 2005 to 56 percent in 2016.[e] These improvements, while significant, reveal how much more room there is for further growth and poverty reduction.

However, debt relief is not a silver bullet, and benefits can vary substantially across countries.

(Box continues next page)

Box 5.1 **Case study: Debt relief to create space for social spending in Rwanda** *(continued)*

Figure B5.1.1 **Poverty-reducing expenditures in Rwanda versus other HIPC countries**

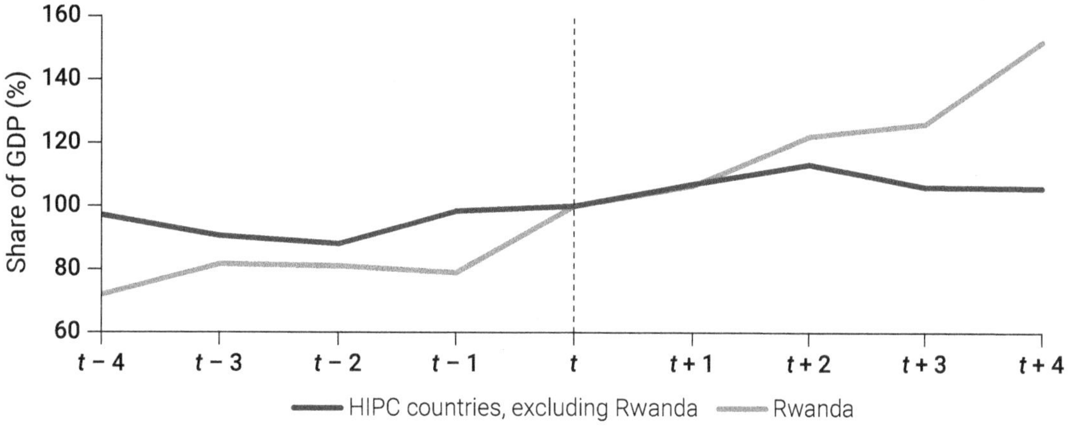

Source: IMF and World Bank 2019.

Note: In the figure, *t* represents the year of the completion point (full debt relief received). The data for year *t* are normalized to 100. The other years should be read in reference to this. GDP = gross domestic product; HIPC = Heavily Indebted Poor Countries (Initiative).

This is especially true of the diverse 38 recipients of HIPC relief. Some countries were in fragile or conflict situations; some were resource-based economies in need of economic diversification; some had better governance structures. For the same debt relief initiative, each of these factors and others can produce different impacts for countries.

Debt cycles and the reversal problem are another issue. Seventeen of the countries that reached the completion point in the HIPC Initiative are currently in debt distress or at high risk of debt distress.[f] Even Rwanda's external debt has been steadily increasing to levels close to the pre-HIPC number (external debt of 76 percent of the gross national income in 1996 versus 62 percent in 2019).[g] Thus Rwanda is now at a moderate risk of debt distress. Debt relief, then, is not sufficient to ensure long-term debt sustainability. Excessive debt is often a symptom of deeper structural and institutional weaknesses that need to be addressed first to achieve debt sustainability

In middle-income countries, such reversals are also evident. Argentina and Ecuador, both participants in the Brady Plan debt relief initiative in 1989,[h] have also experienced these reversals, which involved subsequent defaults and deep economic crises with their tragic effects on social outcomes.[i] These effects highlight the importance of timely and commensurate debt restructuring to ensure debt sustainability in the long run.

a. IEG (2006); IMF and World Bank (2019).
b. Primo Braga and Dömeland (2009).
c. Depetris Chauvin and Kraay (2005).
d. IMF and IDA (2005).
e. World Bank, World Development Indicators (database), https://datatopics.worldbank.org/world-development-indicators/.
f. See World Bank, DSA (Debt Sustainability Analysis) (dashboard), https://www.worldbank.org/en/programs/debt-toolkit/dsa.
g. See World Bank, World Development Indicators (database), https://datatopics.worldbank.org/world-development-indicators/.
h. Under the Brady Plan, banks could exchange nonperforming debt for a new security, a Brady Bond, collateralized by a long-term, zero-coupon US Treasury bond.
i. Farah-Yacoub, Graf von Luckner, and Reinhart (2021); Reinhart and Rogoff (2009).

Figure 5.3 **The lost decade of development in countries defaulting on sovereign debt**

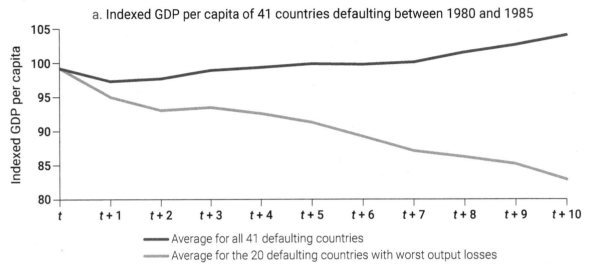

a. Indexed GDP per capita of 41 countries defaulting between 1980 and 1985

Average for all 41 defaulting countries
Average for the 20 defaulting countries with worst output losses

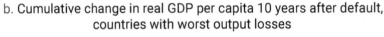

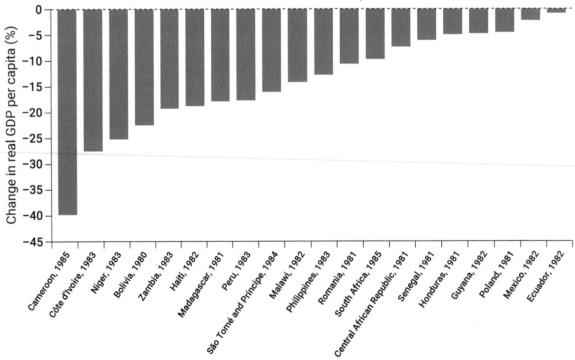

b. Cumulative change in real GDP per capita 10 years after default, countries with worst output losses

Sources: Farah-Yacoub, Graf von Luckner, and Reinhart 2021; International Monetary Fund, World Economic Outlook Data base: Download WEO Data, April 2021 Edition (dashboard), https://www.imf.org/en/Publications/WEO/weo-database/2021 /April.

Note: In panel a, time *t* is defined as the year in which the country defaulted, provided that this initial default occurred between 1980 and 1985. The group of 41 countries consists of all countries defaulting between the two years. The subgroup of 20 countries consists of those requiring the longest time to reach their predefault levels of real gross domestic product (GDP) per capita. In panel b, the country name is followed by the year of the default. Real GDP is the value of the goods and services produced by an economy over a specific period and adjusted for inflation.

incomes and transfer payments, whose purchasing power is eroded by inflation when these payments are not indexed to inflation, and households do not have access to financial tools that would allow them to cope with rising prices. Empirical evidence shows the disproportionate impact of inflation on low-income households.[23]

Exchange rate depreciations have similarly disproportionate effects on low-income households because a sudden depreciation in the value of the local currency can make basic goods inaccessible for most of the population.[24] Because most lower-income countries import a large share of consumer goods, a depreciation of the local currency can render imported goods prohibitively expensive for low-income households. These goods include medical products essential for dealing with the COVID-19 pandemic. Exchange rate depreciations also increase the burden of servicing debt denominated in a foreign currency, resulting in the government diverting more resources from social spending, thereby preventing an equitable recovery.

The most recent systemic debt crisis in emerging economies illustrates the dire economic and social consequences that arise when policy makers delay the resolution of escalating levels of sovereign debt.[25] In the 1980s, many countries, especially in Latin America and Sub-Saharan Africa, suffered a "lost decade" of development (figure 5.3, panel a). Inflation surged, currencies crashed, output collapsed, incomes plummeted, and poverty and inequality increased across these regions. The 41 countries that defaulted on their sovereign debt between 1980 and 1985 needed an average of eight years to reach their precrisis GDP per capita. For the 20 countries with the worst drops in output, the economic and social fallout from these debt crises continued for more than a decade (figure 5.3, panel b).

New challenges in managing and resolving sovereign debt

The COVID-19 crisis has played out against the backdrop of a rapidly changing market for sovereign debt, characterized by the increasing complexity in creditor composition and the legal structures used to issue debt. This situation has reduced the transparency of sovereign debt and made it more difficult for governments to manage, renegotiate, and restructure their debt when debt sustainability problems become apparent.

One of the most significant developments is the increase in the type and number of creditors. As of 2020, countries eligible for the G20 DSSI had, on average, more than 20 distinct creditor entities (excluding bondholders).[26] Some countries had many more. Creditors have increasingly included private and official lenders that are not part of the Paris Club, a standing committee of official creditor countries formed in 1956 that, since its creation, has been instrumental in the majority of sovereign debt restructurings.[27]

There has also been a marked change in the types of creditors that hold claims on sovereign balance sheets. Over the last three decades, these have included non–Paris Club foreign governments, quasi-sovereign entities, SOEs, and corporations not traditionally engaged in sovereign lending, such as commodity traders and producers.[28] They now account for a significant portion of sovereign debt, especially in emerging economies (figures 5.4 and 5.5). The rise of China as a bilateral creditor, for example, is a well-documented trend. In 2000, China accounted for 0.4 percent of the debt stocks of low- and middle-income countries. By 2019, it accounted for 4.8 percent. For low- and lower-middle-income countries, China accounted, on average, for 11 percent of total external public and publicly guaranteed debt, although for 20 countries in this group it accounted for more than one-fifth and up to two-thirds in the most extreme cases.

While the rise of non–Paris Club lenders has given emerging economies new avenues to financing public expenditures, it may also complicate the resolution of debt distress. One concern is the lack of transparency surrounding debt contracted with non–Paris Club lenders. Many new bilateral debt

Figure 5.4 External debt in low- and middle-income countries, by creditor type, 1980–2019

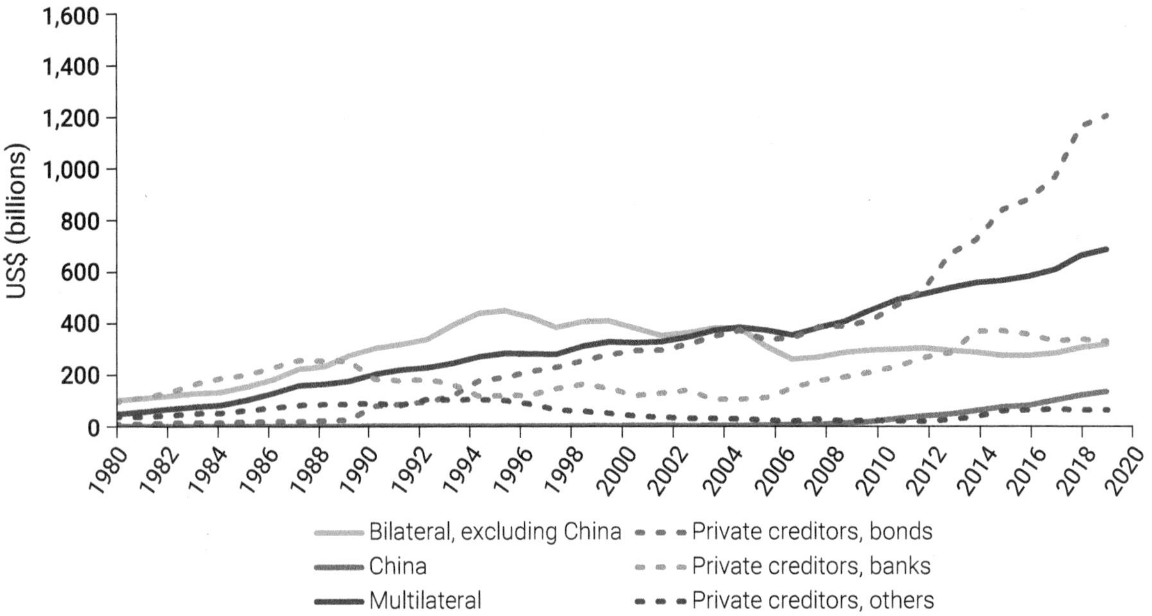

Legend:
— Bilateral, excluding China   • • • Private creditors, bonds
— China   – – – Private creditors, banks
— Multilateral   • • • Private creditors, others

Source: World Bank, International Debt Statistics (database), https://databank.worldbank.org/source/international-debt -statistics#.

Note: The figure shows total public and publicly guaranteed external debt by creditor type in low- and middle-income countries. The data are for 120 low- and middle-income countries, of which 73 are low- and lower-middle-income countries.

Figure 5.5 Composition of creditors in all countries and in low- and lower-middle-income countries, 1989 and 2019

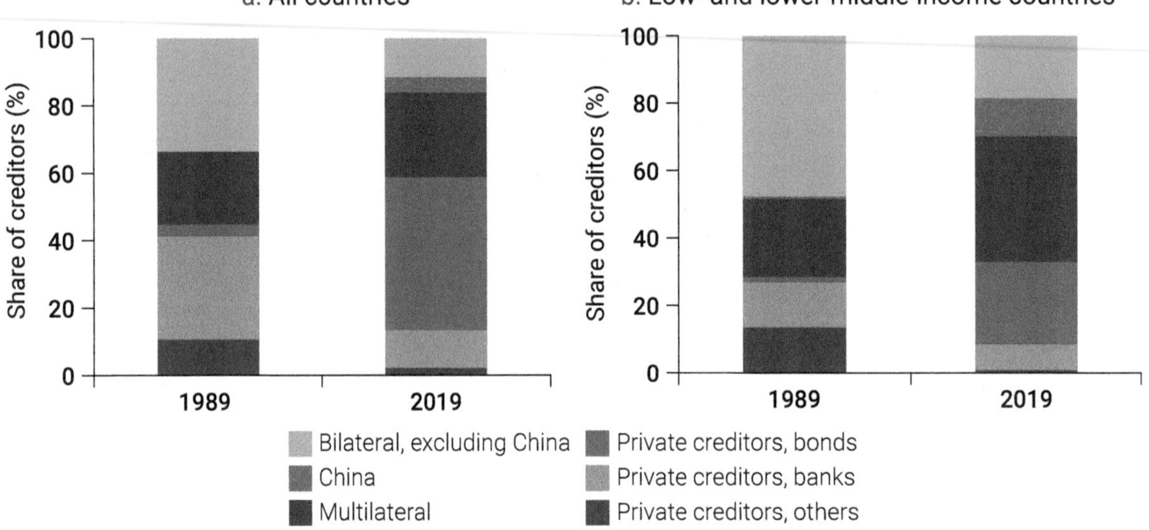

a. All countries

b. Low- and lower-middle-income countries

Legend:
Bilateral, excluding China   Private creditors, bonds
China   Private creditors, banks
Multilateral   Private creditors, others

Source: World Bank, International Debt Statistics (database), https://databank.worldbank.org/source/international-debt -statistics#.

Note: The figure shows the trends in creditor composition overall (panel a) and in low- and lower-middle-income countries (panel b). The data are for 120 low- and middle-income countries, of which 73 are low- and lower-middle-income countries.

contracts contain expansive nondisclosure clauses, making it difficult for other creditors to reliably assess the true financial position of the government or the seniority of one creditor's claim on the government relative to those of other creditors.[29] However, concerns about transparency are not limited to government loans with non–Paris Club creditors. Debts taken on through SOEs or using legal forms not typically recognized as debt have also added to the difficulty of assessing the full extent of sovereign liabilities.[30] Not only does this complicate debt resolution in the event of a crisis, it also may deter lenders from offering loans to countries in the first place.

These issues extend beyond the central government. In many emerging economies, subnational entities, such as SOEs or regional governments, also enter into external credit arrangements. Between 2009 and 2019, debt issuance by SOEs and subnational entities grew sevenfold, to about $140 billion.[31] Such borrowing by SOEs creates a risk of contingent liabilities that may not be reflected in government accounts because the debts of SOEs are often not fully integrated into the public sector's balance sheet. Moreover, not all liabilities of SOEs are structured in ways that make them recognizable as debt, which further obfuscates the true financial position of the sovereign. This approach to liabilities can give rise to significant hidden risks (discussed in more detail later in this chapter), and it is especially important in the current context in which many SOEs are directly affected by the pandemic. Public utilities, for example, have seen a dramatic decline in revenue stemming from moratoria on utility payments or the inability of customers to pay their bills.

There has also been a shift in the type of legal structures used to issue sovereign debt. New debt instruments and contractual innovations have proliferated to meet the needs of particular creditor-debtor pairings. Specifically, secured lending, novel de facto seniority structures, complex guarantees, swap lines, central bank deposits, and commodity-based lending structured as forward sales have become more popular over the last two decades.[32] A recent report on debt transparency finds that commodity-based lending represents 10–30 percent of external debt stocks for the median low-income country in the year following the signing of the commodity-based arrangement.[33] This practice has become particularly prevalent in Sub-Saharan Africa, where this type of lending accounted for 10 percent of new borrowing from 2004 to 2018.[34]

Although syndicated loans (loans issued by a small group of banks organized by an "agent" bank) were the dominant debt instrument in the 1970s and 1980s, they have since given way to bonds as the most prevalent instrument for sovereign debt from private creditors. This shift has direct consequences for debt resolution. For example, because bondholders are more dispersed and more difficult to coordinate than bank syndicates, every time a central government needs to seek debt treatment, a bondholder committee must form.[35] It is also notable in today's context that more than one bondholder committee may form for any given restructuring. This increases coordination problems among debtors and further complicates the management of sovereign debt.

While some contractual innovations can improve the ability of debtors to resolve disputes with specific creditors, they can also hamper coordinated resolution efforts. For example, certain creditor types have become reluctant to participate in broad restructuring initiatives because of their perceived unequal contractual treatment relative to others. One set of contractual innovations is aimed at improving the seniority and security of their claims, including through collateralization.[36] Such innovations can add significant complexity for the sovereign borrower if debts need to be restructured. An analysis of this class of debt contracts found that they often include broader nondisclosure clauses than is typical. Such clauses obscure the true financial position of the sovereign borrower and create significant obstacles in negotiations involving multiple creditors.[37] Although this class of contractual innovations has not been tested in the courts—and it is unclear whether they would prevail—the signaling effect and cost of litigation may be enough to tilt, and lengthen, resolution practices.[38]

Managing sovereign debt and resolving sovereign debt distress

Effective management of sovereign debt can reduce pressure on government finances, free up resources for urgent fiscal expenditures, and avert the large social and economic costs of a full-blown debt crisis.[39] This section reviews tools that governments can use to better manage elevated levels of sovereign debt and resolve distress when it materializes. It also looks at the longer-term policies and reforms that can make government finances more resilient to unanticipated shocks such as the one resulting from the COVID-19 crisis. At times, similar tools can be used for both managing elevated levels of sovereign debt and for resolving debt distress. The difference is often the degree to which the available tools are applied and which combination of available policy options is chosen. The degree of relevance of these tools depends on countries' individual circumstances—for example, their degree of market access and their income level—as well as macroeconomic factors such as the exchange rate regime. Most of the options presented in what follows are applicable across the spectrum because the basic principles of timely recognition of the problem, negotiation, and burden reduction are relevant to all types of debt.

A critical first step is to identify a country's risk of falling into debt distress. International financial institutions typically play a central role in providing debt sustainability analyses (DSAs),[40] which are the basis for classifying debt risks and designing strategies for debt reduction. For example, DSAs are an integral part of Paris Club debt restructurings and often play a key role in restructurings with private creditors as well.

Because a reliable DSA is the basis for successful debt management and debt reduction, it is critical that such an analysis be based on accurate information as well as transparent and realistic assumptions. Accurate assumptions are crucial in three areas. The first is growth, comparing expected growth rates with historical growth rates and allowing for realistic worst-case scenarios, especially in fragile, low-income, and commodity-exporting economies. The second is fiscal. Assumptions should take into account the expenditures needed to achieve development goals—such as reducing poverty, adapting to climate change, meeting the Sustainable Development Goals (SDGs)—as well as assumptions on the amounts and terms of the debt instruments used to fill future funding gaps. The third is realistic discount rates. Assumptions should differentiate between debt due now and debt due in the future.[41] To do this, DSAs use present value estimates, which discount future payments by a given discount rate. Unrealistic discount rate assumptions are often overlooked as a reason that expectations and reality diverge. The use of overly optimistic discount rates that make the present value of a sovereign's liabilities look manageable can lead to surprises when the economic environment turns out to be less benign than the forecast and insufficient relief if debt distress materializes.

Managing sovereign debt

Countries at high risk of debt distress, as opposed to countries already in debt distress, have a number of policy options for making their repayment obligations more manageable. Sovereigns at high risk of default can, for example, modify the structure of their liabilities and the schedule of future payments through negotiations with creditors and the effective use of refinancing tools—whether these creditors are private or official. In this way, proactive debt management can reduce the risk of default and free up the fiscal resources needed to support the recovery from the pandemic.

Debt reprofiling to temporarily free up fiscal resources
One of the primary tools governments have at their disposal to manage debt pressures before they become untenable is debt reprofiling. In debt reprofiling, the sovereign issues new debt in order to change

its debt service profile. Multiple characteristics can be targeted by such operations. Most commonly, debt reprofiling operations modify the maturity or currency exposure of existing debt. This usually happens in one of three ways: (1) new debt is issued, and the proceeds are used to retire old debt; (2) old debt is exchanged for new debt (similar to a debt restructuring, but market-based); or (3) new debt is issued at the time of maturity of the old debt but has significantly different characteristics. The debt is thus rolled over, but the emerging liability service profile is different and more advantageous for the borrower.

Debt reprofiling could, for example, be helpful when a country has multiple loans that come due in the same year and would place an excessive strain on government finances. The sovereign could choose to issue new debt with a longer or more even maturity profile that is easier to service. The sovereign would then use the capital raised from this new debt issue to retire some of the loans for which maturities were bunched in the same year. More typically, the operation would retire debt maturing in the near future and replace it with debt of longer duration. In recent years, some sovereigns have also begun to issue amortizing bonds, which pay principal down at different points of their life. Use of this method helps to manage debt service ex ante by spreading out debt payments over time.

Reprofiling can also target currency composition, which is an important factor in debt sustainability, irrespective of a country's exchange rate regime. In this case, instead of changing the maturity of existing debt, the debt reprofiling operation aims to retire existing debt in one currency by issuing new debt in another currency. In a recent debt reprofiling operation in Ghana, for example, a foreign currency bond was issued to partially retire domestic currency debt. The rationale for this choice was to take advantage of abundant hard currency liquidity to increase space in the aggregate balance sheets of the domestic financial sector.[42] Of course, the risks of greater foreign currency debt exposure, particularly in the context of significant currency depreciation, must be weighed against the costs of domestic debt service in a relatively shallow domestic market. Other operations can retire expensive debt if the sovereign's cost of funds has fallen in capital markets (see box 5.2 for an example).

The details of reprofiling operations vary, depending on the characteristics of a country's debt and debt service profile. Although debt reprofiling receives more attention when pursued with private creditors, it is not uncommon for debt reprofiling operations to involve official creditors. Thus this option is available to debtor countries whatever their creditor composition. Countries with access to bond markets are, in theory, in a better position to take advantage of debt reprofiling, but they may also be more reluctant to do so to avoid risking a downgrade in their credit rating. Designing a reprofiling operation that effectively manages the risks associated with sovereign debt is not trivial and requires extensive analysis, typically carried out by the country's debt management office in conjunction with international financial institutions and possibly other advisers.

Overall, a country seeking to reprofile its debt needs to ascertain whether realistic financing options are available and whether the resulting changes to its debt profile would be sufficient to solve the problem. Although debt reprofiling can free up liquidity and make a country's debt payments more manageable, it typically will not reduce the debt stock and is therefore not a long-term solution for debt sustainability issues.

Preemptive negotiations with creditors to prevent debt distress

Sovereigns that are at high risk of or are in debt distress have the option of initiating preemptive negotiations with their creditors to reach a debt restructuring before they fail to meet their contractual obligations.[43] There are many historical examples of preemptive restructurings aimed at averting outright default, including Chile (1987 and 1990), Algeria (1992), the Dominican Republic (2005), and, most recently, Ukraine (2015–16) and Belize (2020).[44] The option to pursue a preemptive restructuring depends largely on the creditor's willingness to negotiate, the debtor's credibility, and agreement on the debtor

Box 5.2 Case study: Seizing market opportunities for better debt management in Benin

The COVID-19 crisis has had a profound impact on Benin's economy and people. Between 2017 and 2019, Benin's real gross domestic product (GDP) was growing at 6.4 percent per year. In 2020, with the pandemic under way, real GDP growth dropped to 3.8 percent per year. Gains in poverty reduction were partially reversed. According to World Bank estimates, the percentage of people living under the international poverty line of $1.90 a day increased from 45.5 percent in 2019 to 45.9 percent in 2020.[a] Because of this fragile situation, the government now faces greater than usual difficulties in collecting taxes, as well as more demands for additional spending on health and social programs to contain the impacts of the pandemic.

In the years prior to the pandemic, Benin's total public debt increased significantly, from 22.3 percent of GDP in 2014 to 41.2 percent of GDP in 2019.[b] But it was not the only country in this situation: 45 of 48 countries in Sub-Saharan Africa saw an increase in debt levels over the same period.[c] Benin's increase in debt partly resulted from better access to commercial debt. Benin first entered the Eurobond market in March 2019 with an issuance of €500 million ($600 million) and a final maturity of seven years for a coupon of 5.75 percent. The bonds were to be amortized over the last three years of their life (2024, 2025, 2026).[d] These terms placed significant pressure on the government to mobilize the resources needed to meet the debt service demands. In particular, the 2023 external debt service-to-revenue ratio was expected to triple, reaching 20 percent in 2024 due to amortization of the Eurobonds.[e]

To meet the growing financing needs triggered by the pandemic, as well as the looming debt service pressures, Benin looked at different financing options, including reentering the bond market. It issued a new Eurobond in January 2021. This issuance had two tranches: (1) €700 million ($840 million) with an 11-year maturity and a coupon of 4.875 percent and (2) €300 million ($360 million) with a 31-year maturity and a coupon of 6.875 percent.[f] Overall, Benin succeeded in mobilizing €1 billion, which allowed it to buy back 65 percent of the previous Eurobond issuance (from March 2019), reduce its debt cost, and address the debt service

problem. Benin was also able to mobilize substantial funding to address new financing needs arising from the pandemic.

Benin had experience in proactive debt management. In 2018, it was able to obtain commercial loans for €260 million ($312 million) through the World Bank's Policy-Based Guarantee. The terms of these loans were 4 percent interest and 12-year maturities. Benin used the loans to buy back shorter-term domestic debt.[g] Although Benin replaced local currency debt with foreign currency debt, it was able to take advantage of improved financing conditions with a small increase in its exposure to currency risk because Benin's currency is pegged to the euro. Overall, however, this operation is an example of how Benin has effectively used the instruments available through international financial institutions such as the World Bank and the International Monetary Fund (IMF) to optimize market access, as well as to manage its sovereign debt.

Another example of how Benin has been able to effectively combine financing instruments from international financial institutions and the bond market is Benin's July 2021 issuance of a Sovereign Sustainable Development Goals (SDGs) Bond.[h] The €500 million ($600 million) mobilized through this issuance will be used toward achievement of the SDGs as described in the Benin SDG Bond Framework.[i] Benin was able to secure a maturity of 14 years with a coupon of 4.95 percent for this bond, compared with a maturity of 11 years and a 4.875 percent coupon in the previous operation (table B5.2.1).

Benin has also successfully tapped into sources other than commercial funding to finance its COVID-19 response. As a low-income country eligible for International Development Association assistance, Benin has access to concessional loans from the World Bank and IMF. Benin obtained $177.96 million in emergency assistance from IMF in December 2020, in addition to the $103.3 million approved earlier, in May 2020.[j] Benin also secured $50 million in emergency financing from the World Bank in 2021 to fight the COVID-19 pandemic, in addition to the $100 million in budgetary support disbursed in 2020.[k]

Successful debt management requires optimizing complicated contracts with different moving

(Box continues next page)

Box 5.2 **Case study: Seizing market opportunities for better debt management in Benin** *(continued)*

Table B5.2.1 **Benin's debt profile and recent issuances in the Eurobond market, 2019–21**

a. Debt profile

	End of 2019		End of 2020 (est.)	
	External	Domestic	External	Domestic
Nominal debt (US$, millions)	3,623.90	2,611.00	4,055.80	3,247.00
Interest payments (% of GDP)	0.5	1.0	0.5	1.2
Weighted average interest rate (%)	2.1	6.1	1.8	5.9
Average term to maturity (years)	10.9	2.8	10.8	3.6
Share maturing in one year (%)	3.2	24.2	3.4	21.7

b. Recent issuances

	March 2019	January 2021, tranche 1	January 2021, tranche 2	July 2021
Amount (€, millions)	500 ($600 million)	700 ($840 million)	300 ($360 million)	500 ($600 million)
Maturity (years)	7	11	31	14
Coupon (%)	5.75	4.875	6.875	4.95
Used to repurchase maturing debt?	No	Yes, partially	Yes, partially	No

Sources: CAA 2019; MEF 2021.

Note: Panel a considers all external and domestic debt, including concessional lending. Panel b provides further details on bond issuance since 2019. For bonds alone, weighted average coupons evolved from 5.75 percent in 2019, to 5.5 percent in January 2021, and then to 5.35 percent in July 2021. The corresponding average maturities evolved from 7 years in 2019, to 15.5 years in January 2021, and then to 15 years in July 2021. GDP = gross domestic product.

parts—maturity, currency, interest rate, and amortization schedules, among others. Debt management offices need to be aware of market movements, as well as actions and initiatives by donors and multilateral organizations, to find the opportunities that best match their country's interests and financing needs. Benin is a good example of how countries can mitigate pressures on government finances and preserve their ability to meet urgent financing needs through proactive debt management.

a. World Bank (2021b).

b. IMF (2020b).

c. WDR 2022 team calculations, based on data from International Monetary Fund, World Economic Outlook Database: Download WEO Data, April 2021 Edition (dashboard), https://www.imf.org/en/Publications/WEO/weo-database/2021/April.

d. Government of Benin (2019).

e. IMF (2020b).

f. Government of Benin (2021b).

g. IMF (2020b).

h. CAA (2021).

i. Government of Benin (2021a).

j. IMF (2020b).

k. For more details on the financial engagement of the World Bank in Benin, see World Bank, Overview: Strategy, World Bank in Benin, https://www.worldbank.org/en/country/benin/overview#2.

country's needs. For countries with market access, these negotiations usually take the form of convening a meeting with bondholders. When these negotiations are pursued with official creditors, they take the form of either separate bilateral negotiations or a meeting with multiple creditors that could be coordinated by a group such as the Paris Club or an international financial institution. Whatever the creditor pool, the objective is a reduction of the debt stock or some present value reduction of the debt burden through reduced payments, extended maturities, or extended grace periods.

Evidence shows that where preemptive restructuring is undertaken, it is resolved faster than postdefault restructuring, leads to a shorter exclusion of the country from global capital markets, and is associated with a lower decline in output.[45] This option is not available to all governments, however, because it requires a high level of transparency about who holds the country's debts and on what terms. This is important because a preemptive restructuring relies on debtors and creditors agreeing on the probability of debt distress and reaching an agreement acceptable to all creditors.

Although this discussion suggests that countries can reap clear benefits from renegotiating high debt burdens preemptively, the evidence also shows that preemptive restructuring does not make countries more resilient to debt sustainability problems in the longer term. The probability of defaulting within 24 months following a restructuring does not differ between countries that pursue preemptive versus postdefault restructuring (the relapse probability is 39 percent in both strictly preemptive and strictly postdefault restructuring).[46] This finding suggests that in the future countries should use the improved breathing space and stability offered by preemptive restructuring to more rapidly lay the foundation for longer-term debt sustainability.

Resolving sovereign debt distress

Once a government is in debt distress—most often marked by a default—the options to treat the problem are more limited. The primary tool at this stage is debt restructuring. It requires prompt recognition of the true nature of the problem (sustainability), coordination with creditors, and an understanding by all parties that restructuring is the first step toward debt sustainability (that is, reaching a level of debt that allows the government to pay its current and future obligations).

These broad principles for sovereign debt restructuring are very similar to the principles for restructuring private sector debt covered in chapters 2 and 3, with a few important differences. First, there are no bankruptcy or insolvency courts for sovereign debt, which remains a significant gap in the present financial architecture. To restructure sovereign debt, there are, at best, creditor committees (such as the ones set up by the Paris Club, bondholders, or the London Club in the past) so debtors can meet to negotiate and come to an agreement. However, it is often a difficult, lengthy process to enforce such agreements or seize the assets of the debtor as in a regular commercial insolvency case. Typically, the assets of the sovereign are either covered by sovereign immunity (for example, central banks' reserve accounts with other central banks) or outside the jurisdiction of the courts adjudicating the contractual breach. With rare exceptions, only assets pledged as collateral and covered by clauses forgoing immunity are readily reachable by creditors. Second, despite the term *public debt*, there is often a lack of information about a country's lenders and the total amount of debt. Credit registries or credit bureaus track corporate debts. Although these databases may not be perfect, they tend to be more complete than the information available on sovereign debt (see box 5.5 later in this chapter on the hidden debt problem). Third, sovereign debt restructuring involves lenders from different countries, with the result that debt contracts are often established under different jurisdictions with different instruments and different levels of implied seniority. Although corporate debt can also have an international component, this is less common, especially in the case of micro-, small, and medium enterprises.

The importance of timely debt restructuring

When a country is unable to service its debt, there are strong arguments in favor of it quickly acknowledging the problem so it can take steps to reduce debt loads and allow for faster recovery. Evidence from past debt crises shows that the average default spell lasts eight years,[47] and the indebted country typically goes through two debt restructurings before it emerges from default (figure 5.6).[48] Indeed, Jamaica and Poland each engaged in seven debt restructuring deals with private external creditors before resolving their default spell so they are capable of financing the necessary spending. Chad, one of the first three countries to apply for the G20 Common Framework for Debt Treatment beyond the DSSI (see box 5.3), is currently seeking its third debt restructuring since 2014. Such extended timelines have far-reaching social and economic consequences in which development goals suffer significant setbacks, delaying an equitable recovery. This is part of the post–COVID-19 reversal problems many low-income countries are already experiencing (see box 5.1).

The resolution of sovereign debt distress can be a lengthy process for several reasons. First, the increased importance of new types of lenders impedes transparency and makes it more difficult to establish the true extent of a country's outstanding debts, which complicates the coordination of different creditors. Second, governments are often tempted to delay debt restructuring for strategic or political reasons. In addition, creditors are often reluctant to grant debt relief that is extensive enough to permanently solve a country's debt sustainability problem. Although the explanations vary case by case, the common outcome is that the initial restructuring is often delayed and falls short of what is necessary to achieve debt sustainability.

One common—and misguided—approach is to postpone debt resolution efforts until economic conditions improve.[49] However, such a strategy can itself deepen and prolong an economic downturn because the unresolved debt crisis prevents a country from recovering capital inflows. Creditors and debtor governments should thus view debt restructuring as part of the initial resolution and recovery plan rather than as a subsequent step, as is often the practice for private debt.

Sovereign debt restructuring typically involves five steps:

1. The debtor country announces its intention to pursue an agreement with one or several of its key creditors.
2. Creditor committees are formed (if no standing committee exists), and conversations are initiated.
3. The debtors, creditors, and their respective advisers take inventory of the existing claims against the debtor nation and validate them in order to agree on the set of contracts to be discussed—a process called claim reconciliation. This process includes a review of existing contracts to ascertain the truthfulness and validity of the claims. This is often a time-consuming process, and countries would benefit from conducting such an analysis as part of their ongoing debt management efforts.
4. Negotiations cover aspects of the contracts the parties want to change.
5. When an agreement is reached and a debt exchange offer is completed, creditors exchange the old debt contracts for new and amended debt agreement contracts that reflect the negotiated settlement.

This process is applicable to countries at all income levels and to all creditor compositions. What changes is the degree of complexity involved.

When a country defaults because of a temporary shock such as the COVID-19 crisis, sufficiently extending maturities and spreading debt service payments more evenly into the future may achieve debt sustainability. However, it may not be possible to determine in real time whether a shock is temporary, and the cost of erring in favor of a shallow restructuring can extend the duration of default spells and

Figure 5.6 Sovereign debt restructuring and time spent in default, selected countries, 1975–2000

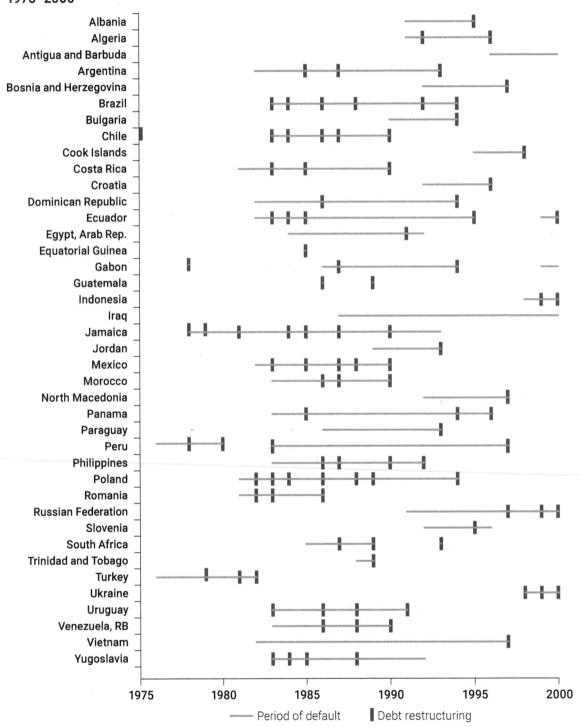

Source: WDR 2022 team, based on Cruces and Trebesch (2013); Farah-Yacoub, Graf von Luckner, and Reinhart (2021); Meyer, Reinhart, and Trebesch (2019); Reinhart and Rogoff (2009).

Note: The figure shows a timeline of sovereign defaults and debt restructuring from 1975 to 2000. The figure excludes countries covered by the International Development Association (IDA) and the Heavily Indebted Poor Countries (HIPC) Initiative.

increase their human and economic costs. Data from recent studies suggest that more than half of the debt restructurings that ended a default spell included a reduction in face value.[50]

The role of insufficient debt reduction in future defaults

One reason why countries typically require several rounds of debt restructuring to emerge from debt distress is that creditors often find it difficult to agree to restructuring deep enough to make debt burdens sustainable and future default unlikely.

From the creditor's perspective, sovereign debt restructuring follows a simple logic: the restructuring should grant sufficient debt relief to ensure repayment but avoid reducing debt more than is strictly necessary. For low-income countries, official lenders equate debt relief with aid, and so they may be more willing to agree to larger debt reductions. However, the debtor country's ability to service its debt depends on a wide range of factors (such as economic growth, international economic conditions, and the ability to raise tax revenue), which are difficult if not impossible to forecast at longer time horizons. In this situation, it is tempting for lenders to buy in to overly optimistic forecasts because those forecasts imply that smaller debt write-offs are required to ensure debt sustainability in the future. In reality, however, by relying on overly optimistic forecasts creditors systematically underestimate the amount of debt reduction needed, thereby laying the foundation for future debt distress.

To avoid this common cause of prolonged debt distress and recurring rounds of default, creditors and sovereigns need to agree on a set of realistic (ideally independently assessed) growth projections, which can provide the basis for a more reliable debt sustainability analysis.

The importance of effective creditor coordination to debt resolution

Debt restructuring requires coordination between the sovereign and its creditors. Because there is typically one debtor and many creditors, a creditor committee is formed to facilitate the process and minimize holdouts and litigation.[51] Whether a restructuring is attempted preemptively or after distress has materialized, negotiating through a creditor committee is the most common approach to resolving sovereign debt distress. Depending on the composition of the creditors, creditor committees can be made up of multilateral, bilateral, and private sector creditors. Coordination problems are typically difficult to resolve for any of these types, but historically multilateral and bilateral diplomacy between official creditors has helped (box 5.3).

Because the growing importance of nontraditional lenders has obfuscated the full extent of countries' debts and made creditor coordination more difficult, new solutions are needed to overcome coordination problems in debt negotiations. Past crises may offer some guidance on how better coordination between creditors can be achieved in a more complex market for sovereign debt. For example, commercial creditors, which account for a growing share of sovereign debt, could be enticed to participate in restructurings by their own governments. During the debt crises of the 1980s, US commercial banks held substantial amounts of emerging market debt, especially in Latin America. Defaults on these assets threatened to develop into a banking crisis in the United States,[52] thereby giving the US government an incentive to offer bilateral debt relief. The result was the Brady Plan, named for US Treasury Secretary Nicholas Brady. Under the program, banks could exchange nonperforming debt for a new security, a Brady Bond, collateralized by a long-term, zero-coupon US Treasury bond. The initiative was, in most cases, a success for debtors and for the United States. After these restructurings, debtor countries experienced higher growth rates, renewed capital inflows, and improved credit ratings.[53] The stock market capitalization of US banks with emerging market exposure also increased substantially.[54]

Today, the debt of emerging economies is not nearly as concentrated in a handful of large banks as it was then. Nonetheless, countries whose commercial banks and nonbank lenders are newly exposed

Box 5.3 The role of multilateral coordination in the looming debt crisis: The G20 Debt Service Suspension Initiative and the G20 Common Framework

Multilateral coordination is essential when many debtor nations are facing distress. It is especially important when the sovereigns in distress are low-income countries, whose largest creditors are governments and multilateral organizations.

The G20 Debt Service Suspension Initiative
Responding to this reality, in April 2020 the G20 (Group of 20), along with multilateral financial institutions, including the World Bank and International Monetary Fund (IMF), launched the Debt Service Suspension Initiative (DSSI), which sought to preempt debt distress from the pandemic by offering 73 low-income countries the option of forbearance—delayed payment—on bilateral loans.[a] Since it came into effect in May 2020, the initiative has provided 48 economies with temporary cash-flow relief, and by the end of June 2021 it had delivered about $10.3 billion in debt service suspension (a national development bank participated as a private creditor). On average, participants in DSSI faced more elevated risks of debt distress than those economies that abstained (see figure B5.3.1).

Multilateral institutions provided much relief through the initiative. From April 2020 to June 2021, the World Bank committed $52.4 billion in International Bank for Reconstruction and Development (IBRD) and International Development Association (IDA) financing to DSSI-eligible countries. Its total gross disbursements to these countries—IBRD, IDA, and Recipient Executed Trust Funds (RETFs)—amounted to $31.1 billion, of which $8.8 billion was provided on grant terms ($28 billion in net transfers). International Finance Corporation (IFC) support amounted to $4.9 billion in commitments (own account and mobilization) and $2.0 billion in disbursements (own account). However, multilateral institution actions alone are insufficient to relieve countries of the debt pressures faced. Commercial creditors, except for the national development

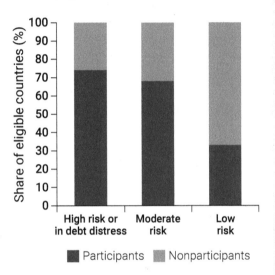

Figure B5.3.1 Participation of countries in DSSI, by level of risk of debt distress

Source: WDR 2022 team.
Note: The figure presents the percentage of the 73 eligible low-income countries participating in the Debt Service Suspension Initiative (DSSI) within each class of risk of debt distress as defined by the World Bank–International Monetary Fund debt sustainability analyses.

bank mentioned earlier, have not offered forbearance under the DSSI. Because private credit is now a much larger share of sovereign debt than when the Paris Club was founded, creditor coordination to date appears more difficult than in the past.

The G20 Common Framework for Debt Treatment
The DSSI was followed in November 2020 by the G20 Common Framework for Debt Treatment beyond the DSSI, which covers the same 73 low-income countries eligible for the G20's DSSI. The Common Framework seeks to expand on the

(Box continues next page)

DSSI's provision of relief by establishing a process to restructure debts, including those held by non–Paris Club official and commercial creditors. The process of debt treatment is initiated by the debtor country. Eligible debt includes all public and publicly guaranteed external debt maturing in at least one year. How much debt needs to be restructured and the related financing needs for the country are determined by IMF–World Bank debt sustainability analyses (DSAs) and an assessment by the participating official creditors in conjunction with the debtor country.[b] Treatment should comport with the parameters of an IMF upper credit tranche loan—that is, the program, amount, and policies should lay the groundwork for a return to debt sustainability. Modifications considered by the process include (1) changes in debt service over the course of the IMF program; (2) debt reduction in net present value terms; and (3) extension of maturities. The framework reserves the right to cancel or write off debts for the "most difficult cases." Determination of such need also follows the IMF–World Bank DSA and the collective assessment of the participating official creditors.

The key driving principle of the G20 Common Framework, much like that of the Paris Club, is the comparable treatment of creditors—that is, upon reaching an understanding with the participating official creditors, the debtor nation is obliged to seek similar debt relief from its other creditors. Still, so far only three countries have applied for treatment: Chad, Ethiopia, and Zambia. Many eligible countries remain reluctant to seek assistance because of concerns about reputational credit risks and access to capital. All three major credit agencies have made it clear that requesting commercial creditor forbearance on G20-comparable terms could lead to a downgrade of credit rating. That certainly would be the scenario if comparability of treatment triggers private debt restructuring.

In summary, the international community can take the following steps in the event of debt distress: (1) determine whether the restructuring deal and policy package returns the country to debt sustainability and thus offsets creditworthiness concerns; (2) ensure participation by all relevant creditors; and (3) advocate for concessional sovereign financing until the state can access finance from the market, including by increasing concessional options. As the historical track record shows, these steps have been difficult to achieve.

a. For the DSSI, see World Bank, DSSI (COVID 19: Debt Service Suspension Initiative) (dashboard), https://www.worldbank .org/en/topic/debt/brief/covid-19-debt-service-suspension-initiative.

b. For the DSA, see World Bank, DSA (Debt Sustainability Analysis) (dashboard), https://www.worldbank.org/en/programs /debt-toolkit/dsa; International Monetary Fund, DSA LIC (Debt Sustainability Analysis Low-Income Countries) (dashboard), Washington, DC, https://www.imf.org/en/publications/dsa.

to sovereign debt are in a position to implement a similar approach. Nonperforming debt could, for example, be swapped for new securities backed by creditors' sovereigns and held in escrow to reduce risk in the same way as the Brady Bonds. Such an initiative could prove fruitful in encouraging commercial lenders to participate in resolving debt distress and at the same time reduce risks to the lender country's financial system, as occurred with the Brady Plan. Nonetheless, Brady Bond–like arrangements require significant subsidies from the government, donors, or international financial institutions and therefore come at a cost to taxpayers. This may help explain why about eight years passed after the onset of Mexico's debt crisis before the first Brady deal in 1990.

The high social and economic costs of liquidating sovereign debt without restructuring

Significantly reducing sovereign debt in emerging economies typically requires debt restructuring, there are other means to achieve this end. The most orthodox approach is fiscal consolidation, which involves reducing government expenditures, raising taxes, or both. Similarly, debt burdens can be reduced through robust economic growth, which improves government revenue, fiscal balances, and debt servicing capacity.

Sovereign debt can also be reduced using less orthodox macroeconomic policies, such as deficit monetization (central bank financing of budget deficits) or financial repression (forcing negative real interest rates and proscribing capital outflows). Such policies have often accompanied debt crises and arguably are a forced response to debt distress in situations where other options are limited.[55] Nonetheless, when policy makers are confronted with unsustainable debts denominated in local currency, held by local creditors, or adjudicated under domestic law, they often see deficit monetization and financial repression as soft options that they should attempt before default or restructuring.[56] Because both types of policies require action by the central bank, they can not typically be applied in countries that are members of a currency union.

Unanticipated inflation has also played a role in debt reduction in both advanced and emerging economies.[57] The degree to which inflation spikes can reduce debt depends on the currency profile and maturity profile of a country's debt stock and the extent to which inflation expectations are well anchored, among other factors. In many countries, particularly in Africa and Latin America, the monetization option has proved to be a slippery slope, often leading to high, persistent inflation.

Financial repression measures, often coupled with higher inflation, are another path that many countries have taken to manage domestic debt servicing costs and reduce debt loads.[58] For example, Ethiopia, one of the first three countries to apply for the Common Framework, has maintained significantly negative real (inflation-adjusted) interest rates since 2006. Financial repression measures also include financial market regulation, such as caps on interest rates, and capital controls. Directed lending to the government by "captive" institutions or public programs has played a role as well. For example, governments may require banks, pension funds, or other domestic financial institutions to purchase sovereign debt, often to the exclusion of other assets, or to lend directly to the government (or government-sponsored enterprises) at below market rates. In short, financial repression is a transfer from savers to borrowers, with government often being the single largest borrower in most low-income countries.

Historically, numerous countries have used financial repression policies to reduce their sovereign debt. Studies document that between 1945 and 1980 financial repression was among the most widely used paths to debt deleveraging in countries as diverse as Argentina, France, India, and the United States.[59] More recently, in some countries financial repression policies have been employed specifically to help finance the COVID-19 response.[60]

Even though they are often used to reduce domestic debt stocks, financial repression policies can have pernicious effects on economic growth, the allocation of capital, and inequality.[61] Forcing domestic financial institutions to finance sovereign debt crowds out credit to the private sector and reduces economic growth in the longer run. It also exposes the domestic financial sector to sovereign risk and can undermine financial stability, and it increases the magnitude of contingent liabilities and the likelihood they will materialize. Perhaps most important, financial repression policies have severe negative effects on poverty and inequality. By keeping nominal interest rates artificially low, such policies punish savers and reward debtors. In addition, they often coincide with high inflation, which further erodes the value of wage income and precautionary savings, with disproportionate impacts on the poor. As described in box 5.4, in Argentina financial repression policies have been used extensively, but this policy choice has had adverse consequences.

Box 5.4 Case study: The social and economic costs of financial repression in Argentina

At the turn of the millennium, Argentina faced one of the severest economic crises in modern history. Accumulated vulnerabilities, delays in pursuing restructuring, and a three-year recession brought about significant economic turmoil. Fiscal vulnerabilities, loss of competitiveness, the rigidity of the currency board system, overly optimistic growth assumptions, and political instability were all cited as key factors leading to this conglomerate crisis.[a]

As a result of the crisis and the delayed policy actions to address it, Argentina's economy shrank 20 percent in 2002 and, according to national statistics, 53 percent of the population was living in poverty in May 2002, up from 38 percent in October 2001.[b] Based on the World Bank's international poverty line of $1.90 per day, the poverty rate peaked at the height of the crisis in 2002 (figure B5.4.1).

In addition to loans from the International Monetary Fund (IMF) and the World Bank, debt restructuring, and changes in tax policy, the Argentine government instituted a number of standard financial repression policies, which effectively distributed losses across the population. These policies included forced conversion of foreign currency deposits, capital controls, and requirements that domestic financial institutions finance the government (see figure B5.4.2). These policies had several objectives. Their primary goal was to stem the flight of private capital, which was gathering steam in 2000 and 2001. In addition, financial repression was used to reduce sovereign debt loads by generating real negative interest rates.[c] In essence, the government forced domestic savers and financial institutions to bear the costs of reducing its excessive debt burden by freezing their capital inside the domestic financial system, forcing savers and financial institutions to convert foreign currency to domestic currency, requiring financial institutions to buy new sovereign debt denominated in local currency, unifying and floating the exchange rate, and maintaining tight control of all foreign currency flows.

These measures had significant social costs. They were accompanied by a rise in poverty, which mirrored a dramatic fall in employment and in household incomes and wealth.[d] On December 1,

Figure B5.4.1 Poverty and financial repression, Argentina, 1995–2002

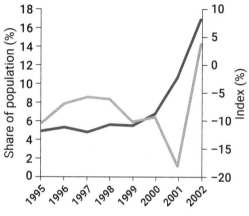

— Poverty rate (left axis)
▬▬▬ Financial repression index (right axis)

Source: WDR 2022 team, based on data from Banco Central de la República Argentina; Ilzetzki, Reinhart, and Rogoff (2019); and World Bank's World Development Indicators Database.

Note: In the figure, the poverty rate is the poverty headcount ratio at $1.90 a day (2011, purchasing power parity–adjusted), expressed as a percentage of the population. The financial repression index is calculated as the parallel exchange rate premium minus the real interest rate on deposits (the difference between the interest rate on deposits and inflation). This measure captures the difficulty in safeguarding liquidity in foreign currency (as expressed by the parallel market foreign exchange premium, which is the percent difference between parallel market exchange rates and official exchange rates) and the implicit inflation tax the government is imposing on this liquidity that becomes trapped in domestic currency (as expressed by the real interest rate, which in these cases is often negative).

2001, the government declared a bank holiday and implemented an array of banking controls to fight the ongoing bank run. This package of measures would become known as El Corralito.[e] Deposits were frozen, savings denominated in US dollars were forcibly converted at the official rate of Arg$1 per US dollar, and weekly withdrawal limits of Arg$250 were imposed. As convertibility ended, the

(Box continues next page)

Figure B5.4.2 Financial measures affecting savers during Argentina's economic crisis, 2001–02

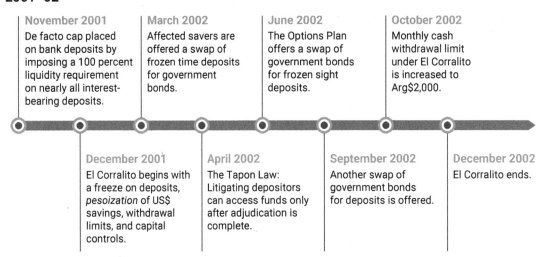

November 2001
De facto cap placed on bank deposits by imposing a 100 percent liquidity requirement on nearly all interest-bearing deposits.

March 2002
Affected savers are offered a swap of frozen time deposits for government bonds.

June 2002
The Options Plan offers a swap of government bonds for frozen sight deposits.

October 2002
Monthly cash withdrawal limit under El Corralito is increased to Arg$2,000.

December 2001
El Corralito begins with a freeze on deposits, *pesoization* of US$ savings, withdrawal limits, and capital controls.

April 2002
The Tapon Law: Litigating depositors can access funds only after adjudication is complete.

September 2002
Another swap of government bonds for deposits is offered.

December 2002
El Corralito ends.

Source: WDR 2022 team.

peso quickly depreciated to Arg$1.8 per US dollar on the first day of unified floating (February 11, 2002), rendering depositors instantly poorer in terms of both the incomes they earned and the wealth they had saved. The central bank also moved to control all sources of foreign currency through a combination of requirements on exports and transactions involving foreign currencies.[f]

Although financial repression measures are likely to have been a factor in the stabilization of the Argentine economy, their effects were not only unpopular but also highly regressive. In Argentina, repressive measures can be viewed as a consequence

of delayed policy action rather than an effective response to the debt crisis. Because Argentina had followed a fixed exchange rate regime (currency board) prior to the crisis, adjustments had to come either from the fiscal side, through increases in sovereign debt, or from the real economy. The resulting vulnerabilities—unsustainable levels of sovereign debt, in particular—continued to accumulate. This accumulation ultimately contributed to the depth of the Argentine economic crisis and left the government with little choice but to resort to policies that had severe negative effects on poverty and inequality.

a. Daseking et al. (2004); Feldstein (2002); Hausman and Velasco (2003); Mussa (2002); Perry and Serven (2002).
b. Cruces and Wodon (2003).
c. Reinhart and Sbrancia (2015).
d. Cruces and Wodon (2003). See Daseking et al. (2004), appendix 2, for a thorough recap of the measures.
e. The term *El Corralito* (a bank account withdrawal limit or a freeze on a bank account) was popularized by Argentine journalist Antonio Laje to refer to the measures. See *La República*, "Argentina: Una década después del corralito," December 4, 2011, cited by *El Economista*, https://www.eleconomista.com.mx/economia/Argentina-una-decada-despues-del-corralito-20111204-0089.html.
f. For example, any amounts in hard currency held by banks or exchange bureaus over a specified limit had to be deposited daily in the central bank. Taxes on exports were increased. Export receipts were required to be sold exclusively to the central bank. The purchase of foreign banknotes or transfers abroad for amounts over $100,000 required the central bank's prior approval. See Daseking et al. (2004).

Looking ahead: Reforms to mobilize revenue, improve transparency, and facilitate debt negotiations

The challenges of managing higher debt levels and resolving a rising number of debt crises in the aftermath of the COVID-19 crisis highlight the need for reforms that can facilitate revenue mobilization, better debt management, debt negotiation, and access to capital markets in the longer term. This section explores how improved transparency, as well as legal and tax reforms, can make sovereign debt markets more efficient and sovereign balance sheets more resilient.

Dependence of sovereign debt sustainability on mobilization of new tax revenue

Prior to the COVID-19 pandemic, most countries saw a sustained rise in tax revenue—in lower-middle-income countries tax revenue as a share of GDP increased from 17 percent to 22 percent between 2000 and 2019.[62] Half of this revenue growth came from indirect taxes (especially the value added tax, VAT), 30 percent from direct taxes on income, and 20 percent from payroll taxes. This upward trend in revenue mobilization was driven by the greater efficiency of tax administrations, technological innovations, and improvements of tax designs.

Can governments continue to increase tax revenue over the next decade? The COVID-19 pandemic has created a short-term but drastic revenue shortfall, but it could reinforce revenue mobilization in the medium term by legitimizing the role of the state as a provider of insurance and redistribution. However, there are no magic bullets—higher tax revenue arises principally from long-term investments in tax capacity and from structural changes in countries' economies bolstered by international efforts to address tax avoidance. Three areas of reforms can nonetheless raise revenue while balancing equity and efficiency considerations. However, progress on mobilizing new tax revenue may be threatened by a delayed or anemic recovery or social backlash, as was seen recently in Colombia.[63]

First, governments increasingly have the capacity to target high earners with progressive taxes. Currently, in low- and middle-income countries personal income taxes and property taxes account for only a small share of GDP (3 percent and 0.5 percent, respectively), which is a much lower share than in high-income countries. The long-run transition from self-employment to employment in firms is a key enabler of modern personal income taxes. However, this evolution in employment structure must be accompanied by investments in a tax administration's capacity to target high earners and to tax their income from all sources (including capital) at rising marginal tax rates. Thus the tax effort is borne principally by those with the means to contribute.[64] Taxes on property are another progressive source of revenue. But despite a visible tax base, the current revenues are low. As urbanization drives property values up in many cities, modern property registries, documented and accessed by means of technology, make real estate valuation and administration easier. Thus taxes on personal income and property are an untapped source of government revenue and simultaneously can help curb inequality.

Second, structural changes arising from the digitalization of economies and the climate emergency present not only challenges but also opportunities to mobilize revenue. As transactions go digital and taxpayers file electronically, tax administrations can compare self-reported economic activity with third-party reports to uncover discrepancies and better target audits. Similarly, large online platforms that aggregate transactions can be used as withholding agents and as mechanisms to formalize smaller firms that want to participate in online markets. Another key evolution is related to the climate emergency; it justifies taxes aimed at limiting energy consumption and could raise additional tax revenue. Policy responses could take the form of removal of energy subsidies and the imposition of fuel taxes or more ambitious carbon taxes. Whatever their shape, taxes must be tailored to each country's tax capacity and energy structure and compensate vulnerable households for any increases in their tax burden.[65] Better use of health-related taxes (such as taxes on the consumption of alcohol and tobacco) could also add more resources to the public purse while aligning personal incentives with a reduction in the pressure on public health systems.

Third, the design of taxes can be simplified to improve their transparency and efficiency. The principal tax instruments (the VAT and corporate and personal income taxes) are riddled with tax exemptions and tax credits. By narrowing tax bases, exemptions reduce revenue collection and the efficiency of taxes and provide opportunities for tax avoidance. Although some tax exemptions are justifiable, other government tools might be more appropriate to address the underlying issues. A contentious example is the removal of exemptions from the VAT base. Typically, products such as food and energy are minimally taxed or not taxed at all to introduce progressivity. However, exemptions also benefit the rich, especially in countries where poor households mainly purchase goods in the informal sector.[66] Zero rating goods is thus a coarse tax instrument for introducing progressivity. Conditional on compensating poor households through transfers, the removal of exemptions could be socially acceptable and would collect revenue while also improving efficiency.[67]

To follow the suggested path to tax reforms, governments will need to overcome political challenges and the opposition of interest groups. To achieve successful reforms, governments must build wide support, clearly communicate the intended effects, and compensate poor households for tax increases. Even then, it is difficult to gather support for even well-designed tax policies, such as removing tax exemptions. Such considerations might dictate the set of feasible reforms. Furthermore, where the informal sector is large, complementary policies to develop the private sector and expand the tax base are paramount. Finally, because of the increased mobility of capital and of high earners, some tax revenue gains will depend on greater international tax cooperation. Recent developments on the minimum taxation of multinational companies hold promise, but it remains unclear how these agreements will be applied in practice and how much they will benefit low- and middle-income countries.[68]

It is equally important to rationalize public expenditures and target public spending and investments effectively. To set priorities for the allocation of public funds and to avoid inefficient spending, waste, and corruption, governments must have a well-designed public finance management system. Effective public finance management can also enhance the transparency of public expenditures and the accountability of government officials. At a time when governments are pressured to increase health expenditures to address the effects of the pandemic, a well-managed public expenditure process can make this task less daunting.

The importance of transparency to debt management and resolution of debt distress

Some of the main obstacles to the prompt recognition and resolution of sovereign debt distress stem from opaque fiscal accounts and unreliable debt data. A prerequisite for expedient sovereign debt reprofiling and restructuring is creditors' access to reliable granular information about the country's overall debt as well as the seniority (when applicable) of their own claim relative to that of other creditors. Transparent data on a country's sovereign debt help creditors and multilateral institutions arrive at better debt sustainability assessments and financing decisions, which are ultimately helpful to both debtors and creditors and to overall market stability. When a country faces problems servicing its debt, better data reduce the time needed to negotiate with creditors to resolve the problem. Hidden debts, in their many guises, have been a recurring obstacle to prompt action, and not just in low- and middle-income countries as the 2011 Greek and 2015 Puerto Rican debt crises highlighted.

Debt transparency has two main dimensions: transparency in debt reporting and transparency in debt operations.[69] For transparency in debt reporting—probably the best-understood dimension—existing and new debt must be disclosed to the public in a timely, comprehensive manner. Transparency in debt operations refers to the process of entering a new debt contract or altering an existing debt contract, which includes but is not limited to having a well-designed legal framework.

Recent studies and proposals related to the international debt architecture have emphasized the central importance of transparency in debt reporting to successful debt management. Building on earlier work by the World Bank and International Monetary Fund (IMF), in 2019 the G20 endorsed a set of Voluntary Principles for Debt Transparency drafted by the Institute of International Finance and targeting private sector lenders. Meanwhile, the Organisation for Economic Co-operation and Development (OECD) is in the process of developing a disclosure platform based on these principles. These developments are a positive step toward further strengthening transparency in terms of both comprehensiveness and accessibility, but more can be done.

Effective, forward-looking debt management requires comprehensive disclosure of claims against the government, as well as the terms of the contracts that govern this debt. In practice, very few countries meet this standard of transparency. In the market for sovereign debt, contracts are often not made public, and some even include explicit nondisclosure clauses.[70] In addition, it is often difficult to develop a comprehensive picture beyond the central government, as this is typically the level of debt reporting. Unfortunately, the majority of low-income countries do not yet have consolidated public sector accounts.[71]

One important prerequisite for transparency in debt reporting and operations is therefore an unambiguous legal framework that clarifies which entities are authorized to contract debt that is enforceable against the sovereign.[72] This framework should also require debt contracts to be made public in a central repository. Although various government agencies can be signatories of sovereign debt contracts, the claims arising from these contracts are ultimately enforced against the underlying sovereign state and its population.

Some recent debt events have highlighted the problem of hidden or undisclosed debt and the possibility of legal disputes about whether a government and quasi-government entities have the authority to enter into debt contracts. Clarifying which state-owned entities are authorized to contract debt on behalf of the government and which subnational entities can raise claims against the government, including through guarantees and debt exchanges, can significantly facilitate debt management and reduce the risk of hidden debts, thereby helping to avoid costly and disruptive disputes. Such clarification would also ensure that any domestic accountability mechanisms that may be in place have sufficient information to operate properly. However, it is important that these legal requirements be accompanied by strong underlying institutions and by a domestic and international commitment to respecting those rules. Otherwise, even if the law clearly states who can approve debt contracts, the enforcement of those rules may be lacking, as in Mozambique (box 5.5).

Improved debt transparency can also contribute to the adoption of debt instruments, such as state-contingent bonds, which are efficient for debtors and creditors, but remain underutilized. One example is GDP- or commodity-linked bonds, which generate variable returns that move with the business cycle or commodity prices. Such bonds automatically reduce the burden on sovereign balance sheets during downturns and could also prove beneficial for investors. At present, these instruments have been used most commonly as value recovery instruments (securities that allow the creditor to share in the recovery of the country if it agrees to restructure debt during times of distress). GDP-linked bonds were used in the 2015–16 Ukrainian debt restructuring. In the past, Nigeria and República Bolivariana de Venezuela have issued commodity-linked warrants. However, the willingness of creditors to enter into such contracts depends heavily on reliable data on a broad array of financial and economic indicators. Although

Box 5.5 Case study: The curse of hidden debt in Mozambique

As in any credit market, timely access to information is essential for a well-functioning sovereign debt market. If there is any hint of undisclosed information about a country's debt, lenders may become less willing to provide financing, and new financing may become more expensive as lenders demand an additional premium to account for the potential risks associated with hidden information. Because of hidden debt, in Mozambique access to funding by the government was significantly reduced and therefore public investment was substantially cut.

In 2013 and 2014, external loans amounting to more than $1 billion were contracted by state-owned companies in Mozambique under guarantee by the central government. In other words, the Mozambique government would be liable for these loans if the state-owned companies were unable to repay them.[a] This publicly guaranteed debt was never disclosed to the public (including debtors and citizens) until 2016, when the media uncovered it.[b]

How did this happen?

The hidden loans, as well as a state-guaranteed bond, were contracted without the proper approvals.[c] In Mozambique, the Ministry of Finance and the parliament have oversight over the issuance of new debt (including publicly guaranteed debt). However, for external borrowing by Mozambique's state-owned enterprises, those checks and balances were not implemented. Because of the lack of proper oversight as well as corruption allegations against the parties involved in these loan transactions, in 2019 Mozambique's attorney general filed a lawsuit to nullify the government guarantee of the loan contracted by one of the state-owned companies.[d] In early 2022, the lawsuit was ongoing because the lender appealed the original court decision. In the meantime, Mozambique has been renegotiating its debt, even as it waits to see whether the court decides the loan and guarantee contracts are illegal in their entirety and thus void.

How has this affected Mozambique's financial standing?

In Mozambique's 2015 debt sustainability analysis, the World Bank and International Monetary Fund (IMF) projected the country's external public and publicly guaranteed debt for 2016 to be 61 percent of GDP.[e] The equivalent document published in 2018 estimated the external public and publicly guaranteed debt for 2016 to be 104 percent of GDP.[f]

These hidden debts had significant implications for Mozambique's ability to service its debt, as it dramatically increased the amount of interest and amortization due in a given year. In particular, prior to the disclosure of these debts, the market was operating under the assumption that 11 percent of Mozambique's tax revenue would suffice to cover the debt service for 2016. With the disclosure of these debts, it was clear that at least 22 percent of tax revenue, or about $600 million, was needed (figure B5.5.1). The projected increase in debt service was even bigger in 2017 and 2018. This increase was too large for the Mozambican economy to endure, and Mozambique defaulted on its debt in 2016.[g] As a result, credit rating agencies downgraded Mozambique to selective or restricted default. Similarly, Mozambique, which had been classified as in moderate risk of debt distress by the World Bank–IMF in 2015, was classified as in debt distress in 2016.[h]

The deterioration of Mozambique's fiscal position and risk rating had far-reaching economic consequences and turned a crisis of transparency into wider economic turmoil that had many characteristics of a conglomerate crisis. The debt crisis was accompanied by a significant real exchange rate depreciation starting in 2014, a rise in inflation, reduced space for fiscal expenditures, as well as loss of confidence by external investors and the international community, leading to an acute downgrade in the country's sovereign credit rating. Concessional lending from international financial institutions—often used to resolve debt crises in

(Box continues next page)

Box 5.5 **Case study: The curse of hidden debt in Mozambique** *(continued)*

Figure B5.5.1 **Mozambique's external debt service projections (2015–27) before and after the 2016 disclosure of hidden debts**

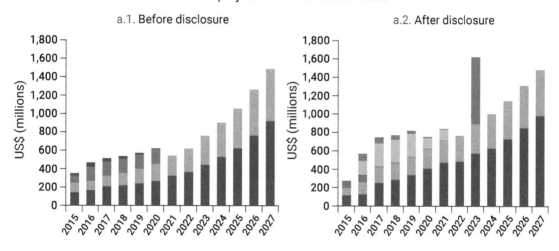

a. DSA projections of amount of debt

a.1. Before disclosure

a.2. After disclosure

b. DSA projections of share of government revenue, excluding grants, needed to service debt

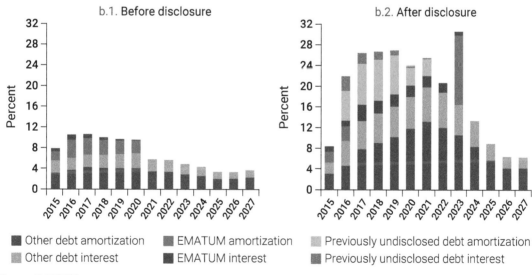

b.1. Before disclosure

b.2. After disclosure

■ Other debt amortization ■ EMATUM amortization ▨ Previously undisclosed debt amortization
▨ Other debt interest ■ EMATUM interest ■ Previously undisclosed debt interest

Source: IMF 2018.

Note: DSA = debt sustainability analysis. EMATUM bonds were widely covered in the financial press as "Tuna Bonds." They were issued by Proindicus, EMATUM (The Mozambican Tuna Fishing Enterprise), and Mozambique Asset Management and were involved in a controversy over authorizations.

(Box continues next page)

Box 5.5 **Case study: The curse of hidden debt in Mozambique** *(continued)*

emerging economies—was no longer available. Only in 2019 was Mozambique's debt classified as sustainable on a forward-looking basis—eliciting enough confidence that the World Bank and IMF provided financing in the aftermath of Cyclone Idai. One important step to rebuilding confidence was improving transparency in debt reporting and debt operations implemented since. Improvements were the publication of periodic debt reports, including information on state-owned companies; a new decree on public investment management; and new government-approved regulations to strengthen debt and guarantee management (including borrowing by state-owned companies). Nonetheless, Mozambique is still in debt distress while renegotiating its debt, and the legal battle over its hidden debts continues. Meanwhile, Mozambique still faces unfavorable borrowing conditions that imply a high cost of credit not just for the government but also for firms and households.

a. IMF (2018).

b. England (2016).

c. The hidden loans from companies covered by a sovereign guarantee were as follows: $622 million for Proindicus and $535 million in favor of Mozambique Asset Management (MAM). The authorities also disclosed the existence of $133 million in direct loans from bilateral lenders contracted between 2009 and 2014. This set of hidden debts was in addition to the EMATUM corporate bond, which was originally issued in September 2013 (also backed by a state guarantee) and then restructured as the MOZAM 2023 sovereign bond in March 2016. The government managed to restructure the MOZAM bond to mature in 2031. Although the EMATUM bond was not a hidden loan, it was part of the same package of projects underlying the undisclosed debt scheme.

d. See Spotlight on Corruption, "Mozambique and the 'Tuna Bond' Scandal," Wells, Somerset, UK, https://www.spotlight corruption.org/mozambique-and-the-tuna-bond-scandal/. See also IMF (2019).

e. IMF (2015).

f. IMF (2018).

g. From the Fitch report on Mozambique in 2016: "On 21 November the Ministry of Economy and Finance published a document confirming that Mozambique failed to make a capital and coupon payment, due 23 May 2016, on the USD535m loan to state-owned enterprise Mozambique Asset Management (MAM). The document also confirms that the MAM loan is guaranteed by the Republic of Mozambique. The arrears on the loan amount to approximately USD175.5m. In line with its criteria, Fitch therefore judges Mozambique to be in default on its sovereign obligations" (Fitch Ratings 2016).

h. IMF (2016).

it is recognized that such state-contingent contracts are a desirable way forward, such contracts remain a minority in existing debt stocks.

Technological advances are another path to improve transparency in sovereign debt reporting and operations. One example is blockchain technology, which has been revolutionizing credit and capital markets. International financial institutions, such as the World Bank, but also sovereigns, such as the government of Thailand, have recently begun to use blockchain technology to issue and trade a subset of their bonds.[73] The key contribution of blockchain technology is that it immutably documents ownership status over tokenized assets in a decentralized and typically transparent ledger that is visible to all market participants. In other words, blockchain technology allows for more transparent and timely information on the ownership and terms of debt contracts housed in this environment. It then makes it possible to trace who owns the underlying asset at any given point in real time. For debt markets, the ability to trace and act on current ownership of instruments in a timely manner implies enormous efficiency gains. If implemented comprehensively, this ability could, for example, drastically reduce the time required to trace and reconcile the full list of claims against a country, which is a necessary step before a country can enter into a restructuring negotiation with creditors. Because of today's architecture, this is an inefficient, time-consuming procedure, and some small creditors remain unidentified even after the restructuring is completed. Thus potential gains in transparency through blockchain due to the ability to identify the holders of a sovereign's outstanding debt instruments could be extremely useful in avoiding delays in debt restructuring.

The role of contractual innovations in reducing coordination problems and facilitating debt resolution

Several contractual innovations can help overcome coordination problems and speed up the resolution of sovereign debt. One innovation is collective action clauses (CACs), which could lead to faster resolution of sovereign debt restructuring and thus more stability.[74] Preliminary studies have found that these clauses tend to reduce the presence of holdout creditors during restructuring. CACs that permit aggregation, in which a majority of creditors can overrule a minority of holdout creditors, appear to be most effective at achieving faster resolutions in restructuring negotiations.[75]

However, it may be too optimistic to assume that CACs are sufficiently embedded in debt contracts to resolve debt crises in the near future. Indeed, it may be too early to claim that debt crises were in fact shortened by the introduction of the newest generation of CACs in 2014.[76] Recent analyses argue that the sample on which preliminary findings were based is too recent and draws heavily from a period of relative moderation.[77] Moreover, shortening restructuring processes and shortening debt crises are two different concepts.[78] First, historically bringing sovereign debt crises or default spells to an end has required, on average, two restructurings.[79] Second, it is difficult to argue that enhanced CACs are the secure, de facto market standard because only about half of the outstanding stock of sovereign bonds is estimated to contain these features, and a substantial portion of this legacy debt stock is still at least 10 years from maturity.[80] In addition, of the 62 countries for which bond data are available, 16 have bonds with no CACs, as well as bonds with second-generation CACs or beyond (figure 5.7). This heterogeneity can complicate debt restructuring and highlights the need for broader changes.

Figure 5.7 **Sovereign bond principal maturation in selected low- and middle-income countries, by share and type of collective action clauses included in the bonds, 2021 33+**

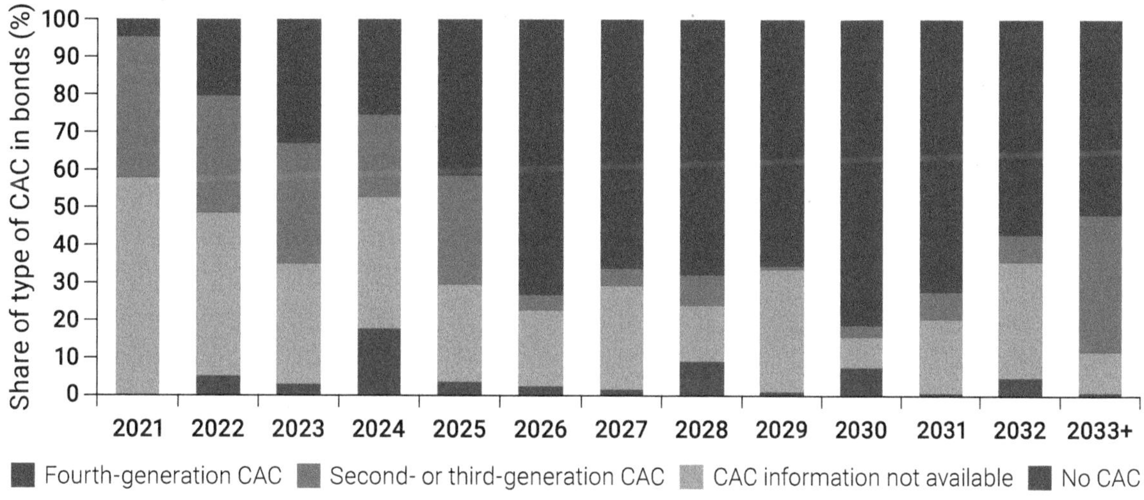

Source: WDR 2022 team, based on data from Munevar (2021); Refinitiv, Refinitiv Data Catalogue (dashboard), https://www .refinitiv.com/en/financial-data.

Note: The data cover 62 low- and middle-income countries and bonds maturing in January 2021 and beyond. The figure shows the share and type of collective action clauses (CACs) included in bonds issued by low- and middle-income countries.

Recent debt negotiations, such as the Argentine and Ecuadorian restructurings of 2020, highlight another practical limitation of CACs: debt contracts can be modified and renegotiated in ways that weaken the efficiency-enhancing features of CACs. In response to Argentina's proposed use of aggregated voting and creditor designation mechanisms, certain creditors demanded a rollback to pre-2014 CAC language.[81] Ultimately, negotiations led to a compromise that included changes to allow for *creditor redesignation* (a provision through which Argentina could choose which creditors would be pooled for voting) and the subsequent launch of a *uniformly applicable offer* (an exchange offer with a menu of options deemed equitable to all creditors) once certain initial approval thresholds had been met.[82] Unfortunately, like state-contingent contracts, only about half of outstanding debt contracts carry enhanced CACs, and the share is even lower for low-income countries.[83]

Another type of contractual innovation that can accelerate debt resolution and shield countries from unanticipated increases in sovereign debt is state-contingent debt contracts that insure the borrower against disaster risk. Such contracts are especially useful as climate risks become more widespread. The recent debt restructurings of Grenada (2015) and Barbados (2018), for example, have included natural disaster clauses. To be effective, contingency triggers should be protected from manipulation or opportunism—that is, the terms of the contract (reduced debt service or access to additional liquidity) should be triggered by an objective and independently verifiable event. By reducing a country's debt service in the event of an unanticipated shock, these types of contracts can free up fiscal resources when they are needed most. In the aftermath of the COVID-19 pandemic or future events that trigger an increase in sovereign debt, this safeguard could be especially useful for countries that are also exposed to heightened risk of natural disasters or climate change.

A final set of legal developments that can potentially improve creditor coordination and speed up debt resolution are legal reforms that address problematic enforcement practices against states. Creditors face legal and practical challenges when enforcing claims against a state. In response, specific creditors (such as holdouts and so-called vulture creditors), have eschewed collective negotiation in favor of individualized enforcement. This approach has jeopardized creditor coordination and payments to other creditors, thereby preventing the prompt resolution of debt distress. Because of lack of a sovereign bankruptcy mechanism that could incentivize coordinated action, several national jurisdictions have taken legislative steps to address problematic credit enforcement practices. These have included profit-capping statutes for vulture fund lawsuits (United Kingdom, 2010) and legal protections for payment-clearing platforms, such as Euroclear (Belgium, 2015). In addition, international bodies have formulated non-binding "soft law" guidelines and resolutions, such as the UNCTAD (United Nations Conference on Trade and Development) Principles on Responsible Sovereign Borrowing and Lending (2012) and the UN General Assembly Resolution on Basic Principles for Sovereign Debt Restructuring (2015). Although such soft law guidelines do not carry penalties for violation, they reflect legal principles in certain domestic jurisdictions and could represent emerging international norms. Further work to solidify these principles into national and international law would be beneficial for market efficiency.

Conclusion

The COVID-19 crisis has highlighted and aggravated preexisting vulnerabilities in public debt, particularly among low-income countries. Addressing debt sustainability problems promptly and proactively is crucial for a strong, equitable recovery. Because the historical track record on this front is not particularly encouraging, it is critical that new initiatives, such as the Common Framework, be strengthened to deliver more expedient outcomes.

Effective management of sovereign debt and resolution of debt distress play an especially important role. In a crisis, governments can essentially act as a lender of last resort to the economy, and well-designed fiscal support can act as a circuit breaker that can reduce financial risks in other sectors and prevent them from affecting the wider economy. Such support, however, requires healthy public finances, which enable governments to spend on public goods and provide households, firms, and the financial sector with emergency support. When the government's ability to carry out this function is compromised by high debt burdens, its ability to support the recovery is limited—a challenge that an increasing number of countries now face because the COVID-19 crisis has outlasted original expectations.

Policy actions to prevent or resolve debt distress depend on many economic, political, and social factors, and no easy one-size-fits-all solutions are offered here. Debt sustainability analyses are the instrument most widely used to determine a country's risk of debt distress and is therefore the right course of action to prevent and resolve debt sustainability problems. For those countries already in debt distress, it is paramount to recognize the problem and not delay the restructuring process. As in the resolution of past crises, fiscal adjustment and structural reforms will be part of the debt restructuring process. Where public debt is denominated in domestic currency (a rising trend in emerging economies), inflation as well as financial repression measures have in some cases been used successfully to avoid default when governments were not able to meet their domestic debt obligations. However, these measures impose significant costs on citizens, especially the poor.

Countries that face sharply increased debt burdens as a result of the COVID-19 crisis have policy options for reducing the risk of falling into debt distress, including debt reprofiling and preemptive negotiations with creditors. For example, countries can take advantage of more favorable market conditions to extend maturities or lower the cost of debt service. Negotiating better terms for a country's debt is much easier when the country still has a relatively solid credit standing than when it is on the verge of default. Tracking credit market conditions can be very fruitful, as can taking advantage of the tools available to low-income countries. Examples include SDG Bonds, which can provide better terms for financing investments (see spotlight 5.1). Most emerging economies will need to make these types of poverty-reducing investments in any case, and, by using these bonds, they can get better lending terms, while improving their ability to attain the Sustainable Development Goals.

Beyond these more immediate actions, increasing debt transparency, adopting contractual innovations that reduce coordination problems in debt resolution, and securing the tax revenue needed to provide public services as well as repay the debt are essential. Although these are medium- to longer-term actions, they can significantly improve the resilience of government finances going forward.

Apart from debt reduction through sustained robust growth, all the approaches discussed here pose their own brand of social and economic costs and aggravate many of the economic fragilities outlined in chapter 1. A realistic assessment of past debt reduction strategies thus offers some guidance but does not deliver silver bullets.

Notes

1. Kose et al. (2020, 2021).
2. Borensztein and Panizza (2009).
3. Baldacci, de Mello, and Inchauste (2002); Furceri and Zdzienicka (2012); Ravallion and Chen (2009).
4. Kose et al. (2021).
5. Kose et al. (2021).
6. Kose et al. (2021).
7. Kose et al. (2021).
8. Although GDP deceleration contributed to the net result, the main driver of the increase was the sheer growth in nominal debt. See International Monetary Fund, World Economic Outlook Database: Download WEO Data, April 2021 Edition (dashboard), https://

www.imf.org/en/Publications/WEO/weo-database /2021/April.

9. In the context of the Joint World Bank–IMF Debt Sustainability Framework, *debt distress* is defined as a situation in which any of the following are observed: (1) arrears in public and publicly guaranteed external debt exceeded 5 percent during the previous three years; (2) a Paris Club restructuring of external debt was undertaken; (3) large disbursements were made in excess of 30 percent of the quota for IMF Stand-By Arrangements or Extended Fund Facilities; (4) a restructuring of commercial debt was pursued; or (5) default was executed on public and publicly

guaranteed external debt. See World Bank and International Monetary Fund, Joint World Bank–International Monetary Fund LIC DSF Database (Debt Sustainability Framework for Low-Income Countries), https://www.worldbank.org/en/programs/debt-toolkit/dsf.

10. Calculations based on International Development Association (IDA) eligibility, including Blend countries (that is, those eligible for IDA funding based on per capita income but which are also deemed creditworthy by the markets), and debt and GDP data from International Monetary Fund, World Economic Outlook Database: Download WEO Data, April 2021 Edition (dashboard), https://www.imf.org/en/Publications/WEO/weo-database/2021/April.

11. Calculations based on data from International Monetary Fund, World Economic Outlook Database: Download WEO Data, April 2021 Edition (dashboard), https://www.imf.org/en/Publications/WEO/weo-database/2021/April.

12. Mbaye, Badia, and Chae (2018).

13. Bova et al. (2016).

14. Bova et al. (2016).

15. IMF (2021).

16. Moody's Investors Service (2019).

17. Brooks et al. (2004); Schumacher (2014).

18. For example, analysis spanning more than a century finds that, for each year a country has been in default since 1900, there was a concurrent banking crisis or an inflation crisis, or both, in one in three of the years. See Reinhart and Rogoff (2009).

19. Borensztein and Panizza (2009); Reinhart and Rogoff (2009).

20. Calvo (2010); Conceição et al. (2009).

21. Calvo (2010); Conceição et al. (2009).

22. Conceição et al. (2009); Ma et al. (2021).

23. See Albanesi (2007); Bulir and Gulde (1995); Easterly and Fischer (2001); Romer and Romer (1998). Binder (2019) finds that, although the relationship between the inflation tax and inequality varies over regions and time, it has remained positive in the Americas and Africa—regions in which a majority of countries are developing.

24. Diaz-Alejandro (1984).

25. See Farah-Yacoub, Graf von Luckner, and Reinhart (2021).

26. This group includes mostly low-income countries.

27. The Paris Club has been involved in over 470 restructuring agreements with over 100 countries. Its members are Australia, Austria, Belgium, Brazil, Canada, Denmark, Finland, France, Germany, India, Ireland, Israel, Italy, Japan, the Republic of Korea, the Netherlands, Norway, the Russian Federation, Spain, Sweden, Switzerland, the United Kingdom, and the United States. Any official or government creditor outside of this group is classified as a non–Paris Club lender.

28. For example, Glencore has been a lender to governments in Sub-Saharan Africa, while Sinopec is a key participant in complex arrangements with Chinese state-owned banks lending to oil-rich countries.

29. Technically, the concept of seniority in the traditional sense is not applicable to sovereign finance because there is no bankruptcy code. However, a de facto quasi-seniority structure exists based on decades of practice and conventions. See Gelpern et al. (2021); Schlegl, Trebesch, and Wright (2019).

30. Consider, for example, the case of commodity-based lending by official or private creditors, which are usually structured as a large forward sale; the case of Chinese swap lines; or the case of the deposit by the central bank of Saudi Arabia in the central bank in Pakistan.

31. See International Monetary Fund, DSA LIC (Debt Sustainability Analysis Low-Income Countries) (dashboard), https://www.imf.org/en/publications/dsa.

32. These practices are not entirely new. Similar types of debt contracts were common during the nineteenth century and the first part of the twentieth century. They were used to borrow through project companies, guarantee debt, and secure loans against government revenue or specific income streams, including commodity sales or tax receipts. However, these lending forms fell out of favor in part due to concerns about giving external actors financial control over domestic affairs.

33. World Bank (2021a).

34. World Bank (2021a).

35. This arrangement is unlike the de facto standing private creditor committees of the 1970s and 1980s. The London Club, for example, was an informal group of private creditors (most of them international commercial banks) that represented its members in renegotiations of the sovereign debt owed to them.

36. Gelpern et al. (2021).

37. Gelpern et al. (2021).

38. Gelpern et al. (2021).

39. See Reinhart, Reinhart, and Rogoff (2015).

40. The World Bank and IMF produce debt sustainability analyses on low-income countries, and IMF produces debt sustainability analyses on market access countries. These assessments are used frequently as a basis for determining the adjustments needed to reach debt sustainability. See International Monetary Fund, DSA LIC (Debt Sustainability Analysis Low-Income Countries) (dashboard), https://www.imf.org/en/publications/dsa; International Monetary Fund, DSA MAC (Debt Sustainability Analysis for Market-Access Countries) (dashboard), https://www.imf.org/external/pubs/ft/dsa/mac.htm.

41. There are other areas for improvement in DSA risk analysis. For example, improvements in the evaluation of contingent liabilities and SOE debt are crucial to the effectiveness of a DSA as a risk mitigation tool. However, for the purposes of this section the focus is on the aspects of a DSA that tend to carry the most importance at both the risk mitigation stage and distress resolution stage because the DSA becomes an integral part of resolution efforts in estimating a country's needs. The three identified factors are the most relevant at both stages.

42. Reuters (2021).

43. Asonuma and Trebesch (2016).

44. Asonuma and Trebesch (2016).

45. Asonuma and Trebesch (2016).

46. WDR 2022 team calculations; Asonuma and Trebesch (2016).
47. Defined as a default on private external creditors.
48. Based on restructurings of defaults since the end of World War II. Farah-Yacoub, Graf von Luckner, and Reinhart (2021); Graf von Luckner et al. (2021).
49. Benjamin and Wright (2009).
50. WDR 2022 team calculations, based on Asonuma and Trebesch (2016) and Farah-Yacoub, Graf von Luckner, and Reinhart (2021). Using a subset of default spells for which the reported default spell end dates in both studies match and restructuring deal details are available, 41 of 68 spell-ending restructurings had a face value reduction. Using only Asonuma and Trebesch (2016) data, 51 of 94 spell-ending restructurings involved a face value reduction.
51. Fang, Schumacher, and Trebesch (2021); Pitchford and Wright (2012); Schumacher, Trebesch, and Enderlein (2021).
52. Friedman (1983).
53. Reinhart and Trebesch (2016).
54. Arslanalp and Henry (2005).
55. Reinhart, Reinhart, and Rogoff (2015).
56. Reinhart, Reinhart, and Rogoff (2015).
57. Reinhart, Reinhart, and Rogoff (2015).
58. Reinhart, Reinhart, and Rogoff (2015); Reinhart and Sbrancia (2015).
59. Reinhart, Reinhart, and Rogoff (2015); Reinhart and Sbrancia (2015).
60. Calice, Diaz Kalan, and Masetti (2020).
61. Easterly (1989); Easterly and Schmidt-Hebbel (1994).
62. International Centre for Tax and Development, ICTD Government Revenue Dataset, Institute of Development Studies, Brighton, UK, http://www.ictd.ac/data sets/the-ictd-government-revenue-dataset.
63. Janetsky (2021).
64. Jensen (2019).
65. Pigato (2019).
66. Bachas, Gadenne, and Jensen (2020).
67. Phillips et al. (2018).
68. OECD (2021).
69. See World Bank (2021a) for a more complete discussion on the debt transparency framework.
70. Gelpern et al. (2021)
71. Aytekin Balibek (2021).
72. For a consideration of issues of sovereign authorization, see Lienau (2008, 2014). Through debt management performance assessments, the World Bank measures several relevant aspects of a well-designed legal framework for debt management. See World Bank, DeMPA (Debt Management Performance Assessment) (dashboard), https://www.worldbank.org/en/programs /debt-toolkit/dempa.
73. Cision PR Newswire (2020); Duran and John (2018).
74. IMF (2020a).
75. Fang, Schumacher, and Trebesch (2021).
76. IMF (2020a).
77. Graf von Luckner et al. (2021).
78. See Reinhart and Rogoff (2009).
79. Graf von Luckner et al. (2021).
80. IMF (2020a).
81. The debtor argued that it could amend the contracts to oblige the pool of voting creditors to redesignation using a voting threshold of 50.00 percent of the principal of each series, as opposed to the 66.67 percent aggregate and 50.00 percent of principal per series, or 75.00 percent of aggregate principal, necessary to amend reserved matters. Under the proposed amendment, Argentina would have been able to pool creditors amenable to its offer even after the votes had been cast and launch a subsequent exchange offer, including to the holders of new exchange bonds and the holders of old bonds who rejected the offer. Creditors argued that, by doing this, Argentina could have forced creditors to gang up and dilute their individual rights. This was dubbed the Pac-Man strategy. The creditors initially demanded a reversion to pre-2014 CAC verbiage as a response. See de la Cruz and Lagos (2020).
82. de la Cruz and Lagos (2020).
83. IMF (2020a).

References

Albanesi, Stefania. 2007. "Inflation and Inequality." *Journal of Monetary Economics* 54 (4): 1088–1114.

Arslanalp, Serkan, and Peter Blair Henry. 2005. "Is Debt Relief Efficient?" *Journal of Finance* 60 (2): 1017–51.

Asonuma, Tamon, and Christoph Trebesch. 2016. "Sovereign Debt Restructurings: Preemptive or Post-Default." *Journal of the European Economic Association* 14 (1): 175–214.

Aytekin Balibek, Arzu. 2021. "Public Sector Domestic Debt Survey Results." With contributions of Malvina Pollock and Evis Rucaj and inputs of the Debt Statistics Team of the Development Data Group, World Bank, Washington, DC.

Bachas, Pierre, Lucie Gadenne, and Anders Jensen. 2020. "Informality, Consumption Taxes, and Redistribution." NBER Working Paper 27429, National Bureau of Economic Research, Cambridge, MA.

Baldacci, Emanuele, Luiz de Mello, and Gabriela Inchauste. 2002. "Financial Crises, Poverty, and Income Distribution." IMF Working Paper 02/4, International Monetary Fund, Washington, DC.

Benjamin, David, and Mark L. J. Wright. 2009. "Recovery before Redemption: A Theory of Delays in Sovereign Debt Renegotiations." CAMA Working Paper 2009-15, Centre for Applied Macroeconomic Analysis, Crawford School of Public Policy, Australian National University, Canberra, Australia.

Binder, Carola. 2019. "Inequality and the Inflation Tax." *Journal of Macroeconomics* 61 (September), 103122.

Borensztein, Eduardo, and Ugo Panizza. 2009. "The Costs of Sovereign Default." *IMF Staff Papers* 56 (4): 683–741.

Bova, M. Elva, Marta Ruiz-Arranz, Frederik Toscani, and H. Elif Ture. 2016. "The Fiscal Costs of Contingent Liabilities:

A New Dataset." IMF Working Paper WP/16/14, International Monetary Fund, Washington, DC.

Brooks, Robert, Robert William Faff, David Hillier, and Joseph Hillier. 2004. "The National Market Impact of Sovereign Rating Changes." *Journal of Banking and Finance* 28 (1): 233–50.

Bulir, Ales, and Anne Marie Gulde. 1995. "Inflation and Income Distribution: Further Evidence on Empirical Links." IMF Working Paper 95/86, International Monetary Fund, Washington, DC.

CAA (Caisse Autonome d'Amortissement). 2019. "Document de Stratégie d'Endettement Public à Moyen Terme (SDMT) 2020–2024." CAA, Cotonou, Benin.

CAA (Caisse Autonome d'Amortissement). 2021. "Benin Becomes the 1st African Country and One of the First Countries in the World to Successfully Issue an Unprecedented €500 Million SDG Bonds." Press release, July 15, 2021. https://caa.bj/benin-becomes-the-1st -african-country-and-one-of-the-first-countries-in-the -world-to-successfully-issue-an-unprecedented-e500 -million-eurobond-on-the-sdgs/.

Calice, Pietro, Federico Diaz Kalan, and Oliver Masetti. 2020. "Interest Rate Repression around the World." Equitable Growth, Finance, and Institutions Insight, World Bank, Washington, DC.

Calvo, Sara Guerschanik. 2010. "The Global Financial Crisis of 2008–10: A View from the Social Sectors." Human Development Research Paper HDRP-2010-18, Human Development Report Office, United Nations Development Programme, New York.

Cision PR Newswire. 2020. "Bank of Thailand Launches World's First Government Savings Bond on IBM Blockchain Technology." News release, October 5, 2020. https://www.prnewswire.com/news-releases/bank-of -thailand-launches-worlds-first-government-savings -bond-on-ibm-blockchain-technology-301145253.html.

Conceição, Pedro, Namsuk Kim, Ronald U. Mendoza, and Yanchun Zhang. 2009. "Human Development in Crisis: Insights from the Literature, Emerging Accounts from the Field, and the Correlates of Growth Accelerations and Decelerations." Social and Economic Policy Working Paper, Policy, Advocacy, and Knowledge Management, Division of Policy and Practice, United Nations Children's Fund, New York.

Cruces, Guillermo, and Quentin Wodon. 2003. "Argentina's Crises and the Poor, 1995–2002." *Económica* 49 (1–2): 55–96.

Cruces, Juan J., and Christoph Trebesch. 2013. "Sovereign Defaults: The Price of Haircuts." *American Economic Journal: Macroeconomics* 5 (3): 85–117.

Daseking, Christina, Atish Ghosh, Timothy Lane, and Alun Thomas. 2004. "Lessons from the Crisis in Argentina." IMF Occasional Paper 236, Policy Development and Review Department, International Monetary Fund, Washington, DC.

de la Cruz, Andrés, and Ignacio Lagos. 2020. "CACs at Work: What Next? Lessons from the Argentine and Ecuadorian 2020 Debt Restructurings." *Capital Markets Law Journal* 16 (2): 226–48.

Depetris Chauvin, Nicolas, and Aart Kraay. 2005. "What Has 100 Billion Dollars Worth of Debt Relief Done for Low-Income Countries?" *International Finance* 0510001, University Library, Ludwig-Maximilians-Universität, Munich. https://ideas.repec.org/p/wpa/wuwpif/0510001 .html.

Diaz-Alejandro, Carlos F. 1984. "Latin American Debt: I Don't Think We Are in Kansas Anymore." *Brookings Papers on Economic Activity* 15 (2): 335–403.

Duran, Paulina, and Alun John. 2018. "World Bank Launches World-First Blockchain Bond." *Reuters: Banks*, August 23, 2018. https://www.reuters.com/article/us-worldbank -cba-blockchain-idUSKCN1L80DP.

Easterly, William Russell. 1989. "Fiscal Adjustment and Deficit Financing during the Debt Crisis." In *Dealing with the Debt Crisis*, edited by Ishrat Husain and Ishac Diwan, 91–113. World Bank Symposium Series, vol. 35. Washington, DC: World Bank.

Easterly, William Russell, and Stanley Fischer. 2001. "Inflation and the Poor." *Journal of Money, Credit, and Banking* 33 (2, Part 1): 160–78.

Easterly, William Russell, and Klaus Schmidt-Hebbel. 1994. "Fiscal Adjustment and Macroeconomic Performance: A Synthesis." In *Public Sector Deficits and Macroeconomic Performance*, edited by William Russell Easterly, Carlos Alfredo Rodríguez, and Klaus Schmidt-Hebbel, 15–45. Washington, DC: World Bank; New York: Oxford University Press.

England, Andrew. 2016. "IMF Halts Mozambique Aid after Finding Undisclosed Debts of $1bn." *Financial Times*, April 18, 2016. https://www.ft.com/content/6c 755214-057f-11e6-9b51-0fb5e65703ce.

Fang, Chuck, Julian Schumacher, and Christoph Trebesch. 2021. "Restructuring Sovereign Bonds: Holdouts, Haircuts, and the Effectiveness of CACs." *IMF Economic Review* 69 (1): 155–96.

Farah-Yacoub, Juan, Clemens Graf von Luckner, and Carmen M. Reinhart. 2021. "The Eternal External Debt Crisis: A Long View." Unpublished manuscript, World Bank, Washington, DC.

Feldstein, Martin S. 2002. "Argentina's Fall: Lessons from the Latest Financial Crisis." *Foreign Affairs* 81 (2): 8–14.

Fitch Ratings. 2016. "Fitch Downgrades Mozambique's LTFC IDR to 'RD'." *Rating Action Commentary*, November 30, 2016. https://www.fitchratings.com/research /sovereigns/fitch-downgrades-mozambique-ltfc-idr-to -rd-30-11-2016.

Friedman, Irving Sigmund. 1983. *The World Debt Dilemma: Managing Country Risk*. Philadelphia: Risk Management Association.

Furceri, Davide, and Aleksandra Zdzienicka. 2012. "How Costly Are Debt Crises?" *Journal of International Money and Finance* 31 (4): 726–42.

Gelpern, Anna, Sebastian Horn, Scott Morris, Brad Parks, and Christoph Trebesch. 2021. "How China Lends: A Rare Look into 100 Debt Contracts with Foreign Governments." CEPR Discussion Paper DP16331, Center for Economic Policy Research, London.

Government of Benin. 2019. "Le Bénin effectue la première émission obligataire inaugurale en euros de l'histoire des émissions internationales africaines" [Benin makes the first inaugural eurobond issue in the history of African international bond issues]. *Communiqué*,

March 20, 2019. https://www.gouv.bj/actualite/234 /le-benin-effectue-la-premiere-emission-obligataire -inaugurale-en-euros-de-lhistoire-des-emissions-inter nationales-africaines/.

Government of Benin. 2021a. "Investor Presentation." Government of Benin, Cotonou. https://odd.gouv.bj/wp -content/uploads/sites/13/2021/07/Benin-IP-July -2021-2021.07.12-FINAL_WEBSITE.pdf.

Government of Benin. 2021b. "Le Bénin réalise la première opération obligataire internationale d'Afrique de l'année avec l'émission d'un milliard d'euros, en deux tranches de maturités finales 11 ans et 31 ans" [Benin carries out the first African international bond transaction of the year with an issue of one billion eurobonds, in two tranches, with maturities of 11 years and 31 years]. Communiqué, January 14, 2021. https://www.gouv.bj/actualite/1128 /le-benin-realise-premiere-operation-obligataire-inter nationale-afrique-annee-avec-emission-milliard-euros -deux-tranches-maturites-finales-11-31-ans/.

Graf von Luckner, Clemens, Josefin Meyer, Carmen M. Reinhart, and Christoph Trebesch. 2021. "External Sovereign Debt Restructurings: Delay and Replay." VoxEU (blog), March 30, 2021. https://voxeu.org/article/external -sovereign-debt-restructurings-delay-and-replay.

Hausman, Ricardo, and Andrés Velasco. 2003. "Hard Money's Soft Underbelly: Understanding the Argentine Crisis." Brookings Trade Forum: 2002, edited by Susan M. Collins and Dani Rodrik, 59–104. Washington, DC: Brookings Institution Press.

IEG (Independent Evaluation Group). 2006. "Debt Relief for the Poorest: An Evaluation Update of the HIPC Initiative." World Bank, Washington, DC. https://ieg .worldbankgroup.org/sites/default/files/Data/reports /hipc_update_evaluation.pdf.

Ilzetzki, Ethan, Carmen M. Reinhart, and Kenneth S. Rogoff. 2019. "Exchange Arrangements Entering the Twenty-First Century: Which Anchor Will Hold?" Quarterly Journal of Economics 134 (2): 599–646.

IMF (International Monetary Fund). 2015. "Republic of Mozambique: Fourth Review under the Policy Support Instrument; Debt Sustainability Analysis." IMF Country Report 15/223, IMF, Washington, DC.

IMF (International Monetary Fund). 2016. "Republic of Mozambique: Request for an 18-Month Arrangement under the Standby Credit Facility: Debt Sustainability Analysis." IMF Country Report 16/9, IMF, Washington, DC.

IMF (International Monetary Fund). 2018. "Republic of Mozambique: Staff Report for the 2017 Article IV Consultation; Debt Sustainability Analysis." IMF Country Report 18/65, IMF, Washington, DC.

IMF (International Monetary Fund). 2019. "Republic of Mozambique: Request for Disbursement under the Rapid Credit Facility; Debt Sustainability Analysis." IMF Country Report 19/136, IMF, Washington, DC.

IMF (International Monetary Fund). 2020a. "The International Architecture for Resolving Sovereign Debt Involving Private-Sector Creditors: Recent Developments, Challenges, and Reform Options." IMF Policy Paper 2020/043, IMF, Washington, DC.

IMF (International Monetary Fund). 2020b. "Benin: Sixth Review under the Extended Credit Facility Arrangement and Request for Augmentation of Access; Debt Sustainability Analysis." IMF Country Report 20/175, IMF, Washington, DC.

IMF (International Monetary Fund). 2021. "Ghana, 2021 Article IV Consultation: Press Release, Staff Report, and Statement by the Executive Director for Ghana." IMF Staff Country Report 21/165, IMF, Washington, DC.

IMF (International Monetary Fund) and IDA (International Development Association). 2005. "Rwanda: Enhanced Heavily Indebted Poor Countries (HIPC) Initiative, Completion Point Document." IMF and IDA, Washington, DC. https://documents1.worldbank.org/curated /en/671031468777935571/pdf/316780Completion 0Point0Doc.pdf.

IMF (International Monetary Fund) and World Bank. 2019. "Heavily Indebted Poor Countries (HIPC) Initiative and Multilateral Debt Relief Initiative (MDRI): Statistical Update." IMF Policy Paper 19/028, IMF, Washington, DC.

Janetsky, Megan. 2021. "Colombians Revive Protests amid New Tax Plan." VOA News, July 21, 2021. https://www .voanews.com/a/americas_colombians-revive-protests -amid-new-tax-plan/6208524.html.

Jensen, Anders. 2019. "Employment Structure and the Rise of the Modern Tax System." NBER Working Paper 25502, National Bureau of Economic Research, Cambridge, MA.

Kose, M. Ayhan, Peter S. O. Nagle, Franziska L. Ohnsorge, and Naotaka Sugawara. 2020. "Can This Time Be Different? Policy Options in Times of Rising Debt." Policy Research Working Paper 9178, World Bank, Washington, DC.

Kose, M. Ayhan, Franziska Ohnsorge, Carmen M. Reinhart, and Kenneth S. Rogoff. 2021. "The Aftermath of Debt Surges." Policy Research Working Paper 9771, World Bank, Washington, DC.

Lienau, Odette. 2008. "Who Is the 'Sovereign' in Sovereign Debt? Reinterpreting a Rule-of-Law Framework from the Early Twentieth Century." Yale Journal of International Law 33 (1): 63–111.

Lienau, Odette. 2014. Rethinking Sovereign Debt: Politics, Reputation, and Legitimacy in Modern Finance. Cambridge, MA: Harvard University Press.

Ma, Lin, Gil Shapira, Damien de Walque, Quy-Toan Do, Jed Friedman, and Andrei A. Levchenko. 2021. "The Intergenerational Mortality Tradeoff of COVID-19 Lockdown Policies." Policy Research Working Paper 9677, World Bank, Washington, DC.

Mbaye, Samba, Marialuz Moreno Badia, and Kyungla Chae. 2018. "Bailing Out the People? When Private Debt Becomes Public." IMF Working Paper 18/141, International Monetary Fund, Washington, DC.

MEF (Ministry of Economy and Finance, Benin). 2021. "Strategie Annuelle d'Endettement de l'État: Annexée à la loi finances, gestion 2021." MEF, Cotonou, Benin.

Meyer, Josefin, Carmen M. Reinhart, and Christoph Trebesch. 2019. "Sovereign Bonds since Waterloo." NBER Working Paper 25543, National Bureau of Economic Research, Cambridge, MA.

Moody's Investors Service. 2019. "Sovereigns, Emerging Markets: Risks from Financial Misreporting Vary, Disclosure Has Major Credit Implications." Sector In-Depth, Report 1146743, Moody's, New York.

Munevar, Daniel. 2021. "Sleep Now in the Fire: Sovereign Bonds and the Covid-19 Debt Crisis." Eurodad Report, May 26, European Network on Debt and Development, Brussels. https://www.eurodad.org/sovereign_bonds _covid19.

Mussa, Michael. 2002. *Argentina and the Fund: From Triumph to Tragedy*. Policy Analyses in International Economics Series, vol. 67. Washington, DC: Institute for International Economics.

OECD (Organisation for Economic Co-operation and Development). 2021. "International Community Strikes a Ground-Breaking Tax Deal for the Digital Age." *Topics: Tax*, October 8, 2021. https://www.oecd.org/tax/international-community-strikes-a-ground-breaking-tax-deal-for-the-digital-age.htm.

Perry, Guillermo E., and Luis Serven. 2002. "The Anatomy and Physiology of a Multiple Crisis: Why Was Argentina Special and What Can We Learn from It?" World Bank, Washington, DC.

Phillips, David, Ross Warwick, Maya Goldman, Karolina Goraus-Tańska, Gabriela Inchauste, Tom Harris, and Jon Jellema. 2018. "Redistribution via VAT and Cash Transfers: An Assessment in the Low and Middle Income Countries." CEQ Working Paper 78, Commitment to Equity, Inter-American Dialogue, Washington, DC; Center for Inter-American Policy and Research and Department of Economics, Tulane University, New Orleans.

Pigato, Miria A., ed. 2019. *Fiscal Policies for Development and Climate Action*. International Development in Focus Series. Washington, DC: World Bank.

Pitchford, Rohan, and Mark L. J. Wright. 2012. "Holdouts in Sovereign Debt Restructuring: A Theory of Negotiation in a Weak Contractual Environment." *Review of Economic Studies* 79 (2): 812–37.

Primo Braga, Carlos A., and Dörte Dömeland, eds. 2009. *Debt Relief and Beyond: Lessons Learned and Challenges Ahead*. Washington, DC: World Bank. https://openknowledge-worldbank-org.libproxy-wb.imf.org/handle/10986/2681.

Ravallion, Martin, and Shaohua Chen. 2009. "The Impact of the Global Financial Crisis on the World's Poorest." *VoxEU* (blog), April 30, 2009. https://voxeu.org/article/impact-global-financial-crisis-world-s-poorest.

Reinhart, Carmen M., Vincent Reinhart, and Kenneth S. Rogoff. 2015. "Dealing with Debt." *Journal of International Economics* 96 (Supplement 1): S43–S55.

Reinhart, Carmen M., and Kenneth S. Rogoff. 2009. *This Time Is Different: Eight Centuries of Financial Folly*. Princeton, NJ: Princeton University Press.

Reinhart, Carmen M., and M. Belen Sbrancia. 2015. "The Liquidation of Government Debt." *Economic Policy* 30 (82): 291–333.

Reinhart, Carmen M., and Christoph Trebesch. 2016. "Sovereign Debt Relief and Its Aftermath." *Journal of the European Economic Association* 14 (1): 215–51.

Reuters. 2021. "Ghana Raises $3 Billion via 4-Year Zero-Coupon Bond." *Middle East & Africa*, March 30, 2021. https://www.reuters.com/article/uk-ghana-economy-bonds/ghana-raises-3-billion-via-4-year-zero-coupon-bond-idUSKBN2BM2XQ.

Romer, Christina D., and David H. Romer. 1998. "Monetary Policy and the Well-Being of the Poor." NBER Working Paper 6793, National Bureau of Economic Research, Cambridge, MA.

Schlegl, Matthias, Christoph Trebesch, and Mark L. J. Wright. 2019. "The Seniority Structure of Sovereign Debt." CESifo Working Paper 7632, Munich Society for the Promotion of Economic Research, Center for Economic Studies, Ludwig-Maximilians-Universität and Ifo Institute for Economic Research, Munich.

Schumacher, Ingmar. 2014. "On the Self-Fulfilling Prophecy of Changes in Sovereign Ratings." *Economic Modelling* 38 (February): 351–56.

Schumacher, Julian, Christoph Trebesch, and Henrik Enderlein. 2021. "Sovereign Defaults in Court." *Journal of International Economics* 131 (July): 103388.

World Bank. 2021a. *Debt Transparency in Developing Economies*. Washington, DC: World Bank.

World Bank. 2021b. *Macro Poverty Outlook*. Washington, DC: World Bank. https://thedocs.worldbank.org/en/doc/77351105a334213c64122e44c2efe523-0500072021/related/mpo-sm21.pdf.

Spotlight 5.1

Greening capital markets: Sovereign sustainable bonds

The economic stress arising from the COVID-19 (coronavirus) pandemic propelled expansion of sovereign sustainable bond issuances. The Climate Bonds Initiative (CBI) reports that the number of sovereign green, social, and sustainable bonds more than doubled in 2020. By the end of the year, sovereign green bonds amounted to $41 billion, or a 65 percent increase over 2019. That trend continued into 2021, with Italy raising approximately $10 billion in Europe's largest green bond debut to date. Other advanced and emerging markets also intend to issue sovereign green bonds.[1]

Sustainable bonds are defined as bonds for which proceeds are used to finance or refinance green, blue, or social projects. A green bond is a debt security issued to raise capital specifically to support climate-related environmental projects.[2] Voluntary best practice guidelines for sustainable bond issuances—the Green Bond Principles (GBP)—were established in 2014 by a consortium of investment banks.[3] Sustainable bonds align with the four core components of the GBP. The current monitoring and development of the GBP guidelines are managed by the International Capital Market Association (ICMA).[4]

As of January 2022, there were no universally agreed-on definitions of green, social, or sustainable bonds, and the GBP do not provide details on what qualifies as such bonds—those definitions are largely left up to the issuers. The World Bank and International Finance Corporation (IFC) use their own criteria and definitions for eligible green and social projects. In turn, the CBI provides separate categories of sector-specific green definitions and criteria.[5]

To ensure the transparency and accuracy of information disclosed by issuers to stakeholders, the GBP recommends pre- and post-issuance external reviews. For any proposed thematic bond, an issuer should appoint external review providers to assess the alignment of its bond or bond framework with the core components of the GBP. After issuance, the GBP recommends that an issuer's management of proceeds be reviewed by an external auditor to verify the allocation of funds from green bond proceeds to eligible projects.[6]

Despite significant growth in recent years, sovereign green, social, and sustainable bonds account for only 0.5 percent of the sovereign bonds market.[7] The first green bonds were issued in 2007 by the European Investment Bank and in 2008 by the World Bank.[8] These pioneer bonds defined eligibility criteria and introduced impact reporting as an integral part of issuance processes. The World Bank issuance also piloted a new model of partnership and collaboration among stakeholders, including investors, development agencies, commercial banks, and private sector players.[9] Currently, the green model is applied to bonds that are raising financing for the 17 Sustainable Development Goals (SDGs).[10] Multilateral development banks were the sole issuers of green bonds until 2012, when the first corporate green bonds emerged. In 2017, Poland issued the first sovereign green bond.

Almost a third of governments worldwide, led by high-income countries, have issued sovereign green, social, and sustainable instruments through a mix of local and national entities.[11] About 60 percent of all high-income countries have government-issued sustainable instruments. This share is significantly lower for upper- and lower-middle-income countries (see figure S5.1.1). Governments in low-income countries have so far not issued any sustainable instruments. As for origination, green, social, and sustainable instruments have been issued both locally and nationally in 15 countries. Government-backed entities have issued sustainable bonds in 34 countries, and in 16 of these countries such instruments were issued only by government-backed entities.[12]

In 2020, about 60 percent of sovereign green and social bond issuances were driven by the COVID-19 pandemic, and two-thirds were issued in domestic markets. Most pandemic-driven sustainable bonds were issued by governments across Africa.[13] These were followed by bonds to finance clean transport projects (17 percent), led by Chile. Proceeds from other green and social bonds have been allocated to aquatic biodiversity conservation, eligible green projects, energy efficiency, and other related areas.[14] Côte d'Ivoire has the highest number of sustainable sovereign bonds issued domestically (25).[15] Meanwhile, Chile has the highest number of sovereign green and social bond

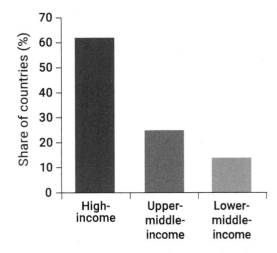

Figure S5.1.1 **Share of countries with government-issued sustainable instruments, by country income group, 2020–21**

Source: WDR 2022 team, based on 2020 data from Climate Bonds Initiative; 2020/21 data from International Finance Corporation; 2021 data from Refinitiv, Refinitiv Data Catalogue (dashboard), https://www.refinitiv.com/en/financial-data; World Bank, World Development Indicators (dashboard), https://datatopics.worldbank.org/world-development-indicators/.

issuances in a nonlocal market (12),[16] followed by Hong Kong SAR, China (8).[17]

Social bond issuance worldwide jumped sevenfold, to $148 billion, in 2020, primarily targeting health care, education, and small and medium enterprises. Most of these bonds were issued by governments and multilateral development agencies.[18] Although public issuers, unlike private ones, have a direct mandate to provide social services, private social bond issuance has also gained momentum. Private issuers of social bonds have aimed to finance programs to support stakeholders, employees, customers, and local communities.[19] These bonds also give firms an opportunity to broaden their pools of investors.[20] Overall, sustainable debt reached a new peak in 2020, amounting to a record high of $732 billion across bond and loan varieties raised with environmental and social purposes for a resilient post–COVID-19 recovery.[21]

Although the global sovereign sustainable bond market is still small, some evidence of "greenium" (a premium in the pricing of green bonds) is beginning to emerge in both developed and emerging markets. In 2020, Germany introduced a unique twin bond structure that included a conventional vanilla bond and a green bond—the only difference between the two was the use of proceeds. The German green bond, priced with a greenium, maintained a lower yield in the secondary market and exhibited lower volatility than its vanilla twin.[22] Green bonds in emerging markets have shown strong performance. For example, in 2020 the emerging market subset of the J.P. Morgan Green Bond index (6.6 percent) outperformed its conventional index (5.4 percent). Overall, the green subset showed lower volatility for similar performance than regular bonds in emerging markets.[23] However, the evidence of green bonds premia—which would provide greater incentives for issuance of green bonds—is still mixed.[24]

Sovereign issuers can include sustainable bonds in their medium-term debt management strategies. This approach offers an opportunity to attract and expand the investor base, while allowing a wide range of funding alternatives. Yet any new borrowing should be consistent with fiscal spending and deficit plans to keep public debt on a sustainable path. Moreover, issuers should have large green expenditures that they can support with sustainable debt. Other challenges include limited impact investing in emerging markets because of credit rating restrictions and lack of understanding of green instruments, coupled with narrow regulatory mandates.[25] Some countries use monetary policy levers to encourage green financing. China, for example, offers green lending incentives by considering qualified green bonds and accepting certain green loans as collateral in its medium-term lending facility—a key monetary tool used to manage liquidity needs in the banking system.[26]

Government-issued green and social bonds often provide longer tenors than corporate bonds. As of August 2021, at least 175 green and social sovereign bonds had been issued worldwide. About 30 percent of these bonds have maturities of at least 10 years (the sustainable bond with the longest tenor—of 50 years—was issued in April 2020 by the government of Indonesia).[27] Similarly, Bulgaria; Chile; Hong Kong SAR, China; Hungary; and Poland have issued sustainable bonds with tenors of 30 years or more. In 2021, green and social sovereign bonds issued in the range of less than 5 years and 6–10 years comprised 50 percent and 30 percent of the issuances, respectively. By contrast, sustainable bonds issued by corporate entities tend to have lower tenors, typically 5–10 years.[28] However, longer term maturities may not be in line with a country's debt strategy because of the implied higher yields.

Although there is no conclusive cross-country pattern, some sovereign green and social bond issuances have paved the way for similar debt issuances by the private sector. For example, in 2017 Nigeria became the first African country to issue a sovereign green bond, which was followed by the first green corporate issuance from Access Bank.[29] Similarly, in 2019 Chile became the first green sovereign bond issuer in Latin America, and, soon after, Banco de Chile issued a green bond to raise funds for renewable energy projects.[30]

In line with bond issuance trends, further analysis shows a strong correlation between the share of green and social bonds in total sovereign issuances and gross domestic product (GDP) per capita (see figure S5.1.2). Lower-income countries usually have less fiscal space for bond issuances because of their limited financing capacity, weaker institutions, lack of strong regulatory frameworks, and limited awareness of and experience in financial markets.[31] Similarly, the extension of domestic credit to the private sector (as a percentage of GDP) is significantly correlated with the issuance of sovereign sustainable bonds—countries that issue sovereign sustainable bonds tend to have more developed financial sectors and stronger macroeconomic fundamentals.[32] Ultimately, determining the specific underlying drivers affecting governments' ability or willingness to issue sustainable debt requires further research.

Figure S5.1.2 Correlation between share of green and social bond issuances and GDP per capita

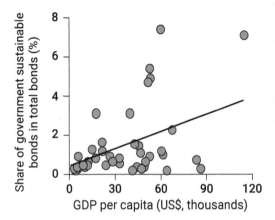

Source: WDR 2022 team, based on data from Refinitiv Data Catalogue (dashboard), Refinitiv, New York, https://www.refinitiv.com/en/financial-data; 2021 data from World Bank, World Development Indicators (dashboard), https://datatopics.worldbank.org/world-development-indicators/.

Note: The relationship is statistically significant at 1 percent; t = 3.3; number of observations = 41. GDP = gross domestic product.

Some emerging markets are noteworthy in their proactive approach to developing green bond markets. In 2016, following the adoption of the 2015 Paris Agreement on Climate Change, Nigeria ratified its Nationally Determined Contributions (NDCs) committing it to reducing greenhouse gases.[33] And, as noted, in December 2017 Nigeria issued Africa's first sovereign green bond—only the fourth globally—of $29.7 million with a five-year maturity.[34] Malaysia's sustainable finance market accounted for 22 percent of the total Association of Southeast Asian Nations (ASEAN) market in 2020.[35] To promote issuances of sustainable *sukuk* and bonds, Malaysia actively participates in the development and implementation of capital market integration and connectivity initiatives undertaken by the ASEAN Capital Markets Forum. Domestically, the Securities Commission has been playing a pivotal role in supporting development of responsible investment.[36]

Sustainable finance regulation has improved recently, especially in emerging markets. In 2020, the central bank of the Philippines issued the country's first sustainable finance framework. Similarly, Colombia's banking regulator established a framework for issuing and investing in green bonds. On a larger scale, in the European Union (EU) the EU Taxonomy and EU Green Bond Standard have increased transparency and comparability, as well as provided further guidance for green bond issuance. The EU Taxonomy also introduced a classification system for environmentally sustainable economic activities.[37] In the meantime, it was reported in November 2020 that public development banks had joined forces to support economic and social transformations toward a sustainable future.[38] The International Financial Reporting Standards Foundation is also working on sustainability reporting standards.[39] But despite these advances, worldwide the overall level of sustainable regulatory development remains low (figure S5.1.3).[40]

To meet their green goals and help channel more financing to sustainable activities, countries need to actively advance sustainable finance. A growing number of high- and middle-income countries have developed sustainable regulatory frameworks, and some emerging markets have made significant progress in implementing sustainable policies. However, much more progress is needed worldwide. In addition, the private sector must adopt sustainable investment practices outside of regulatory mandates. Stock exchanges can support issuers to determine what types of climate-related risks and opportunities need to be disclosed to investors and should have a say in the disclosures required by law. By developing sustainability listing requirements in collaboration with regulatory authorities, stock exchanges can help to ensure compliance among listed companies and set the standard for non-listed corporations. Exchanges should work closely with listed companies to ensure the accuracy and consistency of reported data.[41] Further alignment and implementation of global standards and policy frameworks would help further mobilize capital directed at sustainable economic activities.[42]

Figure S5.1.3 Regulatory coverage of sustainability factors in capital markets, by country income group

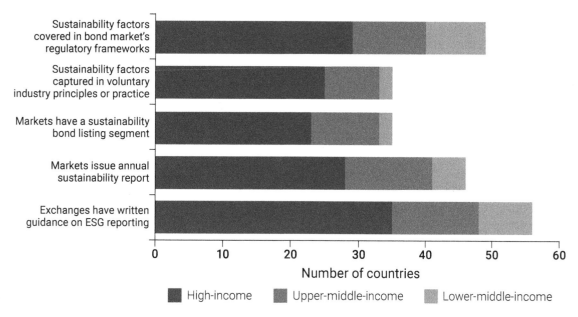

Source: International Finance Corporation sustainability dataset, 2021, forthcoming (see note).

Note: No low-income country has any of these regulatory features. ESG = environmental, social, and governance. The global sustainability dataset was compiled by the International Finance Corporation's Development Impact team between June and October 2021. It covers more than 70 indicators across five thematic areas: government bonds, corporate bonds, equity, regulatory framework, and institutional investors. A variety of primary and secondary sources were used in collecting the data, including desk research (mostly for country-specific sources), Climate Bonds Initiative, International Capital Market Association, Refinitiv, Bloomberg, International Monetary Fund, Asian Development Bank, and Sustainable Stock Exchanges Initiative.

Notes

1. Fatin (2021).
2. World Bank (2015). As defined by the International Capital Market Association (ICMA), *green bonds* are any type of bond instrument whose proceeds or an equivalent amount will be exclusively applied to finance or refinance, in part or in full, new or existing eligible green projects. They are aligned with the four core components of the Green Bond Principles. *Social bonds* are use-of-proceeds bonds that raise funds for new and existing projects with positive social outcomes. The four core components are the same as those set for green bonds. *Sustainable bonds* are bonds that intentionally mix eligible green and social projects. *Sustainability-linked bonds* are any type of bond instrument for which the financial or structural characteristics can vary, depending on whether the issuer achieves predefined sustainability objectives.

3. The banks are Bank of America Merrill Lynch, Barclays Corporate and Investment Bank, BNP Paribas, Citi, Crédit Agricole, Daiwa, Deutsche Bank, Goldman Sachs, HSBC, JPMorgan Chase, Mizuho Securities, Morgan Stanley, Rabobank, and SEB.
4. See Climate Bonds Initiative, "Green Bond Principles and Climate Bonds Standard," https://www.climatebonds .net/market/best-practice-guidelines.
5. Broad green project categories suggested by the Green Bond Principles include energy; buildings; transport; water management; waste management and pollution control; nature-based assets, including land use, agriculture, and forestry; industry and energy-intensive commercial; information technology; and communications. See Climate Bonds Initiative, "Green Bond Principles and Climate Bonds Standard," https://www.climatebonds.net /market/best-practice-guidelines.

6. ICMA (2021).

7. Fatin (2021).

8. IFC (2016). The bonds were issued under the label Climate Awareness Bonds with the proceeds dedicated to renewable energy and energy efficiency projects (World Bank 2008). The World Bank issued its first green bond in November 2008 for a group of Scandinavian investors; it was valued at $267 million with a maturity of six years. The bond was listed on the Luxembourg Stock Exchange. In February 2013, IFC issued a green bond worth $1 billion to support climate-friendly projects in emerging economies. The issue was heavily oversubscribed and marked the largest climate-friendly issuance up to 2013. Through this issuance, IFC was able to change the private placement format of the green bond market to public mainstream.

9. World Bank (2019).

10. World Bank (2018).

11. Between 2007 and 2021, seven countries—China, France, Germany, Japan, the Republic of Korea, Sweden, and the United States—issued over 100 sustainability instruments. The United States has a record number, with over 1,350 issuances, followed by Germany with 162. In terms of volume, France is the world leader, with issuances worth more than $81 billion by 2020, followed by Germany with $23 billion.

12. International Finance Corporation sustainability dataset, 2021, forthcoming. See figure S5.1.3 for a description of this dataset.

13. Refinitiv, Refinitiv Data Catalogue (dashboard), https://www.refinitiv.com/en/financial-data.

14. International Finance Corporation sustainability dataset, 2021, forthcoming; Refinitiv, Refinitiv Data Catalogue (dashboard), https://www.refinitiv.com/en/financial-data.

15. Côte d'Ivoire's economy remains stronger than that of many of its peers. The country was recently upgraded by all three international rating agencies—S&P, Moody's, and Fitch. The political risk diminished significantly after the peaceful elections of March 2021. And the country was able to make a quick V-shaped recovery from the onset of the pandemic (Murdoch 2021).

16. Social bonds are becoming more common in Chile as the government prepares to fight the long-term social impacts of the COVID-19 pandemic. Bond issuances by Chile under the COVID-19 Transitory Emergency Fund focus on social projects as outlined in the country's sustainable bond framework. The government can use the proceeds to fund a wide range of initiatives, including community support through job creation, access to education, food security, essential health services, and programs designed to prevent unemployment derived from socioeconomic crises (BNP Paribas 2021).

17. International Finance Corporation sustainability dataset, 2021, forthcoming; Refinitiv, Refinitiv Data Catalogue (dashboard), https://www.refinitiv.com/en/financial-data.

18. BNEF (2021).

19. S&P Global (2020).

20. Mutua (2020).

21. BNEF (2021).

22. Harrison (2021). Based on secondary market data, the average emerging market greenium stands at −3.4 basis points, which represents 3.5 percent of the average spread of bonds in the sample.

23. Amundi and IFC (2021).

24. A study by the International Monetary Fund suggests that, although some issuers claim that tapping the green bond market lowers their borrowing costs, a discount is rare (*Economist* 2020). A 2019 study showed that, on average, a greenium of two basis points was found in a sample of euro- and US dollar–denominated bonds, while in 2020 another study comparing 640 pairs of bonds revealed no difference in yields of green versus nongreen bonds (Affirmative Investment Management Partners Limited 2021). Some studies project an expansion of the emerging market greenium given the high-yield nature of the market (Amundi and IFC 2021).

25. World Bank (2020). See also Kim (2021).

26. PBC (2018).

27. Murdoch and Jefriando (2020).

28. According to historical data, tenors do not differ based on the market of issue. For example, sovereign sustainable bonds issued domestically are just as likely to have tenors as long as similar bonds issued in international markets. See Harrison and Muething (2021); Refinitiv, Refinitiv Data Catalogue (dashboard), https://www.refinitiv.com/en/financial-data. Within a given market, the sovereign issuer typically issues at longer maturities than firms because the sovereign provides the benchmark yield curve for corporate bond issuers. By this means, the sovereign sends a pricing signal so that firms can price at a margin over the "risk-free" rate at each tenor.

29. CBI (2017); Fatin (2019); SBN (2020a).

30. CBI (2019).

31. SBN (2020b).

32. International Finance Corporation sustainability dataset, 2021, forthcoming.

33. When preparing NDCs, some countries attached conditions to the implementation of some measures. These are referred to as conditional contributions as opposed to unconditional ones. See Jacobsen (2020).

34. Hassamal, Abolo, and Ogaga (2021); Whiley (2018).

35. Nguyet et al. (2021).

36. SC (2021).

37. Amundi and IFC (2021).

38. FiC (2020).

39. IFRS (2021).

40. Amundi and IFC (2021). Since 2012, the IFC's Sustainable Banking Network (SBN) has supported policy and industry initiatives to promote sustainable finance in emerging markets. Currently, 39 countries are members of the SBN and are committed to developing and implementing sustainable finance frameworks in line with international

standards. The SBN supports members through technical resources, capacity building, and peer-to-peer knowledge exchange. According to the SBN's 2019 Global Progress Report, of the 11 low-income countries in the SBN, four are in the "advancing" stage of their sustainable finance journeys (SBN 2019).

41. SSE (2021).

42. Such global initiatives include developing benchmark green taxonomies, establishing the Network for Greening the Financial System, enforcing green bond standards, implementing the recommendations of the Task Force on Climate-Related Financial Disclosures, and building capacity and technical assistance for emerging markets. See Amundi and IFC (2021).

References

Affirmative Investment Management Partners Limited. 2021. "Greenium—Fact or Fiction?" https://affirmativeim.com/greenium-fact-or-fiction/.

Amundi (Amundi Asset Management) and IFC (International Finance Corporation). 2021. "Emerging Market Green Bonds Report 2020: On the Road to Green Recovery." IFC, Washington, DC; Amundi, Paris. https://www.ifc.org/wps/wcm/connect/0fab2dcd-25c9-48cd-b9a8-d6cc4901066e/2021.04+-+Emerging+Market+Green+Bonds+Report+2020+-+EN.pdf?MOD=AJPERES&CVID=nBW.6AT.

BNEF (BloombergNEF). 2021. "Sustainable Debt Breaks Annual Record Despite Covid-19 Challenges." *bnef.com* (blog), January 11, 2021. https://about.bnef.com/blog/sustainable-debt-breaks-annual-record-despite-covid-19-challenges.

BNP Paribas. 2021. "Chile Leads the Way for Sovereign ESG Bonds in Latin America." *Sustainability* (blog), August 5, 2021. https://cib.bnpparibas/chile-leads-the-way for-sovereign-esg-bonds-in-latin-america/.

CBI (Climate Bonds Initiative). 2017. "Nigeria First Nation to Issue a Climate Bonds Certified Sovereign Green Bond." Media release, December 19, 2017. https://www.climatebonds.net/files/releases/media_release_nigeria_issues_certifed_sovereign_green_bond_19122017.pdf.

CBI (Climate Bonds Initiative). 2019. "Green Bond Fact Sheet: Banco de Chile." CBI, London. https://www.climatebonds.net/files/files/2019-08%20CL%20Banco%20de%20Chile.pdf.

Economist. 2020. "What Is the Point of Green Bonds?" https://www.economist.com/finance-and-economics/2020/09/19/what-is-the-point-of-green-bonds.

Fatin, Leena. 2019. "Nigeria: Access Bank 1st Certified Corporate Green Bond in Africa; Leadership in Green Finance." *Climate Bonds Initiative* (blog), April 2, 2019. https://www.climatebonds.net/2019/04/nigeria-access-bank-1st-certified-corporate-green-bond-africa-leadership-green-finance.

Fatin, Leena. 2021. "Sovereign Green, Social, and Sustainability (SGSS) Bonds: How Far and How Fast Could They Grow?" *Climate Bonds Initiative* (blog), March 30, 2021. https://www.climatebonds.net/2021/03/sovereign-green-social-sustainability-sgss-bonds-how-far-and-how-fast-could-they-grow.

FiC (Finance in Common). 2020. "Joint Declaration of All Public Development Banks in the World." Finance in Common Summit, Agence française de développement, Paris. https://financeincommon.org/sites/default/files/2021-06/FiCs%20-%20Joint%20declaration%20of%20Public%20Development%20Banks.pdf.

Harrison, Caroline. 2021. "Green Bond Pricing in the Primary Market H2 2020." Climate Bonds Initiative, London. https://www.climatebonds.net/files/reports/cbi_pricing_h2_2020_01e.pdf.

Harrison, Caroline, and Lea Muething. 2021. "Sustainable Global State of the Market 2020." Climate Bonds Initiative, London.

Hassamal, Komal, Paul Abolo, and Andrew Ogaga. 2021. "NDC Implementation in Nigeria through Green Investments by Private Sector: A Scoping Study." African Development Bank, Abidjan, Côte d'Ivoire.

ICMA (International Capital Market Association). 2021. "Green Bond Principles: Voluntary Process Guidelines for Issuing Green Bonds." ICMA, Paris. https://www.icmagroup.org/assets/documents/Sustainable-finance/2021-updates/Green-Bond-Principles-June-2021-140621.pdf.

IFC (International Finance Corporation). 2016. "Mobilizing Private Climate Finance: Green Bonds and Beyond." EMCompass Note 25, IFC, Washington, DC. https://www.ifc.org/wps/wcm/connect/2996f197-a75b-422a-9e2f-cdc022d8ea96/EMCompass+Note+25+Green+Bonds+FINAL+12-5.pdf?MOD=AJPERES&CVID=lzgXSmr.

IFRS (International Financial Reporting Standards Foundation). 2021. "IFRS Foundation Trustees Announce Working Group to Accelerate Convergence in Global Sustainability Reporting Standards Focused on Enterprise Value." *News* (blog), March 22, 2021. https://www.ifrs.org/news-and-events/news/2021/03/trustees-announce-working-group/.

Jacobsen, Fentje. 2020. "Conditional and Unconditional Climate Action in NDCs." *100% RE MAP* (blog), December 14, 2020. https://100re-map.netconditional-and-unconditional-climate-action-in-ndcs/.

Kim, Jae Ho. 2021. "Investor Demand for Emerging Market Thematic Bonds to Finance a Sustainable Recovery." *Voices* (blog), May 6, 2021. https://blogs.worldbank.org/voices/investor-demand-emerging-market-thematic-bonds-finance-sustainable-recovery.

Murdoch, Adrian. 2021. "Why Côte d'Ivoire's First Green Bond Is So Important." *Capital Monitor: Sector/Consumer* (blog), September 1, 2021. https://capitalmonitor.ai/sector/consumer/why-cote-divoires-first-green-bond-is-so-important/.

Murdoch, Scott, and Maikel Jefriando. 2020. "Update 2: Indonesia Sells Asia's First 50-Year Dollar Bond to Fight Pandemic." *Healthcare* (blog), April 7, 2020. https://www.reuters.com/article/health-coronavirus-indonesia-bonds/update-2-indonesia-sells-asias-first-50-year-dollar-bond-to-fight-pandemic-idUSL4N2BV0XC.

Mutua, David Caleb. 2020. "Goldman Sees Pandemic Spurring Growth in ESG Bond Issuance." *Bloomberg Quint*

(blog), August 20, 2020. https://www.bloombergquint
.com/onweb/goldman-sees-pandemic-spurring-growth
-in-esg-bond-issuance.

Nguyet, Phi Thi Minh, Nabilla Gunawan, Krista Tukiainen, Cedric Rimaud, and Quynh Nguyen. 2021. "ASEAN Sustainable Finance: State of the Market 2020." Climate Bonds Initiative, London. https://www.climatebonds.net /files/reports/asean-sotm-2020.pdf.

PBC (People's Bank of China). 2018. "中国人民银行有关负责人就扩大中期借贷便利（MLF）担保品范围答记者问" [Questions on expanding the scope of collateral for the medium-term lending facility]. June 1, PBC, Beijing. http://www.pbc.gov.cn/goutongjiaoliu/113456/113469 /3549916/index.html.

S&P Global. 2020. "A Pandemic-Driven Surge in Social Bond Issuance Shows the Sustainable Debt Market Is Evolving." S&P Global Rating (blog), June 22, 2020. https://www.spglobal.com/ratings/en/research/articles /200622-a-pandemic-driven-surge-in-social-bond -issuance-shows-the-sustainable-debt-market-is -evolving-11539807.

SBN (Sustainable Banking Network). 2019. "Innovations in Policy and Industry Actions in Emerging Markets." SBN Global Progress Report, International Finance Corporation, Washington, DC.

SBN (Sustainable Banking Network). 2020a. "Case Study 7, Nigeria: Issuing Sovereign and Corporate Green Bonds to Finance NDCs." In "How Low-Income Countries Are Adopting Sustainable Finance to Address Poverty, Climate Change, and Other Urgent Challenges," edited by SBN, 40. SBN Task Force Report, International Finance Corporation, Washington, DC.

SBN (Sustainable Banking Network). 2020b. "How Low-Income Countries Are Adopting Sustainable Finance to Address Poverty, Climate Change, and Other Urgent Challenges." SBN Task Force Report, International Finance Corporation, Washington, DC.

SC (Securities Commission Malaysia). 2021. Securities Commission Malaysia: Annual Report 2020. Kuala Lumpur: SC.

SSE (United Nations Sustainable Stock Exchanges Initiative). 2021. "Action Plan to Make Markets Climate Resilient: How Stock Exchanges Can Integrate the TCFD Recommendations." SSE, New York.

Whiley, Andrew. 2018. "December Market Blog: Nigeria Issues 1st African Sovereign Green Bond and Its Climate Bonds Certified! IRFC and PFC Certified from India: Plus US, Swedish, Italian, German, Malaysian, Japanese and Chinese Issuance and More!" Climate Bonds Initiative (blog), January 19, 2018. https://www.climatebonds.net /2018/01/december-market-blog-nigeria-issues-1st -african-sovereign-green-bond-its-climate-bonds.

World Bank. 2008. "World Bank and SEB Partner with Scandinavian Institutional Investors to Finance 'Green' Projects." Press release, November 6, 2008. https://www .worldbank.org/en/news/press-release/2008/11/06 /world-bank-and-seb-partner-with-scandinavian -institutional-investors-to-finance-green-projects.

World Bank. 2015. "What Are Green Bonds?" Investor Relations, Capital Markets Department, World Bank, Washington, DC.

World Bank. 2018. "From Evolution to Revolution: 10 Years of Green Bonds." News, November 27, 2018. https:// www.worldbank.org/en/news/feature/2018/11/27/from -evolution-to-revolution-10-years-of-green-bonds.

World Bank. 2019. "10 Years of Green Bonds: Creating the Blueprint for Sustainability across Capital Markets." News, March 18, 2019. https://www.worldbank.org/en /news/immersive-story/2019/03/18/10-years-of-green -bonds-creating-the-blueprint-for-sustainability-across -capital-markets.

World Bank. 2020. "Engaging with Investors on Environmental, Social, and Governance (ESG) Issues: A World Bank Guide for Sovereign Debt Managers." World Bank, Washington, DC.

Policy priorities for the recovery

The COVID-19 crisis has given rise to a wide range of new and elevated economic risks, some of which will only become apparent with time. Few governments have the resources and political leeway to tackle all of these challenges at once. Countries will need to identify the risks that pose the most immediate threat to an equitable recovery and prioritize their policy responses. This concluding chapter reviews the most urgent risks and highlights global issues that may arise as countries recover from the economic repercussions of the pandemic at different rates.

Policy Priorities

Pursuit of the following priorities can help set countries on the path to a more equitable and sustained economic recovery:

- **Mobilizing resources for the recovery.** In many low-income economies, high levels of sovereign debt pose the most urgent threat to the recovery. Countries facing this scenario can free up resources for the recovery through improved debt management.

- **Safeguarding financial stability.** In middle-income economies, financial sector risks tend to pose a larger threat to the recovery. These countries should focus on identifying and resolving financial sector risks to ensure the continued provision of credit.

- **Scaling back support in a transparent manner.** Support policies should be withdrawn in a predictable manner and scaled back first for the most resilient households and firms to counteract the highly regressive impacts of the COVID-19 crisis.

- **Managing exposure to global economic risks that threaten an equitable recovery.** These include interest rate and currency risks that are likely to arise as advanced economies scale back stimulus policies.

- **Supporting the transition to a green economy.** Economic policies for the recovery should aim to support sustainable growth by facilitating the reallocation of resources to green sectors and business models.

Introduction

The economic disruption caused by the COVID-19 (coronavirus) pandemic will affect countries for many years to come. As the immediate impacts of the pandemic subside, resource-constrained governments will face the challenge of scaling back support policies in a way that does not threaten the recovery. Because of uneven access to vaccines and economic fragilities predating the pandemic, emerging economies, in particular, face the very real prospect of a slow crisis recovery. Mobilizing the resources needed for proactive management and reduction of financial risks arising from the crisis, as well as for longer-term structural reforms, is essential for a strong and equitable recovery.

This Report has examined the primary financial and economic risks that have been exposed or exacerbated by the pandemic, and it has highlighted concrete steps policy makers can take to address them. In an ideal situation, governments would implement relevant policies for each of the priority areas discussed: financial stability, household and business insolvency, access to credit, and sovereign debt sustainability. However, few if any governments have the resources and political leeway to tackle all of these challenges at once. Countries will have to decide which policy areas to prioritize and how to best allocate scarce resources to support the recovery.

This chapter offers some guidance for doing that within a globally connected economy, taking a thematic perspective on the options and trade-offs available. The chapter emphasizes that the prompt recognition of economic risks is critical for the design of effective policies and highlights how new data and analysis can help evaluate the crisis response and guide evidence-based policy in the future (box 6.1).

Box 6.1 Evaluating the success of the crisis response: A research agenda

The response to the COVID-19 crisis has included many policy tools never applied in emerging economies or tried on this scale. Examples include large cash transfer programs, debt forbearance, and asset purchase programs. Although it is still too early for a conclusive assessment of these policies, a thorough analysis of the successes and limitations of the crisis response is essential to guide future policy making.

Understanding interrelated economic risks

As this *World Development Report* highlights, tracing the economic impact of the crisis response requires understanding the links between the balance sheet risks of households, firms, the financial sector, and the government because policies targeting one sector will have implications for the wider economy. Helping households with government cash transfers, for example, increases pressure on government budgets, but reduces loan defaults and risks to the financial sector. Recapitalizing banks may help them continue to supply firms with credit, but it may come at the cost of reducing the government's ability to support households and firms directly.

Evaluation of the impacts of the economic crisis and the progress toward an equitable recovery thus requires detailed data on the financial positions of households, firms, the financial sector, and the budgets of national and subnational governments. In some cases, such data are already available. In others, they would have to be collected either from conventional sources, such as nationally representative surveys or administrative data, or from newly available "big data," such as mobile banking and digital payments records. These data are useful not only to conduct a retrospective analysis, but also to offer practical guidance on how to best target support and choose between alternative policy approaches.

The use of microdata on household balance sheets is a good example. As shown in chapter 1, when policy makers have access to comprehensive data on the assets, liabilities, and expenditures of

(Box continues next page)

households, they are able to evaluate which types of support policies (income support, debt relief, or improved access to credit) will most effectively strengthen household resilience during a recession. It is also possible to assess how households at different income levels would benefit from each of these policies. However, in most countries standard household surveys do not collect information on household assets that is sufficiently detailed to allow for such an analysis, and, even where such data are available, they are still rarely used to inform policy making.[a]

The distributional impacts of the crisis response

Detailed data on the balance sheets of households, firms, and the financial sector can also be a powerful tool for tracing the distributional implications of the crisis and crisis response. Fiscal support in the form of direct cash transfers has been a lifeline for many households and businesses during the crisis. However, access to these payments typically requires a bank account, and low-income countries in particular have increasingly disbursed payments through mobile money accounts and other digital channels. Although these programs have been very effective at disbursing payments quickly, they also raise concerns that households and businesses without an account may be excluded from such support programs. Combining data on financial inclusion that have become available in recent years with information on household incomes and business revenue can help policy makers assess exactly which households and firms benefit from a given transfer program.[b]

Similarly, government support for the financial sector in the form of bank bailouts and recapitalizations has vastly different implications for inequality, depending on which borrowers are financed by a particular financial institution. In most countries, the currently available data can give researchers and policy makers only an imperfect picture of what share of a bank's lending goes to small and women-owned businesses and low-income and female-headed households. Where such data are available, policy makers can use them to target support to financial institutions instrumental in lending to those segments of the population most at risk of losing access to credit because of the crisis. Such data can be collected by regulators or the private sector. In some emerging markets such as India, some household and firm surveys also collect information on the banking relationships of respondents. Such data collection efforts should be extended to the nonbank financial sector, which accounts for a growing share of lending in emerging economies. This is a promising direction for future research that could not only provide policy makers with practical guidance, but also examine to what extent support of the financial sector actually helps marginal borrowers to maintain access to credit in a crisis.

Transparent government budgets

The pandemic has also had a profound impact on the financial position of many governments. Evidence from past crises suggests that delays in resolving high levels of sovereign debt are associated with lower spending on public goods and worse health and education outcomes. Transparent data on government budgets can be used in analysis of the mechanisms that explain this link. They can, for example, allow researchers and policy makers to analyze which types of government spending are cut first when governments face debt sustainability issues, the extent of the resulting social costs, and how equally or unequally they are distributed across the population. As for fiscal and financial sector policies, this type of analysis can give policy makers specific guidance on the social cost of budget consolidation and the benefits of prioritizing certain types of social expenditures over others.

Better data on the structure and extent of government debt are also crucially important for the management and efficient resolution of high levels of such debt—a task facing many emerging

(Box continues next page)

economies in the years ahead (see chapter 5). One of the most important steps in restructuring sovereign debt is debt reconciliation, which entails reviewing contracts to ascertain the validity of the debt claims. This often time-consuming process could be significantly shortened if more and better transparent debt records are maintained, reducing the time needed for debt restructuring and thereby ensuring a better outcome. Such data could also help researchers to better understand the factors that slow the resolution of sovereign debt, which is associated with severe negative impacts on poverty and inequality.

The role of digitalization in the crisis response
Finally, the pandemic is arguably the first truly global crisis in the digital age. Digital channels, such as mobile money, have been used extensively to disburse support payments, and digital solutions,

including innovations in financial technology, algorithmic lending, and risk assessment, have offered new paths to improving transparency and supporting the crisis response. But for the more vulnerable and less financially experienced, digitalization of government transfer payments and wages also poses risks of informal fees, financial fraud, and predatory lending. Assessing how effective these innovations have been at channeling government payments to households and firms at the bottom of the income ladder and preventing them from losing access to formal credit requires detailed data. Fortunately, data on digital transactions are easily available. A more challenging task is to combine these data with information from household and firm surveys to enable future research to paint a comprehensive picture of the role of new financial technologies in crisis recovery.

a. See Badarinza, Balasubramaniam, and Ramadorai (2019); Badarinza et al. (2021).
b. See, for example, data from World Bank, Global Findex Database, https://globalfindex.worldbank.org.

Tackling the most urgent sources of risk

One of the main themes running through this Report is that the sectors of an economy are interconnected through multiple mutually reinforcing channels. These links create pathways along which risks in one sector can affect the wider economy. However, well-designed fiscal, monetary, and financial policies can counteract these risks, lead to positive outcomes across multiple areas, and support an equitable recovery.

Using the framework of interrelated risks laid out in this Report, countries that need to make difficult choices about how to prioritize resources for the recovery can identify both the risks confronting their economy and where policy action is likely to be most effective at reducing economic fragilities worsened by the pandemic. The areas in which the risks are the most pronounced and are most likely to be the source of damaging spillovers warrant the most attention. This is not to say that countries with a high degree of risk in one area should ignore the other areas, but rather to emphasize the importance of urgent action in the areas where the threats are highest or where a further accumulation of risks is more likely to create spillover risks for the economy as a whole.

A common scenario in low-income countries is that the formal banking sector primarily serves wealthier, more resilient households and larger, more established businesses, while low-income households and small businesses most severely affected by the pandemic are less likely to have access to bank credit. As a result, the possibility of rising loan defaults is typically a less pressing issue in these countries. Moreover, borrowers in low-income countries tend to be more reliant on nonbank lenders, such as microfinance institutions, and so those countries might benefit from guidance on regulating and supporting these institutions (as discussed in spotlights 2.1 and 3.1).

Yet in these same countries, deteriorating public finances threaten the ability of the government to support the recovery and pose a risk to the domestic financial sector, which often holds large amounts of sovereign debt.[1] Low-income countries also tend to face greater external threats to an equitable recovery. As high-income countries begin to recover from the crisis, low-income countries that borrow in foreign currency face the risk that their debt payments and import costs will become more expensive as global interest rates rise and their local currencies depreciate. In this scenario, a focus on improved sovereign debt management can help countries manage existing debt burdens and free up resources for the recovery (as discussed in chapter 5).

By contrast, addressing financial sector fragilities is a more pressing policy priority for many middle-income economies. The financial sector in these countries is typically more developed and therefore more exposed to household and small business debt. As outlined in chapter 1, income losses arising from the pandemic have led to a sharp deterioration in the financial health of households and firms, and could trigger a sharp rise in loan defaults. This could, in turn, threaten the capital position of many lenders. Thus, as outlined in chapters 2 and 3 of this Report, regulators in these countries should take steps to improve the resilience of the financial sector, promote greater transparency of bank asset quality, and expedite the restructuring of bad debts.

Overall, middle-income countries also introduced larger and more encompassing fiscal and financial sector policies in response to the pandemic, including cash transfers, debt moratoria for households and firms, and credit guarantee schemes for businesses. In these countries, policy makers need to ensure that support measures are withdrawn in a careful, predictable manner to avert a wave of loan defaults that will threaten financial stability and create contingent liabilities for governments.

Managing domestic risks to the recovery

Scaling back the stimulus

In the short term, resource-constrained governments face the challenge of scaling back fiscal support to households and firms without dampening the recovery. In many countries, direct payments to households and firms have served as the main pillar of the crisis response and were designed to protect the livelihoods of economically disadvantaged groups—such as workers in the informal sector and those in unskilled occupations—and the survival of businesses in the sectors most severely affected by the crisis. However, few countries have the resources to maintain these policies in the longer term, and in many cases countries will need to phase out support before economic activity has fully recovered.

As governments withdraw stimulus programs, policy makers must balance equity and efficiency considerations. Support should, for example, be scaled back first for firms that are financially resilient and have access to credit and capital markets that can help bridge temporary liquidity problems. Similarly, for households support should be scaled back first for those that are financially resilient, while support that protects the incomes and livelihoods of vulnerable populations that have been especially hard-hit by income losses stemming from the pandemic should be kept in place until their recovery prospects have materially improved. It is, moreover, essential that the withdrawal of support policies is implemented in a transparent and predictable manner to avoid adding to the economic uncertainty that is already dampening economic activity.

Managing risks to government budgets

Governments will also need to mobilize new revenue to pay off debts incurred for the crisis response and preserve their ability to support the recovery. The potential return to economic growth during the recovery will help. However, governments must also pursue complementary, longer-term structural policies to increase their revenue base. Most emerging economies, for example, lack the institutional capacity to tax incomes and instead rely primarily on taxing consumption. This approach is highly inefficient—for example, in 2020 Mexico, which relies heavily on consumption taxes, raised only 18 percent of its gross domestic product (GDP) in tax revenue,[2] while countries in the European Union, relying primarily on income taxes, raised 41 percent of GDP in tax revenue.[3] Taxing consumption is also highly inequitable because it places a disproportionate burden on the poor, who spend most of their income on consumption. Taxing wealth through property, income, and capital gains taxes is an underused revenue generation strategy in most emerging economies and could help mitigate the adverse impacts of the COVID-19 crisis on poverty and inequality. Revenue mobilization strategies should also strengthen incentives for businesses to formalize, which brings additional benefits such as improved access to credit.

Managing risks to financial stability

In many economies, the withdrawal of stimulus programs may also pose a threat to financial stability. Because many support programs will be scaled back before the incomes of households and businesses have fully recovered, regulators and financial institutions should be prepared to address an increase in loan defaults.

Chapters 2 and 3 discuss policies that can counteract these risks and reduce the likelihood of a credit crunch that would disproportionately affect small businesses and low-income households and could weaken the recovery. The policies discussed in chapter 2 focus on managing loan distress and safeguarding financial stability. Those featured in chapter 3 are aimed at improving and establishing a well-functioning legal insolvency framework for households and businesses. Effective policy action in both areas can prevent the risks posed by loan defaults escalating to the point that banks reduce lending. The challenges presented by elevated levels of nonperforming loans require a quick, comprehensive policy response on the three main fronts laid out in chapter 2: (1) improving transparency on banks' exposure to problem assets; (2) developing the operational capacity to address rising volumes of bad loans to ensure the resolute and efficient handling of borrowers considered nonviable; and (3) providing supervisors and bank resolution authorities with the tools they need to deal decisively with distressed banks in a manner that protects taxpayers and ensures the continuity of key financial services. Policies should encourage timely action before nonperforming loans rise to problematic levels. Both regulators and financial institutions should therefore be prepared to address an increase in problem assets as support programs are withdrawn.

An important tool to help resolve high levels of private debts in the economy is a functioning legal insolvency framework (see chapter 3). Because many emerging economies either lack legal or institutional frameworks for debt resolution or suffer from weak implementation or enforcement capacity, they would likely see benefits from concentrating efforts in these areas—notwithstanding the fact that the legal reform process can be lengthy. Even in countries where institutional capacity is limited, small improvements in the bankruptcy code can make a difference. For example, the experience of several emerging economies suggests that reforms that simplify bankruptcy proceedings can improve loan performance and increase the availability of credit.

Ensuring continued access to credit for households and businesses

Many households and businesses are at acute risk of losing access to formal credit as a result of the COVID-19 crisis. Such a loss could dampen the recovery because access to credit is an important insurance mechanism that strengthens the ability of households and firms to weather economic risks that might arise during an extended recovery (see spotlight 1.1 for a review of the evidence). Credit also finances investment and consumption, which are essential to support the recovery.

The ongoing economic disruptions and persistent economic uncertainty resulting from the pandemic have also increased credit risk and diminished the realizable value of collateral as well as other forms of recourse for lenders. Coupled with the fact that government programs have had the unintended consequence of reducing credit market transparency, many lenders are finding it challenging to accurately measure credit risk and have responded by tightening credit conditions across the board. Innovations in financial technology and lending models can help counteract the resulting contraction in lending and stimulate continued lending to households and firms.

Where lenders have sufficient liquidity but are reducing lending, new financial technologies and lending models—often using alternative data sources to assess creditworthiness—can compensate for the lack of credit information. Similarly, better matching the duration of loan terms to the time horizon over which lenders can assess credit risk can facilitate risk management in times of heightened uncertainty. These advances can partly compensate for reduced credit market transparency and help lenders identify creditworthy borrowers. In situations in which lenders are reluctant to issue new credit because of economic uncertainty, governments and central banks could pursue other options such as partial credit guarantees. In these programs, often provided through state-owned banks, a guarantor (usually the government) absorbs part of the credit risk of loans to specific groups of borrowers. Although such programs require the lender to assume part of the credit risk, they must be implemented selectively (as discussed in spotlight 4.1) because they can distort incentives for lenders to collect payments and borrowers to repay credit. They also carry the risk of creating contingent liabilities for the government if borrowers default.

Managing interrelated risks across the global economy

Beyond efforts to support the domestic economy, governments must also consider developments in the global economy that could pose a threat to an equitable recovery. Connections forged through global credit markets, international trade, foreign aid, and other areas create interdependencies. These connections have noticeably affected the recovery, perhaps best illustrated by the disruption of vital global supply chains through the temporary shutdown of factories, shipping, warehouses, and other essential infrastructure.

One important global risk is the uneven pace of recovery between advanced and emerging economies. The faster recovery in advanced economies is likely to precipitate an increase in global interest rates, which will expose public and private sector borrowers to refinancing risks and put downward pressure on the currencies of emerging economies. These risks are especially acute for low-income countries with high levels of foreign currency–denominated debt, and they create a dilemma for the central banks of emerging economies. If they do not follow the interest rate hikes in advanced economies, they face the risk of capital outflows and a depreciation of the national currency. However, if they raise interest rates, they risk dampening the domestic economy by exerting pressure on borrowers and increasing the cost of servicing domestic sovereign debt.

In view of these trade-offs, a carefully chosen policy mix that addresses interest rates, exchange rates, and macroprudential policy is crucial. This is especially important in countries with financial sectors that rely on credit and capital markets for wholesale finance because financial institutions that cannot refinance themselves will have less capacity to supply credit during the recovery. It should also be a high priority in countries where state-owned enterprises account for a significant share of the economy. When state-owned enterprises cannot refinance short-term debt or service foreign currency debt, the risk of contingent liabilities for governments is even higher.

The recovery in emerging economies is also affected by economic growth in the rest of the world, and it could be impeded by slower growth in important emerging markets such as China. In view of China's role as the most important bilateral creditor for emerging economies, a protracted deleveraging of the Chinese banking sector could expose economies that previously borrowed heavily from China to sizable refinancing risks (see chapter 5). Moreover, a slowdown in Chinese economic activity could affect the economic recovery in emerging economies by reducing the global demand for their exports. For example, in 2020 China's share of the total trade of Sub-Saharan Africa was 26 percent, or about equal to the combined shares of the European Union and the United States.[4]

Seizing the opportunity to build a more sustainable world economy

Recovery from the COVID-19 pandemic will call for far-reaching structural changes in economies around the world. This presents an enormous opportunity to accelerate the transformation to a more efficient and sustainable world economy. The consequences of climate change are already affecting lives and livelihoods in all countries. Although climate change is a global phenomenon, its impacts are felt most severely in low-income countries and low-income communities, where they compound existing vulnerabilities such as lack of access to clean water, low crop yields, food insecurity, and unsafe housing.

Governments and regulators have a variety of policy instruments at their disposal to support this transformation and adapt their economies to the realities of climate change, which is a major source of neglected risk in the world economy.[5] Governments can, for example, use the tax code to incentivize green investments, or central banks and supervisors could mandate higher risk provisioning for loans to sectors engaged in unsustainable activities that contribute to climate risks. Governments and central banks can also provide financing to lenders on preferential terms, conditional on meeting specific sustainability targets. Indeed, many countries have begun to use such regulatory incentives to accelerate the shift to a more sustainable economy. Such policies can have an important impact on the reallocation of financing to green sectors and technologies. In China, for example, green lending targets as well as regulation that incentivizes green lending have shifted bank lending portfolios toward sustainable sectors. Similarly, regulatory incentives can help the financial sector and activate a virtuous cycle by recognizing and pricing climate risks so that capital flows toward more sustainable firms and industries.[6] In the aftermath of the pandemic, governments have a unique opportunity to support the financial sector's ability to perform this role by, for example, mandating risk disclosures and phasing out preferential tax, auditing, and regulatory treatment for unsustainable industries.

Notes

1. Daehler, Aizenman, and Jinjarak (2020).
2. Data from Organisation for Economic Co-operation and Development, Revenue Statistics 2021—Mexico (database), https://www.oecd.org/tax/revenue-statistics -mexico.pdf.
3. Eurostat (2020).
4. Data from International Monetary Fund, DOTS (Direction of Trade Statistics) (dashboard), https://data.imf.org /?sk=9D6028D4-F14A-464C-A2F2-59B2CD424B85.
5. See Gennaioli, Shleifer, and Vishny (2012); Stroebel and Wurgler (2021).
6. Carney (2015); Fender et al. (2020).

References

Badarinza, Cristian, Vimal Balasubramaniam, Louiza Bartzoka, and Tarun Ramadorai. 2021. "How Has the Pandemic Affected Household Finances in Developing Economies?" *Economics Observatory: Families and Households* (blog), June 29, 2021. https://www.economicsobservatory.com/how-has-the-pandemic-affected-household-finances-in-developing-economies.

Badarinza, Cristian, Vimal Balasubramaniam, and Tarun Ramadorai. 2019. "The Household Finance Landscape in Emerging Economies." *Annual Review of Financial Economics* 11 (December): 109–29.

Carney, Mark. 2015. "Breaking the Tragedy of the Horizon: Climate Change and Financial Stability." Address at Lloyd's of London, London, September 29, 2015. https://www.bis.org/review/r151009a.pdf.

Daehler, Timo, Joshua Aizenman, and Yothin Jinjarak. 2020. "Emerging Markets Sovereign CDS Spreads during COVID-19: Economics versus Epidemiology News." NBER Working Paper 27903, National Bureau of Economic Research, Cambridge, MA.

Eurostat (Statistical Office of the European Communities). 2020. "Taxation in 2019: Tax-to-GDP Ratio at 41.1% in EU; a One-to-Two Ratio across Member States." News Release 160/2020, October 29, 2020. https://ec.europa.eu/eurostat/documents/2995521/11469100/2-29102020-BP-EN.pdf/059a7672-ed6d-f12c-2b0e-10ab4b34ed07.

Fender, Ingo, Mike McMorrow, Vahe Sahakyan, and Omar Zulaica. 2020. "Reserve Management and Sustainability: The Case for Green Bonds?" BIS Working Paper 849, Monetary and Economic Department, Bank for International Settlements, Basel, Switzerland.

Gennaioli, Nicola, Andrei Shleifer, and Robert W. Vishny. 2012. "Neglected Risks, Financial Innovation and Financial Fragility." *Journal of Financial Economics* 104 (3): 452–68.

Stroebel, Johannes, and Jeffrey Wurgler. 2021. "What Do You Think about Climate Finance?" *Journal of Financial Economics* 142: 487–98.